HIGH RISK

HIGH RISK

Dr. Ken Magid

Carole A. McKelvey

BANTAM BOOKS
TORONTO • NEW YORK • LONDON • SYDNEY • AUCKLAND

HIGH RISK

A Bantam Book / published by arrangement with
M & M Publishing

PRINTING HISTORY
M & M edition published in 1987
Bantam edition / March 1988

Library of Congress Cataloging-in-Publication Data

Magid, Ken, 1946–
  High risk.

  Reprint. Originally published: Golden, Colo. : M & M
Pub., c1987.
  Bibliography: p. 340.
  Includes index.
  1. Antisocial personality disorders—Etiology.
2. Attachment behavior in children.   3. Child rearing—
United States—History—20th century.   4. United
States—Social life and customs—20th century.
I. McKelvey, Carole A.   II. Title.
[RC555.M27 1988]   616.85'82   87-31894
ISBN 0-553-05290-X

Published simultaneously in the United States and Canada

PRINTED IN THE UNITED STATES OF AMERICA

FG 0 9 8 7 6 5 4 3 2 1

TO OUR MOTHERS

And loving mothers

just like them everywhere

Foreword

We live in a time of transition, a demographic revolution that is altering the American workforce as well as the American family.

Sixty-five percent of all mothers with children under 18 years of age work outside the home. There are more single parent families and because of our mobility there is less extended family support to help us meet the demands of balancing work and family.

We have tried to go on about our business as though nothing has changed. We have acted as though the "Norman Rockwell" image is the rule and the rest of us are exceptions forced to make do as best we can.

But everything has changed. As this book points out, the ramifications of these changes can be positive or negative depending on how we respond to the change.

Thanks to the insight of people like Dr. Ken Magid, Carole McKelvey, Dr. T. Berry Brazelton of Harvard, Dr. Foster Cline, Dr. Edward F. Zigler of Yale and others mentioned here, we have been given a unique chance, a gift, if you will. Their research and hard work shows us that we are at a crossroads, and we have a limited opportunity to respond.

Their work *must* convince us to act now before we become entrenched by default, in policies that establish high risk situations for our children. Our task is difficult — to respond quickly and at the same time creatively, with serious thought.

What we do now will have a profound effect on our future as a country and specifically on our children.

This book calls to our attention one change that is too often overlooked. In the past, children with serious problems came almost exclusively from families with serious problems. Today, the challenges faced by average families easily lend themselves to potential "high risk" situations. The dangers appear to be more subtle and the solutions more confounding.

Focus on the bonding process between mother and child is by no means a new idea. Unfortunately it has been presented as something that does or doesn't happen in the first few hours of life. We are led to believe that if it works, your problems as a parent are solved; if it doesn't you have failed. As any parent knows, it is not that simple.

The evidence presented here shows convincingly how important the first few years of life are to healthy human development.

The unattached children, or "trust bandits" described by the authors are heartbreaking examples of what our lack of adequate attention to the needs of children and families has brought about.

Several potential causes for serious breaks in the bonding process are discussed: Day Care, Parental Leave, Adoption, Foster Care, Teenage Pregnancy, Child Abuse and Divorce. There are few families that haven't been touched by one or more of these. If you have not already, it is just a matter of time before you are.

The areas in which most of us share direct experience are child care and parental leave. As the need for child care and leave policies has grown, the response has been to ignore it or search for a quick simple solution. Both responses raise the risk for our children.

An attitude still held by many employers is that if a woman chooses to become a mother she should stay home. The days when that may have been a choice for most of us are long gone. Surveys continue to verify that the majority of women in the workforce are there because of financial necessity.

If you are a working mother reading this book I am sure you will experience, as I did, moments of grief and guilt as you reflect on the difficult choices you have had to make. Pay close attention to the last section. It gives numerous examples of creative ways to approach the challenges we face. I do not believe that the message the authors intend to convey is that women should leave the workplace and stay home. What they are saying is that we must pay closer attention to what is happening to our children, and make the hard choices necessary if we want them to grow up healthy and happy.

We must all face reality. What we are doing now has caused irreversible damage to some of our children. Response must come from many places including the home, workplace, schools and the government.

At the federal level I have introduced the Family and Medical Leave Act. With it we hope to establish a minimum labor standard dealing with leave policy at the time of the birth, adoption or serious illness of a child; the serious illness of an older dependent adult; or personal leave for the serious illness of any employee. My bill makes available an unpaid job-protected leave. It offers a minimum standard upon which employers and employees can build to meet individual needs.

There has been resistance by some members of the business community to this bill. Interestingly enough, the results are just beginning to come in on studies of the actual cost to businesses for implementing progressive leave and child care policies, several of them are quoted in this book. The results show that while there is an initial cost, the policies quickly turn into money savers for the business involved. Some of the reasons for these savings are immediate reduction of the turnover rate, more qualified individuals applying for openings because of attractive policies, less family-related stress on the job and a loyal, more productive workforce.

In many communities around the country there is a renewed interest in the welfare of our children. After you finish reading this book your response may be to wonder what it is that you can do. Let your elected officials and community leaders know how you feel. Educate your friends and neighbors, locate the groups working on these issues and do as much as you can to help.

There is no bond as strong as the love we have for our children. With work we can transform that bond into the support our families desperately need.

Patricia Schroeder
House of Representatives
1st District, Denver, Colo.

*"Evening star, you bring all things
which the bright dawn has scattered:
you bring the sheep, you bring the goat,
you bring the child back to its mother."*
Sappho

Preface

High Risk: Children Without a Conscience is about America's future. It is about babies, parenting, genetics and crime, and how they are vitally connected.

This book has been written for a large and diverse audience, including parents, therapists, psychologists and educators. What you are going to read may at first shock you. Based on extensive scientific data, the prognosis for the future includes the high probability that greater numbers of psychopathic individuals are headed our way.

Wherever these people go a wake of misery and fear usually follows. Unknowingly we may be creating a society in which more and more people without conscience will victimize the innocent. The deviants run the gamut, from child molesters, to abusers, to crooked entrepreneurs . . . to murderers.

This book is about the reasons behind this phenomenon and answers the questions "why" and "why now." The problem starts at the beginning of life, when the scales are tipped toward a future of trust and love, or one of mistrust and deep-seated rage.

The critical factor is bonding. Without effective bonding the infant won't become attached to his or her primary caregiver, the mother and/or father. A growing number of experts now believe this stage in a human's development has much greater significance than previously thought.

Section I of this book explores the disease of psychopathy. Through example and by citing clinical research we explain how psychopaths become ill. Personalized accounts tell you how to recognize those suffering from Antisocial Personality Disorder (APD). We look at adults and children who kill — they personify an attachment process that has gone very wrong. Experts are cited who clearly show how criminality is tied to poor childhood attachment.

Although our deepest concern is the link between criminality and bonding and attachment, this book also shows how psychopathy occurs along a spectrum of deviant behaviors.

We provide helpful information that you can use to protect yourself from being "taken" by someone with this disorder.

In Section II we explain attachment, including why it is important for developing healthy children, how this attachment is formed and how separation imperils this healthy connection. Such separations can result in anger and an unattached child.

We also take a look at the long-term effects of unattachment and what this means for an infant's future. In addition, there are helpful tips on how to detect children who are at high risk for growing up without a conscience.

What kind of attachment breaks are occurring and why at this time in our nation's history are we in a bonding crisis? Section III of *High Risk: Children Without a Conscience* talks about the changing roles within the American family and how this may be imperiling our children. A demographic revolution is occurring which may result in future generations that have huge numbers of detached children. Factors responsible include: the increasing numbers of mothers working outside the home, the child-care crisis, the teen-pregnancy epidemic, a high divorce rate, increasing child abuse and neglect, the shambles of the foster-care system, and too-late adoptions. All of the above, unless handled very carefully, can cause the vital attachment process to become derailed.

The key to prevention is knowledge — a complete understanding of how babies grow emotionally healthy.

In Section IV we discuss state-of-the-art treatments for unattachment from centers around the world. Due to the nature of this subject, the material is of necessity the most technical part of the book. We talk about how far some have come, and how far we still need to go. Most therapists dread having to treat a psychopath. Using their innate charm, psychopaths can con well-intentioned professionals. We discuss — using personalized case histories — several techniques, including a controversial "holding" method some therapists are employing to treat those with APD.

How can this national time bomb be defused? Section V offers realistic preventative suggestions. *High Risk* provides helpful advice on choosing a healthy child-care situation, what you can do about the teenage-pregnancy problem and how to assure that your children are at low risk, should you divorce.

We do not mean to imply that there is a simple solution to this problem. In fact, no single solution will guarantee that all children will grow up healthy and happy. We do offer suggestions for a broad program of sweeping reforms throughout the social structure of the United States.

Additional research on these issues is vital. But it is important to recognize that research takes time, and for some of our children time has run out.

The tragedy of unattachment will not go away. But unconscionable violence does not have to be woven into the fabric of American life. It is our sincere desire that this book will shed light on why some individuals are antisocial, and what can be done to help prevent damage to our greatest national resource: our children.

A word about pronouns

The reader will notice several areas of this text where pronouns of a single gender have been used exclusively. There are two reasons we have chosen to use pronouns this way:

Demographics—When speaking of children's caregivers and attachment formation we have tended to use *feminine* pronouns. Although caregivers may be male, in our society it is still mothers and other females who have the primary responsibility for child care. When speaking of psychopaths, we have primarily used *masculine* pronouns. This reflects the demographic fact that the overwhelming majority of violent psychopaths are male (females, however, are included in this growing problem).

Grammar — The English language lacks entirely *neuter*-gender third-person singular pronouns. The impersonal singular pronouns in our language are *masculine*. While the authors deplore this constraint, we feel the use of "him/her" and similar artificial constructions would impede the flow of the text. We decided to aim for readability and clarity and ask our readers for their understanding.

Statistical clarification

Most of us use statistics to help form opinions and shape plans of action. But how accurate are most statistical studies reported in the popular press and how much should we rely on them? It was Disraeli who said, "There are three kinds of lies: lies, damned lies and statistics."

He wasn't far wrong. Statistics are like witnesses — they will testify for either side. There is a common phrase that with proper treatment one can cure a cold in 7 days, but if you don't do anything, it will hang on for a week. (Huff, 1954, p. 8) The salesmen on Madison Avenue have been aware of the numbers game for decades, hoping the public would never be the wiser.

In the classic book, *How to Lie with Statistics*, Darrell Huff demonstrates how figures can be manipulated. Taking the example of the common cold, Huff tells the over-the-counter medication industry, "You can't prove that your nostrum cures colds but you can publish (in large type) a sworn laboratory report that half an ounce of the stuff killed 31,108 germs in a test tube in 11 seconds . . . It's not up to you to point out that an antiseptic that works well in the test tube may not perform in the human throat, especially after it's been diluted according to instructions to keep it from burning throat tissue. Don't confuse the issue by telling what kind of germ you killed. Who knows what causes colds, particularly since it probably isn't a germ at all." (Huff, p. 74-75)

Many studies purport that products are the "lowest" or the "best." The actual difference is usually negligible and inconsequential. Why do we fall for such claims?

Huff says, "Many a statistic is false on its face. It gets by only because the magic of numbers brings about the suspension of common sense." (p. 138)

For example, statistics show that in 1940 each car on the road had an average of 2.2 persons; in 1950 it was 1.4. If the current trend continues, by 1990 every third car on the road will be empty! Researchers often collect facts, and then draw their own *confusions*.

The popular press frequently reports the results of "scientific studies" without hiring a statistician to check out the accuracy of the statistics. Other "experts" then pick up the information, repeating the data as fact.

We found this to be the case, for example, during our investigation about day-care centers and how they affect infants and children. We found more than a half dozen popular magazine articles with bold titles featuring scientific research that had "proven" mothers and fathers can leave their infants in day care with no adverse effects. Expert after expert agreed there was nothing to worry about. When we asked the publishers to tell us where their scientific data had been obtained, they directed us to several similar studies.

The three most frequently cited studies were given to Dr. Robert Schneider, a professor of statistics and research methodology at Metropolitan State College, Denver. As an example of his findings, Schneider comments on one of the studies, which involved several day care researchers:

> "These authors have produced bad science. . . they have reported results and conclusions that must be taken on faith by the reader. The validity and reliability of various measures are never discussed. They have committed statistical errors of various kinds. . . ."

What is alarming is that these "proven" day-care studies used either too few children or inappropriate samples (one sample was half Chinese children). And none of them studied infants in day-care settings. The observation techniques were either biased or statistically flawed.

The bottom line is that results in the studies could not be replicated as reported nor relied upon as scientifically sound, and yet everyone was acting as if the data was gospel. Parents were being given incorrect information upon which to make one of the most important decisions of their lives: whether or not to place their baby in day care.

It is important to have a healthy amount of suspicion before accepting something as "proven." For this reason, we have included extensive references throughout this book. It is upon these references that we base our suppositions. The book *High Risk: Children Without a Conscience* talks about probability and what might happen.

We do not purport to "prove" anything, but rather to suggest a highly plausible hypothesis about the future based on an extensive review of all the literature we could find on this subject during several years of investigation. A good analogy is that studying how unattachment is linked to crime is similar to studying how cigarette smoking is linked to cancer. We can't prove it yet but feel confident we are on the right track.

We firmly believe that subsequent valid and reliable studies to come will prove our hypothesis true. But the risk factors seem so great for so many families right now, that we decided to inform the public about what we had found.

We have written this book for the layman and for the interested professional in easy-to-understand language. Much of our hypothesis is based on already proven data about the negative effects of abuse and neglect, divorce and crime. We are suggesting the effects on future generations will be far greater than originally thought.

*"Life is a flame that is always burning
itself out.
But it catches fire again, every time
a child is born."*
George Bernard Shaw

Acknowledgements

We have dedicated this book to our mothers, for it is they whom we must thank for our early nurturing.

Writing this book has indeed proven to be a nurturing process itself. As we have researched and written and then rewritten there have been many who have helped and to whom we owe our deepest thanks.

There simply would be no book had it not been for the vision of Dr. Foster Cline. To him we are most grateful for sharing his files, treatment procedures and thoughts. He has asked that we share our thanks with his wife and helpmate, Hermie. Dr. John Allan of Canada must also be included here for the guidance and treatment advice he gave us so freely; he in turn wishes to acknowledge his mentor, Dr. Robert Zaslow. Others in the mental health profession who have been extremely helpful include Connell Watkins of the Youth Behavior Program of Evergreen, Walt Schreibman and Dr. Vera Fahlberg. Educator Jim Fay must be credited and the many legal contributions of Jefferson County Judge Kim Goldberger are gratefully acknowledged.

Our researchers and editors are without peer and we thank them for their relentless work under extremely tight deadlines. Stacey Williams spent long hours researching our thesis and helping organize the materials. Also working on the research team were Gina Thomas of Florida, Angela Dire of Colorado and Jay Croft of Alaska. There are no words that can describe Donna Spevack's dedicated help on this project.

Artists Dan Bulleit and Laurie Riggs helped conceptualize and execute the design of the book and the charts and graphs.

We are deeply grateful for the editing work done by Marlys Duran, Judy Buecher, Margaret Carlin and Verna Noel Jones.

It is to our families, however, that we must give the most credit. Carole's family, especially her husband George and son Ian, never failed to support her in this effort; this has always been the case. And Ken's three sons, Kesson, Justin and Aaron, are now making up for time lost with their father during this marathon.

This book simple could not have been written without the love and support of our families. And this is fitting since trust, love and support are what this book is all about.

Table of Contents

Foreword .... *vii*
Preface .... *ix*
Acknowledgements .... *xiii*

I: *America — A Breeding Ground for Psychopaths?*

1.   The Trust Bandits 1
2.   Kids Who Kill 27
3.   The Victims 37

II: *A Critical Time — Attachment*

4.   What is Attachment 51
5.   The Bonding Cycle, How It Works 71
6.   Childhood Symptoms, A Warning
      of Things to Come 79
7.   The Cycle Continues 101

III: *The Bonding Breaks*

8.   Why Now? 107
9.   Day Care: Simply a Dilemma or a Disaster? 121
10. Parental Leave 139
11. Adoption and Foster Care 147
12. The Teenage Pregnancy Epidemic 161
13. The Cycle of Abuse 173
14. Divorce: Disrupted Children, Disrupted Homes   183

IV: *Treatment*

15. The Trouble With Traditional Therapies 193
16. The Referral 201
17. Defusing the National Time Bomb 207
18. Jeremy: An Abbreviated Case History 215
19. Modified Holding Techniques 227
20. More Therapeutic Options 231
21. Hospital Treatment 237

V: Preventing Children Without A Conscience

22.	Toward Solutions	243
23.	Positive Parenting Practices	245
24.	Teachers of Future Parents	261
25.	The Teenage Baby Boom	269
26.	National Leave Policy: The Time is Now	277
27.	What About Day Care	281
28.	Adoption and Foster Care: Making it Work	293
29.	Interrupting the Cycle of Abuse	301
30.	Relationships: How to Avoid a Trust Bandit	307
31.	Educating the Experts	319
	Poem	338
	Epilogue	339
	Bibliography	340
	Index	351
	Photographs & drawings	182a

I

AMERICA

A Breeding Ground
for Psychopaths?

"Sin is not hurtful because it is forbidden,
but is forbidden because it is hurtful."
Benjamin Franklin

1

The Trust
Bandits

 It is 10:30 a.m. in central Florida. Beads of sweat drip from the foreheads of tourists waiting in long, winding lines at Disneyworld for an exciting ride on the Submarine Nautilus.

Less than 10 miles away, 9-year-old Jeffery Bailey Jr. is also waiting. He is waiting for his young companion to die. After making sure that no one else is around, Jeffery has pushed 3-year-old Ricardo "Nicki" Brown into the deep end of a motel pool. He knows the younger child cannot swim and is afraid of the water.

It is taking Nicki a long time to die. Jeffery gets tired of standing, so he pulls up a lawn chair to the edge of the pool. He wants a better view of how someone drowns. Jeffery stays by the pool until Nicki sinks to the bottom, lifeless. Then he puts on his shoes and shirt and saunters toward home.

A short time later he asks another neighborhood child what the "icky white stuff" is that comes out of someone's nose when they're drowning. He doesn't mention that Nicki is at this moment lying at the bottom of a pool.

Nicki's body is recovered from the pool at 6:40 p.m. by the police. Later, after neighborhood children have told Jeffery's mother about the drowning, the youngster tells his mother about the "accident." (Kissimmee Police Department, June 3, 1986)

Police officer Beth Peturka who investigated the case says she found Jeffery "kind of nonchalant, like he was enjoying all the attention."

On June 3, 1986, the State of Florida charges 9-year-old Jeffery with murder.

*****

America. Land of the free, or a breeding ground for psychopaths? Hundreds of thousands of individuals filled with hatred populate this country. They are people without a conscience, and they hurt—sometimes kill—others without remorse.

1

They are psychopaths, and they possess a poisonous mix of traits. They are arrogant, shameless, immoral, impulsive, antisocial, superficial, charming, callous, irresponsible, irreverent, cunning, self-assured. They are found in jails and mental institutions . . . but they can also be found in boardrooms or in politics or in any number of respected professions. This disorder evades established definitions of sanity or insanity and there is no cure for adult psychopaths.

Haven't you wondered—as you read the morning newspaper or watched the TV news—why there seem to be ever-increasing accounts of psychopathic killers? Almost daily, it seems, we hear of another conscienceless murderer: Gary Gilmore, who was executed by a Utah firing squad; Charles Manson, who directed the Helter-Skelter murders; Henry Lee Lucas, who claimed he was the worst mass murderer in history; Edmund Kemper III, the Santa Cruz Coed Murderer; Kenneth Bianchi, the Hillside Strangler; David Berkowitz, the Son of Sam; Richard Ramirez, the Night Stalker; Donald Harvey, the Cyanide Killer; Juan Corona, who murdered migrant workers . . . The Tylenol Killer . . . Theodore Bundy.

Ted Bundy, one of the most infamous mass murderers of modern times, is a classic example of a criminal psychopath.

For years, Bundy outwitted law officers who hunted him across the face of America. He finally was sentenced to death in Florida's maximum security prison for brutally murdering two coeds and a young school girl.

Bundy arrived in Florida after a deadly rampage in which he raped, mutilated and killed perhaps a hundred young women across the nation. His final victim was a child, 12-year-old Kimberly Leach.

Kimberly did not notice the white van as it slowly circled the school in Lake City, Florida. Her mind was preoccupied with the upcoming Valentine's Day dance, and the new dress she'd wear.

Kimberly had forgotten her purse in her first-period class and went back to retrieve it. She was never seen alive again. Her nude, decomposed body was found two months later in a state park 32 miles from home, under an abandoned hog shed. She had been raped and mutilated before being killed.

Kimberly's killer didn't fit any back-alley stereotype. At the age of 32 Bundy was a former psychology/law student from Washington State. He was a Republican whose liberal leanings and political savvy could have taken him to political office. He had been a promising, confident young man.

Bundy, however, took a different road. From birth he was destined to become a homicidal rapist who killed for the sport of it. His quarries were young women.

Bundy is the ultimate manifestation of the character-disturbed child. He shares a common trait with the 9-year-old from Florida. Sometime, early in their development, something went terribly wrong. They never developed a conscience.

Bundy and Bailey are typical of certain types of criminals who started life as unattached children, perhaps aided by a genetic predisposition.

What happens, right or wrong, in the critical first two years of a baby's life will imprint that child as an adult. A complex set of events must occur in infancy to assure a future of trust and love. If the proper bonding and subsequent attachment does not occur — usually between the child and the mother—the child will develop mistrust and a deep-seated rage. He becomes a child without a conscience.

Somehow, the normal process that causes attachment to occur—the very process that develops a social conscience—was short-circuited in Bundy and Bailey.

Not all unattached children grow up to be criminals, but most suffer some form of psychological damage. It may be that such children simply are never able to develop a true loving relationship, or they end up "conning" others for their own benefit. These, too, can be considered tragedies, for no child should have to grow up without this trust bond and loving beginning.

One mother talks about her unattached son:

"Eddie only loves me when he wants to—on his own terms. Once I was stooping over the oven and he ran up behind me full tilt and threw his arms around my legs. He was great at wanting to hug me at very inconvenient times. Well, I practically shot right into the oven. I told my husband, 'This is like Hansel and Gretel and guess who I am! And I don't like the part of being a witch even a little bit!' "(Cline, 1979, p.90)

In most infants, the affectional bond—the essence of attachment to a parent—develops during the first nine months of life. The most important event occurring during the first year is the formation of these social attachments.

Michael Rutter in *Maternal Deprivation Reassessed* (1981) says the absence of attachment may lead to what Rutter calls "affectionless psychopathy." He describes this as beginning with "an initial phase of clinging, dependent behavior, followed by attention-seeking, uninhibited, indiscriminate friendliness and, finally, a personality characterized by the lack of guilt, an inability to keep rules and an inability to form lasting relationships." (p. 105)

Mary Ainsworth (1973) argues that the most important long-term result of the failure to form an affectional bond is the "inability to establish and maintain deep and significant interpersonal relations." (p.53)

The consequence of this failure can be individuals suffering from Antisocial Personality Disorder (APD). These people, more commonly known as psychopaths, express no remorse if caught in wrongdoings. They are aggressive, reckless and cruel to others. They leave in their wake a huge amount of human suffering. The pain psychopaths wreak on other human beings can be physical, or it can be the mental anguish often felt by those who try to form relationships with psychopaths.

Frighteningly, a growing number of individuals now being diagnosed as mentally ill fits this particular mental health category. These psychopaths comprise an increasingly large increment of the aberrant segment of our population. And they account for a disproportionate amount of deviancy.

We call them the "Trust Bandits" of modern society. They steal our trust.

Many people with APD began life as unbonded, unattached children. Right now thousands of America's children are in danger of becoming unattached. Well-intentioned parents may be unknowingly placing their young infants at high risk.

We all know the stresses that modern life places on the family. Because of necessity or desire, more and more mothers are returning to work, many just weeks after the birth of their babies. Parents need to know that this may be putting their children at risk for unattachment.

This doesn't mean that mothers and/or fathers cannot work, but certain steps must be taken to assure that the proper attachment bond is formed between parent and child.

Other factors can contribute to faulty infant attachment: high divorce rates, day care problems, lack of a national parental leave policy, epidemic teenage pregnancies, too-late adoptions, the foster care system, absence of mother and/or father during critical periods, post-partum depression, infant medical problems, abuse and neglect and infant unresponsiveness. These will be explored in detail in later chapters.

The exact number of people suffering from APD is not known. Respected psychiatrist Hervey Cleckley, whose *Mask of Sanity* is considered a landmark work on psychopaths, states: "I have been forced to the conviction that this particular behavior pattern is found among one's fellow men far more frequently than might be surmised from reading the literature . . . It presents a sociologic and psychiatric problem second to none . . . Although the incidence of this disorder is at present impossible to establish statistically or even to estimate accurately, I am willing to express the opinion that it is exceedingly high." (1982, pp.13-14)

Cleckley, the co-author of *Three Faces of Eve,* based many of his theories on psychopaths from his experiences while teaching at the University of Georgia School of Medicine. He says: "On the basis of experience in psychiatric outpatient clinics and with psychiatric problems of private patients and in the community, it does not seem an exaggeration to estimate the number of people seriously disabled by the disorder now listed under the term 'antisocial personality' as greater than the number disabled by any recognized psychosis except schizophrenia." (p. 14) Our concern is that since most psychopaths work in the shadows, they are undetected and the number may, therefore, be far greater than anyone imagines.

For comparison, schizophrenics are estimated to make up about 50% of state psychiatric hospital admissions, with 300,000 new cases every year. Schizophrenia strikes one out of every 100 people under the age of 55. (Bloom, et al., 1985)

A study of psychopaths in one federal hospital found that almost one-fifth of the total population suffered from psychopathy. (Cleckley, 1964) Because traditional legal and medical rules do not apply to psychopaths, it is hard to pinpoint the numbers. It is also common knowledge that it is only the unlucky or unsuccessful psychopaths who ever allow themselves to be put into a controlled environment, such as a prison or institution.

"Most statistical studies . . . cannot be regarded as even remotely suggesting the prevalence of this disability in the population," says Cleckley (1982, p. 12)

A review of the prevalence of antisocial personalities cites six studies that estimate from 0.05 to 15% of the total adult population in this country suffers some form of APD. (Rosenthal, 1970) One problem in making such estimates is that the concepts of psychopathy vary from investigator to investigator. Because of these problems, it is almost impossible to pin-point the exact number of psychopaths at this time. (Freedman, et al., 1975) The above figures may be conservative estimates, especially if we were to count the conniving entrepreneurs—such as the character portrayed so well on television's "Dallas" as the woman-killer, oilman "J. R. Ewing."

The population of the U.S. is now 260 million. If you consider just 5% of this figure, there could be 13 million psychopaths.

The toll in future years from these individuals will be measured in increased child abuse and neglect, broken homes and hearts, cheating and stealing and criminal acts. Up to one-half of all those currently incarcerated suffer some form of psychopathy. (Cleckley, 1964)

This segment of the population has a huge impact on society, in the time and money spent on either trying to correct APD or on the institutionalization of those with APD. This time and effort is spent attempting to manage their incorrigible behavior as children, dealing with their criminal offenses as adults, or caring for their deserted families. The bottom line is that this is a costly minority.

As society has begun to address the problems of crime and violence it will have to reckon with the antisocial personality. For while crime and antisocial personality are not synonymous, there is no question that a substantial amount of the criminal and violent behavior in this country is committed by those with APD.

The Disease of Psychopathy

It is important, as we explore this illness, to remember that psychopaths run the gamut from mildly impaired to criminal. On a scale showing humanity from its best to its worst the homicidal psychopath, such as Manson or Bundy, would be at one end of the continuum and an exemplary individual such as Mother Teresa of Calcutta would be at the other.

Those on the middle of the scale suffer some problems, but are still able to function in society. Those on the extreme end—those with acute APD—are the most dangerous and inevitably end up doing incredible harm to other human beings.

The degree of psychological damage suffered as a child has a direct bearing on how the lifestyles of people with APD are affected. One telling characteristic is in the area of occupations; both men and women afflicted with APD almost always have problems in their occupations. Typically there are frequent job changes, lengthy periods of unemployment and problems with bosses or peers. Financial dependency may include total or partial support by relatives, social agencies or institutions. Particularly among male APD sufferers one will see an arrest record. The marriages of these people often involve verbal or physical fighting, separation and divorce. Desertion and nonsupport are common. Antisocials also have a higher incidence of alcohol and drug abuse.

Typically school problems are in their backgrounds; Trust Bandits have school records replete with truancy, fighting, suspensions and expulsions.

The Conscience of Humanity

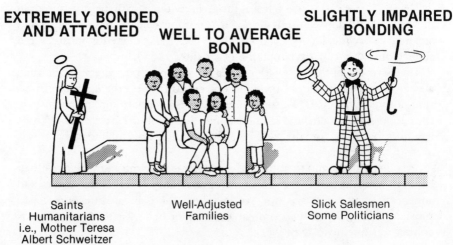

EXTREMELY BONDED AND ATTACHED

WELL TO AVERAGE BOND

SLIGHTLY IMPAIRED BONDING

Saints
Humanitarians
i.e., Mother Teresa
Albert Schweitzer

Well-Adjusted
Families

Slick Salesmen
Some Politicians

Sexual promiscuity is common, particularly among women where it is true in about 90% of the cases. The antisocial personality is always socially isolated without any true friends, although they may have numerous casual aquaintances. (Freedman, et al., 1975, p.1293)

Even among medical dictionaries, the definitions of "psychopathy" are inconsistent and they often conflict with the actual psychiatric use of the word.

It's necessary to understand something about terminology. In the past the terms used to describe this illness have been psychopaths or sociopaths. Some professionals, however, objected to these general terms and a new attempt was made to classify these individuals for clinicians.

The Diagnostic and Statistical Manual (DSM-III) is the "bible" used by mental health professionals when they diagnose patients. The DSM-III is the authorized manual for the American Psychiatric Association and lists the symptoms, histories and other pertinent facts about all classified mental illnesses. In the 1968 edition of the DSM-II, the illness previously called psychopath changed slightly to antisocial personality disorder. (In this book we often use the abbreviation APD.) We will also use the more common and durable term, psychopath to refer to people with this diagnosis. As we quote others, the terms presented above may be considered interchangeable. We will use the name "Trust Bandit" as a generic way of referring to individuals who display behavior which is characteristic of psychopaths, regardless of whether they have officially been diagnosed as having APD. Finally, we often refer to children with this disorder as character-disturbed.

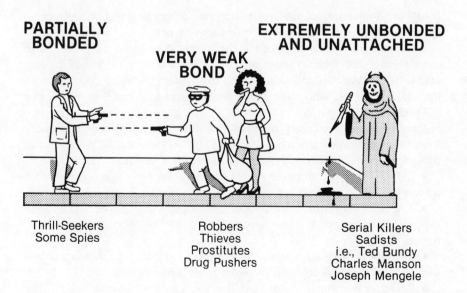

PARTIALLY BONDED

VERY WEAK BOND

EXTREMELY UNBONDED AND UNATTACHED

Thrill-Seekers
Some Spies

Robbers
Thieves
Prostitutes
Drug Pushers

Serial Killers
Sadists
i.e., Ted Bundy
Charles Manson
Joseph Mengele

The concept of the antisocial personality is the end product of a long evolution. It began in 1806 with P. Pinel's case of *manie sans delire.* Pinel described a "mania without delirium" when a French peasant in a fit of rage threw a woman down a well. This description was the first recorded case of antisocial personality. (Freedman, et al., 1975)

It is important to point out that the diagnosis of APD is not limited to the United States. Most countries have their share of these people. Some, however, like Sweden, have lower incidences primarily because of the quality of care afforded their children from a very early age. Sweden in 1987 had a population of 8 million, yet only 740 individuals were locked up in prison hospital wards for mental illness. One of the problems of making comparisons between countries is the fact that the definitions of psychopaths differ. But it can be safely said that the number of high risk people without a conscience who get into serious trouble with the law is much greater in America, relative to the population, than in countries which focus their attention on early childhood, such as Sweden. Sweden has an extremely low rate of psychopathic killers.

One question asked through the ages has been: "Is there such a thing as a criminal personality?" The answer, based on present data, seems to be a heavily qualified "yes."

C. Robert Cloninger feels the diagnosis of antisocial personality " . . . is at least as reliable as that of most other psychiatric disorders . . . There does seem to exist an identifiable personality type, the joint product of genetic and environmental factors, that is highly prone to criminal behavior. The type that . . . is known most commonly as antisocial personality" (1978, p. 97-98).

Just as all unattached children do not turn out to be psychopaths, not all psychopaths commit crimes that put them in jail. There are many Trust Bandits who have lesser degrees of the illness. These may be people who cannot love and often their lives are strewn with a series of broken marriages. Or they are individuals who have found it easy to con their way through life. People who go to prison may be antisocial, but they may not be full-fledged psychopaths.

Among criminals who are psychopaths, there are interesting differences from other criminals. Herschel A. Prins (1977) points to the psychopaths' lack of "affect" and Cleckley (1964) cites other distinctions:

● Criminal activity in psychopaths begins at an early age and pervades their social and personal behavior more than it does in typical criminals.

● The greatest harm done by the psychopath is to others. This often happens because others have a concern for the psychopath but he only rejects them.

● The psychopath often engages in antisocial acts that are incomprehensible and he indulges in these acts for quite obscure reasons.

● Ordinary criminals often have loyalties to friends and family. The hallmark of a true psychopath is that he has no loyalties; he is a loner.

More than a half-century ago Sigmund Freud's student Alfred Adler, noted: "They are suffering from a wrong outlook upon the world, a wrong estimate of their own importance and the importance of other people." Adler said a criminal's crimes "fit in with his general conception of life." (1977, pp. 7-13)

The same might be said of psychopaths.

"All (criminals) regard the world as a chessboard over which they have total control, and they perceive people as pawns to be pushed around at will," says Stanton E. Samenow in *Inside the Criminal Mind* (1984, p. 20) "Trust, love, loyalty, and teamwork are incompatible with their way of life. They scorn and exploit most people who are kind, trusting, hardworking and honest."

Con artist Joe Flynn's specialty was extracting money from well-known individuals and organizations, such as publisher Rupert Murdoch and businessman John De Lorean, bankers, the FBI, the CIA, and various embassies. Flynn admits he is a crook, but he says remorse doesn't keep him awake at night. He believes that politics, banks, finance companies and business institutions are filled with con men, although they may operate within the letter of the law.

"They honestly believe they are honest. I know I'm a crook. Whatever way you flower it up, I'm a crook. But I don't pretend to myself I'm anything else," he says. (Henderson, 1985)

Cleckley wrote his book in part to encourage psychiatrists to acknowledge that psychopathy is a serious illness, despite its "mask of sanity." In it he gives a vivid and succinct account of psychopathy, saying the severe psychopath may seem to be enjoying . . .

> "robust mental health. Yet he has a disorder that often manifests
> itself in conduct far more seriously abnormal than that of the
> schizophrenic . . . We are dealing here with not a complete man
> at all but with something that suggests a subtly constructed
> reflex machine." (1964, p.419)

Mental health professionals have learned to look for certain characteristics when trying to diagnose psychopaths. To help in this identification they use symptoms spelled out in the DSM-III manual. The manual says of the term "antisocial personality":

> "The central feature is a personality disorder in which there is
> a history of continuous and chronic antisocial behavior in which
> the rights of others are violated; persistence into adult life of a
> pattern of antisocial behavior that began before the age of 15; a
> failure to sustain good job performance over a period of several
> years (although this may not be evident in individuals who are

self-employed or may not be in a position to demonstrate this
feature, such as housewives and students); the antisocial
behavior is not due to severe mental retardation, schizophrenia
or manic episodes.

"Lying, stealing, fighting, truancy and resisting authority are
typical early childhood signs. In adolescence unusually early or
aggressive sexual behavior, excessive drinking and the use of
illicit drugs are frequent. In adulthood these kinds of behavior
continue, with the addition of the inability to sustain consistent
work performance or to function as a responsible parent and
failure to accept social norms with respect to lawful behavior."
(1980, pp. 317-318)

As we have said, these individuals are incapable of forming lasting
relationships, never becoming truly intimate and open with others. They
have no enduring friendships and their children often become unattached.
They are usually reliable and often fail to meet financial obligations. They
steal the trust of those around them, with little regard for how they hurt the
ones they leave behind.

Take for example, the case of Frank Abagnale, Jr., one of the best known
"con men" of this decade. Abagnale's book *Catch Me if You Can,* is
dedicated "To my dad." Yet, in an anecdotal introduction to his life,
Abagnale writes:

"The detective confronted me . . . 'You'd con your own father,
Frank.' I already had. My father was the mark for the first score I
ever made. Dad possessed the one trait necessary in the perfect
pigeon, blind trust, and I plucked him for $3,400. I was 15 at the
time." (1980, p. 5)

Perhaps one of the most interesting types of people in the category APD is
the impostor. Often these people are outstanding at the roles they have
assumed. One classic case is that of Ferdinand Waldo Demara, Jr.

Demara ran away from home as an adolescent after a tragic family life. He
first tried to become a Trappist monk and then a teacher. Failing at those, he
began to take on the identities of a number of individuals, eventually ending
up performing surgery as a doctor! He was able to obtain the credentials of a
Dr. French, including a Ph.D. in psychology from Harvard. Demara then
faked his own death and took on the identity of Dr. French. As the good
doctor, he was appointed dean of philosophy in a Canadian college.

He became friendly with a medical doctor and using his identity obtained
a commission in the Royal Canadian Navy. It was there that he was called
upon to perform surgery, after he became the ship's doctor on the Canadian
destroyer Cayuga.

"The self-taught M.D. cleaned and sutured the 16 less seriously wounded men, while gathering his courage for the great ordeal. Then he commandeered the captain's cabin as an emergency operating room. Working hour after hour with slow, unskilled hands, but drawing on all the resources of his great memory and natural genius, Demara performed miracles." (Coleman, et al., 1980, pp. 287-288)

Had the surgeries not made the newspapers Demara might have continued in his role as ship's doctor. But he was found out when the real doctor saw a write-up with his former friend's picture.

A Superficial Mask

"Unless you know what's really going on, these children are the ones you least suspect when something goes wrong. It will take a mother, over a period of time, to notice that there is always havoc when this one kid enters the room. But he always seems to come out smelling like a rose. You would never suspect this particular kid of instigating the trouble. That's how good his cover is." (C. Watkins, personal communication, January 26, 1987)

It often isn't easy, even for a trained therapist, to recognize children or adults who are psychopaths. Even in early years, young psychopaths contain at least two sides to their personalities. The outside, superficial mask is often a likeable character. Usually this charming "public side" is verbally fluent and capable of making short-term friends easily. As one distressed mother of a character-disturbed child put it:

"My son could walk up to perfect strangers and within 5 minutes have them wishing that he was their child and that they could take him home with them." (Cline, 1979)

At first meeting, there may be a sense that something is different about these individuals. Usually the "difference" is misinterpreted. Their eyes often sparkle and they frequently are very animated, compelling, almost hypnotic. They are generally not perceived as bad or evil. More often, they are charming and engaging.

Although these psychopaths are at center stage, they are masters at presenting the illusion that the person they are with is the focus of attention. A curious trait that psychopaths often have is extrasensory perception about others and the ability to pick out personal vulnerabilities with uncanny accuracy. This information they store for later use. They frequently will compliment and praise their new acquaintance, winning him over with their "charm."

Many teachers are at first fooled by these young children when they enter the classroom situation. They believe them to be among the brightest, most promising students, ready and willing to learn. It is only after their devious nature is discovered that the great disappointment of unfulfilled dreams is realized.

A teacher; "At first I thought Paul was a model student; quiet, polite, motivated to learn and thoughtful. You can imagine my surprise when I turned my back one day and he goosed me!" Paul is 7. (Cline, 1979, p.140)

"It must be remembered," said author Cleckley (1982) "that even the most severely and obviously disabled psychopath presents a technical appearance of sanity, often one of high intellectual capacities and not infrequently succeeds in business or professional activities for short periods, some for considerable periods . . . Although they occasionally appear on casual inspection as successful members of the community, as able lawyers, executives, or physicians, they do not, it seems, succeed in the sense of finding satisfaction or fulfillment in their own accomplishments. Nor do they, when the full story is known, appear to find this in any other ordinary activity." (p.102)

"The fake poet who really feels little; the painter who, despite his loftiness, had his eye chiefly on the lucrative fad of his day; the fashionable clergyman who, despite his burning eloquence or his lively castigation of the devil, is primarily concerned with his own advancement; the flirt who can readily awaken love but cannot feel love or recognize its absence; parents who, despite smooth convictions that they have only the child's welfare at heart, actually reject him except as it suits their own petty or selfish aims—all these types, so familiar in literature and in anybody's experience, may be as they are because of a slight affliction with the personality disorder now under discussion." (Cleckley, 1982, p.103)

But how are average people to know when they come across someone afflicted with antisocial personality disorder? Despite the initial charm of these individuals, it is hard to confuse the long-term pattern of behavior of a psychopath with anything else.

There are telling symptoms, some of which may be recognizable right away, and others that will take time to decifer.

Psychologist Walter Schreibman, who practices in Denver, Colorado, has had extensive training in recognizing and treating people with APD. He offers this advice in spotting such manipulators:

> "If someone you first meet, or listen to, sounds or looks 'too good' or 'too smooth' to you or you find yourself becoming spellbound by their words . . . step back and take another look. You may be dealing with a psychopath." (W. Schriebman, personal communication, April, 1986)

The Symptoms

Dr. Foster Cline, an authority on unattached children whose mental health clinic is located in Evergreen, Colorado, has spent a lifetime diagnosing and treating children with attachment problems. He has developed an interesting and comprehensive list of telling characteristics of the unattached child (character-disturbed child), some of which are also found in the DSM-III. If you know of a child with any or all of these symptoms you are looking at a child at high risk for developing APD as an adult. The more symptoms a child has, the more severe his attachment problem may be:

PROFILE OF CHARACTER-DISTURBED CHILD

1. Lack of ability to give and receive affection.
2. Self-destructive behavior.
3. Cruelty to others.
4. Phoniness.
5. Severe problems with stealing, hoarding and gorging on food.
6. Speech pathology.
7. Marked control problems.
8. Lack of long-term friends.
9. Abnormalities in eye contact.

---

10. Parents appear angry and hostile.
11. Preoccupation with fire, blood or gore.
12. Superficial attractiveness and friendliness with strangers.
13. Various types of learning disorders.
14. A particular pathological type of lying—"primary process lying."(Cline, 1979, p.128)

Cleckley was the first to establish a list of characteristics for adult psychopaths, in 1964. Since then the list for psychopaths has been modified and enlarged and has been used to test prisoners for psychopathy. In subsequent research the checklist was confirmed for its high reliability (Schroeder, Schroeder, and Hare, 1983). Notice the correlations between this list of characteristics and that of the symptoms for character-disturbed children.

CHARACTERISTICS OF A PSYCHOPATH

1. Glibness/superficial charm.
2. Grandiose sense of self-worth.
3. Need for stimulation/proneness to boredom.
4. Pathological lying.
5. Conning/manipulative.
6. Lack of remorse or guilt.
7. Shallow affect.
8. Callous/lack of empathy.
9. Parasitic lifestyle.
10. Poor behavioral controls.
11. Promiscuous sexual behavior.
12. Early behavior problems.
13. Lack of realistic, long-term plans.
14. Impulsivity.
15. Irresponsibility.
16. Failure to accept responsibility for own actions.
17. Many short-term marital relationships.
18. Juvenile delinquency.
19. Revocation of conditional release.
20. Criminal versatility. (Hare, 1986)

Although much of the latter listing applies only to adult situations, many children who are unattached display a considerable number of the symptoms.

What is unfortunate is that the DSM-III fails to give a complete list of symptoms, making early identification and treatment more difficult. As Schreibman (personal communication, April, 1986) puts it, "The DSM is totally inadequate in helping the average professional know how to deal with this aberrant personality. For example, the DSM doesn't even allude to some common symptoms, such as viciousness to pets and being 'devil-worshippers.' "

Mass-murderer Kenneth Bianchi, for example, was a master at fooling everyone—even the experts. As the Hillside Strangler, Bianchi had terrorized the Los Angeles area for more than a year in 1977. Bianchi, with his cousin Angelo Buono, raped, tortured and then murdered 10 Los Angeles women and girls ages 12 to 28. Bianchi killed two more after moving to Washington State.

In Los Angeles, Bianchi had used phony police badges to fool his victims; in Washington he worked as a uniformed security guard.

Bianchi, ever the manipulator, almost lied himself out of the murder rap! He fooled the experts into believing he suffered from multiple personality syndrome. Indeed, four "expert" witnesses—renowned psychiatrists and psychologists—testified that Bianchi had a multiple personality and was therefore not responsible for his actions.

Bianchi had studied enough psychology to fool easily most people. (He at one time operated a phony counseling service with framed "degrees" and police found numerous books on psychology at his home.) He even fooled the experts into believing that an evil division of his personality had actually committed the murders and that he knew nothing of them.

It was only when prosecutors brought in a fifth psychiatrist—after irate street-wise police officers had urged it—that Bianchi's deception was uncovered. Martin Orne, M.D., Ph.D., professor of psychology and psychiatry at the University of Pennsylvania, finally used some foolery of his own to ferret out Bianchi's ruse.

Orne made the casual suggestion to Bianchi before a hypnosis session that in cases of multiple personalities there are usually more than two personalities. Bianchi, although quite clever, took the bait. During the next hypnosis session, Bianchi came up with a third personality. The third "personality" turned out to be a real psychologist whose identity Bianchi had used on occasion. Thus, his "pretend world" met the real one. Orne never believed the criminal was actually hypnotized; he says Bianchi faked it.

Orne said he knew Bianchi was faking all along because he made such grandiose efforts to point out differences in mannerisms between his "personalities. He kept referring, time and time again, to the fact that the filter had been torn off the cigarettes in the ashtray, for example. He kept saying, 'Now, how could that have happened? I don't do that,' etc., etc. He kept repeating this over and over again," says Orne, "I knew he was lying." (*Frontline*, 1985)

An in-depth program on the Bianchi murders was broadcast in 1985 on a special *Frontline* television presentation. The program clearly showed why it is so hard for most people to spot a clever psychopath:

Elizabeth Baron, deputy attorney general for the State of California, described the mental picture she had of the murderer while the crimes were being committed.

> "It could have been my colleague at the office . . . someone waiting on a table at a restaurant . . . the person taking the tickets at the theater. This was not a monster but someone who would fade anonymously into all the other people. He was going to be someone who was someone's loving son . . . loving husband . . . sweet neighbor . . . loving brother. People were going to be really surprised when they found out. That really was frightening because you didn't have a way to guard yourself, to protect yourself. It could have been anybody."

He even fooled his common-law wife, Kelli Boyd, who told *Frontline* reporters and police, "The Ken I knew couldn't have hurt anyone. He was helpful with the baby, thoughtful, even helped around the house. He just wasn't the kind of person who could have killed anyone."

In fact, Kenneth Bianchi had suffered from APD since young childhood. Records obtained by the police showed that his descriptions of his mother as a "saintly woman" were far from the truth. (It is typical for adults who were neglected as children—and become unattached children—to deny that their mothers were cruel to them.) Bianchi claimed to have no memory of various events from his childhood, including long periods when he was under psychiatric care.

"Ken Bianchi had a long history, showing a tremendous amount of pathology and difficulties in the family. He was considered a disturbed child," said Dr. Ralph Allison, who at first believed Bianchi to be a multiple personality. The psychiatrist subsequently changed his mind after doing additional work with prisoners at a penitentiary. "Some of these guys change their story every day," he said. "I guess I was wrong; he fooled me."

Bianchi as a child was trotted from one medical doctor to another when he suffered a series of symptoms, including rolling eyes, tics, falling down after petit mal-type seizures. The doctors referred his mother to a psychiatrist. She took him to Los Angeles' De Paul Clinic where records show doctors found Kenneth to be "a deeply hostile boy who has very dependent needs, which his mother fulfills. He depends upon his mother for his very survival and expends a great deal of energy keeping his hostility under control and under cover.

"There seems to be some basic confusion about his own identity. He seems to try hard to placate his mother, but she always seems dissatisfied. He is a severely depressed boy who seems very anxious and lonely."

Like so many young psychopaths—character-disturbed children— Kenneth Bianchi drew pictures of devils and demons. His lawyer uncovered an old sculpture he had done. One side was the image of a man; the other, a horrible demon. He was a child who bore the brunt of his mother's wrath at her gambling husband. She often hit and badgered Bianchi, who at a young age would hide from her. He said his favorite place—"the best place"—was under his bed.

Margaret Singer, professor of psychology at the University of California at Berkeley, studied the case. She told *Frontline*:

"From childhood on Mr. Bianchi's history is that of a typical psychopath. Even his own mother said he had a history of lying, lying, lying. He has a history of lifelong, almost pointless lying—the mark of a psychopath is habitual lying. It seems easier to them to lie than to tell the truth and lying is done usually to try to persuade a person or to try to make the psychopath feel better at the moment."

Bianchi was so good at manipulation he convinced one woman he had known casually before his arrest in Washington to fabricate an alibi for him for the time the killings took place in that state. Angie Kenniberg said she did it because she was in love with him and believed him innocent. (On the advice of Bianchi's lawyer, she withdrew the alibi.)

Amazingly, Dr. Singer said Kenniberg was only one of 12 women Bianchi convinced to stand up for him with alibis. "He even asked his mother to type up an alibi letter—while she wore rubber gloves so they couldn't trace it to her—and to fly to Washington and mail it from there. Psychopaths do not give up . . . they don't stop. Are they sane? Yes, in the eyes of the law. But they exhibit outrageous behavior. The general public may think that is crazy."

After the longest and possibly the most expensive trial in Los Angeles history, Bianchi was sentenced to life in prison. He had plea-bargained his way out of the death sentence by agreeing to testify against his cousin. Judge Ronald M. George was furious at the plea-bargain as he passed judgment, saying:

"If ever there was a case where the death penalty was appropriate, this is that case. Angelo Buono and Kenneth Bianchi terrorized the community for several months, haunting the city like the ultimate and evil spirits, as they abducted children and young women, torturing, raping and, finally, depriving their family and friends of them forever as they slowly squeezed out of their victims their last breath of air and their promise of a future life. And for what? The momentary, sadistic thrill of enjoying a brief perverted sexual satisfaction and the venting of their hatred of women."

In a contemptuous tone of voice, Judge George concluded; "Mr. Bianchi faked memory loss, multiple personality and hypnosis. In this Mr. Bianchi was unwittingly aided and abetted by various psychiatrists who naively swallowed Mr. Bianchi's story hook, line and sinker." George said Buono and Bianchi were "incapable of feeling remorse."

This mass-murderer, a master at deception and assumed personalities, is at the far end of the socialization scale, of course. But he is an example of what 12 innocent girls encountered and of what any of us could someday face.

Examples of other people you may meet in day-to-day life who have APD but to a lesser degree than someone like Bianchi are: the person willing to sell a dangerously defective used car; the ex-husband/wife who plays only by his or her rules; the child who tells bold-faced lies; the boss who steals his subordinates' ideas as his own; the credit card holder who skips town when it's time to pay up; the lover who promises more than a one-night stand, but never calls again; the con men; the fakes; the Elmer Gantrys . . . the Trust Bandits . . .

Another convicted "mass murderer" is Donald Harvey of Cincinnati, whose crimes came to light in June, 1987.

An orderly, Harvey told investigators a tale of stalking hospital halls—on a self-appointed mission to end the suffering of the dying. He plead guilty to the murder of 24 patients at Drake Hospital. And, sources close to the on-going investigation said he has admitted killing more than 50 individuals in seven Cincinnati area hospitals.

In August, 1987, Harvey was indicted for aggravated murder in connection with the cyanide poisoning of one patient at Drake.

It was Dr. Lee Lehman, a deputy coroner, who became suspicious during an autopsy. He detected an odor of burned almonds—the smell of cyanide—and ordered tests. Patient John Powell, 44, of Ohio had died at Drake Hospital on March 7. His comatose condition stemmed from a motorcycle accident and Powell's body had been routinely sent to the Hamilton County morgue for an autopsy.

When the tests came back Harvey was indicted for aggravated murder. (Ludlow, August, 1987, p. 38)

A look at Harvey's childhood brings out a familiar story of abuse. Now an avowed homosexual, Harvey was allegedly sexually molested by an uncle from an early age until he was a teenager. He dropped out of junior high school in his early teens and at 18 joined the Air Force.

Harvey's father died while he was still a small child. This, plus his early sexual abuse have undoubtedly contributed to what the prosecution has called Harvey's "personality disorder."

This latest mass murderer's background fits the profile for an unattached, abused child.

"There are psychopathic personalities in the highest echelons of government, and even within religious heirarchies in America. You can't just assume that, a person with the title 'judge' or 'hospital orderly,' got there honestly and won't manipulate the hell out of you," says psychologist Schreibman. (personal communication, February 10, 1986) He agrees with Cleckley that psychopaths are far more common than thought.

Researchers recently have been gathering evidence of a link between criminality and the interaction between social and certain biological factors. Whether the biological factors (such as low I.Q.s) are caused by genetics or the infant's early environment has not been proven. But one thing has been determined: offenders share some typical characteristics.

James Q. Wilson and Richard J. Herrnstein, in researching their 1985 book *Crime & Human Nature,* found that the temperament characteristics of high-rate offenders were: impulsiveness, insensitivity to social mores, an appetite for danger, and a lack of deep and enduring emotional attachment to others.

As the child grows, these traits, among others, may unfold into a unconventional, deviant or antisocial behavior.

Author Samenow (1984) talks in his book, *Inside the Criminal Mind,* of the parents as victims when they have a child who is going wrong:

> "As the personality of the criminally-inclined child unfolds, his parents are gripped by a gnawing fear that something terrible is going to happen. Their nerves are constantly on edge. Every time the phone rings, their hearts sink. What is it this time—a distraught neighbor, a teacher reporting a fight, the police, or worst of all, a hospital informing them that their child is injured or dead? (p. 42)

He chronicles how the mother is totally bewildered by her son's behavior:

> "One mother in this quandary said, 'At first, we felt that he would just naturally grow out of this disruptive behavior pattern, but as time went on and things began to escalate, it became obvious that there was something else wrong.' She had seen his traits as a young child—his daring, his sense of adventure, his cunning and persistent way of pursuing what he wanted, his occasional tantrums—give way to incessant lying, belligerence, defiance, and destructiveness. 'The cute,' she said, 'gave way to the unbelievable.'" (Samenow, 1984, p. 45)

Lee Robins, a sociologist at Washington University School of Medicine in St. Louis, reconstructed 30 years of the lives of more than 500 children who were patients in the 1920s at a child guidance clinic. She wanted to find precursors of chronic sociopathy. She found that—without exception—adult sociopaths were antisocial before they were 18. The more symptoms manifested as a child, the greater the risk of adulthood sociopathy. (Wilson and Herrnstein, 1985)

One study of a sample of delinquent boys in Denver by John J. Conger and Wilbur C. Miller found that "by the end of the third grade, future delinquents . . . [were] more poorly adapted than their class-mates . . . appeared to have less regard for the rights and feelings of their peers; less awareness of the need to accept responsibility for their obligations . . . and have poorer attitudes toward authority." (1966, p.185)

Indeed, if psychopathy could be prevented or controlled, we believe a significant amount of the serious crime in this country could be prevented.

Of inmates tested for psychopathy, virtually half have been found to suffer from the malady. (Reid, et al., 1986)

Most Americans, unfortunately, don't know how to identify such individuals and do not realize how hard it is to stop a smart, dedicated psychopath. Many criminal psychopaths are so clever that they are not in jails.

Serial killer Bundy once said, "These are people far more successful than I." He, like other psychopaths, envied those criminals who had not been caught for their crimes. Statistically the chances are good that someday you, or someone you love, will cross the path of a psychopath. Whether that psychopath will be similar to a Bundy or Manson is hard to say, because there are so many different degrees of psychopaths and they are so well disguised. What is not difficult to predict is that any encounter with a psychopath is dangerous and usually leads to innocent victims being hurt.

The manipulation used by psychopaths is generally based on charm. The manipulator appears to be helpful, even ingratiating or seductive, but is covertly hostile, domineering, or, at best, neutral in interaction with another, whom he or she considers an object. This object is perceived as an aggressor, competitor, or an instrument to be used. (Reid, et al., 1986)

Psychiatrist M. Scott Peck, M.D., is known for his outspoken writing linking religious beliefs and psychology. His best-selling *People of the Lie* (1983) talks of evil as a disease. The people Peck labels as evil are not, he says, crazy as ordinarily perceived. They are not babbling and demented. "They deny the suffering of their guilt . . . by casting their pain onto others through projection and scapegoating. They themselves may not suffer, but those around them do. They cause suffering. The evil create for those under their dominion a miniature, sick society." (pp. 123-124) He is talking about psychopaths.

APD is a disease of the mind which, in adults at present, is without a cure. Like a cancer, it grows in the dark. It grows in the inner recesses of the mind, its roots imbedded in early childhood. It is the AIDS (Acquired Immune Deficiency Syndrome) of the mental health world.

Most psychopaths at first glance, as we have noted, seem quite well put together—quite normal. They don't suffer from delusions, hallucinations, or memory impairment, their contact with reality appears solid.

Rather, their mental defect—and it's substantial—manifests itself as a chronic inability to behave in conformance with social norms, to defer gratification, control impulses, tolerate frustration, profit from corrective experiences, or identify with others and form meaningful relationships with them. The psychopath must have what he wants, no matter the cost to those in his way.

We Are Vulnerable

It is no secret that many in our quick-paced society are starved for love and affection. The power to capitalize on this is never lost on skilled manipulators, whether they be 6 or 60 years old. Even trained psychiatrists have been fooled.

A distraught mother, who has three other, "normal," children, finally took her very troubled 8-year-old daughter to a child psychiatrist. She wondered how he would deal with this child. This is the account of the first meeting, which the mother later related to a psychologist trained in recognizing and treating unattached children. The psychiatrist first consulted about the child did not have the skills to recognize what he was dealing with when confronted with Laurie.

"Laurie entered the room and immediately took control, but it was so subtle the doctor didn't recognize it. At first, she hung her head and acted frightened, so when he attempted to coax her out, she pretended to be resistant, bashful, and shy (which she isn't at all).

"Then, after a few minutes, she said that it was easy to talk to him: 'Much better than those doctors at school.' While the doctor was taking this in, she commented on how pretty the designs on his tie were, and asked to sit on his lap. Then she proceeded to tell him what he wanted to hear, about how she had gotten into some trouble in school, but it was because no one understood her and how it felt real good to be with him . . . in fant, she asked him if he would be her new daddy! She said all her father ever did was yell at her.

"Afterward, the doctor told me that he had established a perfect rapport with Laurie and that she was a loving child who was just misunderstood! He said we should be giving her more love. I couldn't believe it. Our 8-year-old daughter had conned a psychiatrist."

Just three weeks before this "loving child" had poked another little girl's eye out with a pencil at school after she hadn't gotten her way.

Psychiatrists are often helplessly manipulated by the psychopath; just as are the psychopath's other victims.

These manipulators wear the mask of sanity, but strip away that mask and their other identity is seen. While they can grow up to be seemingly harmless con artists there is also a very dark side, simmering just beneath the surface. It is this dark side that puts us all at high risk.

Charles Manson has been called the most dangerous, feared man alive. There is perhaps no better example in modern times of a petty thief/con artist whose dark side eventually erupted, shocking a nation. Manson always had a black side simmering just beneath the surface. When it emerged the horrible result was the Tate/LaBianca massacre. The two-day killing spree left 7 people mutilated and dead, including movie actress Sharon Tate.

On the evening of the Tate murders, August 8, 1969, Manson says, "I was aware of being totally without conscience. Though I have pointed to numerous circumstances in my life that may have turned my head in the wrong direction, I can't put a finger on when I became devoid of caring emotion." (Emmons, 1986, p. 202)

In his damning book *Manson in His Own Words* (as told to Nuel Emmons, 1986) Manson lays open the life and thoughts of a man whose acts left us trembling.

There is no better living proof of what can go wrong if the attachment bond isn't formed than Charles Manson. He was born in 1934 in Cincinnati, Ohio, to an unmarried 15-year-old girl. His early life was spent in a succession of different homes and with a number of substitute parents. Finally, his mother asked Indiana state authorities to take over his care when he was 12 years old. Since the age of 12 Manson has lived most of his life behind bars. He was first placed in a reform school and, after escaping from there, was sent to the National Training School for Boys in Washington, D.C. He was set free when he was 19 years old.

"Jails, courtrooms and prisons have been my life since I was 12 years old," Manson says in his book. "By the time I was 16, I had lost all fear of anything the administration of the prison system could dish out." (Emmons, 1986, p.21) He sees himself as a person who was dealt a hand that couldn't be played by the rules and values of our society.

"Most of the stories and articles written painted me as having fangs and horns from birth. They say my mother was a whore . . . would it change things to say I had no choice in selecting my mother? Or that, being a bastard child, I was an outlaw from birth? That during those so-called formative years, I was not in control of my life?

"Hey, listen, by the time I was old enough to think or remember, I had been shoved around and left with people who were strangers even to those I knew. Rejection, more than love and acceptance, has been a part of my life since birth." (p. 24)

In explaining why he decided to let Nuel Emmons write the book, Manson says he wanted to answer those who have asked where his philosophy, bitterness and antisocial behavior came from.

There is little doubt that it came from the horrible childhood suffered by the boy who would one day strike terror in the hearts of all mankind. Charles Manson was neglected and used as a child, setting the stage for the conscienceless adult he was to become. "My feeling is, I've been raped and ravaged by society . . . by attorney and friends. Sucked dry by the courts. Beaten by the guards and exhibited by the prisons . . . My body remains trapped and imprisoned by a society that creates people like me." (p.25)

Viewed as a master manipulator who lured young girls and boys to do his dirty deeds, Manson acknowledges that his prison background helped him when he finally was released from Terminal Island in 1967 after serving 7 years time for being a pimp. He stepped into the world of the Hippie Movement in San Francisco to find that his anti-establishment views endeared him to the young street people.

Manson, however, discounts what he calls the "Manson myth" saying he didn't have any special power to seduce people to do his bidding. He says the truth is that "I ain't never been anything but a half-assed thief who didn't know how to steal without getting caught." (p. 226)

He acknowledges there are still victims of the hype portraying him as a charismatic cult leader, guru, lover, pied piper or another Jesus. Manson says his disappointment is "that so many of you are so gullible, that you eat everything you are fed." He ends his book by saying:

> "I want you to know I've got everything in the world, and beyond, right here . . . So, save your sympathy and know that only a body is in prison. At my will, I walk your streets and am right out there among you." (p. 227)

Manson's life points out some of the important differences between psychopaths and more ordinary manipulators. One might consider, for example, entrepreneurs—those who organize, manage and assume responsibility for a business or other enterprise—as manipulative. There is one telling difference between how an entrepreneur views the world and the psychopath does, however. The entrepreneur's manipulation is chosen; for the psychopath, it is an obligation. (Person, 1986, p. 257)

Usually we reserve the term psychopath for those who are "unsuccessful." But there are probably many persons of power and influence who lack morals and guilt who could be termed "successful" psychopaths. Eventually, however, their deeds usually drag them down.

Because the typical psychopath is attractive, impressive and charming, some of the nation's largest businesses may be unknowingly recruiting psychopaths into their ranks. Few businesses, no matter how sophisticated their personnel departments, have had success in knowing how to deal with psychopaths in their midst.

The personality of the psychopath is one of interpersonal manipulator, almost always tainted by antisocial drives. The motivation is to dominate. The psychopath is driven to humiliate the person he is "conning." This can take the form of "using" someone close to the person he is "out to get." He may, for example, seduce a "friend's" girlfriend or spread untrue rumors about a business associate. The situations have a thousand themes, but the outcome is always the same . . . pain and loss.

One example of such manipulation is a young single mother, known to her friends and family to be neglectful of her small children. Yet, when visitors are in her home she feigns love and affection. The mother goes to elaborate efforts to "prove" how responsible she is as a mother. For example, she makes a big deal of excusing herself, saying she has to "give him a goodnight kiss and tuck her in." She makes a great display of cooing and cuddling her babies in the presence of her family.

As soon as she and her children are alone, however, they are treated as virtual slaves, becoming classic "gophers." Only because of stories innocently told by the eldest child does anyone suspect the psychological—and occasionally physical—abuse that is going on in the household. To family and friends this mother presents an outward appearance that seems attractive, impressive and charming. But her only real goal is to dominate. The paradox is that in her mind she must carry out the ruse with her family to satisfy her own anxiety and depression. And she cannot see the inconsistency of her actions.

Ethel Spector Person is an expert on manipulators; she has called the psychopath "a curious mixture of cynicism coupled with a magical belief that fortune will smile on him." (1986, p.265) Although the ultimate effects of psychopathic behavior may be devastating, the underlying purpose of self-destructive acts isn't to fail, but to assuage anxiety and depression. From the psychopath's point of view, then, his behavior is not reprehensible, but self-defense. (Person, 1986, p. 266)

Psychopaths, whether adult or children, lie in the face of absolute reality. For example, a child may have his hand in his mother's purse. The mother sees him and asks "What are you doing in my purse?" The child answers, "I'm not in your purse."

" . . . so he was standing there, holding onto the dog's tail. I told him, 'Let go of that dog.' And Eddie, with the greatest of innocence, looked up to me and asked, 'What dog?' "
(Cline, 1979, p.127)

The psychopath appears to prefer a picture of himself as bad, rather than neurotic or mentally ill. When it becomes impossible to deny the facts, he becomes apologetic and even remorseful and says he plans to make restitution. But any future actions clearly show that anything he feels at the moment is transitory at best and probably is just designed to manipulate the moment.

Both psychopaths and entrepreneurs have personalities that are action-oriented and innovative. A major difference between the two groups is the significant ego split in a psychopath, whose personality is riddled with rage and sadism. The sadism is what ultimately leads to the downward drift in his life, but it may remain well hidden for years. So beware when you come into the presence of a person who seems too slick or charming. You may be dealing with a psychopath.

These Trust Bandits are everywhere. Most don't murder. A few even become powerful figures in the world, politicians or corporate presidents. Since they are not controlled by accepted norms and do not have consciences, the usual rules don't apply. This can give some psychopaths a so-called competitive edge. But the mistake would be in believing that the murderers are the only ones who can hurt us. Nothing is further from the truth. It is what most people don't know about these people that is so dangerous.

What is it that is at the heart of the dark side of these individuals, the simmering volcano, that makes them so dangerous?

At the core of the unattached is a deep-seated rage, far beyond normal anger. This rage is suppressed in their psyche. Now we all have some degree of rage, but the rage of psychopaths is that born of unfulfilled needs as infants. Incomprehensible pain is forever locked in their souls, because of the abandonment they felt as infants.

> It is as if a voice inside their heads is saying, "I trusted you to be there and to take care of me and you weren't. It hurts so much that I will not trust anyone, ever. I must control everything—and everybody—to ward off being abandoned again."

These bondless men, women and children see those around them as objects, targets, stepping stones. Most lie, steal, and cheat without a concern about the consequences on others. They have no conscience and they feel no remorse for their actions. If the suppressed rage ever surfaces, they are capable of much more than a con. The sickest commit the senseless murders so prevalent in the newspapers today. And they do it just for kicks. Dr. John M. Macdonald, a forensic psychiatrist at the University of Colorado Health Sciences Center, talks about what happens when such individuals turn criminal:

> "As the sadistic child becomes an adult . . . you're more likely to see sadistic behavior. He'll pull a stickup, then beat up a cooperative victim. They get pleasure out of it." (Gerhardt, August 31, 1986)

The time to teach obedience
is in the playpen,
and not in the state pen.

2

Kids Who Kill

Psychiatrists don't officially label children as psychopaths. But the consequences of some childhood actions are just as deadly as those of the adult murderer. At an alarming rate in this country more and more children are becoming hard-hearted killers.

Records show that nationally 1,311 people under age 18 were charged with murder in 1986. These statistics reflect only the cases in which formal charges were filed. More often, children are not charged in such crimes, especially if they are below the age of 7. In those cases the child is often just referred for treatment. Children, however, are increasingly committing crimes ranging from armed robbery to murder.

"Ten years ago, it was a shock to see a 7-, 8- or 9-year-old come into the system, now it's not," says Danny Dawson, chief of the Orange-Osceola County State Attorney's juvenile division. "It's a trend." (Thomas, 1987, p. 8)

The wave of criminal horror cases by children has officials baffled. From across the country headlines in daily community newspapers have read:

"Teen-age boy in Colorado waits patiently while two young friends hack and hammer his mother to death"

"Florida police try to determine if 5-year-old knew consequences when he threw 3-year-old off fifth-floor stairwell"

"Kansas City police are baffled by jealous 12-year-old who kills younger sister, mother over birthday party plans"

"Eleven-year-old from affluent St. Louis neighborhood orders 10-year-old out of her yard; when he doesn't leave she shoots him with parents' gun. Playmate dies after surgery"

"Girl, 4, kills twin baby brothers by throwing them to the floor after one of the 3-week-old infants accidentally scratches her during play"

"San Francisco police don't know what to do about 18-month-old who kills playmate with toy truck"

*****

As statistics, the numbers are growing at an alarming rate. Such incidents are humanly unnerving; they raise many unanswered questions. A significant number of these children are unattached. These statistics do not say how many other children are out there with similar problems, but perhaps not the same opportunities to commit crimes. There are many, even thousands.

Prosecutors and judges have long been guided in such cases by the "rule of sevens." Children younger than 7 were thought to be incapable of forming criminal intent and therefore not accountable for their actions. By age 14, it was believed that children can comprehend right from wrong. But this rule is fading.

"You still think of them as children," says Dawson. "But I don't think (the public has) seen what we've seen. They don't see the 7-year-old who has a criminal mind and has the street savvy of a 16-year-old." (Thomas, 1987, p. 8)

When children are delivered from their parents' arms into the arms of the law, what is to become of them? If a child is jailed or otherwise institutionalized as a juvenile, the law reads that his freedom must be restored upon his reaching adulthood. Might the child-turned-adult kill? Some have.

Edmund Kemper is an example of one who did.

Kemper was a troubled child from a broken home; he hated his domineering mother. He was sent to live with his grandparents. At the age of 15, he murdered them.

Sent to a state home in California, Kemper appeared to respond well to treatment. At least, that is the impression he gave state psychiatrists. They pronounced him no longer dangerous and released him. It was then his murderous spree began in earnest. Kemper eventually confessed to killing six California coeds, all of whom he had murdered after picking them up hitch-hiking. He also was convicted in the decapitation murder of his mother.

Kemper's own mask of sanity had so fooled his victims, he said, that one of the coeds had actually let him back in the car after he locked himself out. He then killed her.

How does a life go wrong so soon? There are no clear-cut answers. But experts from around the country are compiling evidence that the violent behavior of children that erupts in murder is rooted in family relationships gone awry. The breaks that cause unattachment—domestic violence, divorce, parental mismanagement—are often to blame.

*****

Little Jeffery Bailey Jr. of Florida, with whom we started this book, has his roots in a far different culture than does Kemper, yet, both seem cut from the same cloth.

Young Bailey was born in a south Florida ghetto in 1977. His mother is a poor black woman, living on welfare and whatever menial jobs she can find. His father is serving his second term in prison; he was convicted in 1978 for auto theft and in 1983 for aggravated sexual assault.

Jeffery Bailey Sr. met Jeffery's mother, Sheila, in 1975 when she was 16, and they began going together. She gave birth to Jeffery when she was 17. The child was not planned. "Things happen," the father said. The three lived together in an apartment on McLaren Circle.

Known as "The Circle," it is a short dead-end street with two facing apartment complexes. Police estimate 90% of the drug trade in the area is carried out here. Street-level marijuana and cocaine peddling has been so blatant for so long that police say people drive up to get "curb service." Tenants either ignore it, engage in it or are afraid of it. There is no park or recreation area nearby. Children play as the drug sales continue around them. One officer said the kids are so accustomed to seeing the cops get harrassed—throwing rocks and beer bottles are common—that "they think police are the bad guys and the drug pushers are the good guys."

It is into this atmosphere that the young Bailey family brought their illegitimate son. Bailey Sr. had quit high school in the 11th grade because "I just got bored. I just got tired of it." He worked jobs in fast-food restaurants while Sheila worked as a maid for local hotels. The baby was passed from one parent to the other, and even to other relatives, as his young parents tried to make ends meet. It is the authors' opinion that the baby became unattached.

Jeffery Jr. often stayed with his maternal grandmother, or his father's aunt, when both his parents worked. Sometimes, when jobs were scarce, his mother obtained welfare. When Jeffery Jr. was about 8 months old his teenage father was charged with auto theft. He stole the car, he says, "because it was something to do."

Osceola County Juvenile Judge Ronald Legendre remembered the name Jeffery Bailey, when the boy came to his attention for the drowning murder of Nicki Brown. But the Jeffery Bailey he remembers was a different one: the boy's father. Legendre was an assistant public defender before becoming a judge and he represented Bailey Sr. on the auto theft charge.

Legendre remembers the elder Bailey as uneducated, but sharp. "He was one of those guys where, if society had given him a break, we might have had a college professor. He had a good head on his shoulders, but he wasn't smart enough to stay out of prison."

Bailey Sr., Legendre says, came from a poor background, but he was too smart "to be trod on. He wasn't about to take the kind of job a dumb person would do." So he stole a car.

Bailey Sr. spent a year in prison for the auto theft. It was during that time that he learned "through friends" that a child-neglect complaint was filed against Sheila for leaving Jeffery alone—while he was an infant—in her apartment in McLaren Circle. Jeffery Jr. was never removed from the home. If Jeffery Jr. wasn't unattached by the time his father went to prison, as we believe; the complaint is certainly an indication that the baby was not doing well during the time his father was in prison.

The father was released from prison in early 1978 and returned to live with Sheila and Jeffery Jr. In March, 1979 the couple married. "I wanted a family and I was in love with her," Bailey Sr. says. In September, 1985, however, he filed for divorce; he said the couple had drifted too far apart.

Bailey Sr. had moved out of the McLaren Circle apartment in 1980 after a spat over another woman he had been seeing. He moved in with the other woman, who has since given birth to his second child, a daughter. Sheila and Jeffery Jr. moved in with Sheila's mother.

Bailey Sr. said in an interview from prison that he saw his son often after the split. "He stayed with me a lot of times after we separated. I took him to the park and played with him. He liked to play—he wasn't no kid to get into no trouble. I'm sorry what happened to that boy (Brown), but I don't believe Jeffery did that. I just don't think he'd do anything like that."

Bailey Sr. was arrested again in 1983 for sexual battery and was sentenced to nine years. Despite his claims that he is close to his son, he hasn't seen the child since "sometime last year." His girlfriend brought Jeffery Jr. to the prison for a visit.

Several days before Nicki's death, Jeffery Jr. had taken a 5-year-old neighbor to a video game arcade about 1½ miles from the Circle. The younger child's distressed mother had reported him missing to police.

She says when she asked Jeffery why he took her son, he responded by cursing at her, saying he "was going to be just like his daddy, a murderer, and to stay out of his business."

During the police investigation of the drowning it was discovered that Jeffery Jr. had perhaps tried to kill once before. Two weeks before the Brown child's death, Jeffery Jr. pushed a 6-year-old girl into a pool at an apartment complex and ran away. A tenant rescued her.

Bailey Sr. says he is worried about his son. He says "if he needs (psychological) help I want him to get it. I feel if he goes to any kind of juvenile home, it would just make it worse."

Looking very much like any other small boy, Jeffery Bailey Jr. was arraigned in Orange-Osceola County Court in November, 1986, for the murder of Nicki Brown. Shackled hand and foot, the child sat in a chair much too large for him, and swung his legs. He was alert, upbeat and talkative—not the least intimidated or frightened. He said he was "embarrassed" by his shackles. His mother had brought him a new pair of sneakers and he wanted to make sure they were the right size. That was his greatest concern at the moment.

The hearing started a little late, but this unattached child's mother waited outside in the hallway—even though she might have come in and talked with him. She didn't seem to care.

Jeffery Jr. didn't seem to mind or be in a big hurry to see her, either. When he answered the court questions, he seemed unaware of the seriousness of the charges against him. The child seemed instead curious about all the fuss.

Juvenile Judge Legendre says he has had minimal contact with the younger Jeffery's case. But he has some impressions "I'm not sure if he doesn't know what's going on as much as he doesn't care."

During the court hearing it was very clear that Jeffery liked all the attention he was getting.

The child's attorney filed a motion during the hearing to have him tried as an adult. Judges and courthouse personnel were stunned when Assistant Public Defender Mike Saunders asked for the ruling. Saunders says the move was aimed at getting a jury more sympathetic than a judge, who would have decided the case alone in juvenile court. Jeffery Jr. was charged with second-degree murder and his case moved from juvenile to adult court.

In March, 1987, the court removed Jeffery Jr. from his mother's custody, to the state's.

Osceola Circuit Judge James Byrd, noting young Jeffery has "serious mental and emotional problems," sent the child to a psychological evaluation center, Seagrave House. Jeffery was declared a "dependent child" of the state after it was determined that his mother had neglected and abandoned him. In urging movement on the case Byrd said: "(This child) has some serious mental problems and we need to get them straightened out." (Thomas, personal communication, March 28, 1987)

Police officer Beth Peturka, who first interviewed Jeffery Bailey, notes, "I'm really worried about the future. I can't imagine what he's going to be like when he gets out." (personal communication, March 15, 1987) (As this book went to press the final disposition in the case of Jeffery Bailey, Jr. was still pending.)

The Roots of Violence

Prosecutors and detectives met in the case of another killer child in early March, 1986. At issue was the question of whether to bring criminal murder charges against a 5-year-old boy from the Miami Beach area who had pushed his 3-year-old playmate off an apartment house balcony to his death. Assistant State's Attorney Abe Laeser said:

> "It's bizarre to even consider the possibility of bringing criminal charges against a child that young. Once I had sat down with the persons involved and determined the type of treatment, the length, and whether there would be continuous monitoring of the child over the course of years, I felt there was no valid reason to bring charges." (Shulins, 1986)

In this case, the 70-pound boy was placed in a long-term residential treatment center for individual therapy. The center is to recommend back to the courts whether the child should be allowed out on an outpatient basis in the future. "He could conceivably remain there until adulthood," says Laeser.

He had confessed to pushing his 3-year-old playmate off a fifth-floor balcony after the 3-year-old had hung on for dear life. The confession was made as the smiling 5-year-old ate three pieces of pizza and drank a Coke.

Police found nothing to support the boy's story that the younger child had told him he "wanted to die because his parents hit him." Psychiatrists, however, immediately suspected the 5-year-old was really talking about himself. "The primary focus of the court was that there had been some abuse in his home life," Laeser says. (Shulins, 1986)

Steve Levine, chief of the juvenile division in the Dade County Public Defender's Office in Miami and a member of the American Bar Association's Juvenile Justice Committee, has predicted that the Miami Beach boy's future will be bleak. Levine said the treatment the boy will receive "is probably not anywhere near the kind of treatment required. As little as the parents could have done or were doing, the state is a poor substitute. I don't think the state will do a whole lot. He will probably go from one foster home to another. He won'd grow up in a warm, nurturing environment, and there will be little or no regular counseling or treatment." (Shulins, 1986)

In other words, this child will become even more unattached than he presently is and more cold and calculating.

Levine says that if this case is at all typical, he will one day meet the child again. "The kids I represented as delinquent kids started off as 6 to ll-year-olds identified as having mental health problems. Now they're back in the system, as adult criminals." (Shulins, 1986)

Many areas need to be studied as investigators probe the reasons for unattached and dangerous children. Among the list of suspected culprits are marital discord, physical, sexual and psychological abuse or neglect; overly harsh, inconsistent discipline; genetic influences; poverty and social disadvantage; the position of the child in the family; the child's individual temperament; and poor child-rearing abilities. We'll explore these topics in greater detail later.

There are, of course, many theories on the source of violence in childhood. The belief that television is a factor is still being explored. Ronald Slaby, an associate professor of education at Harvard University, has done extensive research on causes of aggressive behavior in children. He says the notion that television violence plays a supporting role is backed by studies demonstrating that children who watch a great deal of TV violence are more apt to behave aggressively than those who don't. (Shulins, 1986)

If TV indeed helps to foster violence in youngsters, it would hardly be the only factor. Numerous studies show us that bonding breaks also have the effect of creating disturbed and often aggressive children. Watching too much violent television may aggravate a behavior already established.

Dr. Martin Lazarus of Winter Park, Florida, has worked with more than 50 children in the last 10 years who displayed severe character-disorders. In studying attachment and the problems of unattachment Lazarus has come to the conclusion that "if you have people who can maintain an attachment they are less likely to see other human beings as objects they can kill. These unattached kids are able to suspend the humanity of other people. They take their horrible lives out on others.

"I have a fear for our society. These kids can be Ted Bundys who look perfectly normal. With their mask of sanity these people can be in every profession, such as law, medicine . . . you name it. It is only lucky that Bundy didn't finish law school." (personal communication, June 2, 1986)

"The reason the problem [with children] is so serious is that there is tremendous continuity into adulthood," says Alan Kazdin, Ph.D., professor of child psychiatry and psychology and research director of the Child Psychiatric Treatment Service of the Western Psychiatric Institute and Clinic in Pittsburgh.

Approximately 50% of children will continue to have antisocial behavior into adulthood. A significant proportion of the other half will develop serious psychiatric problems. It doesn't just continue in an individual's repertoire, it is passed on from generation to generation." (personal communication, October 1987)

There are several ways that this behavior can be passed from one generation to another. The first may be a genetic predisposition (although not yet proven), while the second would be a child learning such behaviors from his parents.

Evidence of a genetic component, not yet understood, is mounting but the authors believe the attachment bond continues to be the critical factor. However, studies of twins have shown that even if they are separated from their antisocial parents at birth they are still at high risk for developing antisocial tendencies. It was found that, if one (twin) shows the behavior, the other will most likely show it too. Numerous studies have shown that a child growing up in an antisocial family will have a higher incidence of this behavior.

A genetic predisposition to aggressive behavior has important consequences for infants. Consider how difficult it is for parents to bond and form attachments with a child who is fussy and has hostile tendencies. Parents with such a child find they must be very careful and diligent in the developing attachment process so that tense, emotional walls do not build up between them and the child.

The mother lucky enough to have a cuddly, loving, receptive baby will naturally be more inclined to cuddle and love this adorable infant back. But a baby that is sick or fussy may be harder to love and so a vicious cycle of unattachment can occur. We will deal with this phenomenon—trying to bond to a difficult infant—more fully later in this book.

How Many Character-Disturbed Kids?

Just how many character-disturbed children are there? These children make up the largest single category of emotionally disturbed youth (Robins, 1978). The same researcher found that there is a relatively high prevalence of antisocial children and adolescents ". . . (and) this group also has a poor adult prognosis . . . the poorest of any childhood psychiatric illness." (p. 262)

A very small fraction of all young males commits so large an amount of serious street crime that we can properly blame these chronic offenders for most such crime. In their study of 9,945 Philadelphia males, Wolfgang and colleagues (1972) found that 34.9% had at least one police incident by their 18th birthday. Of this group 6.3% were chronic offenders. Even more telling, the small, chronic group of 6.3% was responsible for at least 51.9% of all the reported crimes. These repeat offenders typically began their misconduct at an early age. We believe most delinquents are unattached children who have not had nurturing environments.

"If children don't get sufficient love early in life, they go crazy," says Erica Manfred, a former probation officer for Family Court in Brooklyn, New York. "If you're baking a cake and you forget to put the salt in while you're baking, you can't sprinkle it on top later. These kids never got salt in their cake. They've never been socialized" (Coplon, 1985, p. 166).

Unattached children, like the unattached psychopathic adults they become, have an uncanny ability to appear attractive, bright, loving . . . helpless, hopeless, lost . . . or promising, creative and intelligent, as may suit their needs at the time. Therefore, strangers, helpful neighbors, even therapists, often see the parents as the problem and believe the winsome child is "beautiful." This can, of course, cause the parents great consternation and frustration and—when police and other child-care agencies intervene— anguish. For these manipulative, intelligent children twist things so that the parent may even be accused of child abuse.

(Cline, 1979, p.119)

Boys, generally, seem much more at risk to become psychopathic than girls. This may be due to baby boys' apparent predisposition to be more aggressive than baby girls.

Eleanor Emmons Maccoby, a professor of psychology at Stanford University and Carol Nagy Jacklin, a psychologist at the University of Southern California, conducted a study reviewing the evidence on sex differences in aggression. (1974) They concluded that data shows the average man is more aggressive than the average woman in all known societies. They said the sex difference is present in infancy—well before evidence of sex-role culturization by adults.

In fact, criminal traits have been traced all the way back to infant behavior patterns, such as hyperactivity and unusual fussiness, as we noted earlier, which make it harder for a mother to bond with her baby.

Premature infants or those born with low birth weights have special problems, researchers have found. These children are vulnerable to any adverse conditions in their environment—including child abuse or neglect. Prematurity and low birth weight may be the result of many factors, including poor prenatal care, a bad diet, or excessive use of alcohol or drugs. Whatever it is in parent and child that leads to prematurity or low birth weight is compounded by the subsequent interaction between them. Premature babies, because of the attendant medical problems, may have a very difficult time getting the right stimulus for proper bonding and attachment to occur. This combination of physical and emotional deficits puts these babies at especially high risk for APD later in life.

When a baby does not become attached the victims are many, including his family. In the next chapter we take a look at several classic cases, and at some victims of those with APD.

> *"Experience declares that man is the
> only animal which devours his own
> kind . . ."*
> *Thomas Jefferson*

3

The Victims

 There was no way that Dorothy could have known about the warning signs of a psychopath. She was a nice, sweet elderly woman who had been protected all her life. Dorothy looked like someone's grandmother. Now she sat on the side of the road in her stalled car; it had flooded out in a sudden downpour.

She thought the attractive young man offering her help that stormy night was a Samaritan, and she was touched by his apparent concern for her safety. He looked "like any average young man coming home from work." She guessed him to be about 30, clean cut, blondish-looking, with a short-sleeved T-shirt. She reluctantly got into his truck at his insistence, "because of the cold." Suddenly, she found herself in the presence of a "demon."

Before she could move, he had a knife at her throat. When she realized what he had in mind, she screamed, "Oh, my God, no!" His whole demeanor was transformed; the person who had seemed like an "average Joe" had turned into a madman. "His eyes, they became slits. He hissed at me to shut up and do exactly what he said."

After forcing the 75-year-old widow to undress he drove to a remote site and repeatedly raped her, saying he was going to kill her and bury her in the deserted field unless she did as she was told. She credits her life with the fact she remained calm and tried to empathize with him. "I kept thinking, God, please help me now."

Dorothy is one of the lucky ones: she is alive. She became a victim because she did not realize the danger; she did not recognize him as a psychopath. Even hardened jailers who deal daily with psychopaths often are sucked in by the initial charm; Bundy's jailers tell of what a nice guy they thought he was.

A Classic Homicidal Psychopath

Ted Bundy, one of the most infamous murderers of modern times, was also destined from the crib. Bundy for years outwitted law officers who hunted him across the face of America. He finally was sentenced to death row at Florida's maximum security penitentiary for the brutal murder-rapes of two coeds and 12-year-old Kimberly Leach. He is a classic criminal psychopath.

Bundy would have gone on killing, but, like many homicidal psychopaths, he finally was apprehended by his own actions. We believe Bundy's antisocial personality disorder had its roots in his early childhood. He started as the out-of-wedlock product of a relationship between his mother and a seaman she thought loved her. She bore him in a hospital for "naughty ladies" during an era that condemned young girls foolish enough to get pregnant without benefit of a husband. Bundy has said that his mother hid the facts surrounding his birth, even from him. It wasn't until he was a college student that Bundy confirmed what he had suspected, that his "older sister" was really his mother. Family rumors had led him to suspect that he was living a lie. When he returned to the family home he discovered the truth. (Rule, 1980, p. 16).

His very birth had stamped the young boy as being different. Eleanor Louise Cowell was 22 years old and a "good girl" who was raised by a deeply religious family. One can only imagine her panic when she found she had been left pregnant by a "sailor." He had left her, frightened and alone, to face her strict family. They responded with shock and sadness. As the baby grew he heard Eleanor referred to as his older "sister," and was told to call his maternal grandparents "mother" and "father." (Rule, 1980, p. 7)

Bundy adored his grandfather/father, Cowell. He identified with him, respected him and clung to him in times of trouble. But Eleanor apparently dreaded what his growing-up years would be like in the working-class neighborhood in Philadelphia. She didn't want to hear Ted called "bastard." So in 1950 she took her 5-year-old son and moved 3,000 miles away from all the people young Ted had loved, to Washington, to live with relatives there until she could get a job. The move was a tremendous wrench for Ted, who had to leave behind his beloved grandfather. There, in May, 1951, Louise Cowell married Johnnie Bundy. Ted attended the wedding of his older "sister" and—when not yet five—had a new name: Theodore Robert Bundy.

It is obvious from his crimes that Bundy had a severe case of APD. His childhood background shows that Bundy suffered a series of bonding breaks in his early years. He says he did not even know who his real mother was!

As Bundy grew in the new home his mother/sister had provided, he became somewhat of a loner. A particular frustration was his inability to establish any close relationships with women. School friends remember him as somewhat introverted and shy. He got good grades, a B-plus average, and was awarded a scholarship to the University of Puget Sound in Tacoma. At first a psychology student, he eventually switched his major to law.

Pierce County records include a card that shows that on at least several occasions he had been picked up by juvenile authorities for suspicion of auto theft and burglary. There is no record that he was ever arrested, but he was known to juvenile authorities.

Bundy began killing when he could no longer contain the rage inside him. The killing spree is suspected of having begun in Washington, then spread to Utah and Colorado—where he was arrested and then escaped—and then on to Florida.

How was Bundy able to lure so many young girls to go with him? Police in several states feel he used elaborate ruses and his disarming and charming manner certainly worked to his advantage, as did the fact that he was extremely handsome and clean-cut in appearance.

It was in Utah that Bundy left the only living witness who could identify him. The fumbled kidnapping of Carol DaRonch took place on the misty night of November 8, 1974.

Carol was looking at some books in a store in the Fashion Place Mall in Murray, Utah, when she noticed the handsome man standing next to her. She told police later that the man asked her if she had parked her car in the lot near the store and she nodded. Then he asked for her license number and she gave it to him. He told her a shopper had reported someone was trying to break into her car. He asked her to go with him to "see if anything has been stolen."

Young and naive, 19-year-old Carol went with him. She assumed he must be a security guard or a policeman, although later she would remember that he smelled of liquor and had slicked-back hair. She followed him out into the rainy night and checked her car. Like most young women her age, Carol had been trained to trust police officers and she felt somewhat foolish questioning him. But she did ask for some I.D. She got only a glimpse of a small badge. He told her he was "Officer Roseland, Murray Police Department." Apparently this was enough to convince her to follow him.

Now the man insisted she accompany him to "headquarters." Instead of a squad car, he steered her toward an old Volkswagen bug. She told officers she debated, but got in. When he told her to buckle her seat belt she refused, thinking about bolting out the door. Carol told officers that she watched cars passing, wondering if she should scream. She also thought of jumping out, but they were going fast. Then the man ground the Volkswagen to a halt, hitting a curb. She remembers looking at his face and seeing he wasn't smiling. As she reached for the door handle he grabbed her right hand, snapping a handcuff on it. Screaming now, she fought back. He grabbed a tire iron and swung it at her head.

Scratching and screaming she fell partly out of the car onto the wet ground. Later she would remember a gun and a screamed threat that he would "blow my head off." As she managed to break free she ran across the road, losing her shoe as she went, screaming and waving her arms in the air.

Wilbur and Mary Walsh were driving down Third Avenue East when the

What Ted Bundy's Handwriting

The writer is given to a high degree of emotional responsiveness; feelings are easily aroused and often become a struggle to contain. Control is maintained when the writer feels that certain behaviors would make him appear inappropriate. The strong feelings will be suppressed until a burst of anger occurs to release them. This person likes with fervence or dislikes intensely. He remembers those emotional experiences that deeply affected him, retaining those memories for a long time, sometimes they are ever present in his thinking. He feels that his rights as an individual are being invaded and is always on the alert for any imposition from others. This hostility influences his thinking and everyone becomes a potential enemy. The deep-rooted hostility goes back into his past and will keep him resisting the forces that he feels stand between him and his desire to be autonomous. The handwriting shows a very hostile personality intensified by his strongly felt emotions.

The basic personality is one of the outgoing nature, able to give and share and interact with others. Because of injustices, real or imagined, of the past it has caused the writer to assess the present in the light of the past indicated by the many heavy lead in strokes beginning below the baseline. This creates an unwillingness or inability to forgive. The resentment can be directed against self, against others or the world in general and becomes a ravaging, overwhelming negative force in the personality.

Reveals...

Impulsiveness is curbed by careful, calculated thinking. A habit of weighing facts before arriving at conclusions prevails rather than making snap decisions. Emotions tend to influence thinking rather than logic. His attitudes and conclusions are inflexible; he will not change his mind regardless of any logic or reason presented. His stubbornness is indicated by the wide open spaces in the "t" and "d" stems. He is protecting his ego by "saving face" and refuses to admit that he has erred in judgement. The writer shows an abnormal need to protect his ego. His defense against imposition is weak, often giving in to the wishes of others against his will in order to be accepted and liked and then feeling used. This adds to the resentment already so strongly felt. Instead of being assertive he has yielded and then anger leads to aggression. A constant feeling of tension and nervousness is deeply interwoven in the personality. He has such extreme hostility which indicates anti-social behavior is evident but there is no means of predicting behavior with handwriting analysis.

A need for nurturing exists indicating that he never felt unconditional love and acceptance. A feeling of "no matter how I do or try, I will never get the love I need" is evident. Acquiring materially and emotionally has become an obsessive need to satisfy the love and approval never felt. This has been pushed into the area of the subconscious and is compulsive. This need for approval controls his conduct and he avoids being conspicious by illogical behavior. He will usually conduct himself in a manner conducive to the approval of those around him. He can be a good conversationalist, meeting people easily but is cunning and manipulative in order to get what he wants. His manipulative tendencies are indicated by the "hooks" in some of his "c's". There is a distortion of reality. The need for gratification of the senses can result in unbridled appetites. Thinking along the lines of self-gratification could overrule logic and morality. There exists an above average need for sensory stimulation, breaks in the area of moral values and strong indication of moral decay.

Once his goals are set, strong self-direction and determination will carry him through no matter what obstacles get in his way. Ideas are put into action with extreme fervence and an over emphasis on action will carry on. This is shown by the intense long downstrokes in some of the lower case letters particularly the "y's" and "g's."

Repression of thoughts, ideas and actions became constant in this personality in order to gain acceptance. A fear of ridicule restricted exploring new experiences and was a limit on expressiveness. A fear of failure stiffled goal setting and a fear of change kept him comfortable only with the known and the constant. These insecurities limit personal growth and emotionally healthy development.

Self-blame for situations in the past and unresolved guilt are ever present. An effort is being made to control the will in order to change some aspect of his personality.

The writer is steadfast in his philosophies and is not receptive to new ideas. He is not one to vascillate but decides on a course of action and is not swayed.

Sallie S. Bolich • Certified Graphoanalyst • Broomfield, Colorado

figure of the hysterical girl appeared in their headlights. The car barely missed hitting Carol. At first the couple wouldn't let her in but then saw how terrified she was.

Mrs. Walsh testified in court later: "When I saw the state this child was in, I realized it couldn't be anything harmful to me. It was harmful to her. I have never seen a human being that frightened in my life. She was trembling and crying and weak, as if she was going to faint. She was in a terrible state." (Michaud and Aynsworth, 1983, p. 95)

The Walshes drove Carol DaRonch to the police department where, after her sobs slowed, she told policemen about her abduction.

Later that night, in Bountiful — seventeen miles from Murray — 17-year-old Debby Kent disappeared after leaving her parents at a school play to go pick up her brother. In the school parking lot police found a small handcuff key; the key fit the lock of the handcuffs removed from Carol DaRonch. And a man who arrived at the high school to pick up his daughter after the play reported seeing an old, beat-up Volkswagen, a light-colored Beetle, racing from the parking lot. No one has ever seen Debby Kent again. (Rule, 1980, p. 120) Although we may never know for certain whether Ted Bundy murdered Debby Kent, we do know that he committed at least 3 murders in Florida.

In a murderous rage, Bundy killed two sorority sisters as they slept in their Chi Omega sorority house. He apparently entered the house in the early morning hours of Super Bowl Sunday, 1978. By the time the rage was spent, those two girls lay battered to death and two others had been beaten senseless. One of the dead girls was found with her brain exposed from the crushing blows; the other had been sodomized with a hair spray bottle. Victim Kathy Kleiner had blood pouring from her mouth and head. "A sorority sister held a plastic pail under the girl's mouth, to catch the streaming blood." (Larsen, 1986, p. 247)

Along the way, Bundy, the promising law student, had left many victims. In addition to the lives he took, Bundy had forever crushed the hopes and dreams of many families.

He fooled people to the end. After his arrest and imprisonment Bundy married a woman who had corresponded with him in jail. Carol Bundy remains convinced that her husband was wrongly accused.

A National Crime Wave

Bundy and others like him represent a national trend toward violence. Those committing serious crimes are doing so more frequently. Since 1961 the rate for death from homicides in the U.S. has climbed sharply, reaching a peak of 10.2 per hundred thousand population in 1974.

Everyone knows someone who has been burglarized, robbed, or had a car broken into. Between 1960 and 1978, robberies more than tripled, auto thefts doubled, and burglaries tripled.

But this book is about much more than body counts and crime. The victims of unbonded men and women con artists grow daily. The effects can be almost as devastating on those who count such people among their lovers, children, husbands and wives, or friends. The charm, wit and cunning of the manipulator is the same as that employed by the Theodore Bundys of the world.

What differentiates the Bundys from the con men is just a matter of degree, from first degree murder to first degree heartbreak. It is impossible to tell which unattached children will become serial killers, but we do know that some will become murderers. Others will become manipulators, thieves, con artists, wife-beaters and child abusers.

The Tip of the Iceberg

The killers are just the tip of a massive iceberg. The message this book has for you is that the chances for increasing numbers of psychopaths are escalating. We must search for answers to the pressing social problems that are helping to create unattached children. We must learn how to prevent unattached children. The solutions will not be easy or cheap, but they *must* be found.

Surely you know people who have used you and then gone on their way. Unless you know what to watch out for, you are at high risk. And unless a prescripton for prevention is followed to reduce the huge numbers of unattached children being raised in this country, we are all at risk.

Psychopaths Wanted

The antisocial individuals who have been studied are usually those who have been institutionalized. But what of the vast majority who are never caught? C.S. Widom (1977) had an ingenious idea for reaching this larger group. She ran advertisements in newspapers that said:

"Are you adventurous? Psychologist studying adventurous, carefree people who've led exciting, impulsive lives. If you're the kind of person who'd do almost anything for a dare and want to participate in a paid experiment, send name, address . . . " (p. 675)

Widom's ads attracted individuals whose responses on a battery of tests were similar to the personality makeup of institutionalized psychopaths.

There are many examples of psychopaths who do not kill, but do spread hurt around. One such man is Giovanni Vigliotto. Henderson writes that Vigliotto was sent to prison for marrying 105 wives, without the benefit of interceding divorce. His mistake was with wife number 104. Sharon Clark may have been foolish enough to fall for him, but she wasn't about to let it drop when he ran off with all her money and possessions.

Unlike the other 103 before her, she tracked him down. Five states and another wife later, she caught up with him. He had lived under about 150 aliases; he said he was born in Sicily and orphaned during World War II. Undoubtedly, this is why he was an unbonded individual.

He confessed to marrying repeatedly, but denied having swindled his wives. The prosecution found another story. They assembled a group of wronged women to testify. A jury found him guilty of bigamy and fraud and sent him to prison for 34 years. In an interview with *People Magazine,* Sharon Clark said, "I figure 90% of them (his other wives) deserved it. I deserved it, too, because I was so gullible. But I'm different from most women. Some of them should have gone out, dammit, and done something" (Neuhaus, 1982).

No one deserves the heartache wrought by such a man. Sweethearts who disappear with a lover's lifesavings, or who leave in their wake a series of broken hearts and shattered egos, are examples of non-violent psychopaths. It is another example of how a psychopath will try to exploit your vulnerability, with no remorse.

Even Benjamin Franklin (1771) wrote about being "taken" by such an individual. As a young man he was put to great inconvenience by a politician who kept promising to help him secure a loan to buy a printing press in England:

> "The governor, seeming to like my company, had me frequently to his house, and his setting me up as always mention'd as a fixed thing. I was to take with me letters recommendatory to a number of his friends, besides the letter of credit to furnish me with the necessary money for purchasing the press and types, paper, etc. . . . " (p.39)

Franklin continues with the story, saying he had appointments to call on the governor a number of times, but "a future time was still named." This went on until the ship was ready to sail.

". . . I call'd to take my leave and receive the letters . . . [the
governor was busy but said he] would be down at Newcastle
before the ship, and there the letters would be delivered to me."
(p.39)

When Franklin arrived in England there were no letters. A friend said that
in all probability the man had not written the letters and that anyone who
knew him would not depend on him. Franklin states:

"But what shall we think of a governor's playing such pitiful
tricks, and imposing so grossly on a poor ignorant boy!" (p. 41)

As an innocent, Franklin learned a lesson about psychopaths. Such
manipulators often target church members and other individuals known for
their generosity and naivete. Often the kind-hearted gestures are repaid
with fraud and betrayal.

Members of the City on the Hill Church in Denver lent several thousand
dollars to a man they befriended and who then skipped town. The American
Indian played on the sympathies of the congregation, telling them how
poor, homeless and troubled he was. He "worked his way into the
congregation," said Pastor Dan Stallbaum and allegedly bilked about a half
dozen of his 150 fellow worshippers out of several thousand dollars. One
woman, who later filed a police report, gave him $6,000 for airline tickets,
lodgings at expensive hotels and other items.

The minister said he was suspicious of the man's boasts about business
ventures, wealth and impending inheritance from a recently deceased sister.
But several months passed before he began checking into his claims; by
then, the Indian had conned the congregation out of cash and owed money
for rent and telephone bills run up while staying at various homes.
Stallbaum said he encounters people seeking assistance and pitching
schemes every week, but he "didn't get on to this fellow very fast. I'm used
to dealing with those type of people, but he was very, very, very slick. He
was a very talented actor." (Goldie, 1986, p. 43)

One member of the congregation said the Indian was "so unkempt and
had rotten teeth, but an unsuspecting, gentle smile. I can usually smell them
[frauds] a mile away, but he was so unsuspecting outwardly. He just had a
real silver tongue . . . he was so slick. And it worked." Although he bilked
people out of money, a district attorney's office investigator said he did not
commit a crime. "I feel badly for these folks, but there's nothing we can do
legally. These people gave him money when he promised them great wealth
was around the corner," said Jim Clement. (p. 43)

It is usually the parents of psychopaths who bear the brunt of their
manipulation, rather than strangers. Walt Schreibman talks about a young
man named Sam who kept fooling his parents over and over again. Because

of their love for him they couldn't bring themselves to believe he was using them.

The parents finally kicked the youth out of the house after they discovered numerous thefts. Their other two children had been slighted for too long while all the attention was placed on this angry and manipulative 16-year-old.

While the boy was away from home he had no trouble finding places to stay. He was very likeable, and had the appearance of seeming warm and caring. He was gone for two years and stayed with a series of friends. The scenario, says Schreibman, was always the same. "Sam would have people take him in after hearing his sad story and then he would mooch and sponge off them—sometimes ripping them off and sometimes not—until they would finally kick him out. Then he would find someone else to take him in. He had no guilt at all. His attitude was that this was owed to him."

After he decided to join the Marine Corps Sam's parents allowed him to come home for a month before he left for the service. They thought the military might help straighten him out.

While he was home the parents brought Sam in for a counseling session. "This kid came in and he talked about all the things he had done before— stealing, lying, hassles at school. And he said it was all because of his mother and father getting divorced. He said he loved his stepfather and his mother and we had a very touching session," says Schreibman. "It ended with everyone crying and happy.

"Well, he fooled everyone. After he left for the service the parents found out he had stolen a neighbor's jewelry, had run up a $400 telephone bill and had taken some antique jewelry of the stepfather's."

Schreibman says the story doesn't end there. Sam was kicked out of the Marine Corps with a dishonorable discharge. He then met a young woman, married her, then deserted his young wife and baby. "He had absolutely no moral problems about leaving her," says Schreibman.

This young man most likely will not end up in jail, but he will continue to manipulate and take advantage of people. "He doesn't necessarily have the underlying rage that is designed to physically hurt people. But he hasn't any guilt and has no qualms about hurting others in an emotional way," the psychologist says.

"In this case there is no joy in hurting like there is with some of the other psychopaths like Bundy. The Bundys, etc., have a trajectory . . . their source of satisfaction comes from physically hurting others." (personal communication, February 9, 1987)

How do you protect yourself from people like this? Certainly, no one wants to go through life suspicious of all their fellow men. But some simple rules apply.

Do not be taken in by people so slick that they seem too good to be true— they probably are. Often just a few phone calls are needed to insure yourself against the heartache a relationship with a psychopath can bring. Check the symptoms of unattached and psychopathic individuals against the characteristics of the person you are dealing with.

It is not fiction when you are dealing with such a person—a Trust Bandit—who is your husband, your wife, your father, your mother, your lover. So far, we have presented adult and child psychopaths and explored some of the ways they victimize us. As we examined the causes of APD, we considered genetic, biological and social factors and we noted how many Trust Bandits start life as unattached children. There is a critical need for every infant to form an attachment to his primary caregiver and, when this basic need is unmet, the consequences can be extreme.

In Section II we shall explore in depth exactly how the bonding process works and why it is essential if children are to grow into healthy adults. We will show how disruption of the attachment formation results in disturbed children. And we'll take a look at the other victims of disrupted bonding— the family.

We believe the link between criminality and unattached men, women, and even children, is real. It is vital to understand attachment if we are to stem the tide of high-risk children growing up without a conscience.

II

A CRITICAL
TIME: ATTACHMENT

*"The proper time to influence the character of a child
is about a hundred years before he is born."*

Dean Inge

4

What is Attachment?

 Danny is an unattached child. He has:
- Murdered three of the family cats.

- Vandalized a neighbor's home so badly that it cost $6000 to clean up the mess.
- Tried to drown a visiting 12-year-old girl.
- Set innumerable fires, one of which almost burned down a neighboring home after consuming a garage and outbuildings.
- Drawn pictures of devils, demons and gore, even while sitting in church.
- Stolen from, lied to, bullied, beat down, and terrified his brothers and sisters and parents.
- Threatened to kill his family by setting the house on fire.

And Danny will probably end up as a criminal, in prison. His former social worker says, "Danny could just as easily kill you as look at you."

*****

Danny's parents, like many of their peers, thought they were helping the world and saving a disadvantaged child when they adopted Danny at age 5 from a Vietnamese orphanage. He seemed an adorable, chubby, loveable little boy. Altruistic by nature, the couple was 26 years old when they first saw Danny. They already had adopted three other interracial children and wanted a baby.

But Vietnam veteran Don Scott fell in love with 5-year-old Danny when he went to Vietnam to escort some other children for the international adoption agency he was helping. "He climbed right up on my lap and cuddled and acted like he wanted to go home with me. It was very flattering. He was a real charmer." But all was not as it seemed.

As an infant Danny had been abandoned by his mother. The orphanage has no idea who she is or was. Like so many others in the Third World, Danny was deprived from his birth of the most basic of needs, the consistent love of a mother.

Fed a meager diet, Danny joined the thousands of other orphans raised amid the squalid confines of an overcrowded and understaffed orphanage. "He started out horribly," says Mrs. Scott. "When I went to the orphanage there were dead children on the sidewalks. Three- and 4-month-old babies were already not responding. You could wave your hands in front of their faces—there would be nothing. They were in cribs on wooden slats. When you picked them up they had patterns on their heads, from the slats."

Those tending the children barely tried to meet their needs. There were far too few workers and too many babies. This meant the infants spent their days primarily lying in the small beds, which filled row upon row, room after room. There was barely enough space to walk between them.

The babies had no one to whom they were attached, no mother to cuddle or pick them up, no one to coo at them. They were fed, changed and then placed back into their small cages, sometimes to cry but mainly just to stare. Most were malnourished.

Babies raised under such conditions become unattached. They do not have the opportunity to bond to any significant caretaker. As a consequence, the children are marked for life.

At age 5 Danny had no speech. He didn't speak Vietnamese; he didn't speak anything but "orphanage talk"—grunts and groans. But he was healthy, even chubby. Later his mother knew why. "He must have done very well taking the other babies' meals. He was not a starving child.

"Those at the orphanage were happy we were taking him. He was destroying the classes. He would get behind other children and grab and push them. He stole anything and everything. He was always punching the other children out of his way. He wanted attention, food, toys.

"We felt," his mother says, "that love would do it. We thought if we gave him enough love he would be all right."

When the Scott family greeted their new Vietnamese son as he stepped off the plane in America, they couldn't imagine that their trials had just begun. At the time they didn't understand unattachment; they didn't even know the term. They didn't know the consequences that can result from a rage-filled child.

When Love Isn't Enough

An infant does not have to be raised in an orphanage in Vietnam to become unattached. This may occur whenever the normal bonding cycle is broken or interrupted. These disruptions come from a variety of sources, which we will cover in the next section.

Children from normal two-parent families can suffer from bonding breaks, so consider what can happen to a Vietnamese baby who spends his early life in a foundling home. Danny's fate was sealed at that orphanage in Vietnam, long before his adoptive parents came on the scene. They were naive; even though they were seasoned parents, they couldn't have been up to the challenge. Danny's story has been included so readers will have a clear picture of the chilling consequences when attachment is not achieved.

*****

From the beginning, Danny was a very difficult child. His initial charm and seeming love at first sight were deceptions. The "honeymoon" never even started.

"I knew from the minute we met him at the airport that we were in for trouble. He was like a wild man. He walked off the plane with no shoes on, and threw them at me," his mother says. "Then he ran all over the airport. It was impossible to calm him down. The doctor who had escorted him from Vietnam was in tears. Others who had been on the plane began to ask us, incredulously, if he was our son."

The Scott family did everything they could think of to win Danny's affection and trust, but he always seemed to stand apart from them. Danny could be so friendly and outgoing with strangers, as he was at the first with them, but he shied away from any affection with members of his family.

"He would actually shrink away, pull away. It was like trying to hold or hug a board," his father says. "Because Danny had never experienced love, never been held or touched, he absolutely hated it."

When Danny was first brought home he screamed constantly. He took food and rubbed it on the walls. He threw food at people. He broke "anything and everything." The first time his mother tried to give him a bath he "screamed like a coyote." A grandmother left the house in tears and the other children were terrified.

"He couldn't speak English at all, so we had to do everything physically," his mother says. "We would take him by the shoulders and say 'no' and we had to do this about 80 times each time."

The first year went by, with little change, then a second. Danny's parents said the one thing they were able to accomplish was to give him good manners, to "civilize" him. But his mother wonders if this didn't really do him a disservice. "The good manners covered up some inside stuff we couldn't handle . . . we couldn't do anything about."

As he grew, Danny's behavior took a frightening turn. At first his parents couldn't believe that their son was responsible for a series of acts perpetrated on the family and the neighbors.

His mother remembers how they turned to the church for help when things "started to get real bad. But Danny hated it. He didn't want to sit with us. We noticed one day he was drawing what I thought was a portrait of the new minister—Dan is a very talented artist—on the back of the prayer manual. Then I got a look at the picture, I couldn't believe it. It was of a demon. It had big pointy ears, evil eyes, blood. This scared us, and the minister, to death. He drew these pictures all the time at home. I think it was then we realized he was pretty sick." (See page 182A)

Close friends and neighbors of the family had a puppy, which Danny teased unmercifully. Finally one day he got the dog so excited that it bit and broke the skin of a neighbor girl. The dog was sent to the pound for 10 days. As punishment for the act, the parents made Danny stay in the house when he wasn't in school during those 10 days.

He managed to get out, even though everyone was trying to keep an eye on him. He went to the neighbor's house, broke in and did $6,000 worth of damage while they were out of town. He smeared bathroom powders, shampoos and cleansers all over the house, turned off the power to the refrigerator and freezer, let the air out of the tires of the car in the garage, let in some cats that also did damage, broke windows, and stole things from the house.

Danny was such an accomplished liar that it took days to finally get him to admit the act, and then he only would admit to portions of it. "All the time," says his mother "everyone felt horribly for Danny, asking us to give him another chance. We gave him lots of second chances."

Both parents said they began to feel like it was they who were going crazy. They would catch Danny in the act of doing things and he would lie, saying he wasn't.

One day, the other children came running into the house, screaming that Danny was trying to drown a visiting girl. "Luckily, this girl was a strong swimmer," says his mother. "She was in the deep end of the pool and Danny had apparently jumped onto her back. As she tried to come up for air, he kept pushing her under. When we ran out to see what was going on, he said he was just joking. But she was terrified. The other children helped her to the side of the pool."

Then Mrs. Scott's favorite, oldest cat was found dead. It had been strangled. Two other cats died similar deaths. At the time they couldn't prove Danny had done it, but he admitted it later to a therapist. He described how easy it was to loop the leash around the cat's neck and pull. He even admitted that he had killed his own cat first so no one would suspect him of the subsequent strangulations.

Always, when mysterious events occurred, Danny was nearby. A series of small fires began to plague the neighborhood. When the fires were discovered, Danny would turn to a sibling and say that he smelled smoke, perhaps someone should check. The Scotts found out later that he had sneaked out of the house, set the fires and then run back in before anyone missed him. "When confronted with these lies he had no remorse, none, not ever. You could have put a loaded gun to his head and he would have died lying," says his father.

When the Scotts confronted Danny with the evidence he denied the charges vehemently. His lying was so slick that his parents often didn't believe he could have committed acts they were certain of. As tension in the house mounted, he told his parents: "You'd better watch out 'cause you just might wake up some night with this house on fire."

Family counselors and therapists who had treated the family did not diagnose Danny's illness. They didn't believe the stories the family told them, but they had never treated a child like Danny before. And he was such a good liar, such a good con, that the parents often came out looking unreasonable and angry, even abusive.

Finally, a therapist accurately diagnosed Danny as suffering from severe lack of attachment. He exhibited most of the classic tell-tale symptoms of a psychopath: a lack of ability to give and receive affection; cruelty to others; phoniness; speech problems; marked control problems; lack of long-term friends; abnormalities in eye contact; preoccupation with fire, blood and gore; superficial attractiveness and friendliness with strangers; and crazy lying. His parents also exhibited the typical anger and hostility of those who have tried to love an unattached child and failed.

The psychologist recommended immediate removal of Danny from the household. He was very capable, the psychologist knew, of harming members of the family next. The therapist found out that Danny had held sharp scissors to his younger brother and sister's throats while they were in bed at night, threatening to kill them if they didn't do what he wanted.

The psychologist talks about the interview with Danny: "I interviewed Danny for an hour. Basically, Danny expressed an intense wanting to leave and live anywhere else but with his family. He stated that he was afraid of what he might do to hurt other family members.

"He described the difference between being angry and being in a rage as 'when I'm angry is when I might throw a few things around and get really mad, but when in a rage I flip out.' He acknowledged feeling rage often.

"Basically he didn't feel he could control the things he did, i.e.; killing the cats; vandalizing houses; lighting fires. He said it made him mad talking about it. He felt people should 'get off his back.'

"Throughout my interview with Danny I saw a young boy absolutely without conflict over his actions and experiencing a smoldering rage towards his family. It is diagnostic to differentiate between rage and anger. Rage is a killing emotion and if not therapeutically released, can endanger himself and others."

The psychologist recommended: "Immediate removal from the family. The other family members are in physical and emotional jeopardy. There is indication that emotional trauma has probably occurred already among the other children in the family. Danny will probably not harm a foster family—as long as they don't try to develop a close, caring reciprocal relationship.

"He is able to maintain, on a superficial level, for a number of weeks, if not months, without becoming actively defiant and belligerent to authority. In placing Danny out of his home strong consideration should be given to placing him outside of the community in which his family is living."

Danny was sent to a foster home. He was relinquished by his adoptive parents, the Scotts, a year after leaving the home. He has been in two foster home situations since the relinquishment. He wasn't able to establish any relationship at either foster home and was at each only a short period of time. Now he is in a more structured group care home, where he will remain until he gets out of high school. "From what we've been able to tell, he hasn't gotten any better," says his father. In fact, the child has vowed to come back and "get" his family after his release from the group home.

It wasn't until Danny left the home that his parents found out the terror he had wreaked on the other children. Weeks after he was gone they began to tell of his threats and bullying. "At first we all felt a sense of relief. We had actually neglected the needs of our other children because we were trying so hard to help this one. All of our time was spent trying to help Danny. Then we felt this sense of real guilt, guilt that we weren't able to love him enough, to help him. But we also felt this overwhelming fear," says Mrs. Scott.

Four years later, the family still lives in constant fear that their adopted son will return to carry out his threats. They have learned that unattached children like Danny are usually vengeful and rarely forget their threats.

The family said the biggest lesson they learned from their seven years of pain and frustration is the lesson about unattached children. They would never adopt an older child again.

In a defeated voice, Danny's father issues a warning: "I hate to say this, because we have been so involved with the adoption movement, and these are kids that need families so badly. But the first three years are so important. If the right care isn't given . . . the end product will be rotten. Nothing you can do, or very little, will help after a certain point. And it simply destroys your family.

"We learned hard lessons. This leaves a person bitter and sad. We poured so much into this child. Now, well, we would never let him live in our home again. We are afraid he will get out and con people—he is a con now. We are afraid for the public, and for ourselves. And there are lots of kids out there like him. It's real scary . . .

"They are kids like Gary Gilmore, who would blow someone's brains out without a second thought. Things an average person couldn't conceive of doing doesn't bother these kids at all.

"It is simply very, very scary."

*****

Bondless men, women and children constitute one of the largest aberrant populations in the world today. And they contribute far beyond their numbers in social disease and disorder. The cure for such diseases is not simple. But the disease of unattachment can be eradicated by ensuring stable human partnerships for each baby.

"If we take the evidence seriously we must look upon a baby deprived of human partners as a baby in deadly peril," says Selma Fraiberg (1977). "These are babies being robbed of their humanity."

As we look at the social problems that are contributing to this national bonding crisis we need to remember that the baby isn't the only one in deadly peril. We are all at high risk.

Situations such as that which Danny came from have been studied by researchers who confirm that such babies grow up quite differently from babies raised by loving parents.

A study by Rene Spitz (1965) showed that babies raised in the inhumane conditions of institutions grow up markedly different in behavior from those who become attached to loving mothers or fathers. The unattached babies vocalized very little. They showed none of the babbling, cooing and crying when in need that attached babies do.

Of one 10-month-old unattached baby, an observer said: "The light in Teddy has gone out."

The unattached babies did not even adopt their postures to the arms of an adult. It is said that they feel like dolls: they move, bending easily at the joints, but they feel stiff and wooden.

What is Attachment?

Have you ever observed a new mother cuddling her baby? In a healthy loving relationship the mother will hold her baby close and gaze into its eyes. The baby will return her gaze and a feeling of rapture will envelope the pair; you will have a sense that they are in love. This is an affectional bond, the attachment. It must be there for a stable relationship to grow between the mother and her infant. Fathers, too, can help foster development of this special bond; this will be discussed in a later section.

Some babies, if treated badly, or left pretty much alone, do not develop this relationship. Social worker Connell Watkins of Evergreen, Colorado, says most psychiatrists and psychologists believe the bond really is not securely formed until the infant is about 3 months old; they believe during this period of time the infant cannot become unbonded. But she knows of the case of an infant who at 2 months of life showed definite symptoms of unattachment. "The baby had been in 5 different placements—her own birth home and then 4 foster homes. She wouldn't look at her foster mother. When she tried to get her to look at her the baby actually scratched her!" (personal communication, January 26, 1987)

The baby was also "stiff" physically. She didn't want to conform to the arms of the foster mother; she was rigid. Watkins said the foster mother finally devised a scheme to bring about the proper attachment for this difficult baby:

"She began using a technique where she would put the bottle on the baby's lips, but she wouldn't feed her until the baby looked at the mother. Of course, she had to be very careful, you can't risk starving a baby of that age." It took from 5 to 7 months of this careful feeding before the mother was able to coax the baby into a proper attachment. Within a week of the successful attachment the infant began responding at the correct developmental level for her age. (C. Watkins, personal communication, January 26, 1987)

John Kennell (1976) defines attachment as "an affectionate bond between two individuals that endures through space and time and serves to join them emotionally." During evolution, the closeness of a baby to its mother was necessary for sheer physical survival. The formation of the attachment bond guaranteed that the baby would remain close to its mother.

Babies must use forces at their command to keep their mothers close;

they cling, cry, smile, and vocalize. It is the same survival technique that infant monkeys use in clinging to their mothers.

This affectional bond or attachment, when strong and healthy, can do much more than ensure the child's physical survival:

" . . . it allows him to develop both trust in others and reliance on himself," says pediatrician Vera Fahlberg, M.D. (1979, p.5). Fahlberg is director of the world-renowned Forest Heights Lodge, a treatment center for emotionally disturbed children. She says "the bond that a child develops to the person who cares for him in his early years is the foundation for his future psychological development and for his future relationships with others" (1979, p.5).

Attachment helps the child to:

- attain his full intellectual potential;
- sort out what he perceives;
- think logically;
- develop a conscience;
- become self-reliant;
- cope with stress and frustration;
- handle fear and worry;
- develop future relationships;
- reduce jealousy. (Fahlberg, 1979, p.5)

Why is attachment important? Attachment is the most critical thing that happens in infancy other than meeting the baby's physical needs. Too much emphasis cannot be placed on this point;

" . . .during the early years of childhood the relationship between emotional state and current or recent experience is often crystal clear." (Bowlby, 1973, p. 5)

Further, Bowlby says:

"There is a strong casual relationship between an individual's experiences with his parents and his later capacity to make affectional bonds" (1979, p. 135).

The development of attachment is at the core of meeting basic social and personality needs, such as maintaining self-esteem and being affectionate toward others. (Fishbein, 1984)

It doesn't seem to matter whether there are blood ties to the baby or whether the primary caregiver is male or female in securing a proper attachment. What is most important is the relationship this caregiver has to the child.

In the book *Attachment and Separation* (1979), Fahlberg says in human societies the initial bonding occurs between the infant and his primary caregiver, who is usually his mother figure. This primary caregiver can be the birth mother, a foster mother or an adoptive mother. In some cases the primary caretaker is the father. It is important that all parents realize that adequate physical care is simply not enough to lead to the development of a physically and psychologically healthy child.

"A primary person to whom the child can become attached, who responds to the child's needs and who initiates positive activities with the child seems to be indispensable," Fahlberg says. (1979, p. 7)

How is Attachment Formed?

During the first year of life the affectional bond which is the essence of attachment develops. A special bonding cycle (described in more detail in the next chapter) takes place between the primary caregiver (mother) and child.

Three phases occur during that critical first year:

1. Initially, in the first few weeks of life, the baby signals his mother by crying, smiling or vocalizing. Those near him respond by picking him up for play or for comforting. The baby attempts to grasp and can suck.

2. As the baby develops he is able to tell a familiar person from an unfamiliar one and discriminate one familiar person (mother) from another familiar one (father). New research is showing that this process is occurring far earlier than previously thought.

3. Still farther along in the process the infant is very actively involved in seeking contact with his mother and/or father (Ainsworth, 1978).

Exactly when this bonding/attachment cycle is complete varies with individual infants. The whole attachment process can take as long as 9 months or even as little as 1 or 2 weeks.

As Michael Lamb notes, "The most dramatic and significant event occurring during the first year of life is the formation of social attachments" (1982, p.185).

How Does Separation Affect Attachment?

Healthy children from thoroughly satisfactory homes, when separated from their mothers for any reason, will undergo protest, despair and detachment. In fact, Bowlby says, "the only children so far observed in such conditions who appear undisturbed (are) those who have never had any figure to whom they can become attached, or who have experienced repeated and prolonged separations and have already become more or less permanently detached" (Bowlby, 1973).

So it is that in normally developing infants separation can produce distress. The phases infants exhibit culminate in detachment; the detachment is a defense mechanism against the pain of separation.

A leading authority on separation and its resulting anxiety is Mary Ainsworth (1978). Her scale for measuring separation anxiety is a widely used tool in determining attachment problems in infants and toddlers. Ainsworth's theory is that humans innately respond with fear in unfamiliar situations. When a child is firmly attached he may have transitional separation anxiety but works through it and develops trust. This gives him a stronger base from which to explore the world.

The age of the infant or toddler greatly affects how he reacts to separation. A particularly vulnerable time is about 1 year of age, when the strength and frequency of fear reactions and anxiety to strangers increases. For example, it is very difficult for a child of this age to develop an attachment to a new caretaker. In healthy relationships, the 1-year-old and his mother will have developed a balancing act between them that mitigates the child's fears.

Studies have found that children between 11 and 36 months of age can show intense anxiety and distress in unfamiliar settings. What is surprising is that children of 2 years of age can be almost as upset as the younger ones. "Up to 30% of children are made angry by their mothers' leaving them alone . . ." (Bowlby, 1973, p. 52)

Why do such separations result in anger and detachment? A child experiencing repeated or long separations learns that his mother is not always accessible. In some cases, the child may learn that he cannot trust others and others will not care for him. Consequently, he fails to learn to care for others and to develop a conscience.

This is the child who has decided in his subconscious that he cannot trust anyone to care for him and so will not trust anyone.

Cline talks of a child who was sexually abused by his birth father and then given up for adoption. The boy is now 9 years old and has been unable, despite intensive therapy, to form any attachments.

"He is a little animal that walks and talks. He gives you what he thinks you want to hear. He is a walking, talking 'Ken' doll. He is really made of plastic." (personal communication, January 7, 1987)

Not all children, obviously, experience this degree of lack of attachment. But healthy children have been found to react strongly to what might be considered typical separations. A study by Christopher Heinicke and Ilse Westheimer (1965) found that children separated from their mothers for one or two weeks (such as might occur if the parents took a vacation without the child) responded quite aggressively.

What sort of behavior can parents look for after such a separation? Likely the child will seem more disobedient, and is quick to retaliate. He can become more or less detached. Many researchers have noted these qualities, and various types of ambivalent behavior after the child returned home.

Foster parents have noticed this sort of behavior in the children they care for. These children often are manipulative and not genuine in their expressions of affection. They are, in fact, unattached. Foster parents have been heard to say: "I give and give to this child, and it doesn't seem to make any difference." (Fahlberg, 1979) These are children who don't feel *real*. They have lost their connections.

If the first relationship a baby has does not set the stage for trust, then later relationships cannot be based on trust. The baby learns from the first relationship what he can and cannot expect from others. If there is no healthy give and take, the baby will not know how to give and take with others. Unattached children do not grow socially. They have great difficulty learning to build any kind of relationship.

Consider, then, this quote from Bundy about his inability to develop socially as a young adult:

"I didn't know what made things tick. I didn't know what made people want to be friends. I didn't know what made people attractive to one another. I didn't know what underlay social interactions." (Michaud and Aynesworth, 1983, p.68)

Bundy, in fact, fabricated the public Ted: scholarly, bright, witty, handsome. He developed the air of cool self-assurance, the look women found irresistible. Authors Michaud and Aynesworth (1983) said Bundy's critical challenge from his teen years on was to perfect and maintain a credible public persona, his mask of sanity.

He was lacking in true adult emotions, so he had to put on the look of normalcy while inside his rage went unabated. It was "like an alien life form acquiring appropriate behavior through mimicry and artifice" (p.68). Bundy obviously missed a great deal in his bonding process.

What Can Happen if Attachment Fails?

It's now clear that one of the primary causes of rapidly increasing crime, particularly by children, is unattachment. Indeed, it may be at the very heart of the crime wave the nation is now experiencing. Many renowned experts now share this view.

Noted author and pediatrician Selma Fraiberg, M.D., states in *Every Child's Birthright: In Defense of Mothering* (1977):

"The distinguishing characteristic of the diseases of non-attachment is the incapacity of the person to form human bonds. In personal encounters with such an individual there is an almost perceptible feeling of intervening space, of remoteness, of 'no connection' " (p. 47).

One of killer Bundy's intended victims said she felt a feeling of "no connection" after he had abducted her. One minute he had been smiling, the next his face had taken on a stony expression.

"The life histories of people with such a disease reveal no single significant human relationship. The narrative of their lives reads like a vagrant's journey with chance encounters and transient partnerships. Since no partner is valued, any one partner can be exchanged for any other; in the absence of love, there is no pain in loss" (p. 47). Fraiberg says some of these individuals are found in mental hospitals, many others in prison. (One warden estimated that fully 90% of the felons housed in his prison were psychopaths.) Many others reside in the slums and other places where an absence of human emotions can sometimes be an advantage. As we have noted earlier, an absence of a conscience can also be helpful to the psychopathic manipulator who is trying to buy into the boardrooms of America. Prime time soap opera plots are full of examples of "successful" business executives who climbed up the corporate ladder by stepping on anyone who got in their way. Women psychopaths use sex as a primary technique of manipulation.

"For the women among them, prostitution affords professional scope for their condition of emotional deadness. Many of them marry and produce children, or produce children and not marry. And because tenderness or even obligatory parental postures were never part of their experience, they are indifferent to their young, or sometimes 'inhumanly cruel . . .' " (Fraiberg, 1977, p. 47)

Imagine the ultimate terror of *not being.* These are people who do not have a sense of their own existence, there is a deadness within. To feel alive, or to get a "kick," many resort to drugs, others to brutality. In the unthinkable acts that result, the victims are often chosen indiscriminately and anonymously. Often there isn't even a motive. There is certainly no remorse.

". . . he was a very nice gentleman . . . I thought so right up to the minute I slit his throat," says one of the killers in Truman Capote's *In Cold Blood.* (1966, p. 302)

When a person has not formed human attachments, he or she may also have a warped sense of sexuality and sexual drives. The person plays out his or her aggressions sexually and violently: hence, the rapist . . . the Ted Bundys of the world.

"His mother's son, Ted always kept himself apart, a device for masking his insecurities. This solitude abetted fantasy, some of it inspired by the late-night radio talk shows he enjoyed listening to," say Michaud and Aynesworth (1983) in their book, *The Only Living Witness* (p. 63). The authors say that Bundy was highly upset when he discovered he was illegitimate . . . "it is possible that it was *Ted,* not [his mother], who bore the true resentment for her single mistake, a hatred at her for committing the impure act that created him. As far as we know, Ted has never shown open resentment or hostility toward his mother. But following the discovery of his illegitimacy, Ted's attitude toward Johnnie [his step-father] degenerated into outright defiance" (p. 65).

The disease of unattachment gives rise to a broad range of psychopathy and personality disorders, including APD. In studies conducted about such patients' histories there usually appears a pattern of no significant human ties.

Often the early childhood of such individuals tells a story of broken connections. A child was farmed out to relatives or foster parents or institutions. These "ping-pong" children shifted beds and families in monotonous succession. Looking back on the records of such people, you can see frequent changes of addresses.

Can such a child be reared in his own family? Unfortunately the answer is yes. The family may have few connections; the child may be unwanted, neglected, and sometimes abused.

Today, as we have stated, the greater fear is that because of pressures on American families, children are becoming victims of nonattachment through ignorance. The mistake may be made by parents leaving their very young children for too long in the care of others. Or it may be made by a teen-age mother, keeping her newborn because she thinks he is cute, or erroneously believing she can adequately care for him. Or the error can be that of a social worker, who removes a small child from a home because of suspected neglect or abuse only to have the child shuffled from one foster home to another, lost in the system.

"More than half of all troubled children we see in our practice have a history of being shuffled and bounced about," says Foster Cline (personal communication, February 16, 1986).

In many cases, by the time the children enter school teachers or counselors report such problems as "impulsive, uncontrolled behavior," "easily frustrated," "can't get close to him," or "doesn't seem to care about anything."

One of the best programs ever instituted in this country for disadvantaged youth, Head Start, has seen a number of these children. They are 3- and 4-year-olds who seem unaware of other people or things. These silent, unsmiling "poor ghosts" of children wander through a brightly painted nursery as if it were a cemetery. Many of those who work with such children count it a victory if, after six months, they can get the child to smile in greeting or learn the worker's name. (Fraiberg, 1977)

The future of such non-attached children is clear if those working with them cannot bring them into a human relationship. They become the permanently unattached men and women of the next generation. Whether that means they will be criminals depends on the extent of their rage. It does mean that these unattached children will go through life devoid of the human emotions necessary to find love and happiness.

Angie is a pretty little blond girl of 7. She will not abide by any of the family rules. Particularly, she is upset with her foster mother, Janet, who is a firm and loving lady. Janet has been trying to get the girl to attach to her, but Angie screams or shuts her eyes when the mother talks to her. When the mother tries to pick the little girl up she is stiff, like a board. Her legs do not naturally wrap around the woman's body as most children's do when picked up, but poke out, rigid. Her mother must tell Angie to wrap her legs around her. (C. Watkins, personal communication, January 5, 1987)

During studies, experts have made an extraordinary and sobering discovery. An unattached child, even at the young age of 3 or 4, cannot easily attach himself despite being provided with the most favorable conditions for the formation of a human bond.

Most expert clinical workers and foster parents can testify that to win such a child, to make him care, to become important to him, to be needed by him, and finally, to be loved by him, is the work of months and years.

Some pioneering techniques are being developed, such as the "holding-therapy" which we will discuss in a later chapter, that are helping reduce the anguish and pain unattachment brings to these children and their families. These therapies have had limited use, however, and are not very effective past the early teen years.

As we urgently note the need to find solutions to the problem of unattached children we are reminded that all this would be unnecessary if proper attachment were accomplished when it normally takes place, during the first years of life. Prevention is always better than rehabilitation.

What Are the Long-Term Effects of Detachment?

Once someone is unattached, what is going to happen to him? Bowlby states that his ability to "make and maintain affectional bonds is always disordered" (Bowlby, 1979, p.72).

In other words, he can forget about having any stable, long-lasting, intimate relationships, such as a marriage. Few psychopaths ever do. Fraiberg says such individuals are so emotionally detached that their distinguishing characteristic is the incapacity to form human bonds. (1977) They are doomed to live a lonely life.

Once again the culprit is seen to be what Bowlby terms "pathogenic parenting," which can include discontinuities of parenting that arouses unconscious resentment and anger which persist into adult life and ultimately find expression in the mistreatment of those who are weaker. "It is useful to remember," says Bowlby, "that each of us is apt to do to others as we *have been* done by" (1979, pp. 136-141).

Three outstanding researchers, Spitz, Bowlby and Sally Provence, all agree on one conclusion—the earlier the break in the attachment process the more damaging it is. In studies of institutionalized infants and children they found that the age at which the child suffered deprivation of human ties is closely correlated to certain effects in later personality and the capacity to sustain human ties. As the researchers sorted out the data they found that the period of greatest vulnerability with respect to later development is under two years of age.

Fraiberg has come to this conclusion: "When *for any reason* [italics added] a child has spent the whole or a large part of his infancy in an environment that could not provide him with human partners or the conditions for sustained human attachments, the later development of the child demonstrates measurable effects" (1977, pp.51-54). The children she studied showed these effects in three areas:

1. These children form relationships only on the basis of need, with little regard for one caregiver over another. There is an impairment of their capacity to attach to any person.

2. There is also retardation, which continues in follow-up testing. Conceptual thinking remains low, even when favorable environments are provided for the children in the second and

third years of life. Language itself, which was grossly retarded in all the infant studies, improves under more favorable environmental conditions. But this area of learning is never fully regained.

3. Disorders of impulse control, particularly in the *area of aggression,* were reported in all follow-up studies of these children.

A review of many studies on the subject shows that the depth of future individual mental illnesses created by the lack of bonding depends on several factors:

● The age of the infant when the bonding cycle is broken is critical. The younger the infant the more disastrous the break will be. The first months of an infant's life are the most important for the attachment process, although the process does not seem to be fully complete for about 2 years.

● The length of time the cycle is broken is also important. If a primary caregiver is gone from the child a relatively few hours, little damage is done. But repeated day-long breaks, or breaks of several days or more, can result in an unattached child.

● The basic genetic predispositions of individual children play a role too, although just what this is has not been determined at this time.

We must caution that it would be a mistake to blame all human ills on failure in early nurturing. There are other conditions which can affect the capacity to love and the regulation of drives. Yet, the implications of maternal deprivation studies are far-reaching and, if properly interpreted, carry their own prescription for the prevention of the diseases of nonattachment.

Supporting the claims of Bowlby and the authors is a study by Craft, Stephenson and Granger (1964) that showed when a mother or father was absent from their child 6 months or more before the child reached 10 years of age that the rate of the diagnosis of sociopath was greatly increased.

Of 67 male inmates in special hospitals for aggressive psychopaths, at least 65% admitted to having such a loss experience. Because psychopaths are routinely over-protective of painful childhoods, we expect that the number is even higher. Other studies have strongly supported this early work, showing that the degree of antisocial behavior rises with this type of childhood loss.

"In psychopaths the incidence of illegitimacy and the shunting of the child from one 'home' to another is high. It is no accident that Brady of the 'Moors' murders was such a one" (Bowlby, 1979; p. 73). Or Charles Manson for that matter.

The research supporting the theory of unattachment is clear. What is still unclear is the degree of maternal deprivation that is necessary to cause this detachment. Just how severe does the situation have to be? No studies have been done on this point at all. There are many unanswered questions:

How can we know if a baby will become unattached because his mother has returned to work too soon? What of child care? Can a substitute mother, in a day-care center or family day-care situation, really replace the mother? How much abuse or neglect is too much? What of infants born prematurely, or sickly babies?

It is too early in the research to be absolutely certain, but child care experts around the country are alarmed.

Among those issuing warnings about the attachment and bonding crisis in the U.S. are such eminent authorities as T. Berry Brazelton, professor of pediatrics at Harvard Medical School and chief of the Child Development Unit at Children's Hospital; Edward F. Zigler, director of the Yale Bush Center in Child Development and Social Policy at Yale University; and Burton L. White, Ph.D., a renowned author and educational psychologist.

Brazelton says it is crucial for new parents to have time to take on the responsibility of creating and maintaining a stable world for their babies. " . . . These early experiences of learning about each other are the base for their shared emotional development in the future."

Parents need to know the precise way in which babies bond so they can carefully bring this process to a healthy conclusion. The bonding/attachment process is a complicated one. There are numerous stages that an infant must be subjected to in continually repeated cycles. In the next chapter we outline in detail this "bonding cycle." The normal stimulation that a loving mother naturally gives her baby is part of a grand plan. Without it that baby is at high risk.

*"I am not impressible, but I
am impressionable."*
Ralph Waldo Emerson

5

The Bonding Cycle,
How It Works

Picture in your mind a newborn infant: red, squealing, totally spastic in his motions.

The newborn human infant is a complete but totally unfocused organism. He has uncontrolled, jerky movements and responses to outside stimuli. Loud noises startle and scare him. He cannot see very well. He is helpless. His only response is often a squall.

Without the loving care of those around him—primarily his mother—he would die.

Yet in a year a miraculous transformation has taken place. The baby has turned into an individual. And what he has learned during the first year is the most important knowledge in that baby's lifetime.

Human beings learn along a logarithmic curve. And it is estimated that half of all our knowledge—our *life's* knowledge—is locked in during the first year. During the second year we learn half as much as we did during the first year, etc. (Cline, 1979).

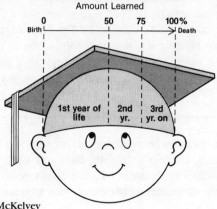

LIFETIME KNOWLEDGE
Amount Learned

The learning process shown in the accompanying chart is critical. In addition to the physical growth of the infant, the process involves the healthy (or unhealthy) growth of the psyche as well.

Although an infant's nervous system is largely complete when he is born, it still needs organization. The newborn during the first month of life will be making adjustments to life outside his mother's body. He doesn't sleep, eliminate or eat on schedule. The interaction between the infant and his parents is a major force in the process of this organization of his nervous system. Vera Fahlberg (1979) says that the influence of parent-child interactions on the child's developing nervous sytem may help to explain why children who are not well attached often have poor cognitive development.

Touch, sound, and visual stimulation occurring between the parent and child helps to begin the process of muscle control. Recent studies have shown that even an hours-old infant is already beginning to respond to the sound of his mother's voice (perhaps already learned in the womb) soon can recognize her face. This learning process usually occurs from the head down and from the central part of the body outward. So it is with the face muscles that the infant begins to respond to the attachment process. (Fahlberg, 1979)

Even very young infants have been found to prefer looking at the human face rather than any other stimuli. This face-to-face contact is very important in the developing bond between parent and child. Spitz (1965) even found signs of pleasure from infants when presented with a mask of the human face. Bodily contact between mother and child also contributes to this process. It has been found that experiencing rhythmic movement encourages growth among premature infants. Cradles and rocking chairs have long been used to soothe fussy babies and the use of such baby carriers as "Snuglis" promotes attachment to the mother.

New research is proving that the loving touch of infant massage can have dramatic results with babies. Premature babies who were massaged regularly gained more weight and had more movement than those who had not been. A study conducted in Dallas by Dr. Ruth Rice, developer of the Rice Infant Sensory Stimulation method, found babies massaged daily for four months were more advanced neurologically, physiologically and pyschologically than those not massaged. (E. Griffin, personal communication, February 5, 1987)

Infants are extremely sensitive to developing attachment behaviors during the early (fourth, fifth and sixth) months of their lives. Studies by Yarrow (1965) confirmed this fact. He found that 86% of infants in his study who were moved from a foster home to an adoptive home when 6 months old showed signs of disturbance. Infants moved at age 7 months or older showed marked disturbance.

Foster Cline (1979) explains that a "magical cycle" that gives birth to the soul begins when a baby is born. He says he uses the word "soul" because it expresses those unique, special human qualities of thoughtful caring for others and the internal belief of something beyond us and far greater than ourselves. A great many past thinkers have written of a cycle or stages of development: Erik Erikson wrote of development of "basic trust"; Martin Buber talked of the "I thou" relationship; some Christian groups talk about a sense of "grace"; and psychoanalysts have spoken about the "internalization of the good parent." This means that the child has accepted the traits of the parent as his own—he has made those traits part of his repertoire.

This cycle repeats about every four hours, as the infant is fed. By the age of six months, the cycle has been completed hundreds of times. It basically "locks in" the first associational patterns. Although unconscious, these associations dictate many of our actions. Cline warns that this cycle is very important. "If, at any step, things go wrong, lasting and severe psychopathology may result" (1979, p.27). Cline says he is frustrated by the lack of concrete action on the problem of unattached children; he believes it is a "very serious threat to society."

"The results of such trauma are not pretty, and they last a lifetime," says Cline. "They last many lifetimes. They warp the fabric of society. It is absolutely essential that those of us with an understanding of these complicated issues raise a united call for effective intervention by society. This is not a problem that needs more study. It is a problem that needs action, now" (1979, p. 129).

There is a growing concern among mental health professionals because psychopathology resulting from deprivation, neglect and abuse during the first year is on the rise. Increasing problems with juvenile delinquents and escalating difficulties within the American family support these fears.

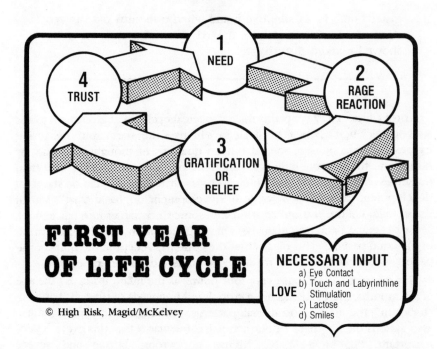

© High Risk, Magid/McKelvey

The necessary bonding or love cycle goes through several stages: Need, Rage Reaction, Gratification or Relief and finally, Trust (Cline, 1979). Others have different names for this cycle. Fahlberg calls the four stages: Need, Discipline, Satisfaction of Need and Quiescence.

No matter what terms are used, the cycle involves the continuing gratification of the needs of the baby being met by the parent. Obviously if the physical needs of the baby are not met, such as food, the baby will die. But there are other needs being addressed here which also must be met for his emotional health. The infant develops trust by having this cycle fulfilled.

The infant expresses his needs in a Rage Reaction, usually by crying. At this stage the parent must respond to try to meet the need. Neglectful or abusive parents may fail at this juncture to consistently respond to the child's overtures and the cycle can be broken. Or it may be that a caregiver in a day-care situation has too many children under her charge and can not meet all of their needs. Other babies who are at risk for the cycle being broken are premature or ill infants. Their behavior may not fit into patterns that promote attachment between them and their parents, or they may have a pain the parent cannot take away.

There is another danger of which parents should be aware. A parent should not consistently meet the child's needs before he is uncomfortable or protect the child from stimuli that would disturb him. To do so would also disrupt the cycle by not allowing the frustration that is necessary to complete the cycle. There are several new infant products on the market that seem to us to be dangerous in this regard. One is a bell, attached to the infant's diaper, which rings so the parent can change the baby the instant he becomes wet or soiled. The use of such a device may foster a disruption of this important cycle.

Adequate satisfaction of the needs happens best in a normally responsive environment and with a healthy child. If the environment is giving and the infant is able to assimilate the satisfactions, then he moves to stage four in which a sense of Trust develops. Basic trust is comprised of three distinct parts—trust of self, trust of others and trust of humanity.

Moving from Rage Reaction to Gratification is where things often go wrong. The cycle can become broken and severe psychopathology can set in; it is necessary for this process to be completed. (Cline, 1979) As we have noted, there are many physical and nonphysical reasons for a break in the cycle.

An example of successful completion of the cycle is when the infant suffers hunger pangs and his mother is there to feed him; that relief leads to satisfaction and a sense of trust. But parents cannot relieve the pain of a chronic illness and they cannot take away the pain of a congenital problem. Cline notes (1979) that such problems in the past have included extreme colic and undiagnosed inner ear infections. Modern medical practices, says Connell Watkins, are easing some of these sources of pain for infants.

When a baby has to be hospitalized during his early months, for whatever reasons, parents must know that he is in danger of becoming unattached. It is extremely important for the mother and/or father to be with the infant to continue the attachment process.

Postpartum depression, parental breakup, parents returning to work too soon—even famines and natural catastrophes—can contribute to a break in this most basic cycle. Consider the sorts of breaks that must be occurring on a daily basis in famine-stricken areas of Africa, or in the refugee camps along the Cambodian border, or in the camps of the Palestinians. From such upbringings come the Moammar Gadhafis of the world. Where there is a lack of trust, proper attachment is impossible. We will discuss more about attachment breaks in the next section.

How is a parent to know if his child is unattached? Usually it will be obvious that something is very wrong. But most parents, particularly adoptive ones, hate to admit that something is wrong with this child so desperately wanted. Parents have, in fact, denied to themselves that they have a problem—often until it is too late to help their child. If a child has become unattached it is important to seek proper treatment as early as possible. The older a child becomes, the more intractable he is.

"The worst case scenario," says Watkins, "would be those children who are unbonded and then are overindulged. These are often kids who are adopted and the adoptive parents give them lots and lots of love. They get this little twerp and they've never had any other children. And they say 'no problem' and begin to give the kid anything he wants. The kid has temper tantrums, you name it, and they still indulge him. These kids end up with no frustration tolerance even though they may have good cause-and-effect thinking." (personal communication, January 26, 1987)

Once the cycle is broken, it is very, very difficult to repair. Such children cannot love or feel guilt. As we have noted previously, they simply have no conscience. Their inability to enter into any relationship means treatment, and sometimes education, can become impossible.

Conventional treatments for mental illness have little effect on an unattached or character-disturbed child. One experienced therapist said "It's like trying to sweep out the tide." (Schreibman, personal communication, February 10, 1986).

Yet the therapist or therapeutic educator can play a decisive role in the lives of such children, if he knows what to do. Cline and a small group of doctors across the world are putting the basics of confrontive therapy (sometimes called rage reduction or holding therapy) into use in selected instances. Others, too, are pioneering treatment for children with attachment and antisocial personality disorders.

Strides are also being made in diagnosis and children with attachment problems are being recognized in increasing numbers. Once diagnosed, they can be sent to knowledgeable treatment centers rather than subjected to fruitless techniques. If not correctly referred, such children become older and more set in their ways. Watkins says a rule of thumb is that these children must be treated by age 7 for therapy to be almost 100% successful. (personal communication, January 26, 1987)

The "vicious cycle of the unattached child" begins when the infant has failed, sometime during the first year, to develop a strong internalized parent. As this cycle continues, babies fail to gain a sense of trust. When children lack trust and attachment, they develop the signs given at the outside of the circle on the next page.

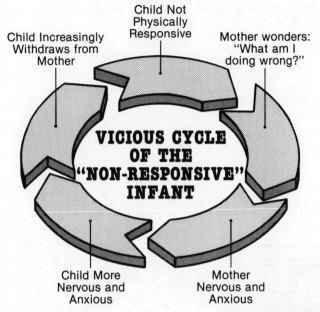

© High Risk, Magid/McKelvey

All civilized cultures are built upon adequate, pervasive internalization of the "object." As noted earlier, normal children learn that they can please their parents by behaving in certain ways: by sharing, by showing love, etc. When they do display such behavior they are demonstrating their parents' values, and the parents reward the children. Over time, and with further emotional development, children internalize their parents' values. The internalization is usually locked in by age 11. From infancy a child goes through predictable stages as he develops his own conscience.

Children who have not formed the proper attachments display a number of telling symptoms. It is important for parents experiencing difficulties with a child to recognize these symptoms. All children at one time or another may display some of these characteristics, but it is the disturbed child who will continually display a number of them. Several of the symptoms are so indicative of pathology, that any child displaying these should be evaluated: preoccupation with fire, blood or gore; cruelty to others or animals; abnormalities in eye contact; lack of ability to give or receive affection; self-destructive behavior.

In the next few pages we will explore the 14 childhood symptoms of character-disturbance in depth, with examples.

*"Hate and mistrust are the
children of blindness."*
William Watson

6

Childhood Symptoms:
A Warning of Things to Come

 You've just walked into a waiting room in a pediatrician's office. Your child is ill with a cold and you're told there will be a 10 minute wait before your appointment.

A little boy playing in the center of the room attracts your attention; in fact, it would be impossible not to notice him. He is zooming around the room, playing with first one toy and then another. Also he is an extremely beautiful child, with a captivating twinkle in his eye. You figure your child is about the same age as he, guessing him to be about 4 years old. Your little girl has picked up a toy truck and sits down to examine it. But before she gets all the way down to the floor, this little boy you initially thought so charming has run over and yanked it from her hands.

As you sit with your mouth agape, he hits her with the truck, smirks and runs to the corner, where he immediately drops the truck and begins climbing on chairs. He pays no heed to your child's cries, acting like he doesn't even notice. Despite his mother's pleas the child does not stop his antics or even acknowledge her. When his mother tries to pick him up to stop him, he shrinks away from her, screaming. The entire time you are in the waiting room the child continues to run around the room behaving impulsively and destructively and causing general havoc. You thank your stars that he isn't your child and think to yourself, "He must be hyperactive."

This child is much more than hyperactive. It is likely you have just encountered an unattached child. The symptoms and bizarre behavior patterns of such a child are not always as easy to identify, however. These are children who continue with infantile behavior long past the appropriate age. They are callous and egotistical; they follow no one's rules or regulations. They are constantly acting out.

When children are unattached they lack an internalized object. Because of this, they do not mature but instead continue to be self-centered, impulsive and "babyish." Their concern is always "What's in it for me?"

79

Like the adults they will become, these children block out the wants and desires of others, including their parents. They keep their distance physically and emotionally. Although the symptoms we will be explaining in this chapter may seem at first very different, they will come into clearer focus if you keep in mind that all these symptoms are ways the unattached child controls and distances himself from others.

The authors at this time wish to express their heart-felt thanks to Dr. Foster Cline, without whose guidance—and generosity in opening his files—this chapter could not have been written. Cline is a leading authority on unattached children, having treated them and taught others to treat them for almost twenty years. Once more we list the telling characteristics of unattachment in children, used by Cline. Then we will probe each in more depth to give you examples of what these damaged children look like.

We also wish to thank the Youth Behavior Program, Connell Watkins and professor Walt Schreibman for submitting case studies. Although all cases we cite are described as they actually occurred, the names of children and their parents have been changed to protect their privacy.

Symptoms of
Character-Disturbed Children

1. Lack of ability to give and receive affection.
2. Self-destructive behavior.
3. Cruelty to others or to pets.
4. Phoniness.
5. Stealing, hoarding and gorging.
6. Speech pathology.
7. Extreme control problems.
8. Lack of long-term childhood friends.
9. Abnormalities in eye contact.
10. The parents seem unreasonably angry.
11. Preoccupation with blood, fire and gore.
12. Superficial attractiveness and friendliness with strangers.
13. Learning disorders.
14. Crazy lying.
(Cline, 1979)

Let us explore in more detail what behaviors you might expect to see in children suffering from the above characteristics.

LACK OF ABILITY TO GIVE AND RECEIVE AFFECTION

If there is one thing that really drives an unattached child crazy, it's being touched and held. These children simply will not allow you to touch or cuddle them. You find babies, barely months old, who will continue to arch their backs when parents try to hug them, long after normal babies grow out of this behavior. Or they will squirm and wiggle and scream, trying to get away. Imagine how a mother feels when her baby won't accept her loving embraces. She feels shocked and rejected and incompetent. Parents tell of infants who are content only when they are left alone in their cribs.

Some babies and young children even refuse to be held for feeding. They will only eat when the bottle is propped up in their cribs. Having such a child is a mystifying experience for a parent who knows—as all the baby books say—that infants are supposed to be held and cuddled. Some babies are predisposed to this kind of reaction and parents must work extra hard to get the infant to attach in a proper way. Others have been ill or are adopted or have experienced other breaks. One mother, talking about how confusing her experience was, said:

"Some of my friends were having babies at the same time, and I felt a little weird when we would get together and they would be holding their babies and Tommy was lying over in his crib—able to be content only if he drank alone." (Cline, 1979, p. 90)

"The only way I could hold and rock Jim when he was small was if I clutched him desperately to my breast. And he had to be in one of those baby blankets, so tightly wrapped that his arms and legs couldn't get free. If I didn't do that, he would grab the arms of the chair and try to pull himself free of me! This was when he was only about 4 months old."

"I tried to kiss Katie when she was small, but even when she was very little she moved her face away. You can't kiss a baby who is jerking away from you all the time. It got worse as she got older. Sometimes I just broke down and cried because my beautiful little girl seemed to hate me. I'll tell you, I told my baby doctor about it and I know he thought I was going crazy."

"Do you know how hard it is to hug a board? That is exactly how it felt when you tried to hug Danny. He stiffened and pulled away from you. I guess he just didn't know what it was to love."

These are children who cannot stand to be loved and held. Although this seems strange indeed, this behavior meets the need of an unattached child—to keep others at a distance so the child cannot be hurt either psychologically or physically.

SELF-DESTRUCTIVE BEHAVIOR

Most of us cannot imagine how anyone could take a knife and carve on his own arm. But therapists have seen unattached children with horrible scars and scabs, most from self-inflicted injuries. One little girl happened to get chicken pox and by the time the illness had run its course she was scarred for life. She had picked and picked at her arms until they bled.

Parents tell horror stories about children who seem to have no fear of heights or dangerous situations. It is almost as though these children see themselves as invincible. They think the mountain will move for them. A child, for example, will think he doesn't have to go around a curb, but will try to ride right over it on his bike and, of course, fall off.

One family took a trip to the Grand Canyon and caught their son just as he was ready to scoot beneath retaining wires. They had warned this 10-year-old repeatedly of the danger. Self-destructive behavior can combine with other obsessions, such as a preoccupation with fire, to create extremely dangerous situations, not only for the child but the family.

Added to this sense of "devil may care" is another peculiar trait. Many of these children seem to have an unusually high tolerance for pain, or at least a distorted tolerance.

"A child like this may complain a lot, for example, about a small thing, like a sliver in the finger," says Watkins. "But he can have a broken arm and not say a thing. One child had to have 150 stitches in his face after he tormented the family dog—he kept sitting on it—and it attacked him. He didn't cry, not once. There is such an unconscious drive to not allow themselves to feel vulnerable or helpless or hopeless that they literally do not feel pain." (personal communication, January 26, 1987)

"Terry was always trying to burn himself. One day he found my cigarette lighter by the bed and I guess he tried to burn his hand, but he dropped it. Anyway, when I ran into the room the entire mattress was on fire. He almost burned himself up along with the house and all of us!"

******

"The baby kept hitting his head against the bars on his crib. We couldn't stop him. We padded it with pillows and anything else we could think of. Then he got old enough to climb out and he would fall on his head. He did it over and over again. I was afraid he was going to get brain damage or something."

Because they do not believe they can feel pain, either emotionally or physically, these children are much more likely to hurt themselves. Sometimes the injury is intentional, as stated, and other times it happens because of the belief that they are above pain.

CRUELTY TO OTHERS

Perhaps one of the worst characteristics an unattached child can have is the tendency to be cruel to others or to animals.

These children are very sneaky, however, in practicing their cruel deeds. It is always an "accident." The acts of violence that befall other children in the family or family pets are denied as being their fault. The blame is always put on others.

The unattached child, because of his conniving nature, is often the last to be suspected. Other children can sometimes get the blame for the acts perpetrated by the culprit. It is often only over a period of time that a parent will discover who is at fault. One mother noticed that when this one child entered a calm room where the other children were playing quietly, havoc would inevitably erupt, with someone getting hurt. Only after seeing a pattern did she discover what was really going on.

Teachers and parents have told of children blatantly hurting other children or adults. One child was kicked out of nursery school—he bit everyone in sight. The final straw was when he bit the teacher.

In most families with unattached children family pets are the target of cruelty. There is a common saying among therapists working with such children: The family pet is an endangered species in the home of an unattached child. Pets will die with no explanation. One mother said her son would run after neighborhood dogs and cats, teasing, kicking and hurting them.

"I didn't know, until George was no longer living with us, that he was killing the animals," said one foster mother. "Before he came we used to have all kinds of little ducks and chickens in the spring. I didn't think anything of it when he told me the dogs were getting them. Then, after he left, we had a veritable menagerie. I know now that he was killing them."

*****

"He was my favorite old cat. I loved him so much . . . I'd had him for so long. I was just sobbing when I found him like that. When the vet said he had been strangled I couldn't figure it out. It was so senseless. It was too horrible to think that Andrew had done it, but I knew that he had. If he could do that, my God, what else was he capable of . . . "

*****

"We didn't find out until later all the horrible things he had done to the other children. They were too afraid to tell us; Matt had said he would hurt them again if they did. I am so angry inside. I feel this experience has damaged our other children; they were terrified."

*****

"Right after we adopted Tom I found him outside by the house lighting his little brother's hair on fire. He burned about half of his hair off before I put the fire out. That first six months we all thought we were going to go crazy."

One parent told of her son's repeated fights at school. Whenever the child got an opportunity he would bully someone, usually smaller than he, into a fight. He was a better fighter (he had a lot of experience) and inevitably would send the other child home with a bloody nose or black eye. Teachers said he enjoyed hurting other children, humiliating them.

PHONINESS

Because these children do not have an internalized object, providing them with a model of behavior, they really do not know how they are supposed to respond to other human beings. Often they come across as "phony" or "not right" or "unreal." They are so insincere in their love and emotions that they come across as manipulators. One parent says, "It's like living with a robot, instead of a real child."

The character-disturbed child bases interactions with others on what he thinks will fool people. He really doesn't know how to feel.

Such children use manipulative love. They might say "I love you" when it serves their purposes, but not mean it. When character-disturbed children are small, their parents usually can tell the phony love from real love. But as these children get older, they get better at living the lie. Their mask of sanity isn't real, but they often are so good at playing the part that at first their victims don't realize they are being manipulated.

"This is a kid who certainly did not wear well," a psychologist noted after trying to evaluate a child. "All through the test, he would say, 'I'm not for sure.' I actually felt he was really saying, 'I'm not for real.' " (Cline, 1979, p. 97)

*****

"It was so hard for me to feel warm toward this child. I felt cold. I felt so bad feeling that way. I wondered what on earth was wrong with me. But . . . inside . . . I felt so uncomfortable, so strange. I knew this child wasn't like our other children. She had this plastic, phony smile. It wasn't like a real smile at all."

Unattached children such as those described come across as unreal. These are children who simply do not know real love and cannot relate in an honest way with other human beings.

STEALING, HOARDING, GORGING

"The closest these children can come to feeling loved is eating sugar. They get that exhilaration—sort of like being loved." (Watkins, personal communication, January 26, 1987)

These children have a chronic emptiness inside. They have emotional wants that need to be sated. Some may try to fill this emptiness with food and this often can take the form of stealing and hoarding food. Watkins says some of these children, when asked to draw a picture of a heart, will put things in the heart, like food, trying to fill it up.

This emptiness doesn't mean that the child was deprived of food as an infant, although it can. Often the hoarding or gorging is an unconscious reflex brought on by the terrible, unexplained empty feeling inside. Although food is often the item hoarded, the child can also steal and hide other items, like toys.

Like someone on the outside looking in, they see another child who is happy, doing well. They think if they take what that child has they will have that happy feeling. They actually think they can rip off happiness. It is impulsive, like a craving.

The greater the need, the more the child will hoard. The food often isn't even eaten, but placed in a safe cache.

One 8-year-old child said during a therapy session: "I don't sneak food for food. I sneak to be sneaking."

This child had been provided with her own box of cookies—a box which her foster mother had kept filled in a futile hope that it would prevent the rest of the kitchen from being ravaged at night. It didn't work.

A father speaks of his 6-year-old: "If there is a milligram of sugar in the house, John sniffs it out. He's uncanny. We can't leave him for a minute. Yesterday we had a typical example. My wife and I were outside only for a short time. When we came back in, John had somehow unlocked the pantry door and was sitting on the floor with food crumbs and open boxes and jars all spilled out. Food was all over his face and shirt. The pantry looked like some kind of animal cage and I thought, 'My God, he's an animal . . . this is another expression of his animalness.' "

The father continues about the thinking defect: "John doesn't look retarded, but so help me, over and over he pulls the same stunts with the same kind of disastrous consequences. He must be retarded! For example, he puts empty candy wrappers back in the candy drawer . . . there they are, all lined up and blown up . . . all in a neat row—but they are empty!" (Cline, 1979, p. 100)

Because these children steal food to fill up a chronic emptiness, the symptom cannot be removed by providing more food. In fact, the more food provided, the greater the hoarding is likely to be.

SPEECH PATHOLOGY

We've all heard children 3 or 4 or even 5 years old use "baby talk" on occasion. It's a natural thing for children to do, especially when they are tired or sleepy. But unattached children use these speech patterns as manipulation. Some unattached children rarely speak at their age level, *except when they are angry*. When screaming in anger, their speech pathology disappears. Most don't talk to communicate, they talk to control. In addition to baby talk they slur words, or mumble, or even talk real low. And they love to take a word and say it wrong so their mother will correct them.

"One child loved sopapillas—a sweet Mexican dessert bread—which her mother made for her often. We worked on the pronunciation of the word until she knew it. But at home little Angie would always say it wrong, on purpose. She simply wouldn't say it right. She wanted to make her mom try to correct her. She wanted to agitate the mom," says Watkins. (personal communication, January 26, 1987)

These children use anything and everything at their command to get the best of the adults around them. Baby talk is simply one of these techniques.

Their speech difficulties manifest themselves in both inflection and articulation. Because it is unclear what the child is saying, he is in "charge." Adults around him are always saying, "What?" or "Please say that again." Equally frustrating, these children do not give direct answers to questions; they give unclear ones.

Before being diagnosed as unattached most of these children have had numerous hearing tests and I.Q. tests. They are often diagnosed as learning disabled. People think they are dumb, but what is happening is that they really are choosing not to do something right. "No one," says Watkins, "would believe that a 6 or 7 year old is sitting there and not getting something on purpose." Of course, some children are so severely unattached that actual speech impediments do exist as a result of early isolation from others.

A therapist can take a little unattached child and ask him to follow the therapist's lead in drawing a picture. The therapist will explain she wants the child to do as she is doing and then, for example, will draw a circle. Most little kids like to have fun with adults and will be eager to draw the circle. Not these children . . . they won't do it. They will draw anything else, anything, but what the adult has drawn. When you say "draw in the circle" they will deliberately draw outside the circle. Then, when you tell them "do not draw in the circle" that's when they draw inside the circle.

Some of the symptoms exhibited by these children are similar to children who have been diagnosed as having "minimal brain dysfunction." Children with this dysfunction can be hyperactive, easily distracted, impulsive, subject to emotional ups and downs, and have learning disabilities. They act before they think and overreact to what is going on around them. These children have a low tolerance for frustration and trouble moving from one task to another.

Children coming into foster care have been found to have a higher incidence of minimal brain dysfunction than is found in the normal population. Fahlberg writes: "One can speculate about whether these children were born with certain organic problems that made it difficult for them to form attachments or whether the lack of attachment between the child and his parent precipitated certain organic problems." (1979, p. 46)

It is believed that minimal brain dysfunction has one of two basic causes: It may occur from genetically determined structural or biochemical reasons. Or it may occur in a child who has not experienced the mothering necessary to get a reasonably organized nervous sytem. It is through the first year of life and the child's relationship with his mother that the child learns how to learn. This is why it is so important for the attachment process to proceed in an orderly way. In unattached children the ability to learn how to learn is impaired, especially impacting cause-and-effect thinking.

Children with this problem also do not easily tolerate changes in their environment. Their behavior can make it more difficult for their parents to deal with them in a way that encourages attachment. This response from a parent can make the infant even more anxious, thus perpetuating a never-ending negative cycle.

A high percentage of these children continue to have difficulties in adult life. Hyperactivity per se usually diminishes, but the children can remain unstable and unable to tolerate frustration. The literature affirms that many juvenile delinquents have a history of school problems and of learning disabilities. (Fahlberg, 1979)

EXTREME CONTROL PROBLEMS

Unattached children cannot tolerate other people's limits on them. They are constantly testing, baiting, to see what kind of a reaction they will get. They act out to push the limits. Parents of these children "reach their limit" many times in a single day. Such children will create major disturbances when asked to comply with absolutely reasonable parental requests. But while they outwardly appear to need to be in control, inside they really feel quite insecure. Children who have been abused in particular feel they have little control over their lives.

Nancy was an obnoxious and demanding child. Her covert ways of controlling were much more intellectually astonishing than her overt mechanisms:

" . . . at times," says her mother, "Nancy is good, but it's only when she wants something or she's being threatened. And she does such weird things to be the center of attention. Once, we had a group of relative strangers over and John (Nancy's foster brother) had been sharing one of the things that he had done that really pleased him. Well, this group of strangers was talking and laughing about John's experience, and Nancy marches into the middle of the room. Clear as a bell she says, 'Last week Kenny took me down into the basement and pulled my pants down and played with me.' Well, you can imagine the conversation just came to a sudden, embarrassed, violent halt! Nobody knew what to say. I mean, what could they say! Then Nancy marches over to the sofa and sat there with this smug grin on her face which was a definite 'I gotcha' grin. And the other thing, her speech was absolutely clear. You know how Nancy usually talks in her baby-talk way. When she said that, it came out clear as a bell." (Cline, 1979, p. 106-107)

******

"I had told Jimmy (age 15) that I wouldn't see him again until he finished taking the MMPI (personality test) that he had refused to take. The next session he came marching in the office with this young man in tow. 'This is my lawyer who says that I don't have to take your test,' he said triumphantly. I looked at the lawyer who had obviously been duped into representing this young con man. 'Counselor,' I said, 'you might want to talk to your client's parents before this goes any farther. There are a whole bunch of things you need to know.' Jimmy started to protest and the attorney said, 'Shut up, I'm going to make that phone call.' "

Obviously, the more severe the character disorder of the child, the more control problems the parents will have. Thought disorder plays a large role in how uncontrollable unattached kids become. Oddly, in many difficult children the control issues may be very subtle. This is because they have become so good at the manipulation that it is hard to identify.

LACK OF LONG-TERM CHILDHOOD FRIENDS

What childhood playmate is going to stick around and continue to be hit over the head with toys before he decides to leave the unattached child alone? It doesn't take other children very long to figure out that there is something really wrong with these kids.

Unattached children are often the "bullies" of the play yard. Other children know that they will be hurt if they go near them. Sometimes a child without too many friends, or one new to a neighborhood, will try for a few months to be friends with an unattached child. But he, too, soon finds it is too difficult a task. These children are usually "loners."

"Little Johnnie came home complaining that none of the other children would play with him. Well, no wonder, he was so rough no one could play with him. He had actually knocked out the two front teeth of this one little girl. Thank goodness they were her baby teeth!"

*****

The grandmother of one little boy talks about the friends he has in the neighborhood.

"He always plays with the older children. He's too rough with little kids his own age. They always seem to end up getting hurt. Really, none of the children his age will play with him."

*****

A teacher, talking about an unattached child in her classroom:

"John has chosen to be non-verbal with teachers and classmates. He physically isolates himself from his class, to show noncompliance with school rules and standards. He is physically aggressive with classmates. He can be verbally demanding when he wants others to do things for him and if it works he becomes even more demanding. Once, when he felt slighted he left the classroom. When he returned he hit, pinched or pushed every child within range. The other children do not want to work with him and he has had to complete many class assignments on his own.

"One thing was very weird. John was called upon to give his answer to a problem and although his performance this time was of high quality, it was the way he did it that was strange. He verbally demanded total silence and the attention of each and every classmate before he would proceed."

What normal child would want to be friends for a long period of time when faced with a manipulative, self-destructive, and cruel "friend"?

ABNORMALITIES IN EYE CONTACT

Unattached children will not look you in the eye. The only time they do have good eye contact is when they are extremely angry, or want something and are being very manipulative. Then eye contact can be terrific.

Therapists find that establishing eye contact with these children is one of the major tasks that must be accomplished before the therapy can proceed. "The eyes are the windows of the soul" is a most apt and revealing proverb for these children. When therapists or parents try to look these children in the eyes Cline says they often get a response called "motor eyes." The children roll their eyes all over the place, moving them all around in the sockets.

A curious phenomenon has been noticed in both adults and children with antisocial personalities—an intense change can be seen in their eyes when they are enraged. Many victims of adult psychopaths have remarked about the look they saw in the criminal's eyes before the act was committed. The look is that described by our elderly victim, Dorothy, in Section I. She said it was the look "of the devil." The eyes become slits and appear very dark; they are constricted, and a look of intense hatred is seen.

Terry Storwick, a childhood acquaintance of Bundy, recalls:

"It was really easy to see when Ted got mad. His eyes turned just about black. I suppose that sounds like something out of a cheap novel, but you could see it. He has blue eyes that are kind of flecked with darker colors. When he gets hot, they seem to get less blue and more dark. It didn't have to be a physical affront, either. Someone would say something, and you could see it in his face. The dark flecks seemed to expand." Bundy as a child was known to have a bad temper, a short fuse. It got him into many childhood scrapes. (Michaud & Aynesworth, 1983, p.62)

These children are extremely resistant when asked to look a parent or therapist in the eye.

THE PARENTS SEEM UNREASONABLY ANGRY

The parents of unattached children describe them as bratty, demanding and obnoxious. These are parents who have had it. They don't know where to turn next or what to do. Usually they are mentally and physically exhausted; it takes a lot of energy to chase after a little monster all day.

Often, the child's teacher shares the frustrations that the destructive behavior patterns of such a child can bring. The parents and teachers feel hopeless and helpless. They feel no one really understands them and what they are going through. Because of the superficial charm of these children, adults not dealing with them on a day-by-day basis cannot understand the parents' seemingly inappropriate anger. One mother was criticized by her mother (the child's grandmother) for not loving the child enough. The grandmother felt the child just needed more hugs. The young mother grabbed up a nearby chair, held it out to her mother and said "How would you like to hug this?"

It is often the mother who is having the hardest time with an unattached child. These are children who seem bent on "getting" their mothers. This can even cause divisions in the marriage. Sometimes the father, who may just be around the child two to three hours a day, feels there is nothing wrong with him. One mother said: "No one, not even my husband, thinks anything is wrong. I'm the one they think is crazy." She told a therapist, "This is the first time anyone has believed me or understood what I live with." Her husband had said to the therapist: "I come home and she's mad and she tells me all the things this kid has done. No wonder he has problems, she's such a bitch."

Some parents of unattached children have been wrongly accused of child abuse or neglect because of their seemingly inappropriate angry attitude. And these young psychopaths are quick to take advantage of situations where police or social services workers are called in. They play the role of the poor, abused, little kid very well.

Many therapists talk of couples who come to them for help and how angry the parents seem.

Cline consulted with one couple he called typical. "They did not vibrate their natural, relaxed and open potential. They were angry. They felt frustrated and misunderstood. For years they had been searching for concrete and helpful answers out of their private hell with their son, Tony.

"And, for years, they received good, sensible advice which seemed to work for all children but their son . . . the problem slowly worsened.

Because of the ineffectiveness of their efforts with Tony, they now doubt their own competence." (1979, p.111)

The Scotts—the adoptive parents of the Vietnamese child, Danny—explain some of their frustration and anger:

"We spent more than 7 years trying to love this child's hurt away. We exhausted ourselves and almost ruined our family. We virtually ignored our other children and spent all our time on Danny. Our friends and family didn't understand the problem. They accused us of picking on Danny. When he got into serious trouble, like the time he vandalized our neighbor's house, they wouldn't press charges because they felt sorry for him. He caused more than $6,000 in damages!"

Is it any wonder that the parents of unattached children should feel frustration and deep anger? They often have a feeling of hopelessness after being perceived by family friends, school counselors and even some therapists as the cause of the problems.

PREOCCUPATION WITH BLOOD, FIRE AND GORE

As we noted before, extremely disturbed children can profess an allegiance with the devil. The rage inside is so intense that the child blames everyone else for his problems, but never himself. This rage manifests itself in an allegiance with evil. Blood, fire and gore represent evil.

Deep down inside his psyche the unattached child knows it is he who is bad. He will not admit it—except under intensive therapy—but he knows that somehow he is *made wrong*. It is an unconscious recognition. He is constantly battling the world of good, of right, and all the people who represent it.

The child's preoccupation with blood and gore often comes out in drawings, frequently of horrible monsters or devils. One family realized how very ill their child was becoming when they found such drawings all over the house.

Dr. John Allan of the University of British Columbia uses artwork in his therapy with these children. He says that as they get better you see a dramatic change in the thrust of the artwork. One little girl's drawings started out being a black scribble. As the child progressed in the treatment a girl emerged in the middle of her drawings; the blackness subsided from each subsequent drawing. A later picture, when the child was beginning to respond, shows the girl crying. Progressive drawings clearly show the progress the child is making. In one she pictures a pretty girl in a new flowered dress and, finally, she draws a picture of her mother and father. (personal communication, December, 1986)

Danny was preoccupied with fire, blood and gore. From the time he was small, he drew pictures of demons. He would put them where his parents and brothers and sisters could find them. He was a talented artist, but his parents worried about the way he was using that talent. "These were not just pictures of dragons and such, but real gross drawings of horned creatures with blood coming out of their eyes," said his mother. "They were very frightening in appearance."

The pictures unattached children draw reflect the bad they feel inside. In rage reduction and other similar therapies used with these children a main goal is to help the children bring the "mad" or "bad" to the surface so it can be dealt with.

One formerly unattached child, years after therapy, remembers what he was thinking as he did cruel things to others. He remembers that he was bad.

"Before the treatments I was mean. I didn't like anyone and felt like no one liked me. I tried to burn up my little brother. I did bad things to dogs and other animals.

"One time, some people were visiting and they had a little puppy with them. I took it to my room and beat it up for awhile. Then I picked it up and it peed on me. I learned a little lesson there.

"I used to throw rocks at kids, try and fight with them. I really thought I was a bad guy . . . there was no way I was going to be good. What difference did it make anyway?"

This child could not act appropriately, because of the rage he had locked inside his small head. After treatment brought out and dealt with the rage, he knew that it wasn't his fault that he felt bad. He learned how to love.

SUPERFICIAL ATTRACTIVENESS AND FRIENDLINESS WITH STRANGERS

> "It is really good that these kids are beautiful," Watkins says, "because no one who was ugly would live long doing what they do." (personal communication, January 26, 1987)

Just like psychopathic adults, character-disturbed children can work a good con. They are manipulators who appear cute, loving, helpless, smart or beguiling, as suits their needs at the time.

Policemen, social service workers, potential adoptive parents—all are sucked in by the attractive appearance and friendly nature they perceive in these children when first encountered. The extent of the superficial attractiveness and cunning depends on several factors, such as whether the child has a thought disorder or is capable of cause-and-effect thinking.

Children who have no internalized object but are capable of cause-and-effect thinking can be the most manipulative of all. An example is from William March's book, *The Bad Seed* (cited in Cline, 1979).

> "The child went to her, put her arms around her neck and kissed her with an intensity that seemed to engage all her consciousness. She laughed softly and rubbed her cheek against the cheek of the entranced woman. 'Aunt Monica,' she said in a shy, sweet voice, drawing out the name slowly as though her mind could not bear to relinquish it. 'Oh, Aunt Monica.'
>
> "The mother turned and went into the drawingroom, and thought, half amused, half concerned, 'What an actress Rhoda is. She knows exactly how to handle people when it's to her advantage to do so.' "

In the book a psychiatrist spoke of the child as the most precocious child he'd ever seen: "her quality of shrewd, mature calculation was remarkable indeed; she had none of the guilt and none of the anxieties of childhood; and of course, she had no capacity for affection, either, being only concerned with herself. But perhaps the thing that was most remarkable was her unending inquisitiveness. She was like a charming little animal that can never be trained to fit into the conventional patterns of existence . . ." (pp. 118-119)

This transcript is excerpted from a telephone conversation between a therapist and an unattached child's mother:

Therapist:	What's the problem, Peggy?
Mother:	Well, Susie is back home. She ran away and then found a police officer, and am I ever in trouble!
Therapist:	What do you mean?
Mother:	Well, she took Sarge (her puppy) and told the officer that I kicked her out of the house and wouldn't let her have her puppy. He read me the riot act. He said that you had tortured her and that I had tortured her too. She had told him that during our sessions we had made her tell lies about talking to the devil. You just wouldn't believe it. He wanted to know who the therapists were. He took your name and the others.
Therapist:	Just great.
Mother:	He got so hooked. I'm so mad—I mean really mad. He tried to get me to promise I would not get rid of the puppy. Now, Sarge has been vomiting blood since Susie brought him home. I don't know what she fed the poor thing. I tried to tell the police officer that there was a chance Sarge wouldn't make it if Susie kept him. I don't think he understood a bit. I can cope with Susie's running away, but these stories she tells are just too much.
	One time when she ran away I know she pulled her seductive act. When a man brought her home, after questioning my fitness as a mother, he kept looking at me with this surprised look on his face, saying, "Are you sure she's 11? I can't believe that she's only 11 years old!" (Cline, 1979, pp.120-121)

These manipulative children can twist events to suit their own purpose. They can appear to strangers to be the poor, helpless baby or the sweet, bright child. Appearances can be very deceiving.

LEARNING DISABILITIES

Many unattached children exhibit signs of learning disabilities. Some are truly learning disabled, especially if they suffered from severe deprivation as infants. Others, however, are wrongly diagnosed as slow or developmentally retarded when they are simply refusing to learn. Sophisticated testing is often required to tell the difference.

Some truly neglected and abused babies never recover from damage that occurs during their early lives. Others, with consistent and loving care, can sometimes overcome or compensate for this sort of early deprivation.

"We were warned before we adopted Bob that there would be problems. The adoption agency told us he had emotional problems and said he was borderline retarded. They warned us that he would never function at a normal intelligence level. But when we got him home we knew they had been at least partially wrong. The retarded label didn't fit at all. There was a spark in his eyes and a quickness that belied what they had told us.

"No, Bob wasn't retarded. But there was something wrong with him. We finally got the diagnosis ... he was unattached. We feel the years of neglect had taken their toll on him. After treatment, and years of our love, he is doing just great."

Consider these facts: Prior to birth the fetus possesses a full complement of neurons and if these neurons are damaged there is virtually no regeneration. Before the infant is born, then, his maximum intellectual potential is set. The goal during the latter months of pregnancy and during infancy and early childhood is to get the neurons organized into patterns of responsiveness.

At birth the baby does not recognize objects in his environment or the feelings he is having. He does not know, for example, that the discomfort of hunger is relieved by eating or drinking. But when his mother consistently identifies the discomfort with an empty stomach and fills that need, the child learns to perceive the feeling as hunger for food. It is through the relationship with his mother that the child first learns cause-and-effect. (Fahlberg, 1979)

Infants deprived of this important sensory stimulation during the first months of life suffer dramatically. Severe mental retardation is often the result.

Investigators who studied infants who were fed but otherwise neglected found that the babies turned into virtual "vegetables." (Mussen, 1979)

Basic trust is necessary, then, for development to proceed. It has been proven that delinquency and learning disorders are a matched pair.

For the brain to function properly and development to be completed unhindered, the bonding cycle must spin uninterrupted.

In severely disturbed children who have been deprived as infants, a combination of symptoms is often found and eating disorders, personality defects and disorders of cause-and-effect thinking are almost inevitably present.

CRAZY LYING

This is a particular type of lying that flies in the face of reality. Unattached children lie even when caught red-handed. They can be caught with their hand in their mother's purse, stealing money and they will say "What purse?" They can be collared by the store security guard walking out the store with a candy bar and deny it is in their hand.

Cline says it is almost as if the child confuses the way he *wishes* life were with the way it *actually is*.

Unattached children lie all the time, not just once in a while. They lie when it just doesn't make any sense. For example, they will lie about what they had for lunch, or the color of the socks they are wearing. A child will say he has on green socks when they are red; this is a child who does know how to tell colors apart.

All normal children lie at some point in their young lives. But they outgrow the tendency when they realize that lying displeases their parents. They want to do what pleases their parents because they have a solid internal object.

It is very different with unattached children, however. They don't care what the parents, or anyone else for that matter, think and they continue to lie consistently.

" . . . I told him to stop punching his little brother in the mouth and he actually denied he was doing it. There he is, sitting in the middle of the playroom floor, on top of his baby brother, with his hand poised to hit him again. And do you know what he said? He has the nerve to say he was minding his own business!

"I actually thought maybe I was losing my mind!"

This kind of lying cannot be logically explained. These children are born liars. And the most infuriating thing about the lying for parents is not just that it continues, but the blatant manner in which they lie.

*****

All the symptoms we've been discussing are consequences of the broken life cycle we described earlier. They result from "breaks" which happen during the first year of life.

As we have stated, the extent of these psychopathologies depends on factors like age, ego strengths, the child's genetic strengths and the length of time the cycle was broken. It is the failure to reach these milestones which puts children at high risk for later psychopathology, particularly for developing APD. In any case, the first year of life is critically important for proper developmental stages to be attained. But the development started in the first year must be continued in a consistent way as the child grows into his second and subsequent years. Even after proper attachment has occurred it is still possible for a break to occur.

"If a man harbors any sort of fear, it perculates through all his thinking, damages his personality, and makes him landlord to a ghost."
Lloyd Douglas

7

The Cycle Continues

 The second year of life is also important if *continued* personality building is to occur. The foundation laid down during the first year develops the strength and stability of the personality. But during the second year of life construction of the personality continues. (Cline, 1979)

The toddler's main task is to recognize that he and his caregiver are two separate individuals. This is easier at this age because the child can physically get around on his own. Separation and becoming an individual are the bywords of the 2-year-old, just as are newly learned actual words such as "Me" and "Mine."

It is understandable that if the child has had a poor first year, he will almost inevitably have a poor second year. But there also are many ways for the child and parents to have a relatively good first year and still have a poor second year, when the child is seeking autonomy and independence. The second year correlates well to the teenage years. In fact, if you want to know how a teenager will be, then simply consider what life was like when the child was 2. How the child reacts to this phase depends upon the degree of parental control. The clamps of parental discipline may be too tight or too loose, or put on in the wrong manner.

The second cycle is called the *anal* cycle. Freud (1949) called the second year of life the *Anal Stage* because, for practical reasons, parents begin then to concern themselves with the lower gastrointestinal tract and toileting behavior. This provides an excellent vehicle around which the parent and child fight out control battles and fill themselves with bad feelings. Feelings of guilt, anger and stubbornness may follow the child all his life if this period isn't successfully resolved.

According to Foster Cline (1979) the second year cycle goes through several stages:

In the first stage a child expresses his *wants.* (In the first year it was needs, now it is wants.) To some of these wants, the mother says "yes" and to others she says "no." Even at this stage things can go wrong. The child must be able to have some way to express his wants, verbally or nonverbally. His parent must understand his wants and accept or deny them.

If the child has not experienced resolution of issues during his first year, his wants will be skewed. Such wants likely will not be gratified by the parents. In any case, the child normally experiences more frustration during the second year than he will at any other time in his life.

The second stage involves experiencing "optimal frustration." Some infants can handle tough situations and cope with them adequately; others are easily frustrated and express their irritability quickly. Parents vary in their responses. Many parents say "No" when another would say "Who cares." Different parents will gratify and frustrate their children in different degrees.

Next is the stage of acceptance. If the parents frustrate the child appropriately, when it is for his own good, and help him enjoy the good feelings of pleasing the parent, the child comes to a point of "joyful acceptance."

The final stage is the "development of increased autonomy." With healthy parents, the more the child accedes to the parents' desires, the more likely the parent is to say yes. A number of studies on exploratory behavior in children have demonstrated that the better the parent-child relationship, the more likely the child is to be an exploring and risk-taking individual. However, toddlers with poor mother-child relationships (unattached children) are clinging and nonexploratory.

According to Erik Erikson (1965), the second year is really about increasing autonomy vs. control. It is a time when a child tests the limits and then acquiesces to the majority of lessening parental demands. Ideally and normally, the search for autonomy doesn't break down into continual control battles.

A child can suffer from "breaks" at any stage along this growing process, in his first or second year. As each succeeding year builds on the personality laid down before, certain breaks, such as trauma, abuse, neglect, loss, etc., can endanger the entire attachment process.

Our hypothesis is that antisocial personality disorder—APD—can result from breaks or delays in the development of the child. This usually occurs during infancy but can occur later, particularly if the original attachment is not a strong one.

K. G. Kegan says, "Persons diagnosed sociopathic (or with antisocial personality) overwhelmingly illustrated the same developmental diagnosis" they do not have a conscience. " . . . The development of conscience . . .

frees one of having to exercise so much control over an otherwise unfathomable world. It frees one of the distrust of a world from which he is radically separate." (1986, pp. 46-54)

A reporter asked psychopath Willy Sutton, "Why do you rob all those banks, Willy?"

Sutton's reply: "Because that's where they keep the money." (Kegan, 1986, pp. 46-54)

Sutton was completely sincere. His reasoning demonstrates the concrete, naive thinking typical of development stuck at this level. Kegan's view recognizes that judgments of sociopathic behavior are not so much *amoral* as at a developmentally lower stage of moral reasoning. Psychopaths can sometimes delay gratification and can form goals; they possess intentions. (Consider that psychopaths are capable of planning their criminal activity and waiting for the "right" victim or circumstance.) Finally, his view implies that psychopaths have never had an adolescence—that treatment should facilitate growth.

"The implication is that something has gone terribly wrong with the normal process of development at a highly conspicuous cost to those who are connected to the individual, but at an equally high, if less conspicuous, cost to the individual himself," says Kegan (1986, pp.70-71).

In this section of the book we have explained what attachment is, why it is important, what happens if separations occur and what happens to make unattached children. We have gone over the bonding cycle and the importance it plays in the growth of healthy babies. And we've given the warning signs, the symptoms that tell if a child is unattached.

Without the successful completion of the attachment process the consequences are dire for a child's future. We started this section with the story of the adoption of Danny, a Vietnamese child. In the case of Danny and his adoptive family, everyone was a victim. But, as we have noted, an infant does not have to come from a Third World orphanage to suffer bonding and attachment breaks. In Section III we look at the demographic revolution occurring in this country and its effects on the family.

III

THE BONDING BREAKS

*"Part of the problem today is that
we have a surplus of simple answers
and a shortage of simple
questions."*
American Proverb

Why Now?

 She hounds you constantly.

She is obstinate.

She always has to have her way.

She is driving you crazy.

You love her.

But she can't be cured without help.

Laura is an unattached child.

During her young life she has suffered numerous "bonding breaks," any of which could have caused her condition. She suffers from severe childhood psychopathology.

As we stated in Section II, the extent of such pathology depends on a number of factors: how old the child was when the bonding break occurred and how long the break lasted. The longer the break, the better the chances that the child will be at high risk of developing without a conscience. Also, John Bowlby (1979) sees treatment of unattached children as extremely difficult, if not impossible:

"There is an inability to love or feel guilty. There is no conscience. Their inability to enter into any relationship makes treatment or even education impossible. They have no idea of time, so they cannot recall past experience and cannot benefit from past experience or be motivated to future goals." (pp. 127-160)

Laura was at high risk even before her birth. Laura's mother and father were married during their teens, after the mother became pregnant at age 15. Both dropped out of school. Like many such marriages, theirs was destined for failure. The mother told social workers that she and the young father fought constantly, usually about money. The situation escalated after a second child was born. It seems the mother blamed Laura for the problems, however.

Because of the mother's feelings toward the child, and her depression, Laura suffered from neglect. After divorce, the mother said she had an even harder time making ends meet and often couldn't feed her children properly. She told social workers she felt a sense of relief when she finally moved in with a boyfriend. She "overlooked" complaints of abuse from her daughter because she was afraid she would lose the security the boyfriend offered her.

It was because of the sexual abuse of Laura by the live-in boyfriend that the child was finally removed from her home. Since then, Laura has "burned out" two foster homes. The social services department suspects the child was abused again at one of the foster homes. The physical abuse was to "make her mind."

Laura is now living in a foster home with a mother considered to be one of the best available. But she has brought Laura into the social services department, begging for help. She laments that "this is a very unusual child. She will not mind, period!" She describes a typical day:

"Laura constantly asks questions, repeating the answers and questions over and over, like a mimic. She does this all day long. She terrorizes the other children, chasing and hitting them, and they are all older and larger than she. When she is caught lying— and she does this constantly—she just continues to lie, bold-faced lies. She teases the dog, hurting it. Finally the dog bites her and then she just goes back at teasing it. Physical pain doesn't seem to deter her one bit. She's constantly in motion, will not sit still. And she's into everything, pulling things out, especially in the pantry.

"I try to make her look at me when I'm talking to her, but she can't. She closes her eyes, just squinches them tight. Nothing seems to work. I've tried to reward her and she hates it. When I praise her she just mimics me. I've spanked her and that doesn't mean anything. Standing her in the corner and making her stay there doesn't help either."

Laura is an unattached child; she suffers a character disturbance. If she were an adult, the clinical diagnosis would be APD.

There are numerous reasons for such maternal-infant breaks, as we have stated in the section on attachment. The cycle can be broken by a woman who is suffering from severe post-partum depression. Or perhaps the mother, through no fault of her own, can't tend to her infant as she should. The baby may be premature or in chronic pain from an undiagnosed inner ear infection and the mother cannot provide the relief the baby needs. It is also not unusual to find cases of nonattachment that stem from poor parenting, often because the mothers themselves received poor mothering.

We have explored the long-term implications of unattachment in Section I. In Section II we showed what bonding is and why it is important. In this section we will look at the reasons why, at this time in our history, we are seeing increasing numbers of individuals with antisocial personality disorder. How do these bonding breaks occur and why are we in the throes of a bonding crisis now?

Child advocates across the country are beginning to issue warnings. Some hard questions that need to be answered are:

• How do these bonding breaks occur and why are we now in the throes of a bonding crisis?
• How can we deal with and recognize those with APD?
• What must parents know to prevent their children from becoming APD victims?
• What can be done to stem the tide of character-disturbed children?
• Can those who have never become attached be helped?

*****

Children who grow up to have psychopathic personalities often come from very seriously flawed families. A pattern of personal abuse or exposure to extreme violence in the family or community has always led to the creation of some children with the hard hearts of killers. But the new challenges facing many American families today may be creating a volatile situation.

Our research reveals that in the United States right now, pressing needs are not being met for parents and their children. We need solutions to these problems:

• The demands on working parents' time, particularly mothers, must be recognized. If women are expected to achieve on the job, and at mothering, they need help.
• Poorly run and understaffed day-care centers are often the only choices available for working parents who need help caring for their preschool and

older children. There are also not enough affordable child-care centers for day-care situations to serve all who need them.

● Prenatal and postnatal leaves without loss of jobs or other serious penalty are unavailable to the vast majority of working mothers and fathers who need this time to prepare for, *and care for*, children adequately. New parents should have time to get to know their newborn or adopted children and to care for ill children.

● The child adoption system in the U.S. has been the direct cause of thousands of children being injured, perhaps permanently, through bureaucratic delays and bungling. Unwittingly, delays in permanent placement of adoptable children are causing them to become unattached.

● The social services boondoggle is causing many breaks. The current foster home system is simply not working. Abuse and neglect also have been found to be statistically more prevalent in some foster homes.

● Action must be taken to stem the pervasive and epidemic teenage pregnancy dilemma. Today's youth desperately need help, before they spawn another generation of "mistakes."

● The cycle of abuse must be broken. Families with a history of abusive backgrounds are passing abuse, like a genetic defect, from parent to child.

● It is imperative that new joint custody divorce arrangements take into account the attachment process. A high number of marriages ends in divorce, and the toll on children is staggering. Compounding the problem are custody battles and uninformed judges and lawyers who are throwing the baby out with the bathwater.

The authors do not pretend to have the answers to all of these dramatic situations facing the American public. These are problems which have been brewing for many years. But we have suggestions we believe will help mitigate the increasing numbers of unattached children resulting from these bonding breaks. At the very least we believe each of these areas deserves further long-term, detailed study.

The Bonding Crisis

We are in the midst of a bonding crisis. Children are becoming unattached across the nation. In your hometown. On your block. In the house next door. Perhaps, in your own home.

Factors are at play that, for the first time in the history of this country, are interfering with the basic bonding needs of America's infants. Society is in the midst of a profound demographic revolution. In the way that it affects the lives of our children this revolution is as significant as the industrial revolution that changed the course of history at the turn of the century.

In 1982 Hunter College president Donna Shalala, in opening remarks to the Association of Junior League symposium, "Women, Work and the Family," predicted:

"The role of women will change dramatically in the next two decades. In 1950, women made up 29% of the work force and today they represent 40%. By the end of the 1980s, half of the American workers will be women. Many of these female workers have children; more than half of all mothers with children under 18 are in the labor force, and it's predicted that by 1990 only one out of every four women with children will remain at home" (p.5).

In the 5 years since Shalala made that prediction women have entered the work force at even greater numbers than imagined.

Between 1950 and 1981, the number of working mothers tripled. In the last decade alone, the number of working women with children under the age of one has increased by 70%. Never in the history of the world have so many children been raised by strangers.

The combined effect of this demographic revolution and the stresses now faced by the family may be that we are unwittingly raising a generation with a dramatically increased risk of becoming unattached. On the one hand are mental health professionals and child specialists who are issuing warnings. On the other hand are feminists and working mothers, saying that being a working mother isn't harmful. Both sides want the same thing: healthy, happy children.

But some important questions have not yet been answered by research: Are children helped by day care? How early should they be placed in substitute care? Will we find out the answers too late?

Do not jump to the conclusion that this book is another diatribe saying women should abandon their careers and go home to the family — one of the authors is a working mother. Rather, this book warns that things are not as they should be with this nation's children. And we offer some sane suggestions that will work for many of the insane situations causing problems today for families.

Let us look, for a moment, at the family and how it is changing. American society continues to cling to the image of the stereotypical nuclear family as the unit of choice. But reality is far different.

"The description of the typical family as one with two children under 18 years of age, the father in the paid labor force, and the mother at home fits only 5% of all families," says Dr. Lenora Cole-Alexander, director of the U.S. Department of Labor Women's Bureau. (1982, p.4) "These statistics aren't just interesting sociological facts; they represent staggering changes in human lives which have produced not only a new set of opportunities for women in America, but also a new set of problems that demand immediate and serious attention."

Interestingly, a recent study conducted by *Redbook* magazine asked: "Do children need a stay-at-home mother?" The magazine's editors couldn't believe the impassioned outpouring that resulted. Responses, often consisting of five to six pages, were received from an astonishing cross section of women from Texas to Alaska, from New Hampshire to Florida. Respondents ranged from 20 to 50 years old and had from none to six children. (Gaylin, 1986)

Overwhelmingly, respondents favored a woman staying home with her small children. Not surprisingly, 74.5% of non- working mothers agreed that when a mother works outside the home, her children almost always suffer. But 49.5% of *working* mothers also held that opinion. (Gaylin, 1986)

Why is it that mothers know so much more than researchers? It's like they all know something deep inside about the importance of being with their children . . . even before scientific proof about bonding and attachment.

Then why do so many mothers go to work?

Necessity is often the answer. The Yale Bush Center in Child Development and Social Policy in 1984 convened the Advisory Committee on Infant Care Leave to evaluate the impact of the changing composition of the work force on families with infants. Among the conclusions:

"The majority of parents work because of economic necessity. The employed mother's salary is vital to the well-being of families." Further, the committee noted, "A growing proportion of American families do not have the means to finance leaves of absence from work in order to care for their infants." (October, 1985, p. 1)

The *Redbook* survey supported these findings. Virtually all of those responding—96.4% of the non-working and 86.5% of the working mothers—said mothers work because they need the money. One Wisconsin mother said, "I wish I could stay home, but it just isn't realistic. We have no other choice."

The decision to leave her children and go to work is a difficult and painful one for almost any woman, no matter how dedicated to her career she may be. A theme running through many of the letters received by *Redbook* was deep frustration with a society that forces women—but not men—to make that decision. (Gaylin, 1986)

Says Patricia McBroom in *The Third Sex*, (1986) "Men, whose role in reproduction can be limited to twenty minutes, remain fertile. Women, who must put their bodies on the line for a year or more and figure out how to maintain that life after birth, do not. No matter how sanguine working mothers may be about the ease of combining the two roles, being a parent does change the singleminded focus of a professional, not only because of the time it takes, but because people care less about their work. The pleasures and responsibilities of having a family restore the balance between love and work. But our present definition of careers requires an imbalance." (pp.239-240)

One of the situations that makes being a working mother particularly difficult is the lack of a national parental leave policy. In today's world, thousands of children are suffering due to the fact that their mothers are forced to return to work too soon.

A recent study by T. Berry Brazelton suggests that the present situation is folly. His research as associate professor of pediatrics at Harvard Medical School and chief of the Child Development Unit at Boston's Children's Hospital has found that critical stages in mothering must be addressed. "These are critical months for a baby's development. Each stage of learning between the mother-infant pair takes committed time together. (Brazelton, 1985, p. 55-56)

"Unless a baby is allowed to experience fully these stages of trust and attachment, his or her ability to attach to important others (either father or mother) will be either endangered or diluted." (October, 1986)

Jerome Miller, president of the National Center on Institutions and Alternatives, says the potential in the future, with more working mothers leaving their children with others, is for "a lot of depersonalization. Children will tend to be more shallow." (personal communication, April, 1986)

Problems naturally result when a young mother is torn away from her baby too soon. "If we can predict with that kind of accuracy, can't we also prevent? It is especially important that parents today give their babies a good self-image. We as a society should also be doing all we can to give the parents a good self-image," Brazelton told a conference on parental leave sponsored by the Association of Junior Leagues in 1985.

Brazelton also is fearful that early separation will cause a mother to set up three defense mechanisms crucial to her personal survival:

1. Denial or distortion of the importance of the change in her life. Many young career women are denying the reality that having a child will change their lives. They tell colleagues, "It isn't that big a deal." They do not realize that after having the baby, they will feel a deep sense of loss if they do not

allow themselves enough time for proper attachment to take place. They also seem not to realize the investment in time that an infant requires.

2.   Projection is a young mother's second defense mechanism. For example, she might blame a day-care center or family care providers for any problems.

3.   Detachment is the third. Mothers may say, "I need to work. I have to work. The baby doesn't miss me. I don't miss the baby." (Brazelton, 1985, p. 5)

Others agree. "One of the long-lasting structures that is supposed to be shaped during infancy and early childhood is a sense of emotional security—an idea closely related to the notions of trust, attachment and love," according to the authors of *Infancy: Its Place in Human Development* (1978). "[This is] one of the primary concerns to mothers who are considering day care for their children." (Kagan, et al., p. 29)

Just for a moment, imagine a scene as Norman Rockwell might have painted it. Mom kisses dad goodbye as he heads off to work down the cottage path; the kids (the requisite boy and girl) wave happily from the doorway of their suburban hideaway.

Well, it isn't like that anymore.

Some of the latest figures on women facing these dilemmas, from the Yale Bush Center Infant Care Leave Project (1985):

85% of all women with school-age children have moved into the marketplace.

85% of all working women in their child-bearing years will become pregnant at some time during their working lives.

46.8% of the married mothers of infants in 1984 were in the work force; in 1970 that figure was 24%.

Argues Sylvia Ann Hewlett, author of *A Lesser Life: The Myth of Women's Liberation in America*, "Such views are outdated. Most women work because they have to." (Peterson, 1986, p.30) But many government policymakers and employers choose not to notice. They instead cling to outdated views of the American family. In their minds, it is still mostly a man's world, despite overwhelming evidence to the contrary.

It is time for the U.S. to reckon with the great and steadily growing presence of women in the work force. Almost half of the country's women are now working outside the home, a total of 49 million of them. (Hellwig, 1986, p.129)

The new reality for most working women today involves remaining in the labor force, despite pregnancy and childbirth.

All industrial nations have experienced a steady and rapid growth in the number of working women, but the United States stands almost alone in its failure to develop a national program for dealing with the profound consequences.

European women don't have to quit their jobs to have children.

The results of one of the most comprehensive surveys of working and non-working women done in recent years were announced in June, 1986, by the firm of Yankelovich, Skelly and White for *Women's Day Magazine.* "This survey," says editor-in-chief Ellen R. Levine, "reveals that American families are in the middle of a major domestic crisis. Women want to hold jobs; they have to hold jobs. Yet, neither men or society is giving them the help or flexibility they need to handle all their responsibilities."

Three critical areas were covered in the 77-question survey: marriage, children and work. More than 60,000 women responded. They said the big winners of the women's movement have been men. The big losers have been children. The typical respondent is likely to be balancing marriage, children and work: she is under 45, a wife and mother and has or expects to have a job.

The survey's biggest finding was that *women simply need more help.* They need help from men and help from society in general—particularly where children are concerned. About 60% believe that mothers of young children are caught in a squeeze play:

● Those who stay home with their children aren't as respected as those in the *work* world, but . . .

● Those who do have jobs are made to feel guilty for not staying home.

Three-quarters of the respondents said that public officials aren't paying enough attention to day-care. Large numbers also declared that employers have at least some responsibility to provide flexible work schedules (82%), part-time work (70%) and a day-care program (66%).

"We can no longer afford to think of the issue of home versus work as only a private matter," says Ethel Klein, associate professor of political science at Columbia University and a special consultant to the*Woman's Day* study (1986). "Women are facing problems that have critical implications not just for their own lives but for the well-being of their children and the future of our country. Men need to change if women are to have any hope of resolving the difficulties—but so do business and government policies."

The survey found that an astonishing *84% of those responding reported feeling overworked and tired,* 41% said that they felt that way frequently. A clear majority (70%) said the ideal marriage is one where spouses share responsibilities for earning money and raising a family. Most, however, did not have such an ideal arrangement.

Overall, 62% of the mothers surveyed have had to decide whether to get a job or stay home with their children. Very few said the decision was easy.

Mothers of children under 3 years of age are the fastest growing segment of the work force. When employed, 60% of mothers of toddlers under 3 years of age work full-time. (Yale Bush Center Infant Care Leave Project, 1985)

Professional women deciding whether to have a career and/or children face an even larger dilemma. Research, in fact, suggests that U.S. society actually makes childbearing difficult for professional women. Among women executives, one in five has never married, one fifth are separated or divorced, and only 46% have children; 99% of male executives are married and 95% have children. (Levine, 1987, p.31)

McBroom interviewed 44 successful women in New York and San Francisco for her book, *The Third Sex* (1986). She found that women are maintaining equality with men by sacrificing reproduction.

McBroom further found that women are accepting the grief of trying to integrate careers and families without protest, and they are suffering alone. "Throughout recent history, the vast majority of professional men have had families; the majority of professional women have not. Current attempts by an avant-garde group of women to have it all only indicates how far we still have to go in creating a world where women have access to a full life" (p.161). Yet, many women's magazines carry cover articles suggesting that "You can have it all," aggravating the frustrating dilemma.

The fact is, women are giving up the option of having children, rather than sacrifice their careers. Says McBroom: "Women's thorough integration into business and professional roles presents institutions with a critical choice. They can either move in fundamental ways to balance their requirements with family life or watch reproduction dwindle among the daughters of the middle class" (p.249).

Brazelton says something else sinister is happening. In the past 2 to 3 years he has seen a change in many young pregnant women who have come to him for prenatal advice.

"I've had young women sitting in my office and they won't share. They don't want to get into the subject (of their babies) in depth any more. I began to realize that what they were saying to me, when they were not willing to share the deeper emotional feelings about the turmoil of pregnancy or not wanting to talk about nursing, was that they had to return to work too soon.

"They were already guarding themselves, in pregnancy, from too deep an attachment. Now, that scares the hell out of me. That scares me to death. That young women today have to guard themselves in pregnancy because they don't dare get too close. These young women are grieving for what they might have had at a time when they ought to be investing themselves so emotionally and passionately that, of course, it is going to hurt to leave. But at least they would have loved and lost. Isn't that better than never having loved at all?"

Brazelton asks, "If you can guard yourself like that, then what kind of a nurturing person are you going to be?" (1986)

It is a simple fact that most working women today must remain working, despite pregnancy and childbirth or child caring and rearing responsibilities. "Women work out of economic necessity," says Marsha Hurst, M. D., adjunct assistant professor of community medicine at the Mt. Sinai School of Medicine. "I don't think we can say that too many times" (Association of Junior Leagues, 1982, p. 5). She notes that in 1979 nearly two-thirds of working women were heads of households or had husbands earning under $10,000 per year. "Poverty is still a women's issue" (pg. 5). Poverty brings on depression to women immersed in it, which definitely affects children in the home.

One of the most dramatic changes over the past decade has been the sharp rise in the number of women who have primary responsibility for the welfare of their families—an increase of about 66%. This reflects the corresponding and equally dramatic and unprecedented divorce rate that has resulted in millions of women left to struggle as sole support for themselves and their children. Many of these women have become America's "new poor." Women in 1987 still earned only 60 cents for every dollar men earned. There is also a rising number of "never-married" women who are having babies without husbands (Association of Junior Leagues, 1982). Many young children are being raised in single-parent homes.

Working mothers — and the possibility that their children are suffering bonding breaks — are simply not being given enough attention. These women are not being given sufficient time to spend with their very young infants. Adding to the problem is the continued disenfranchisement of fathers. Fathers, whether married, divorced or never-married, can help assure that their children bond and attach.

"If the family of today is to survive intact, fathers *must* take on a larger role in the raising and bonding of their children," urged Brazelton in an October, 1986, talk to a group of Colorado parents.

Some social scientists have called for restructuring the work environment to accommodate families. For women to be truly equal in the work force, and still be able to manage at home with small children, industry must help make fathering easier also. The priorities of the workplace must change dramatically to allow men and women the time and energy to rear families.

When parents work 8 to 10 hours a day, they barely have time for themselves, let alone children.

"The majority of American women now must scramble to find adequate day-care help and must be able to find the right husband, and right employer, to enable them to have a job and a family," says McBroom (1986, p.240).

Dual-career families have been with us for decades; the 1970s and 1980s, however, are the first in which the acceptance of male supremacy has been so broadly questioned. The dual-career lifestyle has been criticized for contributing to divorce, to troubled children and to physical exhaustion. Jo-Ida C. Hansen, a psychologist at the University of Minnesota, says the dual-career lifestyle is also stressful. The most relevant finding of Hansen's studies so far is that much of the success of women's careers depends on their mates' ability to emphasize family and career, she told a meeting of the American Psychological Association in late 1986 (Ode, 1986).

To be closely involved with their children, parents need more time on a daily and weekly basis. Work, argues Kenneth Keniston in a 1977 Carnegie Corporation study on children and the family, should be changed to fit the needs of the family. "It should no longer be assumed that families are not the business of employers or public officials" (McBroom, 1986, p.250).

The latest Bureau of Census survey found that labor force participation rates for women who had a baby within one year increased more than 40% in 7 years. (Rogers, 1984)

At the heart of problems facing America is the question: What effect is the profound demographic revolution now taking place on so many fronts in this country having on our children? In the next few chapters we will explore separately each of the stresses being placed on the formation of attachment: child-care needs, lack of parental leave, adoption and foster care, teenage pregnancy, abuse and neglect, and divorce.

Never before in the history of this country have so many parents been away from home and their children at the most critical times.

With so many mothers working, just who is taking care of the children? Proper bonding and attachment cannot occur when the infant's significant caregiver isn't around, and the baby has no reliable, *consistent,* loving substitute caregiver. Without suitable answers, these problems could result in a national attachment crisis, thus putting a future generation at high risk.

"The difficulty in life is the choice."
George Moore

9

Day Care, Simply a Dilemma or a Disaster?

Just what is the harm of dropping off a child before work in the morning and then picking him up after work? It may be plenty, according to many experts.

Infants put in day-care centers may be harmed by sensory deprivation and trauma caused by separation from their mothers, comparable to "psychological thalidomide," child development expert Edward F. Zigler of Yale University warns ("Day care infants," 1985).

Harvard's T. Berry Brazelton predicts that the problem will worsen because infant care is the fastest growing part of day care. Zigler and Brazelton estimate that tens of thousands of very young infants — from 3 weeks to 2 months old — are being checked into infant care centers of questionable quality in America every day ("Day care infants," 1985).

These dire warnings come just as day care has become a fact of life for many parents. And day care for infants is steadily increasing. The National Commission on Working Women's 1986 Child Care Fact Sheet shows the highest increase in the rate of labor force participation was in women with children under 3 years old.

"There is a shortage of child care slots for every age group, with a particularly acute need for infant care," the Fact Sheet states. In many instances, parents must join long waiting lists for especially desirable day care facilities as soon as the mother learns she is pregnant.

Most working parents agree that finding satisfactory (let alone excellent) child care tops their list of problems. There is an urgent need now for more and better day care options for preschool children and other children outside school hours. If the child care options desperately needed by working parents are to be realized, additional financial help is vital. Federal and state governments must be more innovative, and special plans designed for working parents must be set up and partially funded by employers.

Notes Alexis Herman, chairman of the National Commission on Working

121

Women, "Child care is a working women's issue, but fundamentally it is a social issue." She says she has a recurring fantasy, "that one day every working mother and father in America would take their kids to work in the office or the plant. I imagine that the 'crisis' in child care would become top priority when employers saw clearly the link between their employees' work lives and their family lives . . ." (National Commission on Working Women, 1985).

It is obvious that with the explosion of mothers into the labor force, the supply of child care has not kept up with the demand. There are now about 5 million child care providers, almost 3 million of them working full time. Statistics tell us the following: more than 96% of all providers are female; their average annual wages range from $2,200 to $12,500 (many of them live below the poverty level); they come from a wide variety of educational backgrounds but most have little or no special training when they begin their work. The child care industry is ill-prepared to deal with the deluge of children headed their way. (National Commission on Working Women, 1985)

MOTHERS IN THE WORK FORCE

Percent of working mothers.

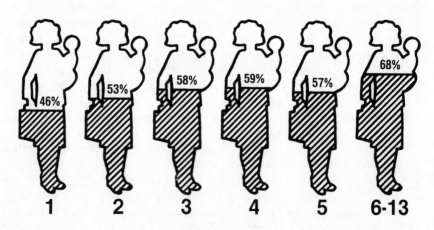

1   2   3   4   5   6-13

**Ages of Children
(Years)**

© High Risk, Magid/McKelvey

The fact is, the middle class and poor in this country are in the middle of a child-care crisis. Fifteen years ago, President Richard M. Nixon vetoed a bill providing for a national day-care system. Since then the American family has been through an economic and emotional wringer. The demographic revolution occurring in this country has seen more than half of all mothers go to work. But many of the friends and relatives who used to be available to babysit working mothers' children are now also at work. This puts working mothers and their children in an even tighter squeeze.

Says Elizabeth Ehrlich in Business Week (1986); "Despite the urgent need for more child care, what has emerged is an ad hoc, fragmented, inadequate network that bewilders parents with services that too often range from minimal to dangerous or bad. The once private matter of child care has become a public policy issue that demands action . . . No one is suggesting a uniform, monolithic federal program. For one thing, it would cost tens of billions of dollars.

"But," continues Ehrlich, "the private sector is not meeting the sheer size of the need or coordinating the various services. It can't assure quality care or serve the growing numbers of poor children" (p.52).

Child care in this country consists of five basic categories of care-giving situations: in-home care, shared care, family day care, group homes, and child-care centers. The lowest paid caregivers are in family day care. This type of care is also the most used — 40.2% of all children, especially infants and children under 3 years old, are in these homes. Next in outside-of-home use is the child-care center, with 14.8% of children in infant, preschool and mixed-age centers. (National Commission on Working Women, 1985)

The child-care industry in this country is not healthy. It's rare to find an excellent day-care center. Most fall into the inadequate range. Extremely important for the physical and mental well-being of infants and toddlers is the ratio of caretakers to children. That can range from a low — and the child care expert's recommended—ratio of three infants to one caretaker to as many as ten or more infants for each staff member.

The low ratio of caregiver to infant is important if the children are to get the proper stimulus and loving attention necessary for the attachment process to proceed in a healthy way (White, 1985).

Everyone has heard horror stories of babies left lying in cribs or sitting in high chairs in front of television sets. These babies can suffer the same ill effects as infants raised in poorly-staffed institutions; they are at high risk of becoming unattached.

The child-care industry has argued that if standards for caregivers are raised, or the ratio of caregivers to children is required to be higher, they couldn't afford to operate. Susan H. Law, executive director of the North West Child Development Council Inc., says "if you make it one-to-four, nobody could afford to put their kid in there — even if you pay minimum wage." (Ehrlich, 1986, p.53) Therefore, the frequently quoted "excellent day care" is largely a myth.

When Zigler told the press in 1985 that "we might be handing out psychological thalidomide" he was concerned about unattached children. Zigler says child development damage could result "from sensory deprivation and trauma when infants are separated from mothers. By we, I mean the providers of infant care."

Zigler notes that, even if quality infant care were available everywhere, few could afford the $6,000 annual cost.

In the low risk infant-care center, he says, there would be one worker for each three babies. "By contrast to this ideal, consider two overworked women taking care of 24 infants. All these women do is feed babies and diaper and keep them in a darkened room. We know about the harmful effects of sensory deprivation" (Meredith, 1986, p.42).

In the typical state, Zigler says, there are eight infants to one day-care worker, who may be a 17-year-old with no training, making less than the minimum wage and perhaps carrying a communicable illness or infection. "What I am saying," Zigler explains, "is that mothers are working, and they will continue to work, and we have to make sure that we have infant day care of good quality" (Meredith, 1986). We are not talking about the intellectual development of children—that type of development does not seem to be stunted by alternative care situations.

"The research evidence is compellingly consistent in demonstrating there is absolutely no adverse effect of out-of-home care, be it in centers or in families, on children's *intellectual functioning*," says Jay Belsky, professor of human development at Pennsylvania State University.

But, like the authors, Belsky finds the picture very different when you look at a child's emotional development as it relates to the quality of the attachment to the mother.

"Today I cannot conclude, as I did in 1978 and again in 1982, that the data shows no apparent adverse effects on infant care," Belsky said in 1984 as he testified before the U.S. House of Representatives' hearing on child-care services. (Hunter, 1986)

Findings in a recent Belsky study support his earlier concerns. He has concluded that babies who spend 20 hours or more a week in care away from parents—during their first year—face a risk of becoming more insecure than other infants.

Belsky said his findings put full-time day care babies at risk of "heightened aggressiveness, non-compliance and withdrawal in the preschool and early school years" (Belsky, 1987). Research, he said, has linked insecure infants to problematic children.

He began his study on nonmaternal care in 1982, gathering data on child care arrangements and parents' employment in the cases of 149 infants during their first year of life.

The infants were videotaped in "strange situation" episodes so that secure and insecure attachments to the babies' mothers and fathers could be measured.

In this type of research the baby is separated repeatedly from the parent, introduced to a stranger, then reunited with the parent. Belsky and his associates measured the reactions of the babies.

The research showed that 43% of 58 infants who had extensive non-maternal care during their first year (20 hours a week or more) were classified insecure. Of 51 infants with extensive non-parental care, 49% were determined to be insecure. Belsky's research found that babies who became insecure had mothers who were less sensitive and in less-than-satisfying marriages. This may help to explain why certain babies cannot overcome a certain amount of maternal deprivation.

Interestingly, babies found to be insecure at one year were considered "fussy" by their mothers at 3 months of age.

Zigler, in commenting on Belsky's latest findings in an Associated Press story, said he has found similar warning signs in reviewing first-year day care studies, but none as ominous as those reported by Belsky. Zigler told A.P. writer Maud S. Beelman that he was personally more concerned about directing attention toward the crucial issue of establishing quality day care in the U.S.

Belsky's study relied on the parents' evaluations of their day care situations and their level of satisfaction with that day care. It did not measure the quality of the care arrangements; the day care used by the parents ranged from centers to babysitters to in-home day care.

Belsky said he is not trying to debunk day care, despite the findings. He is instead calling for parental leave, the availability of high-quality child care and part-time work which will go back to full-time work after the baby reaches one year of age.

Belsky said he is finding families in stressful circumstances and that these problems need attention.

Writing in the September 1986 *Bulletin of the National Center for Clinical Infant Programs,* Belsky noted the results of an investigation of kindergarten and first graders reported in 1985 by R. Haskins in *Child Development.* (p. 700) The children had been reared since 3 months of age in an extremely high-quality day care center at the University of North Carolina. He said these children, who received center-based care in the first year of life, where compared to those receiving care any time thereafter. They were found:

" . . . as more likely to use the aggressive acts of hitting, kicking, and pushing than children in the control group. Second, they were more likely to threaten, swear, and argue. Third, they demonstrated those propensities in several school settings—the playground, the hallway, the lunchroom, and the classroom. Fourth, teachers were more likely to rate these children having aggressiveness as having a serious deficit in social behavior. Fifth, teachers viewed these children as less likely to use such strategies as walking away or discussion to avoid or extract themselves from situations that could lead to aggression" (Belsky, September, 1986, p. 1).

The bottom line of this new study? That the "risk of insecure infant-mother attachment under conditions of extensive nonmaternal care (as it is routinely experienced in this country) increases when infants from relatively well-functioning, two-parent families are reared in these particular circumstances." Belsky further cautions in his study, however, that "while the current investigation clearly reveals that extensive nonmaternal (and nonparental) care in the first year is a risk factor in the development of insecure infant-parent attachment relationships, it just as clearly indicates that complete understanding of conditions of risk requires a focus upon the child, the family and the particular rearing situation" (Belsky, 1986, p. 22).

In helping the family with child-care difficulties, the U.S. has historically compared poorly with other nations. In Sweden, for example, the federal government has set up centers to care for *all* preschool-age children of working parents and before- and after-school care for all children ages 7 to 12. In the U.S., however, only about 10% of the 23 million children whose parents are working get care in comparable centers. So the U.S. government is helping less than 10% of America's children while Sweden helps 100% percent of its working families. (The Swedish Institute, 1982) This disparity is reflected in the difference between Sweden's and the U.S.'s rate of APD victims.

Although the U.S. is the world's wealthiest nation, other nations have forged far beyond us in the provision of early childhood services. For example, Israel provides kindergarten for all its 5-year-olds, child care for 50% of its 3- and 4-year-olds and comprehensive health care through neighborhood Mother and Child Clinics for 90% of its infants and their mothers. In Hungary, nurseries are provided for half of the 3- to 6-year-olds. Pamela Roby, writing in the book *Child Care — Who Cares?* (1973) notes, "Americans entering Scandinavian or Israeli children's centers are immediately struck by their hominess . . . and by the seriousness with which their hosts explain that child-care center policies should be considered only in the context of a *comprehensive* social policy for the promotion of children's well-being and development and the well-being of their parents" (p.300).

America's children, in contrast, are given only lip service, while the comprehensive children's services of Sweden, Israel, Hungary and other nations are built on the belief that all human beings, including children, have the right to a decent level of well-being. These countries also seem to believe that the nation must concern itself with the welfare of its children today, because they will be its citizens tomorrow. In Finland and Norway, "park mothers" provide year-round, daily, supervised playground and park activities, and Scandinavian "child visitors" look after sick children in their homes when their parents are at work. (Roby, 1973)

American families aren't nearly so lucky. Most can't even find adequate child care for their children and, even when parents don't have problems obtaining child care, they must realize that the jury is still out on the benefits of the average day care available in this country. Research in this area is still extremely limited and doesn't represent the full range of substitute care being used. It tells us that we *really don't know* the effects of various substitute systems.

Psychologist and child advocate Burton White has said he *feels* such practices may not be in the best interests of children, especially when the substitute care is full-time and the children are under 3 years of age. And Zigler says he feels it is "a high risk gamble."

In a 1984 letter to the editor of *Young Children,* Michael K. Meyerhoff of the Center for Parent Education, Newton, Massachusetts, challenged a column by Joanne Curry O'Connell that stated that a review of the research shows day care is not harmful to children.

Meyerhoff states: "It is presumptuous of O'Connell to conclude that there is even a shred of hard evidence for her position that there is nothing harmful about substitute care . . . I doubt that any intellectually honest person who has reviewed the research on early child development or who has worked with parents and babies would not be concerned about the growing trend toward placing infants and toddlers in substitute care for 8 or 9 hours a day, five days a week" (p.2).

Like Meyerhoff, the authors have found some articles in professional journals and the popular press seriously flawed and misleading. For example, most studies have tested only small numbers of children in ideal day care situations. The hard data just isn't there to support their claims. These ideal situations don't exist in large numbers and are not available to most of working parents seeking alternative child care. We also doubt that any caring individual reviewing these studies would not be sympathetic to the plight of parents trying to find excellent child care.

Meyerhoff sees mothers as being in the proverbial "hot seat." He says mothers are usually alone when it comes to making the tough decisions that must be made about substitute care. Meyeroff concludes his letter: "The rights and plights of working women in our society should be addressed emphatically and effectively . . . After all, if not us, who will speak for the children?" (p.2)

Brazelton agrees that present day care research is "biased and overinterpreted. We need randomized, controlled trials to see if it really makes a difference and when it does make a difference and what kind of day care makes a difference." He says one thing is clear: "The kind of day care we have for most kids in this country is devastating. Poor quality day care exists and it is clearly harmful and destructive" (1986).

The truth is that we can't wait another decade for research to find out how deprived our children have become.

There are many mothers who are dropping their infants and small children off at day care each morning, worrying that they are leaving them in an unsafe and unnurturing place.

As Congresswoman Patricia Schroeder, D-Colo., and sponsor of the Parental and Medical Leave Act (reintroduced in February, 1987, after failing to pass in 1986), states: "There are just a tremendous number of guilt-ridden mothers out there who want to do the best for their children but simply don't know how." (personal communication, September 15, 1986)

More than half of all children under age 5 in the United States are in second-rate day-care situations. In 1980, the turnover rate of child-care providers in centers was almost 42%; for family day-care providers, the rate was even higher. In 1984, there were an estimated 2 to 3 million child-care providers in the U.S.; the majority earned minimum wage, or less. (National Commission on Working Women, 1986)

Educational psychologist White is known for his outspoken opposition to women working outside the home during the first three years of their babies' lives. Many of his beliefs are built on information about the poor quality of substitute care in the U.S. today. He wrote in 1985:

"Given the current incomplete state of knowledge about children's needs and substitute care, I firmly believe that most children will get off to a better start in life if they spend the majority of their waking hours during the first 3 years being cared for by their parents and other family members rather than in any form of substitute care" (p. 27).

The reason for this substandard day care is simple: day-care workers are underpaid and undertrained. "What person," Brazelton asks, "is going to work a 40-hour week with small kids all day for $8,000 a year if they could do anything else?" (1986)

In addition to the overwhelming evidence supporting parental care of very small infants, parents have something else to fear when considering day care options. Recent events reported in the news have caused many professionals and parents to wonder whether children being cared for in inadequate day-care homes and child-care centers may be suffering more than deprivation of mother-infant bonds. Reports of incidents of child sexual abuse in day-care centers in California, New York and other areas have spotlighted the child-care profession negatively.

In the summer of 1984, the parents of a 3-year-old girl discovered to their horror that their daughter had been sexually abused at the prestigious West Point Child Development Center.

What followed were years of anguish for that family and others as they sought justice. At first, only the one West Point family spoke out; others followed. In all, it was alleged that 11 children were sexually abused. The parents of the 3-year-old were initially ostracized until other parents learned their children were also involved.

In 1986 parents of 8 of the children filed a civil claim against the U.S. government for $110 million in damages on behalf of the 11 children of West Point. The reason? No criminal charges were ever brought against two teachers. A federal grand jury's reasons: "We concluded that although there were indications that children may have been abused at the Center, there was insufficient evidence to prosecute anyone as the perpetrator of that abuse . . . Although a few children have identified one or another former employee of the center, the extremely young age of the children raises a serious issue as to the evidentiary strength of their potential testimony . . . "

The suit was filed by the parents to seek justice, since they found it lacking in the criminal court system. A similar outcome has occurred in most of the celebrated child abuse cases across the country. The children have been ruled too young to testify accurately.

For the affected families no amount of money will ease the torment of families who trusted that they had placed their children, as one mother in the West Point incident put it, "in the safest place in the world." (Michaels, 1986)

Parents need to have a safe, healthy environment in which to place their child. And there are other pressing questions that must be answered. What is the optimal age for children to be left in day care? Can parents leave a child too early? The fact is that no one knows what *too early* is yet. The best recent research says that under no circumstances should any child be left with anyone other than a primary caretaker during the first 3 to 4 months. Brazelton says, "In my opinion that would be the absolute youngest age." (1986)

After reviewing all the literature, it is the authors' opinion that no child should be left for any significant period of time during the first year of life. After the initial attachment period parents can safely use substitute care if they follow careful guidelines. Parents should remember that bonding breaks and trauma can occur during the second or third years as well.

"In the eyes of most students of human development, the first three years of life are extremely important and like no others . . . Clearly, what most of us (including parents) worry about most is the emotional development of babies," says White (p.27).

Few would debate the almost mystical significance of the mother-infant bond. Research from many fields, including psychiatry, child psychology, ethnology and from studies of other animal species, has confirmed our intuitive respect for mother-infant attachment. Studies cited previously in this book show that the first two years of a baby's life are when that bond forms. It is our opinion that parents of small infants must proceed with extreme caution when they are considering turning care of their baby over to someone else, whether it be a babysitter or a relative. These are the most important moments of your baby's life.

Some babies, particularly those who may have been ill or had other problems very early, seem to have a tendency not to bond and attach to their parents. These infants are at particularly high risk and would not do well under the supervision of another caregiver. Parents of infants who have avoidant behavior — poor eye contact or who seem stiff or reluctant to "mold" to the adult body when held — should probably not use substitute care until these problems have been solved.

Two recently completed research projects support the premise that too-early day care can actually be harmful to infants. Schwartz (1986) reported in *Child Development*: Of 50 infants studied, those in full-time care displayed more avoidant behavior than did either part-time care babies or the study's control babies. The study focused on Bowlby's work (1972) and found that "More infants attending day care on a full-time basis displayed avoidance on reunion than infants cared for primarily by their mothers" (p. 1076). Belsky's research cited earlier supports these studies.

The 1980 study by Brian Vaughn of the University of Illinois at Chicago supports similar conclusions. He and his colleagues found that about 50% of babies in sitter-care were insecurely attached to their mothers, compared with 30% of babies cared for by their mothers.

The study further found that " . . . mothers who work may, because of problems associated with their employment, be less psychologically available to their infants, as well as less physically accessible because of separations, than mothers who remain at home" (p. 1210). Of course, mothers have felt this for years; it causes them much guilt.

The researchers concluded that "during the first year, when the attachment bond is being formed and consolidated, regular, daily separations resulting from out-of-home care are associated with the development of anxious-avoidant attachments . . ." (Vaughn et al., 1980, p. 1212).

The bottom line in this study was: "For infants who enter child care before 9 months of age, the length of daily separations from the mother may influence the nature of their original relationship." (Schwartz, 1983, p.1076)

In contrast to the studies that show that infants do poorly if their mothers or fathers go back to work too soon, there is mounting evidence that children whose mothers return to work after the children are of school age actually may do better when their mothers work.

Two recent studies found evidence that employed mothers' children can do well, if the mothers wait until after the children are of school age.

A large scale study, led by project director John Guidubaldi of Kent State University, focused on grade-school children from 38 states. It is the first broad-based national research done on the highly controversial issue of mothers in the work force. The study clearly demonstrated that school-age children's classroom behavior and academic performance are positively — not negatively — related to maternal employment.

It wasn't the mothers who worked full-time whose children did best however, but rather those whose mothers worked only part-time. "They were also more successful if their mothers held a high-status job with flexible hours and were satisfied with the dual roles of working woman and mother," Guidubaldi says.

Interestingly, job satisfaction does appear to play a role. Lois Wladis Hoffman, a psychology professor at the University of Michigan, concluded that "When a mother is satisfied with what she is doing, the children seem to fare better. If she's working and she prefers that arrangement, the children score higher on adjustment scales than if she's working and doesn't want to be, or if she's staying at home and doesn't want to be" (Seliger, 1986, p. 77).

The timing of the mother's reentry into the work force is very significant; the longer a mother can wait to reenter her career field, the better.

"Child care does have an affect on the job, and that's probably going to worsen unless we do something about it," Ellen Galinsky, a psychologist who led a symposium on child care told the annual meeting of the American Psychological Association in August, 1987. ("Day-care worries," August 30, 1987)

Galinsky's research shows that one in four working parents with preschool-age children has trouble finding day care. And this difficulty is making these parents less productive, increasing their absenteeism and affecting their health adversely.

Other studies presented showed that 38% of parents said their child-care arrangements affected productivity. Marybeth Shinn of New York University surveyed 644 parents with children younger than 17. Family incomes were from $30,000 to $40,000. Those responding to the survey said they missed work or were late for work once every three weeks because of problems with child care. Difficulties seem even more severe when parents have lower incomes and younger children. And women are more than twice as likely as men to miss work when a child-care emergency arises.

Shinn said these events are stressful for the parents, but men who missed work because of child-care problems were even more stressed and had a greater health and well-being reaction.

The health symptoms related to child-care problems, Galinsky said, include: shortness of breath, pounding or racing heart, back and neck pains, overeating or increased use of alcohol, cigarettes, or tranquilizers. ("Day-care worries," August 30, 1987)

What is known is that children today are facing an entirely different home social environment than children of the previous generations. If predictions hold, by 1990 only 14% of children under the age of 18 will have a stay-at-home mother. The most important thing to remember when reading about working mothers in the Guidubaldi study is that it dealt primarily with children whose mothers had returned to work only after their children began school. This offers little solace for mothers forced to go to work, leaving their very small infants in substitute care.

A second recent study, this one of middle-class children, was done by psychologists Adele E. Gottfried of California State University at Northridge,

Allen Gottfried of California State University at Fullerton, and Kay Bathurst of the University of California at Los Angeles. It concluded that children suffered no negative effects when their mothers worked. They found birth order, home environment and socio-economic class had more effect. This is an interesting study, as it looked at children through their first 7 years; but the study did not look at children under 1 year of age. And the children were mostly from white, middle-income families that included both employed and homemaking mothers. The California study did not include day care as a specific factor and did not consider the effects of substitute care on very small infants. (Meredith, 1986).

In contrast to this "good news" for older children, experts are noticing an unfortunate and disturbing trend as they look at younger children in day care. These children appear to be more aggressive than other children. A study recently completed by Alison Clarke-Stewart, a psychology professor at the University of California at Irvine, found "They tend to be more aggressive with other kids and assertive in general. They're less compliant — even with their parents. That's the price you pay." (Seliger, 1986, p. 77)

Dr. Ron Haskins of the University of North Carolina found similar results on the trend toward more aggressive children. "On balance," he concludes, "there is reason for concern about the effects of day care on social development." (Bracey, 1985, p. 227) He found that group day care is associated with increased levels of aggression and resistance to adult authority.

Research itself on the day care issue has now entered a new phase. The first studies simply compared the effects of mother care with high-quality center care, and were indecisive as to whether day care harms or helps children. Now researchers are sharpening their focus, attempting to evaluate different forms of day care. Unfortunately, the good news about older children and working parents does not translate to infants. Parents cannot leave infants with much certainty or comfort. The results of the very few studies done on infants have been so controversial that the effects of infant day care remain murky at best.

"The first wave of research made everybody feel pretty sanguine." But the early studies were all conducted in high-quality settings and were not representative. The second wave of studies shows that there seem to be some problems in mother-infant attachment with babies in day care," Zigler says (Meredith, 1986, p. 39).

Vaughn's research has also shown problems with infant day care. The findings "don't mean that all children in non-maternal or day-care groups have an insecure attachment, it's just that the probability is higher" (Meredith, 1986, p.39). In other words, they are at higher risk.

For parents who work, the term "day care" has truly become a double-edged sword. They couldn't work without it, yet many parents feel they are shirking their parental responsibilities, or worse, when they put a child in day care.

We now know that during their first months of life babies need a great deal of prompt, loving attention. "What's at stake is the basic human capacity for loving other humans," says White (1985, p.28). In other words, the babies are at high risk of becoming unattached and then never being able to experience the most important human emotion — love.

What makes it so hard to predict how children will turn out is that we are entering a new era of parenting. White further cautions: "Even though first reports of research show no obvious harm being done to infants in high quality programs, I cannot endorse such practices . . . None of the few evaluations performed to date have addressed the question of what is *very good* for young children" (1985, pp.28, 30).

"Put simply, after more than 20 years of research on how children develop well, I would not think of putting a child of my own into any substitute care program on a full-time basis, especially a center-based program," White says (1985, p.30).

What is a parent to do who has no choice but to work while his child is still small? How can you choose the best day-care situation for your infant or small child? We'll give some tips later on for ways you can make this difficult quest easier. It's a task parents must largely handle alone because federal and state governments do so little regarding day care.

*****

If the federal and state governments in the U.S. have been lax in helping families, America's businesses aren't much better. Only a few corporations provide some form of day care. About 3,000 companies across the country (out of millions) now offer some type of child-care help (Basler, 1986); only 570 businesses operate child-care facilities at their work site. Other options open to employers include vouchers, vendor discounts, flexible benefits and spending (or reimbursement) accounts. (National Commission on Working Women, 1985)

It is a fact that in the past four years the number of companies providing child-care benefits has quadrupled. Yet, that number is *fewer than 0.1%* of the nation's 6 million employers. (Stautberg, 1986)

Businesses have always said they can't help with child care for employees because of the cost. But there is growing evidence that companies offering some form of day-care help actually save money through increased productivity and higher employee morale. It turns out that business can actually *benefit* financially from helping to provide such care.

Washington Post columnist Judy Mann writes that Dr. Deanna Tate, chairman of the Child Development and Family Living Department at Texas Women's University, has done cost-benefit analyses of three companies that had such detailed personnel data that she was able to determine the impact on productivity and profit of child-care assistance to employees. "The results of her studies are striking arguments that this kind of employee benefit makes good business sense," said Mann.

"A small textile manufacturing plant she analyzed had 87 employees, many of whom were women in low-skilled jobs. The turnover rate was running at the 40% level, in a community that had an unemployment rate of about 1.5 to 3%. The company paid $42,500 to buy and modify a nearby house and set up a child-care center. It budgeted $30,000 for ongoing costs with the rest to be paid from parent fees. The center provided care for 36 children, and 26% of the employees used it.

"The company calculated that it spent $1,000 to train a new production worker and $2,000 to train a new office worker. Turnover rate after the first year of operation of the center dropped to 7%, and absenteeism went from 10% to 1%. The company was able to reduce its payroll by 10 production workers and 5 office workers, saving salary and training costs of 15 employees, reducing its workspace, and lowering administrative costs for turnover and training. While it had four applicants for each position before the center was started, it had 20 afterwards, with 90% of them saying it was because of the child-care center." Every $1 spent yielded $6 in costs containment (Mann, 1984).

Tate's cost-benefit analysis of a print shop that was considering child-care assistance for its 50 employees showed it would save $4 for every $1 invested. She projected that a hospital with 4,000 employees would save $3 for every $1 invested in a center (Mann, 1984).

The bottom line of this study is that business can benefit from providing child-care benefits. And business interest in child-care assistance for employees is certainly growing.

But the cost of instituting on-site centers can be prohibitive for smaller companies, going well into the hundreds of thousands of dollars. So some companies have sought other, less expensive ways to help (Kantrowitz, 1986).

One program, for example, allows flexible leave policies, so parents can use sick leave when their children are sick.

In between are a variety of options: IBM, for example, has recently contracted with a Boston firm for a nationwide child-care and information referral system; banks in New York, Iowa and Ohio have developed working-parent seminars; Proctor & Gamble and the American Can Company offer employees flexible benefit plans with child-care as an option; the Polaroid Corporation and the Ford Foundation in New York give financial assistance to their employees for child-care. And other companies, including broadcasting stations in Washington, D.C., have formed a consortium to set up centers, which are then operated by nonprofit boards of employees. (Mann, 1984) Unfortunately, such companies are in the minority, but certainly they are forward-thinking. They are also finding out what Tate discovered: programs helping workers with child-care result in contented employees who are productive. Implementing policies to accommodate working parents can result in reduced employee turnover, better morale and company loyalty, lower absenteeism, increased productivity, and good word-of-mouth publicity, which attracts the most desirable applicants.

Once again, the bottom line rules. A study summarized by Rosabeth Moss Kanter of Goodmeasure, a consulting firm in Cambridge, Mass., concluded that "companies with a reputation for progressive human-resource practices were significantly higher in long-term profitability and financial growth than their counterparts" (Stautberg, 1986).

What parents need is a reliable and flexible arrangement for child care that has a contingency plan for times when the primary caretaker is unavailable due to bad weather, illness, or personal problems. Until recently, if parents had child-care problems, the company didn't want to know about them. Yet results of a study by Child Care Systems, a Pennsylvania consulting firm, show that each employee with a child under 13 years of age loses approximately eight working days a year because of child-care problems, and 39% of those workers have considered leaving their jobs because of difficulty in finding good child care (Stautberg, 1986).

Child-care problems, in fact, have as much impact on an employee's productivity as his relationship with a supervisor or even job security, a new survey in *Fortune* magazine reveals. The survey was nationwide and covered 400 working men and women with children under age 12. About

41% of parents surveyed said they lost at least one-day's work in the last 3 months due to care of a sick child or to attend to other child-related needs.

Nearly 10% of the parents said they had taken from 3 to 5 days. The survey said that fathers were almost as likely as mothers to say their jobs interfered with family life. Nearly 25% of the fathers and mothers said they had sought a less demanding job to spend more time with their families. ("Child-care strongly," p. 79)

Despite the fact that working parents are making new demands for more humane policies, however, most of the nation's employers still have not jumped on the bandwagon of this benefit, which has been touted as the "perk of the '80s." Even when companies offer some help, parents are finding child care isn't free. Usually parents will realize a 10 to 20% discount (Meister, 1986).

Child care isn't the only major problem working mothers and fathers face, however, when trying to combine their roles as employees with their responsibilities as parents. Perhaps the biggest problems are faced during pregnancy and after childbirth. The next chapter talks about the vital need for a national parental leave policy.

"It is a wise father that knows his own child."
Shakespeare

10

Parental Leave

Today's woman is plowing new ground, and it hasn't been particularly productive soil in the quest to "have it all."

Two case histories bring the inequities in America's family-leave "system" into clear focus:

During her second pregnancy, Ann was working as a computer operator for a small company. Because her husband was unemployed, she planned to work right up until the day of delivery. When she began having complications during the seventh month of her pregnancy, her doctor told her that she had to have complete bed rest.

She asked for, and received, a three-month unpaid maternity leave. Medical benefits covered part of her hospitalization, but the company had no plan to cover lost wages. Luckily, she had a normal delivery and her baby was healthy. Although still ill, Ann was back to work when the baby was 3 weeks old. Her boss would not guarantee her job any longer than the three months she had already been off, so she could not afford to stay home any longer. Then because she was frequently sick, she was fired.

*****

In contrast, Sue, who works as a staff assistant for a large telephone company, was able to leave her job long enough to recover fully from childbirth and to help her family adjust to the new baby. She had no medical problems, but if she had, she would have continued to receive disability payments until well enough to return to work.

Sue's job was also guaranteed during an extended period of unpaid "care-of-newborn-child leave." She was encouraged to

139

phase into her time at work as soon as she felt she could by working part-time. When she returned to work full-time, Sue was healthy and rested and her family had had ample time to decide how to care for the new baby while she worked. (Lang, 1985)

Female employees in past decades usually dropped out of the job market—permanently—when they became pregnant. Today 93% of women in the work force will bear children sometime during their working lives and, because of economic pressures, more than half will remain at work during the pregnancy and will return to their jobs before their children are 1 year old.

More than three out of four working women will experience a pregnancy at some point in their working lives.

Despite the fact that the fastest-growing segment of the work force is women with young children, there is currently no federal policy addressing these demographic changes in American work and family patterns.

Employers are ill-prepared to deal with this new phenomenon. The nation's response to the influx of working mothers has been for individuals, a few large corporations and a few state governments to create a hodgepodge of policies surrounding the circumstances of childbirth and adoption and the parents' return to work.

According to the American Association of Junior Leagues, only about 40% of working women have an official leave for complications of pregnancy, childbirth, and care of the newborn child. In 1984, 60% of all working women had no paid parental (maternity) leave of any kind. (National Commission on Working Women, 1986)

On January 15, 1987, the Supreme Court ruled that states may require employers to give pregnant workers job protections not available to other employees. The court ruling upheld a California law requiring employers to grant unpaid leaves of absence of up to four months to women whose pregnancies leave them unable to work—even if leaves are not granted for any other disability. The ruling was hailed by those seeking work equality for American women. The ruling did not, however, mandate such leaves nationwide.

In 1978, Congress passed an act requiring employers who provide disability insurance coverage to treat pregnancy as a disability. But that act only applies to about half of the country's employers and to an even smaller proportion of those with the highest concentration of female employees.

Disability benefits, in any case, are typically much less than the worker's normal pay. Those "lucky" enough to get the disability benefits are still not necessarily guaranteed a return to their jobs. The Pregnancy Disability Act of 1978 prohibits discrimination because of pregnancy and requires insured wage compensation for the period (usually 6 to 8 weeks) a woman cannot work, *if* her employer provides other kinds of short-term disability coverage.

Some employers do have a paid or unpaid "parental leave" policy (generally 4 to 16 weeks) which allows a woman time off from work to care for her newborn child. Women not covered by any policy (the majority of working women in the U.S.) are forced to use a combination of sick days, vacation days and leave without pay during this period. (National Commission on Working Women, 1986)

So a majority of American working women are faced with a total lack of policy on day care, maternity leave, and parental leave. In the U.S., in fact, 80% of all working mothers are not having their day care or their maternity needs met.

What is deplorable is that 75 other nations, including all other advanced industrial societies (France, Britain, Sweden, the U.S.S.R., East and West Germany, Canada) have statutory provisions that guarantee infant care leave of some kind.

Many women in this country can kiss their jobs goodbye when they discover they are pregnant. There is no statutory provision protecting the right to return to work after taking a pregnancy leave. And, the U.S. has no regulations providing that even a portion of the salary be paid to a parent on leave to care for a newborn.

AFL-CIO secretary-treasurer Thomas Donahue has said that most parents are denied the option of staying home with a new child, "because to do so will endanger their employment." Those not faced with loss of their jobs for staying home are frequently faced with a loss of income they can't afford. (Meister, 1986)

Donahue is one of dozens of employee representatives, child-care specialists, parents and others who spoke out during hearings that four House subcommittees held in 1986 on The Parental and Medical Leave Act.

A similar bill, sponsored by Patricia Schroeder of Colorado, was reintroduced into the 100th Congress on Feb. 3, 1987. Schroeder, co-chair of the Congressional Caucus of Women's Issues, says the bill was designed to combat some of the most serious problems of working parents by requiring employers to provide job-protected unpaid leaves for certain serious family or medical reasons. Employers with less than 15 employees were exempt from the legislation. The proposed law would provide an employee up to 18 weeks of unpaid leave for the birth, adoption or serious illness of a child or dependent parent; the leave would be available to any employee—male or female—who requests it. "Without a doubt, parental leave is the family issue of the '80s," Schroeder says. "This act is the answer to the harsh choice men and women face between economic security and the family." (Stautberg, 1986)

"Families today are under increasing stress. In order for families to maintain the standard of living their parents enjoyed on one income, it now takes two. Having a baby, trying to adopt or getting seriously ill, jeopardizes their economic security," says Schroeder.

"We show returning veterans and reservists how we honor them when they serve their country by guaranteeing these men and women the right to reemployment with a private employer, the federal government or a state or local government after completing their tour of duty, lasting sometimes up to four years. Now it is time to show American families that we value them and the contribution they make to our society by providing them with the same kind of job protection." (personal communication, February 3, 1987)

The bill would also provide a medical leave of up to 26 weeks if the employee is unable to work as a result of a serious health condition. Pre-existing health benefits must continue to be provided during the leave period.

An editorial in the November, 1986, issue of *Glamour* magazine said of the bill: "No single measure is as important to working women. Right now women lose one-fifth of their earning power when they leave a job to have a baby." ("The parental leave bill," 1986, p.194)

Contrast this with Sweden, where a mother can step right back into her career without a loss of earning power. In that Scandinavian country, the mother takes a 6-month leave and then she and the father can divide up another 6 months between them. "With more mothers working in the U.S.

each year, we are going to have to establish more family-oriented policies that will be good for parents and their children so that people can better balance a career with a home life," says Brazelton (1985, p.71).

The bill proposed by Schroeder and supported by many child specialists would not grant paid leaves or child-care allowances to parents, as has been done in other industrial nations. Schroeder said in early 1987 that it would be impossible to pass such a law at that time. But the bill would create a commission to investigate the possibility.

The fact that this bill did not pass in 1986 is a sad commentary on the status of children in America. Our legislators are fearful that we, the most powerful and rich country in the world, can't afford to ruffle the economic feathers of big business, to protect future generations by providing the same type of parental leave that more than 100 poorer countries already provide.

"Parents are not super beings, they are human beings," says Schroeder. "I think they should have an option to do what is best for their families. Today they have no choice— just a very painful decision to keep their job or stay with their baby." (personal communication, February 3, 1987)

The major impact of the bill would be to require private companies with 15 or more employees and all public agencies to grant an unpaid disability leave to workers of either sex before a child's birth and unpaid leave for them to care for newborn, newly adopted, or seriously ill children.

Those taking leaves would be guaranteed the same or a comparable job on returning to work, without any loss of seniority.

Backers of the bill include child advocates Brazelton and Edward Zigler and economist/author Sylvia Ann Hewlett, the American Academy of Pediatrics and the National Organization for Women. Leading opponents have been the U.S. Chamber of Commerce and the National Association of Women Business Owners.

To business owners' arguments, Schroeder replies: "Business interests have historically opposed any legislative changes to improve employee rights. The United States is in the Dark Ages compared to most other nations. Our employment policies must begin to reflect the changing reality of parenthood in this country" (Schroeder, 1986).

Many child-care experts say the bill doesn't go far enough, and that parents need up to 2 years to properly nurture their infants. Sheila B. Kamerman, professor of social policy and planning, Columbia University School of Social Work, says, "The vast majority of workers would be unable to take advantage of it," because the leave is unpaid. "To think this legislation will make a significant difference is really unrealistic." (personal communication, March 14, 1986)

She feels the issue of parental leave is critically important, however; "Women's jobs are important to family income, but infant care is very inadequate, and very expensive. Furthermore, protective legislation is limited." (Orr & Haskett, 1985, p. 2)

With its faults, the Family and Medical Leave Act (HR 925) still represents one step, albeit a tentative one, toward a more equitable child-care policy in the U.S.

We agree that it is a necessary step but believe that eventually it will be necessary for American business to bite the bullet and allow a full year paid leave for working parents to care for and attach properly with their children.

Sally Provence, professor of pediatrics at the Yale Bush Child Study Center, hopes to see more part-time job opportunities for professional and blue-collar workers and job-sharing plans. These programs would allow parents more time with their infants, she says. "Many [parents] feel pressed, and indeed are pressed to come back to work in a few weeks [after having a child]. This happens less in the better-paying careers than in factory worker jobs." (personal communication, March 14, 1986)

Notes Hewlett in an article for *Glamour* in 1986: "Right now 60% of working women have no rights or benefits when they leave work to have a baby, and they routinely lose their jobs and their seniority when they try to return to the work force" (p.194).

The majority of working women in the U.S. are not guaranteed the same job or a comparable one on their return to work, nor is there a law that mandates some type of income replacement for women who are on leave.

Hewlett tells the story of a young professional woman whose substantial salary was affected by her decision to have a child:

"Three years ago, when she was 30, Louisa Thomas [not her real name], an associate in the litigation department of a New York City law firm, became pregnant with her first child. Now she is pregnant again. Louisa has worked part-time, usually three days a week, since her daughter was born, and plans to keep her part-time schedule until her second child turns three.

"Louisa has not been promoted to partner; indeed, it is unclear whether she will ever be considered for partnership. She is being penalized for stepping off the conventional career ladder. When she returns to work on a full-time basis, she will be in her late 30s, too old to advance quickly in her chosen field, if at all. Louisa now earns a fraction of what her male contemporaries earn, and she fears that she will never close the gap." (Hewlett, 1986, p.194)

In Italy, Louisa Thomas would get 2 years credit toward senority when she gave birth to a child—in effect a reward for becoming a mother. If she lived in Sweden she would be entitled to a 6-hour working day until her youngest child was 8 years old. She would then have the right to go back full-time with her job future as bright as it was before. (Hewlett, 1986)

A 1986 report from Catalyst, a New York City research group that studies family and work place issues, states that even among large firms, some do a better job of helping the employees cope with pregnancy or parental leave than do others . The survey of 384 companies sought to discover whether the firms offered parental leave, and if so, what kind. Most (95%) offer only short-term paid or unpaid disability (maternity) leave. But 13% don't guarantee "a comparable job" or "some job" when the woman returns. (Peterson, 1986)

Says Secretary of Labor William Brock: "The family is under a great deal of stress. We have to make sure we aren't part of the problem." (Kantrowitz, 1986, p.54) Unfortunately, the labor department and business are part of the problem.

It still is a pretty grim picture for working parents. But the future may be better. Some policymakers are asking the right questions—parents are eagerly awaiting the right answers.

All happy families resemble one another,
Every unhappy family is unhappy in its own fashion.

11

Adoption and Foster Care

John is a child who was adopted by his current family at 20 months of age from an orphanage in Brazil. His parents did not have a chance to visit with him before the adoption, having hastily purchased airline tickets after getting a phone call saying he was available. When they arrived the adoptive parents found John to be cute and cheerful and were delighted. "All we could think about was that he was going to be our little boy," his mother says.

Things soon went wrong. "He was the perfect definition of the Tasmanian Devil. He was a whirlwind of action and all we saw was a little blur go past us as he got into everything, pulling things out of drawers and 'accidentally' breaking things in our home."

John's parents thought he was acting like this because he was confused and everything was so new. They thought everything would be all right as soon as he got adjusted to their home.

"One day he came up to me with a big smile on his face and handed me a goldfish he had taken out of the tank. It was squished and lifeless. It was like he was giving me a gift, but it was a gift of pain. I didn't know whether to feel sorry for him or spank him."

Unlike many foreign adoptions, language wasn't a problem; the mother and father both knew Spanish. They just couldn't control this new son they had wanted so desperately. For the next few years John's frantic parents went from therapist to therapist trying to get proper help. But no one diagnosed John properly.

"By the time he was in school John was frankly incorrigible," says his father. "He was stealing from everyone; he was caught stealing money from his teacher's purse. He ripped up anything he could get his hands on." Once, he tried to set fire to the house. "I ran into the living room," says his mother, "and the drapes were all on fire.

"And, I was getting phone calls from his teacher, saying he wasn't in school. He was cutting class in the first grade! He fought with and bullied other children unmercifully and absolutely controlled our lives. We couldn't go anywhere with him and were really prisoners in our own home with this uncontrollable kid."

John is an adopted child. He is also unattached.

*****

Adopted children, or children who have spent some of their childhood in foster child care, account for a disproportionate number of unattached children. This isn't surprising to those who know that the proper bonding cycle is not fostered in children who have had significant breaks early in their lives. These are children who have been put at particularly high risk.

Infants and toddlers have much faster "internal clocks" than adults do. You just can't make an infant wait too long to begin the attachment process. If you do, it may never happen. The tragedy of the present adoption and foster-care system is that it often makes children wait, in limbo, before trying to settle them into a new home.

To prevent such breaks from occurring in children already at risk, a total revamping of the child-adoption and foster-care industry is needed. Hundreds of thousands of children have been injured, perhaps permanently, through bureaucratic delays and bungling caused by the current system. Unwittingly, delays in permanent placement of adoptive children are causing them to become unattached. Some critics even say delays are not caused by bureaucracy gone astray but by profit seekers. They charge that foster care is more profitable than permanent adoption so children are therefore kept in temporary homes.

As a psychiatrist, Foster Cline knows the horrible tragedies that result when we make babies wait too long: "Fully two-thirds of the sociopathic youngsters I have had in treatment for bonding difficulties are adopted children." (personal communications, January 5, 1987)

Compelling proof of the difficulties adopted children have is recorded in an abstract appearing in a recent issue of a professional psychiatric journal. Of 160 12- to 19-year-old first-admission psychiatric patients in one facility, 21.2% were adoptees, with a high incidence of major depression among them. (National Association of Homes for Children, 1986)

Social worker Connell Watkins issues a warning to future adoptive parents: "You really need to be aware of the potential difficulties." In addition to the emotional toll parents pay when they attempt to help a child who is unattached, the costs of therapy can be crippling. Watkins says the Youth Behavior Program, which treats character-disturbed youngsters through trained treatment families, costs about $24,000 a year. Residential [in-patient] treatment is even costlier, running about $30,000 a year. Some insurance plans pay part of the costs, others do not. This unwieldy financial burden falls on either the parents or the state. (personal communication, January 26, 1987)

Cline and Watkins agree that the chances of therapy being successful are greatly increased if the child is diagnosed while still young—preferably under the age of 7. "Over that age, the chances of success go down to about 50%," says Watkins. Over age 11, the chances of recovery for character-disturbed children are not good.

Youngsters with this condition who are not treated successfully often end up in group residential homes; the law says they must be released when they reach the age of 18. These are children who have often been relinquished from their adoptive homes because their parents couldn't control them.

Because of the difficulties they have had in foster homes and other placement care, many such children suffer bonding breaks. They often end up as part of the failed adoption statistics. Estimates by members of the National Association of Homes for Children (NAHC) say failed adoptions today range from 10% of all adoptions to 33%.

These are the most damaged of children. Some suffer from "adopted child syndrome" in which the child, after multiple rejections, becomes very resistant or highly, sometimes dangerously, antagonistic. (National Association of Homes for Children, 1986)

Watkins gives the example of a young girl, now 7, who is in danger of a failed adoption by her second adoptive family:

The birth mother gave up custody of Nancy and her two younger sisters when Nancy was about 5 years old. The mother was deemed unfit—she is retarded with a very low functioning level. She severely neglected and abused the girls. An aunt finally reported the problem to social services after discovering that the mother, or one of her numerous "boyfriends," had broken one of the younger children's legs.

After being placed in several foster homes, the sisters were adopted. But the couple who adopted the three girls were young and couldn't deal with the anger and hostility displayed by Nancy. This unattached child carried a deep-seated anger, aggravated by the pain of being given away by her birth mother. There were other complicating circumstances.

Because she had always been required to care for her younger sisters, Nancy refused to allow the new mother to take on this role. Finally, the adoptive parents brought Nancy to the Youth Behavior Program for treatment. But after three or four months, no progress had occurred. This pretty, blond, waif-like little girl was capable of despicable behavior. In addition to suffering from learning disorders and having extremely aggressive and agitated behavior, she was very sexually oriented. Perhaps because she had seen her mother in numerous sexual encounters, Nancy at age 7 approached most adult males in a teasing, suggestive way. (This is a common symptom for young, unattached females.)

It was decided to remove Nancy from her adoptive home and place her with a Youth Behavior trained-treatment family. She has been in treatment for nine months and is showing progress.

There is still a long way to go for Nancy and her sisters, however. The adoptive parents have gotten a divorce and relinquished all three girls. The two sisters have been placed in another adoptive home. At the time of this writing, it was not clear whether that family would also take Nancy. That decision depended largely on the outcome of her therapy. (personal communication, January 26, 1987)

Unfortunately, there are many high-risk children in the system just like Nancy.

An associate director of a child-care agency talks about a child who had the horrifying experience of 10 failed foster homes, four failed adoptions and four failed group homes. "This type of youngster 'bad mouths' adoption to other children, creating a very poor climate for any type of adoptive effort."

One 8-year-old child in foster care was asked to give his definition of adopted children: "Rotten kids who've been taken away from their parents." (National Association of Homes for Children, 1986, p.5)

Many children in foster care or adoptive homes are unable to form normal, healthy attachments to their new "parents." The attachment problems often originate in their birth families. However, the instability of foster-home placements and the series of moves that many foster children experience give them further problems in developing trust in others and a sense of appropriate autonomy. Complicating these factors is the directive given to many foster parents that they should not become close to these children. In the past social workers have felt that a child shouldn't become attached to foster parents, because of the pain to the child, or the parents, when he is removed from that home. Child-care experts now believe this is faulty advice; they say any attachment a child can make is a healthy sign.

The signs and symptoms of attachment problems that one may see in a particular foster child are a result of the way his parents behaved toward him, his environment and his own particular psychological traits. In general, children who have been severely neglected are the most apt to suffer from a true lack of attachment. Children who have experienced less severe neglect, intermittent physical abuse or emotional abuse are most likely to exhibit signs of an imbalance between dependency and autonomy.

As for John, the child with whom we began this chapter, he was referred to Cline's offices in Evergreen by a concerned school principal after the child was caught stealing money from a teacher's purse in the second grade. Cline used rage reduction therapy with John (also called reattachment therapy), described in a later chapter.

The result?

"The first session lasted four and a half hours," says his adoptive mother. "At the end he came over, sat in my lap and snuggled in my neck like a baby does. I remember weeping with joy. It was the first time his love really felt real to me. Afterwards I held him and rocked him twice a day for ten minutes at a time.

"Thus, I rocked him to sleep for the first time when he was 7½ years old!

"His behavior improved dramatically. We did followup faithfully and confronted old behavior patterns and supported behaviors we liked. Our life as a family was as dramatically changed as John's was. We began doing more and feeling better about it.

"We have been so encouraged that we have adopted two more children." (Cline, personal communication, August 6, 1986)

John, had he not been properly diagnosed and treated, could have ended up as a "failed adoption." The most injured children, indeed, may be those who have suffered the loss of their original family, then have been placed in a foster or an adoptive home, and have failed there as well. Evidence is beginning to surface that suggests that failed adoption is on the rise and is already a problem of considerable consequence. Most of the affected children are unattached and are just more than most adoptive parents can handle.

In exploring the reasons such adoptions fail, NAHC members cite several factors, among them: inadequate preparation, of both the adoptive families and the child; inadequate on-going support; transracial adoptions; and low level of commitment by adoptive parents.

Many adoptive parents, after a failed adoption, feel anguish and frustration and blame not being "told the truth" about the child's problems. Adoptive parents in many cases have not been told about, and do not understand, the attachment process—what is required on the part of the parent and child to permit attachment, if it can take place at all!

We are talking in most cases of children who have not had a successful early bonding experience. Said one director responding to the NAHC survey: "In cases where children have experienced multiple placements, there may be an inability to bond at all with adults." (National Association of Homes for Children, 1986, p.5)

When a single child experiences multiple failed adoptions, interpreted by him as multiple rejections, the child's attitude becomes negative toward the very idea of establishing any type of relationship with adults. Can there then be much hope for adoptive success? The answer is often no.

In fact, the adopted child syndrome can lead to tragic antisocial behavior. In one case, an unattached child was charged with murder and arson in the death of his adoptive parents. The defense psychologist told the jury in the trial of the 14-year-old:

> "Patrick's behavior pattern was a classic, though extreme, example of the adopted-child syndrome, something which I have observed in perhaps 200 patients over the last 20 years of practice" (p.6).

The youngster he was defending had been taken from his birth mother at age 3, removed from his foster parents at 5, and most recently been made a ward of the court by his adoptive family. They had threatened to send him away from home.

In commenting on the case, the defense psychologist struck the same note now echoing through the professional halls of voluntary child-care: "The importance to society of further research on this problem is that only by acknowledging that it exists can we obtain the data and understanding to treat, and we may hope, to prevent further tragedies. . ." (National Association of Homes for Children, 1986, p.6)

Transracial adoptions and those which mix ethnic and cultural backgrounds also pose special attachment problems. Said one NAHC director, "In mixed racial and ethnic minority adoptions, bonding can be a real problem." (p.6) He explained that this leads to a failed adoption rate as high as 65%. "Sometimes neither the agency nor the adoptive family fully understands the genetic, biological and cultural needs of such a child." (Refer to the case of Danny with whom we started Chapter 4.)

The number of Americans adopting foreign children is rising. There were 5,818 such adoptions in 1982. The number rose to 7,350 in 1983 and to 8,273 in 1984. (*Cosmopolitan,* 1986)

The authors do not want potential adoptive parents to feel they should not proceed with adoption efforts. That would make an already terrible problem even worse. These are the children, especially those with a mixed ethnic or cultural background, who most desperately need a loving home.

But social-service agencies should fully disclose to adoptive parents the background of the child and fully prepare prospective parents if they are going to receive an unattached child. With early therapy and consistent loving care these children can have a chance at a new life. But no one benefits when parents adopt a child and have incomplete information on the child's history.

In the example of Danny, the Vietnamese child, his new foster parents were not told about his condition or the previous death threats. Imagine having a potential murderer living in your house and not being warned about the danger. How many other families is this happening to?

There are many good reasons for adopting abroad, especially with the scarcity of healthy adoptable babies in the U.S. The costs of such adoptions can run as little as $3,500 (for Korean infants) to more than $15,000 (a fair-skinned baby from Chile). In monetary terms, about $5,000 is average. (*Cosmopolitan,* 1986) But, as we have seen, foreign adoptions can be risky, both in the costs that may result in emotional damage to the child, and in financial expenses to parents from disreputable adoption officials or lawyers. Regardless of ethnic background, the younger the child is when adopted, the better the chances for success.

When difficulties and problems in adoptions are not overcome, the outcome can be dire. Emotional and psychological problems can develop into major disturbances, with numbing consequences.

Children and Their Responses to Separation

What problems do children experience who have been placed in foster care? Already, these are children in crisis. They have been removed from the presence of the only people to whom they have related, however bad the situation.

In her book *Necessary Losses,* author Judith Viorst writes of the connection between mother and child, no matter how bad a mother she is:

"A young boy lies in a hospital bed. He is frightened and in pain. Burns cover 40% of his small body.

"Someone has doused him with alcohol and then, unimaginably, has set him on fire.

"He cries for his mother.

"His mother has set him on fire.

"It doesn't seem to matter what kind of mother a child has lost, or how perilous it may be to dwell in her presence . . . Fear of her loss is the earliest terror we know." (Flynn, 1986, p.4-M)

There are a number of reasons why foster homes have been the cause of many attachment "breaks." For one thing, abuse and neglect can occur in foster homes, just like in the homes from which the children were originally taken.

Many foster-care home placements result in "ping-pong" children. It is important that children have a stable and consistent environment and a caregiver who will nurture them, promoting the formation of attachment. Vera Fahlberg (1979) writes, in *Attachment and Separation*, that many children in foster care have moved from one family to another and have not experienced relationships with members of a family over a long period of time. She feels it is the *continuous but constantly changing* contact with the same family members that is important to provide a solid base for the children's lives.

"Two out of every five children in care have experienced more than one placement and for an unfortunate 20% of the sample, children have gone through four or more placements. Extrapolating to the total foster-care population of the U.S., we find 200,000 multiple-placed children and 100,000 who have been bounced from home to home at least four times." (Pride, 1986, p. 244) Such irresponsibility is begging for future disaster when these rage-filled children hit the streets as adults.

Critics of the foster-care system see a monetary reason for these multiple placements. They note that nationwide, the average annual government payment per child to agencies is $6-$10,000. Children with handicaps or special problems may be worth up to $250,000 (Powledge, 1985, p. 47).

Keep in mind that if an agency places a child for adoption, the government pays the agency a one-time fee, as high as $3,000 but often much less. It is easy to see how in some situations child-care agencies have a poor record in placing kids quickly for adoption. They make much more money if they have children in foster placements.

The U.S. Department of Health and Human Services 1980 overview, *Adoption Services in the States,* notes that "While twice as many [waiting] children are receiving adoption services, there are now three times as many children in foster care (502,000 nationwide) than there were in 1961." Data in the report shows that:

"Foster care is seen as a permanent arrangement for 32% of children currently in care. One hundred ten thousand children had been in foster care more than 6 years. An unknown but significantly large number of children in foster care are not free for adoption and no efforts are being made to find adoptive homes for them. As many as 215,000 children then in foster care might benefit from adoption services but are not receiving them." (Powledge, 1985, p.56)

In 1981 in New York City, for example, 78% of children in foster care who were cleared for adoption still waited for placement. Nationally 50% of the tax money supplied for each child goes for salaries of social workers and maintenance of organizations. (Hester & Nygren, 1981, p. 178) Many babies stay in hospital wards waiting; this waiting sometimes lasts months or even years. (See box on next page.)

The costs for foster care are enormous. It is estimated that federal and state governments spend as much as $1.5 billion a year on the estimated 500,000 foster children in the U.S.

After entering foster care children are supervised by social workers who are often young, inexperienced, underpaid and overworked. The recommended number of children per social worker is 20 to 30 but the nationwide average is actually 70 to 90. Overburdened personnel obviously cannot give systematic reviews to the children in foster care. It has been estimated that as many as one third of all children in foster care have fallen through the cracks. (Hester & Nygren, 1981, p.178)

Glenn Hester writes in *Child of Rage* of his personal experience growing up in a series of foster homes and institutions. He says he was bumped from foster homes to orphanages to institutions and, in the process, was severely abused. He tells how his being moved from place to place "destroyed my trust to the point that at age 9 a psychiatrist diagnosed me as a child who neither loved nor trusted anyone.

"I feel," says Hester, "I was suffering from mental illness caused by my ill-fated experiences as a foster child." Hester credits his salvation from his rage, literally, to God. He says he is a born-again Christian. (1981, p.181)

Most judges handling foster-care cases don't know what is happening in America. They make rulings that cause emotional breaks in children. They are damaging children as a result.

As Douglas Bersharov, former director of the National Center on Child Abuse and Neglect, a division of the U.S. Department of Health and Human Services in Washington, D.C., points out: "At the present time, there are no legal standards governing the foster-care decision. Juvenile court acts, for example, give judges unrestricted dispositional authority ... decision-making is left to the ad hoc analysis of social workers and judges." (Pride, 1986, p.243)

Even social workers don't know what is going on. Young, zealous and inadequately trained caseworkers often are too quick to snatch children from innocent parents without thorough investigations, or too slow to take children from homes where they really are in danger.

What is worse, children who are placed in foster care—rightly or wrongly—may be victims of abuse there or at the least may languish for months, years or their whole childhoods, in a legal and emotional limbo that can literally turn them into criminals.

A Worse Case Scenario

For some babies, there simply is no love. These infants live, and die, where they came into the world—in a hospital ward. A modern tragedy, they are AIDS babies. About one-third of children born with AIDS are orphaned or abandoned at birth. Some infants die without ever leaving the hospital, because foster or adoptive parents cannot be found.

What is particularly troubling is that the numbers of AIDS babies is steadily growing. In mid-1987 the Centers for Disease Control in Atlanta said there were 550 children in the U.S. with AIDS. Researcher Dr. James Oleske has predicted the number of AIDS-infected children could reach 20,000 cases nationwide by 1991. A new study released in September 1987 indicated the AIDS virus, once thought to be a manageable single entity, is a complex group of rapidly mutating viruses which constantly changes its weaponry, camouflage, defenses and even its targets in the body. The current epidemic has already created havoc in the foster care system, especially when you consider that 80% of infants born with AIDS are minorities, many from drug-abusing mothers.

People resist taking in an AIDS baby, because they fear the disease and are unable to face the thought of losing a child. "These children are born in the hospital, they suffer in the hospital and then they die," said Penny Ferrer, special assistant to the deputy commissioner of the Department of Human Resources in New York City ("Aids babies," Sept. 4, 1987, p. 4).

Children differ in the way they respond to being separated from their parents. This response ranges from severe depression in children who are well-attached to their parents and then abruptly separated from them to almost no reaction in children who have been emotionally neglected and have virtually no attachment to their parents. The reactions of most children entering the child welfare system fall between these two extremes, and into a dark forgotten crack in the impersonal world of bureaucracy.

There are several important influences on how individual children react to separation, including how strong the child's original attachment is, how strong the parent's attachment is, what sort of separations the child has experienced in the past and the circumstances of this separation.

Whether or not the child has been prepared for the move and the situation from which he is being removed are also important factors which influence how a child will react to separation.

Well-attached children go through different stages than do nonattached children when they are separated from the person they love. Bowlby (1973) describes three stages most evident in the younger child:

1. The child protests vigorously and makes attempts to recover his mother, such as going to the door and trying to find her.
2. The child despairs of recovering his mother, but he continues to be watchful. He appears to be preoccupied constantly and is depressed. When a car drives up or when there is a noise at the door, he becomes alert, hoping that his mother is returning.
3. The child becomes emotionally detached and appears to lose interest in caretakers.

A case example of a child who was well-attached and then separated:

John had lost his mother when he was 18 months old. His father became his primary caretaker. The father planned a major move across the country. While moving and getting settled, he left John with an aunt. John had had almost no contact with the aunt before he was left there and he was very fussy with his aunt. He regressed in toileting and smeared feces. He alternated between being very depressed and having temper tantrums. The aunt placed John in foster care.

John was 4 and had been in foster care for about 3 months. During his first six weeks in care, he was in a foster-care receiving home. While there he was fussy and cried constantly. In his second foster placement he was not so much fussy as withdrawn. He played for hours by himself, talking to himself in baby voices and making peculiar sounds. He had good eye contact when examined, but he seemed indiscriminately affectionate: he seemed to respond equally warmly to all adults. He was performing at his age level on developmental tests and was in good contact with reality.

When John was in the second foster placement, his father came for his first visit with the child. John's face "lit up" when he first saw his father. He then looked apprehensive and acted ambivalent about getting close to his father. His father initiated many positive interactions with John. Eventually, John was able to say, "Don't ever leave me again, Daddy." (Fahlberg, 1979, p.31)

John's history illustrates the stages Bowlby describes as common in well-attached children who are separated. It is possible, because such strong attachment is rare in children in the social-services system, that such a child could be wrongly classified as mentally disturbed.

As we stated earlier, studies show children raised in institutions do not get the proper stimulus to develop into physically and psychologically healthy children. Many foster homes fortunately do provide the right atmosphere for day-to-day loving care by a primary caretaker. But there are some aspects of normal family care that foster care *cannot* provide.

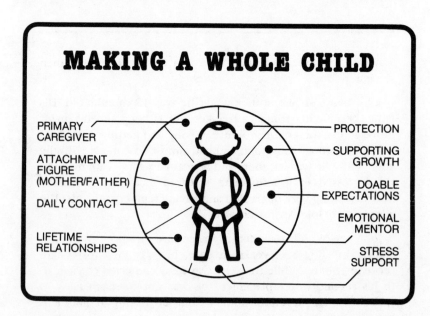

MAKING A WHOLE CHILD

PRIMARY CAREGIVER

ATTACHMENT FIGURE (MOTHER/FATHER)

DAILY CONTACT

LIFETIME RELATIONSHIPS

PROTECTION

SUPPORTING GROWTH

DOABLE EXPECTATIONS

EMOTIONAL MENTOR

STRESS SUPPORT

Children who are bounced from one foster home to another, are actually being hurt much more than those responsible may know.

What is most important is the growing and changing relationship between the parent and the child. For example, that relationship changes when a child grows from an infant to a toddler. Then, when the child is of school age, the give-and-take changes again, and it continually changes throughout the child's life.

It is the consistent relationship, *over time and space*, that truly cements attachment. A strong sense of identity and responsibility is achieved with this changing nature of attachment. People who lack such long-term attachments have more difficulty sorting out what to attribute to their own actions and what to attribute to changes in their environment.

*****

In this chapter we have shown the sorts of breaks that can be anticipated when children are either adopted too late or have suffered from numerous foster-home placements. In the next chapter we look at the pervasive problem of teenage pregnancy and the effect it has on the thousands of babies born each year into the arms of young and ill-prepared mothers.

*"Bright youth passes swiftly
as a thought."*
Theognis

12

The Teen Pregnancy Epidemic

"Hi, Daddy" the voice on the other end of the long-distance call said. "I, um, just wanted to call to talk to you, about, um, something. I'm sorry I haven't called for awhile. You see, Mom said I had to call you and see what you thought about me coming to stay with you for awhile.

"You, see, um, I'm pregnant."

The call was from his 14-year-old daughter.

This pretty, baby-faced teenager was calling her father to see if she could move in with him and his new wife . . . "just until the baby comes."

Red-haired Linda had become part of a national problem. She is one of the two-thirds of pregnant teenage girls who become unintended, unwed mothers.

In many ways, her case typifies the experiences of teenagers who are having children in this country today. She lived in a single-parent family headed by her divorced mother. She dropped out of high school after the baby was born. After leaving her father's home—when her son was 6 months old—Linda joined the ranks of teenage mothers living in poverty, with no education and few opportunities. She exists on Aid to Families with Dependent Children (AFDC).

The father of the baby was never determined. Like many young mothers, Linda was destined to have additional babies. The second baby, however, wasn't unplanned. She said she wanted a girl, "so I didn't bother with contraceptives." She was afraid to take the pill, she said, because "it is bad for you." Her logic is common among teenagers, who fear the pill because of rumors they have heard. What they don't recognize are the dangers that pregnancy, childbirth and motherhood hold for them and their children.

In some ways Linda and her baby are lucky. Many babies born to teen mothers die in the first year of life. The risk of having an ill or low-birth-weight infant is considerably greater among teenage mothers often because of poor or non-existent prenatal care. Her son was healthy.

But the outlook for teen mothers and their children is not bright; it is one of the biggest challenges facing America today.

The babies of teenage mothers are more likely to become unattached than are the children of the general population. This is the result of a number of factors, primary among them is the fact that these mothers are children themselves and they do not know how to properly interact with infants. Dr. Tiffany Field, a neonatal specialist and researcher who teaches mothers bonding and attachment in Florida, says, "Teenage mothers are very vicissitudinary, they don't interact with their babies well. They have a flat affect, they do not stimulate their babies. The interactions just don't look good."

Field says mothers who have inappropriate behavior usually adopt the position of an entertaining or "clowning" mother. She plays teasing or hostile games, such as placing the pacifier in the baby's mouth and then yanking it out.

The flip side of a teasing mother is one who Field describes as "flat. This mother doesn't engage the baby at all but will just sit there looking at the infant." Field says teenage mothers are much more likely to adopt one of these two deviant approaches to their children, as are the mothers of premature or handicapped children. (personal communication, February 10, 1987)

Educational programs and birth control are desperately needed by today's youth before their children become tomorrow's "mistakes." They are children raising children, and they are not very good at it.

*****

Teenage pregnancy is epidemic in the U.S. and the implication this has on future generations of children cannot be underestimated. Perhaps the most critical of all high risk babies are being born to these child mothers. Fully 554,000 babies a year are born who look into the face of a mother who is still a child herself. There are now about 1.3 million children living with 1.1 million teenage mothers. More than half of these children are living with unmarried mothers and two-thirds were born to mothers age 17 or younger. An additional 1.6 million children under age 5 are living with mothers who were teenagers when they gave birth.

The comprehensive report, "Teenage Pregnancy: The Problem That Hasn't Gone Away," issued in 1981 by the Alan Guttmacher Institute states that more than 1 million young girls a year are becoming teenage mothers. This phenomenon is happening despite the fact that 84% of American adults regard teenage pregnancy as a serious national problem.

The report further states that 82% of girls who give birth at age 15 or younger are the daughters of teenage mothers. Young blacks are much more likely to become pregnant than are young whites; nearly half of black females in the U.S. are pregnant by age 20.

The impact of teenage pregnancies is not just with the young mothers. In addition to being at high risk psychologically, the babies of teenagers are at much higher risk medically; the infant death rate is 200% higher among babies born to teenagers than to those born to women in their 20s. (Sanko, 1986)

The problems faced by children of teen parents begin before these children are born. Only one in five girls under age 15 receives any prenatal care during the first three months of pregnancy. The combination of inadequate medical care and poor diet also contributes to problems during pregnancy. Teens are 92% more likely to have anemia and 23% more likely to have premature babies (Wallis, 1985, p. 87).

Low-birth weight babies (those who weigh under 5.5 pounds) are at increased risk for serious mental, physical and developmental problems. These babies can require costly and even lifelong medical care.

Some teenage mothers have been helped in the past by low-cost prenatal programs. But in 1982 the Reagan Administration reduced funding for the Feeding Program for Women, Infants and Children. Under the program nutritional supplements and medical care to low-income expectant mothers was provided. Some critics say the cuts will cost more in the long-run, because of increased costs to care for undersized, sickly infants through Medicaid.

It is no secret that teenage pregnancy breeds more than babies—it also breeds poverty. Teen mothers, for example, are many times more likely than other women with young children to live below the poverty level. The study states that these young mothers are 7 times more likely than other families to live in poverty; fully two-thirds of single mothers ages 14 to 25 live in poverty.

The Guttmacher Institute studied 37 countries, comparing them to the U.S. Why, as the study found, does the U.S. lead all other developed countries in teenage pregnancies? The answer can be found in the way other countries deal with teenage sexuality.

"While European societies have chosen to recognize sexual development as a normal part of the human development, we have chosen to repress it. At the same time, we behave as if we're not repressing it," says Fay Wattleton, president of the New York-based Planned Parenthood Federation. (Wallis, 1985, p.82)

There are many experts who feel that it is this very ignorance of sexual development which dooms American teenagers to a persistently high out-of-wedlock birth rate.

We could learn something from our foreign neighbors: Elise F. Jones and her colleagues, writing in *Teenage Pregnancy in Industrialized Countries* (1986), found the factors most important in their effect on low teenage fertility to be:

- High levels of socioeconomic modernization

- Openness about sex

- A relatively large proportion of household income distributed to a low-income population (important mainly for younger teenagers)

- A high minimum legal age at marriage (important for older teenagers only)

The U.S. fits the pattern for high teenage fertility because we are far less open about sexual matters than most countries with low teenage birthrates, and a smaller proportion of our income is distributed to families on the bottom rungs of the economic ladder.

Other factors in the U.S. which lead to teenage pregnancy include:

1. Overwhelming media presentation of sex; we are selling sex to our teenagers.

2. Peer definitions which say it's cool to be sexually wise at a young age and uncool to be a virgin.

3. Spoiling and protecting teens from the consequences of their acts by either the welfare system or their parents.

The Guttmacher Study found the two key factors in the United States' pervasive teenage pregnancy problem are:

- An ambivalent, sometimes puritanical attitude about sex;

- The existence of a large, economically deprived underclass.

Teenagers in the U.S. are literally caught. They are in a bind between the puritanical beliefs of past generations and today's adolescent environment. Those not sexually active by their late teens are viewed as strange and out of step. If they have contraceptives on hand before a steady relationship is established, they may be considered sexually promiscuous, but those who don't have a method of contraception are viewed as irresponsible. Teens clearly are exposed to conflicting messages. Confounding the situation is the difficulty teens have finding providers of information about sex and contraception.

The consequences of these mixed messages are approximately 1 million teenage pregnancies each year. Fully 86% of the 749,000 pregnancies among unmarried teens and 51% of those among married teens were not planned. None of the 30,000 pregnant girls under age 15 intended to get pregnant. Black teenagers are more likely than whites to have unplanned pregnancies: 82% of their pregnancies and 70% of births were unintended.

Teenage pregnancies and birth are compounded by adverse health, social and economic outcomes. Often a teenage girl who has missed her last period because she is pregnant misses out on a lot of other things. She will be at high risk for also missing her high school graduation ceremonies. In fact, one poster trying to fight teenage pregnancy shows a young girl holding her infant in her arms. [The mother is on the left, the baby on the right.] The message under the picture says: "The one on the right will graduate from high school first."

These young mothers drop out of high school at an alarming rate. Only half of those who give birth before 18 complete high school. Compare that with the 96% of those who postpone childbirth. Even young fathers drop out of school at a higher rate than normal!

A young teen mother can expect to earn half as much as women who first gave birth in their 20s. Marriage disruption is three times more likely in these families. (Guttmacher Institute, 1981)

In addition, studies have shown that many children of teenage parents suffer from educational and cognitive deficits: They tend to have lower I.Q. and achievement scores than children of women who delayed childbearing, and they are more likely to repeat at least one school grade. These are babies who are much more likely to have psychological and social problems. They are far more likely to be unattached than are children born to more mature parents. They are at high risk.

"The art of mothering is not inborn. It's a learned process. The young women of today tend to be ill-prepared for the role of mother," says Florence Clark, an assocate professor of occupational therapy at the University of Southern California. (USC News Service, 1986, p.1)

These "ill-prepared" young mothers think they are going to be getting an adorable plaything. When the reality of the situation hits them—as they combat the terrible two's—they often change their minds. Far too often the babies of these teenage mothers end up as burdens, rather than bundles of joy, especially for the families of a mother who has decided to desert her child.

Imagine the anguish of a grandmother, who has nurtured and attached to an infant, only to find that several years down the road her daughter has returned to claim the child. Imagine the anguish of this baby who is being taken away from the only mother he has ever known.

A psychologist's files reveal the example of Kim, and her parents:

Jenny was carrying laundry downstairs when the air was pierced with an anguished scream—coming from her 16-year-old daughter's bedroom. She dropped the clothes and ran to Kim's room, finding the teenager lying on the bed holding her stomach. "Mom, I . . . I . . . think I'm going to have a baby now." This mother hadn't even known her child was pregnant! Kim had concealed the fact by wearing fashionably loose-fitting layers of clothes.

After baby Shawn was born, however, the real trouble began. Kim decided to return to school and friends and the baby's care fell to mom and dad. Jenny quit her job so Kim could finish high school. Friction increased as Kim, assuming she had adult status, stayed out late at night. The arguments escalated — then, one snowy winter night, Kim grabbed Shawn, saying she was going to disappear forever with her baby! She walked out the door without a coat, the baby in her arms, heading nowhere. The police brought them back.

Baby Shawn clearly had attached to his grandmother and grandfather, because of consistent nurturing. Yet all legal rights remained with the biological mother, Kim. In desperation, the grandparents sought custody. An incredible legal battle ensued, with attorneys for the grandparents, Kim, the uninvolved teenage father and the baby. The case dragged on — and the bills piled up — as attorneys haggled over the custody issue. Weary and frustrated, Jenny and her husband told Kim "we can't take this any longer. If you want full responsibility for parenting, we feel you need to get started right away by finding a job and your own place. If you want us to pay the bills and raise Shawn, then we must have legal control." Realizing she no longer had a free ride, Kim signed over custody. She went to college, visiting Shawn on weekends. For many grandparents, however, similar nightmares continue.

Often these babies of teenage mothers are shunted from the mother's living arrangement to the grandparents. There is a great lack of stability and resentment builds not only between the mother and her parents but within the child. These are infants who simply do not know where or with whom they actually belong.

Teen pregnancy impacts mother, child and society. Many of these babies are victims of child abuse at the hands of parents too immature to understand why their baby is crying or how this plaything could suddenly develop a will of its own.

These children of children also have an increased tendency to drop out of school and perpetuate the cycle by becoming teenage parents themselves. Many sociologists have noted that the so-called "feminization of poverty" actually is a reflection of these teenagers having babies. "So many can't rise above it to go back to school or get job skills," says Lucille Dismukes of the Council on Maternal and Infant Health in Atlanta. (Wallis, 1985, p. 84) It becomes a vicious cycle of welfare children begetting welfare children.

The Guttmacher Institute found:

• The U.S. leads nearly all other developed countries in its incidence of pregnancy among girls ages 15 through 19.

• American adolescents are no more sexually active than their counterparts in Sweden, Holland, France, Canada and Britain but are many times more likely to become pregnant.

• Whites alone had nearly double the pregnancy rate of their British and French peers and six times the rate of the Dutch.

• Statistics in the study show that the incidence of sexual intercourse among unmarried teenage women in the U.S. increased by two-thirds during the 1970s.

• The highest teenage pregnancy rates were in countries with the least open attitudes toward sex.

• Black American teenagers have the highest fertility rate of any teenage population group in the entire world. (Jones et al., 1986)

It is perhaps in the area of sex education (or rather the lack of it) that America is doing the most harm in the fight against teenage pregnancy.

In Sweden, for example, teens are sexually active much earlier than in the U.S. and Swedish teens see much more explicit sex on television. But the Swedish National Board of Education has provided curriculum guidelines ensuring that, starting at age 7, every child in the country receives a thorough education in reproductive biology.

By age 12, each child has been introduced to various types of contraceptives. Annika Strandell, the board's specialist in sex education says, "The idea is to de-dramatize and demystify sex, so that familiarity will make the child less likely to fall prey to unwanted pregnancy and venereal disease." (Wallis, 1985, p.82)

Sex is similarly demystified in Holland. There teens can obtain contraceptive counseling at government-sponsored clinics, for a minimal fee. In contrast, in the U.S. it is very difficult for teens seeking contraceptive advise to find it without their parent's knowledge.

Often, in America, teens go to family doctors with their questions. One teenager found out this was a mistake. The family doctor immediately called the young girl's parents, to tell them what their daughter was asking. Instead of sitting down with the girl and discussing birth control methods with this sexually active teenager, the parents' reaction was, "You are grounded." It would be a long time before this teen ever opened up to her parents about such intimate matters.

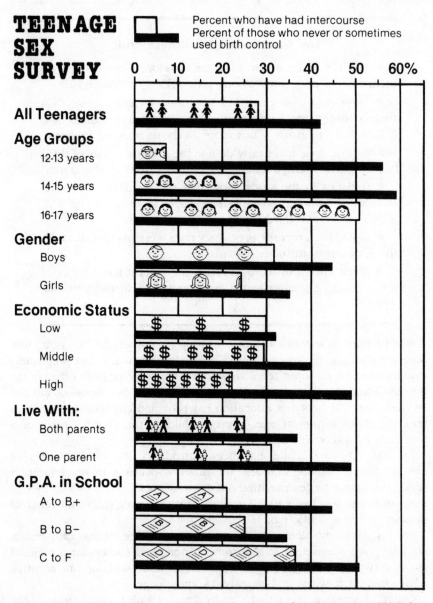

© High Risk, Magid/McKelvey

In our society a new mother bringing her baby home from the hospital is ill prepared to deal with the child. For many, panic sets in. And, says Clark, her fears are probably justified.

In an extended family, the young woman has an opportunity to observe or assist in the caretaking of children before becoming a mother herself. When that first child is born, experienced family members can give support and guidance. But many of today's young mothers have little such experience or guidance. Post-partum depression is a common occurrence in young mothers; left ignored it can have disastrous effects on the mother and her relationship with her child.

Worse yet is the young teenage mother. Maternal preparation programs are valuable for any first-time mother, Clark says, but especially so for the growing number of teenage mothers who lack the maturity, experience and resources to care competently for a child. (USC News Service, 1986, p. 1)

• Studies show that in the U.S. teens wait an average of 12 months, after first becoming sexually active, before seeking contraception.

• Most recent statistics show that almost 30% of all U. S. abortions are performed on teenagers.

• About 15% of pregnant teens become pregnant again within one year; 30% do so within two years. (Guttmacher Institute, 1981)

Some measures to reduce teen pregnancies have proven successful. Ask yourself whether you favor sex education in the schools, including birth control information. If you answered "yes" you are in the majority of adults polled by Yankelovich, Skelly & White, Inc. They found that 78% of the American population supported sex education in the schools.

Schools initiating their own clinics and giving out information on everything from treatment for veneral diseases to immunizations to contraception advice have reduced pregnancy rates. Four St. Paul, Minnesota, high schools have had dramatic results with clinics in the schools. Births to female students fell from 59 per thousand to 26 per thousand during the seven years the clinics operated. The dropout rate at one of the schools fell from 45% to 10%. A controversial clinic at Chicago's DuSable High School and others at schools around the country have been fashioned after the St. Paul program.

The bottom line here is that the chances there will be additional unattached children go down along with the pregnancy rate.

PREGNANCY PROFILE

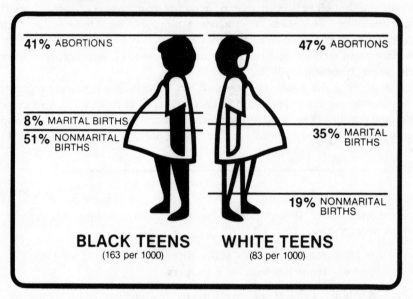

41% ABORTIONS

47% ABORTIONS

8% MARITAL BIRTHS

51% NONMARITAL BIRTHS

35% MARITAL BIRTHS

19% NONMARITAL BIRTHS

BLACK TEENS
(163 per 1000)

WHITE TEENS
(83 per 1000)

© High Risk, Magid/McKelvey

The costs in tax dollars for unwanted teen pregnancies are staggering. The total cost in direct federal, state and location funds may run to more than $200 million annually. And, "never-married mothers turn to welfare more often than other women and use it an average of 10 years, twice as long as other recipients," according to a study by Harvard economist David Ellwood. (Burling, 1986, p. 6)

These are just the direct, monetary figures. The costs in quality of life for these mothers and their children, and their reduced opportunity for productive futures, are enormous.

Many of these teenage mothers are forced to grow up too fast. They suffer not only the missed opportunities afforded by an education, but those they would gain in a normal rite of passage from childhood to adulthood. These are children robbed of their adolescence.

One teenage girl talks about the anger she feels toward her unwanted baby boy:

"Sometimes I would get so mad at him, I could just knock him out. But I just watched my temper with him. Sometimes I get mad and I say, 'Dang, my life is messed up. I can't take it any more'... Sometimes I just feel that way because most teenagers my age be having fun, and now I seem tied down." (Burling, 1986, p.35)

When a child is forced into motherhood too soon, the losses range from monetary to emotional for both her and her child. As we noted, these are often the babies who suffer the most from lack of bonding. Closely associated with teenage pregnancy is the issue of child abuse. We examine this national tragedy in the next chapter.

"Cruelty has a human heart."
William Blake

13

The Cycle of Abuse

Andy is a 3-year-old black boy presently living with a foster family. His early history is not known, but as far as social workers know, he had a normal birth and early development. It is believed he crawled at about 6 months and walked at about 9 months.

His natural mother, Donna, was said by her family to be "a problem" from adolescence on. She was truant, a runaway and often shoplifted. When Donna was 13, her mother married her present husband and Donna rebelled. The girl stayed with a boyfriend, who is believed to be Andy's father.

After the baby's birth, when his mother was 15, she lived with her mother and stepfather for a while. But Donna appeared very depressed, isolated and was drinking heavily. She worked on and off but mostly supported herself with Aid to Dependent Children and, from what her family could tell, prostitution. When Andy was about a year old, despite the pleas of the grandmother, Donna took him and moved to Texas.

During the time he was in Texas his grandmother reported he was "talking" and could say "Hi, Grandma" during phone calls. But when the grandmother traveled to Texas for a visit when Andy was 2½ she found a changed child.

The baby had been severely neglected and she said Andy had numerous bruises on his head. He had also lost all speech. The grandmother felt the baby had severely regressed. His walking was "clumsy" and "He wouldn't let anyone touch his head."

The grandmother brought Andy back home with her, but found him uncontrollable.

This neglected and physically abused baby was tested at a nearby children's hospital and found to need both speech therapy and a hearing aid. It is unclear whether Andy suffered loss of hearing due to his mistreatment, but that is suspected.

During an evaluation on this child by therapists he was found to be "squirmy" and did not like being held.

Therapists initially diagnosed Andy as being mildly mentally retarded with poor speech patterns and a lack of ability to follow simple directions. But they were unable to tell if the difficulties were due to organic deficit, hearing loss or resistant behavior. The overall diagnosis of this child: unattached due to an abusive childhood.

*****

Andy is but one example of what can happen to a child through abuse and neglect. There are thousands of children in foster care who exhibit the scars, emotional and physical, of mistreatment. For most, unattachment is the result and its effects are almost always permanent if the abuse or neglect started early in life and the children are not diagnosed and helped when they are very young.

Children who are abused tend to be abusive as parents. This pattern of abuse must be broken. Families with a history of abusive background must be singled out for help and education.

These families must know that the consequences of their acts will come back to haunt them.

The cycle of abuse now is passed down, like a genetic defect, from parent to child. Jerome Miller of the National Center on Institutions and Alternatives (1986) notes that the situation is even worse among poor and neglected inner-city kids, especially with "a very young mother who is a child herself and who relates to the kid much the same way as a baby doll or teddy bear." (personal communication, March 14, 1986)

Child abuse incidence has been estimated at anywhere from one out of every 200 children per year to one out of every 40 children per year. (Pride, 1986)

Nationwide about 2 million children were reported to be abused in 1985—up a whopping 158% since 1976. But only 35% of those cases have been substantiated. (Hulse & Bailey, 1986)

The most accurate statistics on child abuse in the U.S. are probably those compiled by the American Humane Association, which keeps track of child abuse for the federal government. The AHA put the national rate in 1984 at 27.3 per 1,000.

These figures include a high percentage of serious crimes perpetrated on these children. Major physical injury accounted for 3.3% of substantiated cases and sexual maltreatment for another 13.3%. This means about 10,000 cases of major physical injury, several thousand cases of incestuous rape, and several thousand more cases of starvation and other serious neglect occurred that year.

Altogether, more than a million cases of some kind of neglect or abuse are reported annually. (Pride, 1986) Most of us are aware that sexual abuse of children is on the rise in the United States. There were more than 123,000 reported cases in 1984. This figure was up 35% nationally between 1983 and 1984, according to AHA.

Mistreatment of this kind leads to maladjustment because it disrupts the attachment formation.

Dr. Richard Krugman, a pediatrician who heads the Colorado-based C. Henry Kempe National Center for the Prevention and Treatment of Child Abuse and Neglect, says, "We've got a problem in the area of abuse and neglect that is far greater than anyone suspected when the system was set up. We're asking social services to bail out the ocean with a couple of buckets." (Hulse & Bailey, 1986, p.6)

Talking about abusive families and their tragic progeny, Miller says there is no question that poor bonding results in later maladjusted behavior. He says that in each case of a child murderer he has studied, there was something very, very wrong in the family, particularly with the mother or the father.

What does Miller think about the thesis that bonding and attachment problems harm children for life? He says the general thesis is "very true." Miller says even if poor bonding doesn't lead to violence it could cause "a schizophrenic type of withdrawal, retreating into a total psychotic state. I don't think in most cases of children who kill that there would be much experience with a normal bonding situation." (personal communication, March 14, 1986)

In homes with very young mothers, many times the mother can't give the child what is expected, so she passes the child around to other people, often extended family members. Miller sees such a family as "very immature and laced with a bit of violence and neglect so that you don't have the kind of family situation where the mother is even involved much. It's not uncommon at all for their kids to be alienated from their mothers and raised by others." That can lead to further problems because the other family members have responsibilities of their own. The cycle of neglect continues.

Miller has found that families of killers are different even in social context. They have a lot of violence, neglect and abuse with little likelihood of much bonding. Inconsistency is the overriding characteristic. As expected, it happens more among the poor but, ironically, "the middle-class kids who commit murder come from even more pathological families, because it's even more out of sync with their culture."

One example of a mass murderer who was abused as a child is Steven Judy. Miller described a horrifying scene in which Judy's father skinned his pet dog in front of him. Imagine the child's reaction to such a barbaric act. Rage begets more rage.

In another atrocity, future killer John Spenkelink's father put a shotgun to his own head and killed himself, making the boy watch.

"We have yet," says Miller, "to have one (murderer's background) in which one does not find these sorts of incidents. It's just routine." (personal communication, March 14, 1986)

Indeed, in the cases we have been citing, the children are tragically abused. But there are circumstances when the tables are turned and the parents are the injured parties.

Some cases of suspected abuse spring from accusations made by children—often against foster families. People tend to believe children, even if those children have demonstrated very bad behavior in the past. In effect, some cases of alleged abuse of children, particularly in foster-home situations, are false; the accusers are unattached children who are pathological liars. Who wouldn't believe a sad-faced little 7-year-old who is telling her desperate tale of abuse at the hands of her parents or foster parents? Police and social service workers would have no reason to suspect the truth, that this child is an accomplished liar who will do anything to have control over her family.

There may be other reasons to doubt the word of children suspected of having been abused. Some experts say those working with these children can put words in their mouths through suggestion. Gordon Barland, a nationally known Salt Lake City polygraph operator, has studied taped interviews with children. "A number of times, the caseworker is obviously asking leading questions. Even when the child has denied (the allegation), the caseworker comes back sometimes a third time, almost trying to break down the child." (Hulse & Bailey, 1986, p.61)

Victims of Child Abuse Laws (VOCAL) have charged that huge numbers of false allegations are occurring.

They say social service agencies are amassing blacklists of suspected abusers and once a name is on a blacklist it's not easy to get off, even if the individual is acquitted of child abuse charges.

"The state has you registered as a criminal," says Irwin Zook, president of the Colorado chapter of VOCAL. (Hulse, October 27, 1986, p.6) Barland says there is "no question" that the national concern over child abuse has caused an increase in the number of false allegations of abuse, especially sexual abuse. (Hulse & Bailey,1986, p.61)

In addition to some figures being inflated and others being too low, accurate reporting of cases is confounded by different definitions of "child abuse" used in this country. Public Law 93-247, which became effective in 1974, defines child abuse and neglect as "physical or mental injury, sexual abuse, negligent treatment or maltreatment of a child under the age of eighteen . . . " (Pride, 1986, p. 226) Many say this law is too ambiguous.

For example, it isn't "official" neglect when a mother leaves her infant too long with a variety of caregivers, but the consequences of becoming unattached are all too real.

Who are the real abusers of children and why do they do this? Studies have shown that parents engaging in maltreatment appear to be younger at the birth of the first child than nonmaltreating parents (Bolton, 1983). This raises also the potential for a longer childbearing career, during which a large number of children are born in close succession. The more stress, the greater the potential for abuse.

It is interesting to note that parents of babies born prematurely or with low birth weight or handicaps are more prone to abuse those children. This may be because the prematurity or low birth weight in some cases is attributable to neglectful practices before birth, such as bad prenatal care (or none), a bad diet or excessive use of alcohol or drugs.

Premature, low birth weight or handicapped infants are more difficult to care for and therefore place greater strains on their parents. Parents must be prepared for the task of caring for such children; if not, parents may vent frustrations at the infants' unresponsiveness by hitting or neglecting them.

Whatever it is in parent and child that leads to prematurity or low birth weight can be compounded later.

This same problem may occur between parents and children with low IQ's who may have difficulty understanding rules. If their parents also have poor verbal skills, the communication between the parent and child will be poor, possibly leading to child abuse. (Wilson & Herrnstein, 1986) Hyperactive or even excessively passive babies may also touch off hostile mothering. It is possible that neither kind of child reinforces a mother's friendly overtures. Closely spaced children in large families are also more at risk, as are stepchildren. Bonding to your new mate's children is often far more difficult than stepfamilies realize; this problem can lead to the breakup of the new family.

Nearly all studies conclude that while abused children can be found in all social strata, they are disproportionately found among lower-status families. The prevalence and severity of child abuse and neglect are strongly related to poverty. Abuse is more common and more serious among the poorest of the poor.

According to the available literature, abusive parents have quite often had physical and emotional deprivation in their own childhood (Bolton, 1983). This background leads to skewed emotional needs in them as parents (Bolton, 1983).

These parents can view a child as a competitor, even when he or she is not. Often isolated from sources of physical and emotional support, these parents can turn to their children with the expectation that parenthood will enhance them emotionally. Parenting skills that might have helped compensate for their great needs are largely unavailable.

The net effect is change in the child's normal role in the family from that of consumer of resources to one of provider. This new role isn't familiar to the child, who is bound to fail at it. Parents in this situation often react with frustration and aggression. (Bolton, 1983)

It is indeed hard to imagine how a seriously-abused child will not suffer ill consequences from the experience. Abuse in its most dramatic form ends the life of many children each year in the U.S. Estimates put the toll of children who die from abuse at 2,000 per year. For many others, it means permanent physical disability.

But the risk for most is increased likelihood of psychological and social problems that often carry into adulthood. "In many ways these are the most costly effects, because they are the most widespread and affect society as a whole," say James Garbarino and Wendy Groninger, (1983) authors of *Child Abuse, Delinquency and Crime.* (p.1)

Some studies show that it is possible for children raised in abusive or neglectful homes to grow up to be healthy and productive adults, just as some children manage to emerge intact from childhoods spent in orphanages or in refugee camps. But most seriously abused or neglected children face serious problems, as do many adopted children or those who have faced foster care.This may be where a strong genetic component pulls children through. But the majority of vulnerable children will be consumed by such a background.

One of the best predictors of whether abuse victims will repeat the pattern and abuse their own children is whether they form supportive relationships with nonabusive adults and peers. "The same is probably true of the link between abuse and other problems, such as delinquency and self-destructive behavior. That is, victims can avoid later trouble if they form other attachments. It's hard to tell in advance whether the victim of abuse is going to respond with antisocial behavior," say Garbarino and Groninger. (1983)

Of course, the big "if" here is whether an abused child can form other attachments. In most cases, if the developmental cycle has been broken, the answer is no, unless the child is given adequate early help through therapy.

One of the few long-term studies to prove the connection between attachment behavior and abusive parents has been under way for a number of years at the Minnesota Mother-Child Project. The 200 children in the study were picked more or less at random without prior knowledge of whether they were abused. All came from lower-income urban families with mothers who were mostly young, unwed, and relatively uneducated; they have been followed from just before birth for two years.

These families were especially at risk, but there was no effort to choose families in which abuse occurred. Abuse and neglect were detected after observation began.

The mothers were divided into five groups: physically-abusive, verbally abusive, neglectful or uncaring, psychologically unavailable (withdrawn, unemotional or unresponsive) and normal.

Researchers found that by 12 months, the physically-abused infants were less than half as likely as the normal ones to be securely attached emotionally to their mothers and three times more likely to be "anxious/ avoidant." The same pattern persisted at age 18 months. The abused children were also more prone to express anger and frustration.

Abusive or unavailable mothers can also result in children who have lower performance on certain measures of infant intellectual and verbal development, though the relationship between this and adult intelligence or language skills is unclear.

One startling fact came out of the study: The children of the psychologically unavailable mothers formed even weaker attachments than did those of the abusive ones.

Even worse, by 18 months *none* of the infants with unresponsive mothers had developed an attachment (nearly three-fourths of the children with normal mothers had). Similar findings have been reported in other studies. (Wilson & Herrnstein, 1985, p. 255)

One of the worries of child advocates like T. Berry Brazelton is that mothers who have to return to work too quickly will become "psychologically unavailable" to their children.

The central conclusion is that physical maltreatment (as well as some forms of psychological deprivation) impedes or even prevents the formation of a strong and confident attachment between infant and parent. Maltreated children also tend to display more aggression in both psychological tests and play situations. (Wilson & Herrnstein, 1985, p. 254).

It must be remembered that children placed early in day-care situations have also been found to display a higher level of aggression, independence and reluctance to follow adult leads. Any abnormal aggression in a child— that which goes beyond the normal patterns of children his age—should be cause for concern.

It may be that once a bully, always a bully. Children who frequently bully others grow up to be adults who display patterns of aggression. Researchers who studied 860 children in Columbia County, New York, over a 22-year period, found this to be the case. (Bridgman, 1987)

Researcher Leonard D. Eron cautions that children who are aggressive to other children or who tell lies to get others into trouble may be headed for other problems. It was found that children who were aggressive at 8 were still aggressive at 19 and by 30 *they were more likely to have committed crimes, been arrested for traffic violations, acted aggressively toward spouses and failed in school and on the job.*

These findings have been confirmed in study after study when nonabused children are compared to abused children. (Bridgman, 1987)

Delinquency and abuse are part of a self-sustaining destructive cycle which promotes more unattachment.

The link between child abuse and juvenile delinquency is well documented; 97% of male hardcore delinquents have a history of severe physical punishment and assault in the home. Abused delinquents, in fact, are 24 times more likely to commit arson and 58 times more likely to commit rape. (Garbarino & Groninger, 1983)

Life with abusive parents is a far cry from life with the supportive style of child rearing that encourages competence.

There are survivors, of course. Not all abused children grow up to be abusing adults, or even aggressive ones. It is believed that certain inherent ego strengths help some abused children overcome their handicap. One such survivor is Sandy Meyer, author of a book on her life story, *The Song of the Phoenix.* Meyer, now a married mother of three children with a Ph.d. in human behavior, tells her story:

"At the age of 2, I was thrown against the wall. At 10, I was raped by my father. At 12, pregnant by my father, I had an abortion. At 13, I had a baby [her father's] and was beaten by him while I was in labor. The baby died."

She talks about how she overcame her horrifying childhood:

"At first you rage and get it out . . . then you let it go in peace and forgiveness; anything you hate has a power over you. From the moment you get a hurt, it's your job to fix it. Until you let it go, you'll re-create it."

All proceeds from Meyer's book go to the Sandy Meyer Clinic for Human Advancement in Virginia. She has devoted her life to making sure that others get help in overcoming their tragedies. (Lamm, 1986)

Meyer is a survivor, but she is a flower in the desert. Many others are not so lucky. The facts are often appalling. Ninety percent of adults sentenced to prison were abused as children. And many of the institutionalized mentally ill come from backgrounds of abuse and neglect. (Lamm, 1986)

Abuse also plays a significant role in juvenile delinquency problems. Many runaways are the products of abusive homes, particularly sexual abuse. It plays a role in both suicide and drug/alcohol abuse.
Depression, self-hate, anger and a sense of futility are often the result of abuse. One study found that among a group of female drug abusers, nearly half were victims of sexual abuse. Among prostitutes, close to 80% were sexually abused as children. Records show that as many as one-third of all homicides reveal a history of abuse in the perpetrator's background. (Garbarino & Groninger, 1983)

"All in all, it seems clear that abuse is linked to juvenile delinquency and adult crime. Early abuse can produce a variety of psychological problems and social deficits that set in motion a pattern of behavior that leads to delinquency. Juvenile delinquency can trap the youth in a pattern that leads to adult crime." (Garbarino & Groninger, 1983, pp. 5-6)

The authors believe that preventing abuse (and neglect) is a critical and necessary step in preventing more angry and unattached children from "recreating" their inner rage through delinquency and aggressive crime.

Just as abuse is an obvious high risk situation, so is the dissolution of families. Divorce in this country is endangering thousands of children. We explore the implications of this in the next chapter.

Children Without A Conscience

Fig. 1

This picture of a devil (Fig. 1) was drawn by the adopted child Danny discussed in Chapter 4. He began drawing on the back of a church bulletin one Sunday. His parents thought he was drawing a portrait of the minister. This picture was the portrait!

182a

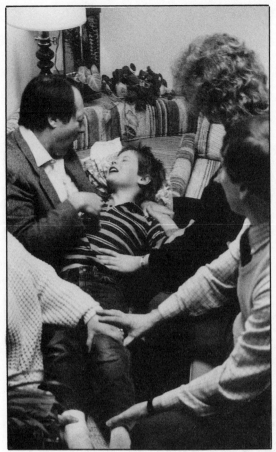

In this series of photos Dr. Foster Cline illustrates how a Rage Reduction Therapy session is conducted. In photo at left (Fig. 2) Cline stimulates subject toward rage reaction. Child is being held by "holders." Below (Fig. 3) child screams how much he hates the therapist.

Fig. 2

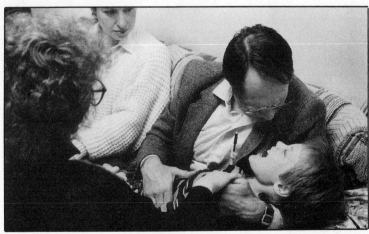

Fig. 3

182b

Rage Reduction Therapy

Fig. 4

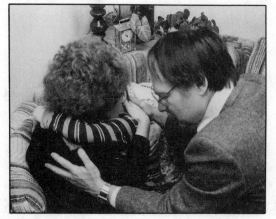

Fig. 6

Fig. 5

Younger children, or those who have successfully completed previous rage therapy sessions, may just sit in the therapist's lap (Fig. 4) as they discuss progress. Above (Fig. 5) child is comforted after reaching a rage reaction. Left (Fig. 6) mother and child begin the rebonding process after the child has reached rage peak.

Fig. 8

Professor John Allan
of Canada uses
drawings in his
therapeutic work with
unattached children.
The drawings show
a child's progress. In
the drawing at top left
(Fig. 7) the girl has
drawn herself behind a
curtain of scribbles. At
top right (Fig. 8) the
drawing shows the
progress she has
made in therapy. A
child drew herself in a
cage (Fig. 9) before
therapy and (Fig. 10)
out of the cage after
several sessions.

Fig. 7

Fig. 9

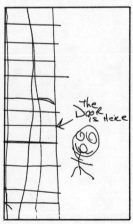

Fig. 10

Fig. 11

Drawings above (Fig. 11) were done by a boy severely physically abused by his father.

Fig. 12

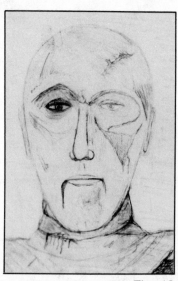

Fig. 13

A child who killed his sister during a fight drew pictures (Fig. 12 & 13) of a creature he saw in a dream. These drawings helped the boy resolve his guilt and anger.

14

Divorce
Disrupted Children
from Disrupted Homes

Scott Darwin Michael, an eighth grader, cried out to his assailant, "Don't shoot, it's loaded." He was then knocked backward by the force of the bullet as it hit his chest. He had been shot point blank by Jason Rocha, then 14, a bully who had threatened other students with knives and guns before he killed his classmate.

With his good looks and pleasant smile, Jason Rocha could be any typical suburban teenager. But he has been called by a prosecuter "an extremely dangerous threat to the community."

When he was brought before the court, Jason was grinning. He shook his head, covered with thick sandy brown hair, several times as the events leading to the fatal shot were recounted. Moments before killing 13-year-old Scott, Jason had paraded through the hallways of the school, displaying a chrome-handled gun sticking out of his pants. He had stolen the weapon as well as a .22 caliber rifle from his grandparents' home.

Jason told the judge, before being sentenced to 12 years in prison at the young age of 15, "I never intended to shoot Scott Michael, because I didn't have anything against him. And even if I did, I would never hurt anybody."

The judge, noting that Scott would have no chance at rehabilitation because "he is gone for all time," rejected four hours of defense testimony and pleas for a lesser term. The sentence, however, was no solace to the victim's family. Scott's father, after hearing the sentence, said, "Scott would probably like to be getting out in six years (the minimum time served). But Scott is dead." Since then, the father has called Jason "a cold-blooded murderer, and he will always be one. . ."

Jason's divorced parents were blamed by the judge for many of his problems. He told Jason before the sentencing that his parents were "uncaring, unnurturing" during his early years. Two court-appointed psychiatrists said the young man had a personality disorder resulting from a disruptive childhood during which he was separated from his mother several times.

They described him as "mistrustful of other people, depressed, angry, and often unable to control his impulses." They said he was not only suicidal, but will continue to be a threat to others unless he receives "intensive, long-term therapy."

Jason Rocha was born after his parents divorced. He started life without his father. Then, when Jason was 15 months old, his mother was injured in a serious accident and Jason was raised by relatives for six months, at a time when he was at a critical stage in the bonding process. The quality and consistency of that care is not known, but the amount of time spent away from his primary caretaker (his mother) was significant.

It is clear that these separations caused a break in his bonding process. Jason Rocha had become an unattached child with a personality disorder.

Then, when Jason was 9, another break occurred—his mother's second marriage began to fall apart. At that same time, Jason was attacked by his own dog. He twice had plastic surgery on his face and began seeing a psychiatrist, to recover from a dog phobia.

Meanwhile, his mother was working up to 70 hours a week, similar to the long hours put in by his stepfather. Two older brothers were sent to live with relatives because of the family's problems. To make matters even worse, his mother moved to the Virgin Islands. She left Jason to live with his stepfather. To punish the teenager for bad grades in school, his stepfather stopped the youth's visits to the psychiatrist, despite objections from both.

Only five months before the shooting, Jason had hysterically called the psychiatrist, saying he needed help. He said he was hanging out with tougher students at school. He saw the psychiatrist once, but a second appointment—only days before the shooting—was cancelled when Jason went on a trip to New Mexico to visit his grandparents.

It was there he stole the guns.

It is possible that Jason didn't actually mean to pull the trigger at point-blank range on his classmate. But when he was face to face with his victim and saw the horrified, helpless and hopeless expression on Scott's face it may have reminded him of his own previous helplessness and all of his own rage suddenly surfaced. Then there were no controls, as another child died and another killer was born.

*****

Jason Rocha is an extreme example of the worst that can happen in today's world of divorces and separations. Obviously, this killer child is also a victim.

Many marriages are strained with the result being divorce and the toll on our children is astounding. Twelve-million children under 18 now live in homes marked in some way by divorce. Many of these children have been found to have lower academic scores, problem friendships and emotional turmoil lasting years, even decades, beyond the initial separation.

It has been estimated that, at the present rate, approximately 40% to 50% of all children will experience a single-parent family in the next few decades. (Guidubaldi, 1983) There also seem to be sex differences in how well children handle divorce; young boys are at higher risk than girls largely due to the lack of nurturing from a consistent male role model. (Talan, 1986)

Compounding the obvious problems of divorce are the ways in which it is handled; custody battles and visitation arranged by uninformed judges and lawyers can set children up for unattachment and subsequent disaster.

Young children in particular cannot be safely out of the care of their primary caregivers for too long a time. Still, in courtrooms across the nation children are daily placed in visitation arrangements taking them away for too long from their primary caretakers—even to other states. This practice is breaking natural bonds that have already been established.

Just how long a child can safely be away from his primary caregiver depends on the age and social growth of that child.

Throughout the last 10 to 15 years, the effects of divorce on children have been studied and documented. These effects include depression, guilt, denial, overdependency and anger. (Levitin, 1983) Most seriously affected are the youngest children who are vulnerable to difficulties resulting from divorce trauma, particularly because optimal development requires both parents. (Kaplan, 1978) There is simply no such thing as a disposable parent.

A recent study of attachment quality among children of divorce found that the disruption in parenting had discernible effects. David Stevenson (1985) reported that parental disruption is tied to an increase in anxious attachment and is characterized by uncertainty about the continued availability of mother or father. The degree of the anxious attachment was found to correlate with the child's age at the time of the breaks in parenting.

"Some but not all broken homes will also be characterized by a weak parent-child attachment and inconsistent discipline, and children in these families will be less likely than those in affectionate and consistent families to internalize rules and temper their actions to the consequences." (Wilson & Herrnstein, 1985, p.261)

For many children, the disruption in parenting caused by divorce is followed sometime later by a parent's remarriage. While making the adjustment to the divorce, the child must then adjust to a stepparent. In fact, *by 1990, more than one-fourth of American children under the age of 18 will be a part of a step-family,* according to Paul Glick, a demographics expert formerly with the National Institutes of Health. (Krasnow, 1986)

Additional breaks can occur when a child bonds to a new stepparent and then that attachment is broken.

"There is this myth of instant love [in a stepfamily], that everybody is going to get along just because the couple is in love. Well, that just doesn't happen right off the bat. Sometimes it never happens," says Barbara Mullen, director of the Stepfamilies Association of America.

In the modern stepfamily a stepfather generally enters the household, since 90% of child custody awards are granted to divorcing mothers. Mullen says, "In the '70s it was single parenting and divorce. The stepfamily is the family of the '80s. Everybody you know is somehow touched by this."

The roles placed on stepfamilies aren't just on the children. The new parents feel the pressures too. "The call I get most often is from the instant stepmother like me who had never been married before," says Mullen. "The question is 'what is my role'? You are not the mother and you are not the big friend and you are not the aunt, but you're supposed to discipline and do all this stuff." Mullen remembers one night crying "because she was hurting." The reality wasn't what she thought it would be. (Krasnow, 1986)

In stepfamilies in trouble often times the problem is a conflict between an adolescent stepson and the stepfather. John Guidubaldi, a professor of counseling and school psychology at Kent State University, Ohio, says "In many cases, the adolescent son has a sense of rivalry for leadership in the family, rivalry for the mother's affection, for being the man in the family." (Krasnow, 1986)

When it comes to divorce, parents are damned if they do and damned if they don't. Some parents, for example, elect to remain married just for the children's sake. But this is not always a wise decision either. It is well known there is always a cost to a child who is raised in a home with continuing marital disharmony. This price may be an increased probability of psychiatric disorder for the child. (Schwarz, 1979)

"Every other weekend and half of Christmas Day" . . . It sounds like a recipe for fairness, but few are happy with the product. With the rocketing divorce rate in this country, one of the most glaring omissions in the nation's judicial system is the absence of sound guidelines governing . . . shared parental responsibility. The questions for the courts have been, and still are, "what solution is in the best interest of the children and what is the most equitable custody arrangements for the parents?"

It is hard to know what is best for the children and is still fair for the parents, however. There haven't been any long-term studies on the best arrangements for divorced children so judges are forced to predict the future based on uncertain guidelines and hazy theories, rather than to rule on clear and conclusive evidence.

Just what is at stake when children are the victims of a divorce?

To find out, Guidubaldi (1986) compared 700 children in the first, third and fifth grades. Half were from divorced homes and half from intact families. The children were studied after an average length of four years had passed since the divorce. Guidubaldi felt this was long enough for the initial shock of separation to subside.

In most cases the first and third graders from divorced families had lower grades, poorer teacher assessments and spent more time in school counselors' offices.

In addition, these children of divorce did worse on all social competency indicators. These included teacher ratings of peer popularity, the degree of withdrawal and dependency, and inattention and negative feelings about themselves.

In looking for factors that can mitigate the problems of divorce Guidubaldi says he found children with more structured lives—less television, regular mealtimes with parent, early bedtimes—did better than children from chaotic home settings. (Talan, 1986)

The more *consistent* the home environment, the better the children did. This finding supports the authors' viewpoint that consistency in the home, particularly with the primary caregiver, is the most important factor in helping young children handle the trials of a divorce. Of course, as everyone knows, the most chaotic time in an adult's life is when he is undergoing a divorce.

Among the factors that determine how a very young child will react to the divorce and the subsequent visitation problems that may occur is the attitude of the mother about the separation.

"How upset the custodial mother is about the separation and divorce may be far more important in determining the effect of the separation on the infant. Mothers who are tremendously upset will upset the infant. In addition," says William F. Hodges, author of *Interventions for Children of Divorce* (1986), "the routine and responsiveness of the infant may be extremely disrupted." (p. 12)

In Guidubaldi's study he found that boys did equally well in three circumstances: if they grew up with their fathers rather than under the sole guidance of their mothers; if they were in contact with the non-custodial male parent; or if the mother was satisfied with the parenting and emotional support of the father. (Talan, 1986)

Consistent visitation, timed with the child's "internal clock," seems to work best.

Persia Woolley, author of *The Custody Handbook*, (1979) says "A toddler who doesn't see a parent for a week or two may have lost contact with the emotional and psychological relationship they once enjoyed and perceive the separation as a form of abandonment" (pp.103-104). Therefore, to maintain a child's main relationships following divorce, time-sharing should coincide with the child's time perspective so it isn't so traumatic.

The trend has been toward lengthy visitations in the belief that they would allay young children's rage. However, just the opposite is true. Long visitations are high-risk situations for all young children, especially for infants. Dr. Parker Oborn, family therapist and an expert on custody and visitation, says, "In light of this fact, traditional visitation schedules are outmoded and dangerous." (Magid & Oborn, 1986, pp. 331-341)

Parents, judges, attorneys and child psychology professionals should be concerned about the risks of serious potential trauma to young children resulting from such inaccurate assumptions concerning attachment.

These new studies are showing that the father's impact upon child development is greater than has been previously assumed. This is especially true with younger children. Thus, there is a need for guidelines for the involvement of both parents in cases of divorce.

It must be noted that some, but not all, homes touched by divorce will also be characterized by weak parent-child attachments and inconsistent discipline. Obviously, children in these families are less likely than those in affectionate and consistent families to internalize rules and temper their actions to the consequences.

In one study, researchers noted that in situations of high father absence, both boys and girls displayed significant decreases in four areas of paternal influence: emotional development, moral development, disciplinary role models, and financial decision-making. The support for more father-child involvement in divorce has grown and the evidence clearly indicates that it is in the best interests of the child to have frequent access to both father and mother. (Lamb, 1981) As Guidubaldi's study indicated, boys seem to be more affected by a lack of a father than girls.

"Highly visible mothers' rights and fathers' rights groups have inadvertently headed in the same direction: less against each other and more toward what is now termed shared or mutual parental responsibility." (Magid & Oborn, 1986, p.332)

Heavily populated, progressive states like California and Florida stand at the vanguard of efforts toward this new, shared parental responsibility. Laws governing this process, however, have been drafted largely without precedent and need to draw heavily upon the available research and respected professional opinion on joint custody arrangements.

In the past, custody of the child was based primarily on the "tender years doctrine" which in effect recognized the importance of early bonding and attachment between a mother and child as critical to the healthy survival and developmental progression of the infant. Judges almost always placed children during their so-called tender years (very young children) with the mother. This new move toward parental equality was initiated largely to help the adults.

Now that there are more shared custody arrangements certain factors *must* be taken into consideration for helping the children:

- How children understand and integrate varying time frames;

• How this factor combines with a child's varying cognitive levels and support systems; and

• The effect of this combination on a child's ability to adjust to a shared parental responsibility agreement.

The work of researcher Jean Piaget (1956) indicates that prior to the age of 7 or 8, due to their immature organizational thinking, children's time conception is prone to systematic errors. Younger children are certainly more unclear about time perspectives and even a fundamental understanding of the future and past tenses does not form until later.

Adults, in contrast, have the ability to anticipate the future and to deal with delays. With children it is different. Their built-in time sense is based on their own immediate emotional needs.

When a shared parental living arrangement for the child is not tailored to the child's time perspective, the child is less able to comprehend the transitions and is thus more susceptible to trauma, including regression, developmental delays, acting out and maladjustments.

The reasons for effectively balancing shared parental living arrangements become even more critical when we look at the recent research on how deprivation can seriously affect a child's development. This research shows *infants have a surprising awareness of their environment.* (Roman & Haddad, 1978) When an infant senses that its relationships with others have been disrupted and parental consistency is lost (as is frequently the case in unbalanced parental responsibilities in divorce), the infant is very likely to call forth a self-surviving instinct. This emotion is called rage. It is this rage and sadness that is at the core of the unattachment syndrome.

This unresolved rage can simmer for years and manifest itself in a number of ways, ranging from antisocial criminal acts, to suicide, to abuse or neglect of their own children, perpetuating the cycle.

As we have shown earlier, 2- and 3-year-olds with secure attachments who come from stable homes are more competent and independent, more likely to be peer group leaders, to be empathetic and to enjoy learning new skills than are 2- and 3-year-olds with insecure attachments.

To make sure infants and small children do not succumb to rage, adequate and reliable guidelines are needed to help the legal system and parents implement low-risk but effective shared parental responsibilities. We'll give specific information on visitation schedules and timetables a bit later.

*****

In this section we have reviewed the areas where attachment breaks can occur. Among these are: attachment problems for infants whose working mothers or fathers have to return to work too soon after childbirth or adoption; difficulties brought on by inadequate or inconsistent substitute child care; the hardships the system places on adoptive or foster children; the special needs of teenage mothers and their babies; and the dire consequences abuse and divorce have on young children.

There are ways to mitigate the effects of these breaks. America must find the answers to the problems it faces as it tries to stem the tide of ever-increasing numbers of unattached children.

There are a few treatments being pioneered which are attempting to reach and rescue some of the damaged children. In the next section we look at conventional treatments and their failures as well as promising new techniques, such as "rage reduction" therapies, that are successfully helping unattached children regain their abilities to love.

IV

TREATMENT

15

The Trouble with
Traditional Therapies

The first real choice a human baby *must* make is whether to trust or mistrust other humans. This basic trust-versus-mistrust stage is the first building block upon which all later love relationships are formed.

Babies simply must know that adults around them will care for them and can be trusted to meet their needs. Perhaps Erik Erikson said it best in 1968 when he described this phenomenon:

> "A sense of *basic trust* . . . is the first and basic wholeness, for it seems to imply that the inside and the outside can be experienced as an interrelated goodness" (p. 82).

Certainly the best known expert on attachment is John Bowlby. He echoes the same concern about bonding and predicts dire consequences for unattached children as they go through life untrusting, controlling and filled with rage.

> "The psychopath always show[s] an impaired capacity for affectional bonding, one that is severe and long-lasting" (1977, p.71).

193

As previously noted, it is through this strong attachment that the central nervous system is regulated, feelings of trust and security are established, and the child begins to develop a sense of expectancy that a consistent caregiver (usually the mother) will be there when he needs her. Through this consistency of care the child will begin to show more spontaneous behavior and will soon want to be more autonomous and move away from parents and into normal play with other children. He will begin to master interpersonal skills.

But breaks in attachment lead to feelings of anger and rage, grief and hopelessness, poor impulse control and a failure to learn the basic social and cognitive skills necessary for a healthy life.

When there are such breaks the child fails to develop deep feelings of trust and becomes instead locked into negative behavior.

Eminent therapist Dr. Robert Zaslow of San Jose State University in California originated a therapeutic technique for treating psychopaths, known as "Z Therapy." He says the infant perceives his parents as the cause of tension and builds a shell around himself to avoid it.

But the walls we build around ourselves to protect us from pain also imprison us. This is the plight of the Trust Bandit. His defensive walls are 10-feet thick.

This supershell forms early and hardens to become almost impervious as the child blocks out the world. Some curious aspects of the psychopath may be explained by this hard shell. His anxiety level is much lower than that of normal individuals, and his pain tolerance is extremely high.

In studies of psychopaths' brains a startling discovery has been made: they have low levels of a mood-altering chemical called serotonin (Brown, et al., 1986). It is possible that this partially explains their constant desire for kicks or stimulation, often of a criminal nature. These are people who must live on the edge. They frequently test themselves, and others, regardless of future consequences or physical pain. (Linnoila, et al. 1983)

Hare (1965), for example, found that psychopaths were not alarmed (like most of us would be), when told they would be administered electric shocks. It was as if they could distance themselves from future pain, actually putting pain out of their minds!

It has even been reported by jailers that the voltage required to execute psychopathic killers in the electric chair has sometimes had to be increased. In Russia, the feared psychopath Rasputin was stabbed and then shot numerous times and then had to be drowned before he died.

How a pyschopath manages to survive against all odds is baffling. These and other aspects of APD leave mental health experts confused and divided on how best to treat Trust Bandits.

As we saw in the last section, the causes of this illness are many. Neglectful and abusive parents are two of the most dramatic precursors of attachment problems. And the process of drawn-out adoption is another.

What is appalling is that children can become unattached from apparently normal two-parent families for any number of reasons.

Certainly, prevention is the best possible solution. But lacking that, what can be done? Adult psychopaths file in and out of mental institutions and jails, pigeonholed as criminals, misfits, addicts and alcoholics.

Let's not forget, they can also sit in boardrooms, or function in a number of respectable occupations; only if their manipulation catches up with them will their lives hit the downward trail. No matter their station in life, Trust Bandits share two traits: they are psychopaths and they are *legally competent.*

THROUGH THE CRACKS: HOW IT HAPPENS

It is an all-too-familiar story. A psychopath with a pattern of criminal behavior is caught. His lawyer successfully argues that the psychopath's history shows he is a victim of madness and is not *legally* accountable for his crime. The judge orders the criminal confined to a mental hospital.

Once evaluated at the hospital, however, the psychopath is found to be sane and competent. Diagnosis reveals no nervous or mental disease. The hospital is then *legally* compelled to release him. This psychopath has fallen through the cracks that exist in our legal and medical definitions of insanity — because the *psychopath* does not meet the current definition of *insanity.*

He escapes any responsibility or accountability for his antisocial behavior, and goes free.

What is unfortunate is that psychopaths are uniquely suited to take advantage of this loophole. A recent study by Darwin Dorr and Peggy Woodhall (1986) offers intriguing insights. They found psychopaths to be like normal people "with regard to their capacity to experience external events as real and with regard to the sense of bodily reality. They generally had good memory, concentration, attention, and language function." (p. 128) So, psychopaths *resemble* normal people and can be classified as reasonably sane. But Trust Bandits differ dramatically in other areas studied, scoring even below schizophrenics.

What it boils down to is that psychopaths don't have disordered thought processes, but they do show poor judgment, poor impulse control and an inability to get along with others. They are neither psychotic nor schizophrenic. But they are clearly disordered. Being neither legally sane nor insane they *fall through the cracks,* continuing to commit crimes and go free, leaving us a society at high risk.

These Trust Bandits may not display psychosis. Nonetheless their lives are headed for disaster, as are the lives of all those with whom they associate.

The psychiatric community knows of no cure for these adult sufferers of APD. Trust Bandits evade being defined as either sane or insane. Psychiatrists and psychologists are just as often helplessly manipulated as are their other victims.

We will examine traditional treatments in this chapter, and the failures of such treatments. Then we will look at the intensive treatments that are having limited success with character-disturbed children. There is some hope—but a very long way to go—for treating the child on his way to becoming a pyschopath.

*****

"The number of ways people can go awry are countless. So wide is the range that almost any theory of emotional disturbance and therapy will find at least a few examples that make sense according to its terms."

Dr. Joel Kovel

Good Theories that Don't Work

Take your pick: Psychoanalysis, Behavior Modification, Client-Centered Rogerian Therapy, Transactional Analysis, Reality Therapy, Gestalt Therapy. These are just a few of the choices of traditional therapies available to the consumer.

Each one has a claim to fame and a place in the mental health market. Depending on the skills of the therapist and the problems at hand, some of these treatments work better than others.

Freudian psychoanalysis, for example, caters to an educated middle-and upper-class neurotic who is well spoken and patient enough to wait for results that may take years and thousands of dollars. This certainly excludes the Trust Bandit, who is impulsive, cannot delay gratification and will not give up control to others. "Analytically-oriented treatment of the true psychopath is of dubious value," says Dr. Ethel Person. (1986, p.271)

Similar criticisms can be launched against other therapies and their lack of effectiveness for Trust Bandits. The Client-Centered therapy pioneered by Carl Rogers works wonders with people suffering from stress and needing a good friend and listener. Given time in a trusting atmosphere, the therapy can be successful. But the keys to this therapy are *mutual trust and empathy.* The problems with such therapy in treating APD are obvious. The Trust Bandit desperately needs direction because his skewed manipulation of others has kept things around him in constant crisis. But the average therapist cannot possibly empathize with a full-blown psychopath.

How does one empathetically listen to and remain non-judgmental toward a client who has just disclosed that he has brutally killed a 2-year-old with a ball peen hammer . . . and that he'd do it again, just for kicks?

There are many traditional therapies we could critique, but suffice it to say that all of them fall short when dealing with the true Trust Bandit.

On closer examination even the most touted and widely-used systems have chinks in their therapeutic armor. Behavior Modification therapies and their offshoots have been widely accepted for use in hospitals, juvenile centers and prisons. By definition, Behavior Modification looks at behavior. It works on rewards and consequences and does not look into the murky waters of the patient's history. Rather, it deals only with the present—what can be observed, measured, and tightly controlled.

It is the control aspect of this treatment approach that is its greatest strength and its greatest weakness. Inside prisons this process has demonstrated rapid changes in behavior, especially when coupled with therapies which force the Trust Bandit to confront faulty thinking and make him responsible for his own life.

In prisons and closed hospital wards a tightly-controlled program of rewards, consequences and conversations can be carried out. Usually "talk" therapy is employed that deals with the client's irrational thoughts and goals, along with a "token" economy. If the patient does the right thing he gets a token, which can be exchanged for something he wants — food, cigarettes, privileges, etc. Tokens are taken away for bad behavior. It's not unlike the real world where we do a good job, get paid and if we don't we sometimes get fined or fired.

Behaviorists sometimes apply punishment, such as electric shocks or solitary confinement. But these punishments can have undesirable side effects, such as making the patient angrier and more violent. It's like the adult who spanks a child for fighting with his brother and then says, "Now, I don't ever want to see you hitting anyone again."

If there is a strong desire on the psychopath's part to change, and a continually-controlled system is set up of fair and desirable rewards, Behavior Modification therapies can work. Their greatest weakness, however, is that they must have tight controls. This is not possible outside of institutions.

" . . . There is little evidence that they (token reinforcement programs) result in long-term maintenance of behavior change once the program is removed and/or the institutionalized person is discharged to the community . . . (p. 175). Target behaviors changed desirably within the prison but recidivism at 18 months followup was not better than for a no treatment group" (Barley, 1986, p. 171).

The truth is that Behavior Modification has many useful applications, but it hasn't been the treatment salvation for Trust Bandits.

One might conclude, as many mental health workers have, that the odds are just too stacked against these people. But the American spirit has always thrived on tough challenges. The brook of life would lose its song if we removed the rocks.

Only a handful of therapists have picked up the gauntlet and considered the challenge of APD as an opportunity for growth. These opportunities come carefully disguised, however, as very hard work. The few who have attacked the problem realize the enormity of the challenge and that we are just beginning to understand how to treat Trust Bandits.

Not unlike the war on cancer, there are as yet no fool-proof cures or solutions or simple answers to the disease of psychopathy.

In fact, those touting a cure for APD should be highly suspect. Psychiatrist Joel Kovel notes: "I distrust dramatic cures and therapeutic breakthroughs. For all their razzle dazzle they seem as tedious and old-fashioned as the tidings of a new Messiah or the miracles of Lourdes." (1976, p. XIV)

So the average consumer of mental health services is caught in a bind, between those who say they have a cure for APD and those who say nothing works.

Why can't a consumer get a straight answer to the question, "Will your therapy work with my unattached child or not?" Unfortunately, mental health "scientists" are not like physicists who have laws like gravity to guide them. They are more like weathermen. They can use scientific principles to predict the chances of rain, or the chances of helping most people. But they can't tell how much rain will fall or how many will be helped. There are just too many individual variables.

There is another problem: a majority of therapists in this country have not followed rigid scientific processes to study and evaluate their work. Most of them rely on theories and successful cases. They don't have the expertise or the time to set up lengthy, controlled experimental designs or to check out each patient's progress scientifically.

Therapists are more practitioners of an art. They take pride that they are on the cutting edge of new breakthroughs in helping solve some of mankind's most difficult interpersonal problems. Bertrand Russell once said: "The only true joy in life is being used for a purpose recognized by yourself as a mighty one." (Hubbel, 1987, p. 66)

Certainly, the parent with an unattached child faces a mighty challenge. Unfortunately the therapist who sees the APD patient is in the same boat.

"Most therapists in America don't know how a patient with Antisocial Personality Disorder operates and are sucked into nonproductive therapeutic sessions that seldom help the client and often have disastrous effects on the unwitting therapist."

Ken Magid

16

The Referral

Let's pretend for a moment that you are a psychotherapist who has just received a new referral from a colleague. At first you wonder why this friend would send you a referral, but you are pleased for the additional income. As you pick up the phone to call this new patient you glance down at the referral note and see the following message: "DSM-III, 309.20, have fun!"

You can't quite remember what these code numbers represent so you grab your DSM book and look it up. Suddenly it hits you like a brick as you see the words "Antisocial Personality Disorder." A jolt of anxiety and disappointment rushes over you.

You were taught in graduate school that an APD patient routinely rejects help and often bites the hand that feeds him. He tries to discredit those attempting to help him and uses any means possible to make the therapist look bad. This doesn't jibe with the skills you were taught—to try and help people and establish a good working relationship.

You were taught to be honest and to recognize honesty in clients. But the APD patient thinks therapists are fools and he lies whenever it suits him. This patient lies about the past, present and future. Unless you painstakingly check out all his stories against reality and third parties you'll never know the truth.

You also realize that an APD patient will blame all his faults on others, including his therapist, when things don't go well. He has a limited capacity for self-observation and will not stick to plans and commitments, although he swears that he will.

By definition, APD patients have long histories of delinquency and problems with the law. Their crimes run the gamut from assault, robbery and arson to sex offenses and murder. Substance abuse is a common problem.

You think of yourself as a loving person who instills a sense of caring in others. But the APD patient doesn't understand love, except as a vulnerable spot to exploit in others. He thinks only of himself. For him, it's a question of survival and the therapist is one of two things: either the enemy or a victim.

You now remember how much you would rather see a neurotic middle-class patient than a full-blown Trust Bandit. As you reflect on how APD patients seldom respond to any of the therapies you were taught in school you wonder how you will keep from either hating yourself or this new patient.

The Therapist Traps

Let's stop the pretend therapy game now. In real life the situation is more complicated and tragic. All of the problems of dealing with psychopaths in therapy can be boiled down to one word: "countertransference." This refers to how the *therapist* emotionally responds to a patient.

But first let's look at transference. This is how the *patient* emotionally views the therapist. For example, a patient might see his therapist as a rescuing parental figure or even as the enemy. In countertransference the therapist's personal tendencies and reactions are brought into play. He may be mad, sad or glad and not aware of how these strong emotions occurred. Countertransference can get in the way of a therapist making good treatment decisions. When the therapist is dealing with a Trust Bandit, he may enthusiastically enter into treatment unaware that it is he, not his client, who is going to change.

Diagnostic Dilemma

The first mistake most therapists make is in diagnosing the Trust Bandit syndrome. They just don't know what they are dealing with and usually over- or underestimate the problem.

The therapist who underestimates his client's power will not be prepared for the manipulation and crisis-oriented events to come. This can lead to dangerous, even life-threatening, confrontations. For example, most therapists learn in school that controlled anger is an acceptable emotion for a troubled client to express. The APD patient can have an uncontrolled, violent rage reaction on the spur of the moment. Not only is the naive therapist in danger but so is the general public. On the other hand, overestimating the patient's power can actually lead to a scenario in which the therapist might over-medicate, over-restrain or develop a phobic response to a patient he considers untreatable.

The Fear Game

Fear begets fear and when both the patient and the therapist remain afraid little progress can be made. Even in hospitals and prisons, where the staff's safety is more easily assured, many experienced therapists have high anxiety levels. One psychiatrist shared her feelings about treating an APD patient whom she calls a "terrifying, homicidal maniac":

> "Today was my first meeting with Jim. Perhaps now that I have gone inside the hospital, the nightmares that woke me the last few nights will stop. The session itself was brief. I am still too frightened to spend the requisite 50 minutes with him . . . Both he and I had to resolve enough of our fear to develop a proper working alliance." (Obekirch, 1985, p. 499)

One variation on the Fear Game theme is for the patient to insinuate or threaten to have uncontrollable urges to do bodily harm to others. The client may gaze out of the window and say, "I wonder if I will ever molest a child again." You can bet the therapist is also wondering about this, and worrying too.

"I feel like I'm taking care of Great White Sharks. All I can do is feed them and stay clear of their pearly whites," says one hospital psychiatric worker.

The Guilt-Gotcha Game

Patients who put therapists in a helpless condition are often reflecting their own fears and helplessness. This type of patient will hone in on any perceived weakness he senses in his therapist and try to get the therapist to buy into his problems. This is the Guilt-Gotcha game. The patient seizes the slightest opportunity to play the victim. For example, if the therapist is late or takes a call during a session the Trust Bandit jumps in to play the rejected party. This puts the guilt on the therapist for not being a better role model.

Because most therapists strive so hard to do a good job, they can get caught in this countertransference trap. A skillful Trust Bandit can escalate this game. He may not pay his bill or will come late to his sessions. Then, when confronted, he will accuse the therapist of being callous, hypocritical and cold-hearted. The guilt-ridden helper is then more vulnerable to taking on the APD patient's problems and trying to "rescue" the "poor soul."

Progress with APD patients, if any is made, is very slow. "The more I saw him, the worse things got," laments one psychology student. "It was like I was working with a tarbaby; the more I tried the more stuck I got." (Wiggins, personal communication, 1987) This can lead to frustration, burnout and even depression.

The Mad-Glad Ploy

There is another game up the Trust Bandit's sleeve, called the Mad-Glad ploy. When the patient makes the therapist mad at him it makes the patient glad, because the patient is in control. The patient assures himself that he is not being ignored and that if someone hates him, someone can also change and love him too. This is especially dangerous when the therapist has unresolved personal problems and allows himself to become defensive. The therapist may steadily withdraw all interest and emotional support toward the client.

The Mad Hatter

If the therapist doesn't go for that bait, the patient may try the Mad Hatter. Here the Trust Bandit tries to overwhelm the helper with such a litany of personal problems that even Solomon would seek to refer him elsewhere. The therapist who lets the APD patient spin his web of confounding tales long enough is allowing the real issues to be passed over; the patient remains safe and unthreatened. Trust Bandits are masters at creating problems and if given enough freedom will continue to generate crisis after crisis.

The Join Me Game

Another game occurs when the patient gets the therapist to join him in his fantasies, as if to say "Watch my exciting life." Sometimes the Trust Bandit is actually able to draw the therapist into his warped world. A female APD patient, for example, may use the lure of sexuality to establish control. One anonymous therapist recalls such a patient:

> "Beside being a knockout, she was dressed to kill. She wore see-through blouses, short skirts, and had a seductive line. She started off by telling me that she had been to several doctors before me, but none of them seemed to know how to help her and that she felt especially lucky to be seeing me now. Before I knew it we were talking about how she was having trouble with her car and she wondered if I could give her a lift home after the

session. Fortunately for me, I had other patients to see and this broke the spell. For a moment there I was willing to follow her anywhere."

Unfortunately, some therapists do follow their patients home, unaware of the trap into which they have fallen.

If the therapist is unwilling to play one game, the patient simply dips into his bag of tricks and pulls out another. The average therapist—armed with only traditional treatments — is no match for a well-armed Trust Bandit.

Rage Reduction Therapy

In a few avant-garde clinics around the world—including some facilities in Italy, England, Australia and Japan—an innovative technique has been developed for dealing with youthful Trust Bandits; it is a most radical treatment for a radical problem. Rage Reduction Therapy is a moving emotional experience for the therapist, patient and patient's parents. In some quarters, Rage Reduction Therapy has been criticized as being close to brainwashing. But Foster Cline, one of the few experts in the world to use this treatment, answers such critics with, "Some of these kids need their brains washed." (personal communication, June 6, 1986)

Cline has hundreds of successful cases to support his methods. While rage reduction is the most direct and confrontive way of dealing with psychopaths, there are other modified therapies that attempt to arrive at the same point. In Canada, John Allan, Ph.D., has been working for 20 years on a modified therapy that gets similar results to Cline's treatments with less rage response.

In the next few chapters we will look at Cline's and Allan's successes with children without a conscience, including Allan's work with a killer child.

Basically, Rage Reduction Therapy involves physical holding and control of a patient who is confronted with his death-grip resistance to accepting love and acting responsibly. The therapy contains explosive dialogue as the psychopathic patient is encouraged to work through his unbelievable rage and anger while being forced to accept another's total control.

Other Treatments

There are many paths up a mountain, and other therapeutic trails are being forged by those first sparked by the creative genius of Dr. Milton Erickson, the legendary hypnotist and metaphor maker. Erickson shared his wizardry with many family therapists, including Jay Haley and Cloe Madanes. Most family therapists view the psychopath's dilemma as a problem of misunderstandings between family members that can best be solved by dealing with the family's crossed messages and cross purposes. Their use of "double binds" and metaphors is fascinating to observe. We will show how their therapies are used in helping severely troubled children.

In the following chapters we will also cover spiritual therapy, which can make a difference in changing the cold, hate-filled heart of a psychopath. We will talk about one of the most instructive parents of all, Mother Nature, and how outdoor experience is helping psychopathic adolescents in a new approach called Wilderness Therapy. Finally, we look at how traditional hospitalization therapy attempts to deal with the AIDS of the mental health community.

"Two hours after the reattachment therapy
began my son's rage reached a climax and he stopped
screaming and began making deep gutteral sounds that
ran a shiver up my spine. My God, I thought, what next
. . . is he going to turn his head around and become
the devil, like in The Exorcist? *And then his eyes*
turned black with hate as he coldly told us that
he prayed to the devil every night."
                                                        "Ruth"

17

Defusing the National Time Bomb

It was 3 a.m. when Dr. Foster Cline fumbled for the telephone in the dark next to his bed. He remembers hearing a woman's shaky voice on the other end of the line. The call sounded like it was long distance.

"I'm . . . I'm sorry for calling you so late and you don't even know me, but we've got to have some help. My son has threatened to burn down the house tonight and no one will believe me. I have other children and I just can't stay awake another night. Please, please help me!"

It didn't take Cline long to get the all-too-familiar story. The emergency call was from a single parent named Ruth who had an out-of-control teenager.

Ruth explained that her 13-year-old son Jeremy had been getting into a lot of trouble over the years, stealing and lying and not following anyone's rules. He could usually talk his way out of problems, blaming them on others or saying that he had learned his lesson. He recently had been caught trying to set a fire at school and was now threatening to burn the house down while everyone slept. Ruth knew he was serious because he had followed through on previous threats, including killing the family cat. She had called social services in her city but she had been rebuffed. And local therapists had been of little or no help. She spent about 10 minutes spilling out her account of hell on earth. Cline interrupted her with a barrage of short questions that she later said "hit the nail right on the head."

"Ruth, is your son adopted or did he have any serious illnesses as a baby?"

"Adopted, why yes. How did you know?"

"Did Jeremy ever resist cuddling and eye contact with you?"

"Yes, he never cuddled as a baby."

After 10 or more questions, the psychiatrist suspected he had an unattached child on his hands. All the symptoms pointed in that direction. Cline reasoned that if Jeremy was an unattached child, then he might carry out his murderous threat. Something had to be done, and quickly, but the crisis was happening in the middle of the night in another state. An understaffed and overworked social services department there didn't understand unattached children and, frankly, didn't want to be bothered.

Cline's strategy that night was simple and direct.

"I simply called social services and told them that I was phoning them out of concern because the parent had talked with me and as a psychiatrist and a professional I found this child dangerous. I told them that if they didn't take immediate action to get this kid out of the home that when things did go wrong, and it looked to me like they would, that social services and the staff on duty would be liable for a horrendous lawsuit.

"I informed them the situation was dangerous and I wanted to go on the record as having fulfilled my obligation to notify them. I said this was so I wouldn't have a lawsuit against me also. And then I asked them again to help me spell their names for my records and urged them to do what was in their own best interest because I was concerned about them."

Jeremy was promptly removed that night to a temporary juvenile facility. His mother was so relieved when Cline called her back that she couldn't stop crying. Interspersed between the sobs she told the exhausted psychiatrist that he must be a magician. Cline agreed to meet with her son later that week.

For the first time in four nights, Ruth allowed herself to fall into a deep sleep. In the next chapter we will recount Cline's therapy session with Jeremy. But first we'll explain how the therapy process works.

Attachment Process

It wasn't magic but training and experience that gave Cline the background and diagnostic skills to deal with this crisis. Not long after his psychiatric residency Cline met and studied with Dr. Robert Zaslow, a man with a mission.

In 1966 Zaslow looked like most other professors on the campus of San Jose State University. He did not stand out as a handsome man but, up close, in his eyes, there was a vibrancy and excitement about life. When he spoke it was in staccato-paced sentences that required listeners to be particularly attentive. His enigmatic style was often confrontive; he asked as many questions of his students as he answered. This style upset many people who characterized him as abrasive, arrogant and stand-offish. His independent thinking particularly upset bureaucrats — they wanted him to be more of a team player.

But those who took the time to penetrate his gruff exterior found a warm and caring individual who tried to help anyone in need. This may be the reason he was motivated to enter psychology—to help others and to challenge his students to learn more about what makes people tick.

Then one day it happened. Several of his students turned the tables and challenged their professor to come up with a better understanding of how severely disturbed children are created. Zaslow not only took on the challenge but developed a therapy for treatment.

He had been amassing data about the attachment process and what happens when this natural bonding fails or is broken. From this data, Zaslow hypothesized that all mental disorders that are not clearly organic can be traced back to some abnormality in the attachment cycle.

He felt that the only hope for normality was in a rebonding process. This process he called Rage Reduction or Z therapy; it requires forcing the patient to complete successfully the attachment cycle. Zaslow's theory was formed after he studied autistic children; they seldom look others in the eye and prefer to stare silently into space or to talk in unintelligible ways. These children seem to want to follow their own solitary paths and concentrate on their own bizarre fantasies in which they attach to things rather than people. Effective treatment for autistic children was virtually non-existent and most therapists preferred not to work with them. But Zaslow was determined to reach them.

He quickly found that talk therapy did not work with these children. He wondered what would happen if they were physically held and confronted face-to-face. They tried to avoid him and became enraged when held. From this strategy was born his rage-reduction therapies, which forced these children to be vulnerable and trusting. Zaslow hypothesized that these children's rages were really like a sound barrier that could be broken through, with peace and resolution on the other side. From his theories about autism, Zaslow began to conceive of a way to use holding to treat unattached children. (Zaslow & Menta, 1977)

This holding treatment breaks down those paths of resistance and allows the unattached child to reach painful hidden emotions. Once these emotions are released the child can go on to attach to other human beings and experience the joy of life.

The Treatment Structure

In Rage Reduction Therapy total control is accomplished by asking the patient to lie down between two rows of trained body holders. The positioning is important. Generally it includes 2 to 4 adults who sit on a couch with pillows on their laps. The same number of people sit across from them on chairs. (For very small children, the therapist may act alone.) The patient then stretches out on their laps, with his head on a pillow cradled by the therapist. This positioning reconstructs the face-to-face position of an infant and mother when attachment normally occurs.

The therapist must orchestrate the session with the precision of a surgeon. The session may last up to 8 hours. With the child's head lying in his lap, the therapist controls resistant responses and provokes rage reactions by stimulating the patient's rib cage with his fingers. The motion is similar to when one teases and tickles another person. At first the motion tickles the patient but soon it becomes irritating, much as it does when someone is tickling you and won't stop. As the irritation builds the therapist talks and shouts along with the child, drawing out the rage inside. The anger begins to surface as the patient struggles with giving up controlling behavior. Eventually reasonable behavior starts to emerge, as the child surrenders to the control of the therapist. But this state can only be reached if the therapy is correctly administered.

The previously uncontrollable child is restrained by the body holders so that he cannot get away from the therapist's treatment. They also gently keep the child from hurting himself or others.

Such children hate this control and resist by squirming, raging and generally being resistant. One mother talks about her unattached son and his reaction to the therapy: ". . . He began doubling up into angry contortions. Within seconds, he was [like] a baby, red and furious, flailing and convulsing with frantic baby rage." (Cline, 1979, p. 192)

It is during times of tenseness or movement that the body holders are able to relay even the slightest twitch or jerk to the therapist. This tells whether the patient is resisting, no matter how slight the signs might be. All the time, the therapist interacts in a close face-to-face way. He alternates between confronting the child and then supporting him when he shows positive efforts.

The first major confrontation in the therapy revolves around who is the "boss." No matter how distasteful, it soon becomes obvious to anyone that, with 4 or more people physically holding him, all directed by a therapist, that the therapist is in charge of the situation. But an unattached child cannot imagine that anyone can have control over him and he may blindly insist that he's in charge. His history of negativism, lack of trust and always being in control makes it difficult for him to be vulnerable.

" . . . During the session I actually feel like killing the people that are there. During the session I also feel like the people are actually trying to hurt me . . . But I know it is helping me get my

head on straight. It has helped a lot," says one previously
unattached child following treatment. (Cline, 1979, p. 190)

Resolving the "who is boss" issue is primary. It helps the therapist
understand the depth of the child's illness; its goal is to help the patient
figure out when he has been a "good" boss or a "bad" boss of himself or
others. The more resistance displayed by the unattached child, the greater
his mental disturbance. Working through these resistances, Zaslow believes,
is the only way to health.

When the patient resists giving appropriate responses by hesitating or not
speaking loudly enough the therapist stimulates the rib cage and insists on a
more correct response. For extreme resistances, he may direct the patient
to "kick your legs until you're ready to give me another response." This
maintains control by the therapist and reduces the need for rib cage
stimulation. (A word of caution: Parents should *never* attempt to stimulate a
child in such a manner since it can cause severe trauma if not done
properly.)

During the therapy unattached children typically resist by offering
evasive or vague answers, such as pretending not to know "What comes
after 4?" or not answering when the therapist asks "How do you feel about
me being boss?"

While the child gets continually more agitated and angry the therapist
maintains his cool; he is understanding, light-hearted and even humorous.

"That's a pretty good kick, but if you were kicking someone
you didn't like I'll bet you could do it even better."

A good therapist is a "good boss" for the patient and is fair and sensitive in
helping the patient resolve his deepest problems. Some resistances take the
form of "motor overflow" which simply means the child refuses to answer
questions by sticking out his tongue, closing his eyes, coughing, blinking or
looking away.

A skilled therapist must be able to detect other areas of resistance and
insist on correct responses. If bodily resistances are picked up by the
holders, the therapist requires the patient to make the correct face-to-face
response in a natural way until the body and face responses balance.

For example, the child may be required to maintain good eye contact and
the therapist will then check with the body holders to see if they detect any
tension. If they do, the therapist will continue to work with the child so his
facial expressions and body language match. This balance is extremely
important to maintain. It rarely occurs until the patient is so highly aroused
that he has no control over what his body is doing. This sets the stage for the
full orchestration of rage reduction. It is here, usually an hour or more into
the session, that the most dynamic and important confrontations occur.

The process has been likened to an exorcism in which the child enters with the devil inside him and then emerges at the end of the therapy as a loving, tender and responsive individual.

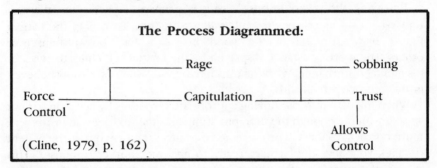

The Process Diagrammed:

Rage ————— Sobbing

Force —————— Capitulation —————— Trust
Control

Allows
Control

(Cline, 1979, p. 162)

The goal of the therapist at this juncture is to explore the family history of the patient and his attitudes about rejection, sexual identity, and male and female authority figures.

The therapist, for example, will bring to the surface the hate the child has deep inside but cannot express and the reasons for that hate. It may be that the child was physically abandoned as an infant or that he suffered some unknown physical pain. Out of this grew his aloneness and lack of attachment. These issues must be addressed and the confusion of love versus hate (especially concerning the patient's mother) must be confronted.

In this controlled, loving situation the unattached, untrusting child can explode into a more primordial rage and hate. This rage appropriately frightens most untrained observers, because they are uncomfortable when the child becomes violent, or they fear that he will go insane. Emotions run high.

A typical session with a severly disturbed child might have the child, for example, reacting with tremendous resistance, struggling and fighting for long periods of time.

> When asked questions the girl refuses, twisting her head from side to side and trying to bite, punch and kick the holders. When asked, "What is your name?" or "How old are you?" the child just keeps repeating "I won't say it. I won't say it. I can't say it. I refuse to say it." This child clearly understands the questions, but is refusing to answer them. When she does finally answer the therapist it is between deep sobs; she has finally relinquished control. She now knows who the boss is.

Rage reduction, then, allows pent up feelings to surface under controlled conditions so the patient can deal with them once and for all. This reduces the ever-simmering suffering and psychological pain locked deep within. One parent describes the experience:

> "If I didn't see it with my own eyes I wouldn't have believed it. First there was this ungodly rage when his whole body tensed up and he screamed that he hated me and admitted that he prayed to the devil. I was scared but after he got it out he said he really hated himself and he started crying and sobbing uncontrollably. That was when I held him. I really held him for the first time in my life. It was like he could trust me to hold him."

Because the child has juxtaposed love and hate, where he hates the things most of us cherish (caring and God) and loves the things we loathe (killing, manipulation and evil), a fascination with gore and the devil often comes out in the sessions. These children want to align with a powerful ally since they feel weak and helpless, and the concept of witchcraft and the devil fits perfectly.

It is important to remember that the therapist leads the child into expressing his deepest rage and sadness about being unattached:

> "Why are you mad at your birth mom?" the therapist asks.
> "Because she left me," the child screams.

This is when the skillful therapist supports and cradles the sobbing child and says, "Thanks for letting that out. You're a beautiful person when you tell the truth."

The resolution toward the end of the session is often extremely emotional; after the "break through" the child is sobbing and exhausted. Parents often cry with their child. One parent spontaneously began singing a little song with her daughter — a song she had remembered singing with her mother when she was small.

After many hours of lie-down therapy the severely unattached child is ready to undergo the reattachment process with a loving parent or caregiver who looks the teary-eyed child in the face and hears this previously uncontrollable child plead, usually for the first time, "I want you to love me. Please love me."

> "When I heard my child say those words I cried," one parent says. "All I could do was hug him and cry out loud, 'Oh, yes, yes, I will love you. By God you can count on it.' "

The new attachment process has started. By this time, the child is in the last stage of the session; all of his controlling mannerisms and resistance have given way to cooperation and comfortable give-and-take talk.

The therapist now summarizes the session for parent and child and asks the child how his behavior now compares with that before the session. The therapist will confirm with the body holders that the patient's body is finally relaxed. "Do you all think this person is acting more loveable now?" he will ask. The group will shout their resounding support of the child's progress.

More than one session is needed and the therapist will set up specific tasks for the child between sessions, such as, "You agree to not play with matches," or "You will not threaten anyone."

Parents are counseled to ensure that they know in what age-appropriate ways the child can express normal anger so he won't have to repress his feelings or resort to manipulation. Finally, the therapist will ask the child if he feels close to the group and is ready to try some new behaviors.

Followup is essential for success. What has been established in the first session must be reinforced and new or unresolved pathologies must be addressed.

Three or four lie-down sessions of 2 to 4 hours each may be required for an unattached child, all occuring within a two-week period. Cline suggests that it is critical to have at least one follow-up session within a week. The sessions become less intense as time goes on and gradually the child does not require restraints or stimulation. Often follow-up sessions will find the child being held in the therapist's lap as they engage in conversation about problems and progress. Then the patient can be seen on a weekly, bi-weekly or monthly schedule. Later sessions center more on nurturing and establishing healthy cause-and-effect thinking and autonomy.

"Little did she know that inside young Jeremy's head the wheels were already turning and a script was being written that would make his life and the lives of all those he came in contact with pure hell."

18

Jeremy: An Abbreviated Case History

Jeremy has no conscious memory of the painful events that occurred when he was 11 weeks old, although bringing those events to a conscious level and dealing with the rage inside is the primary task of his therapist. His birth mother, Sharon, was 16 when she put Jeremy up for adoption. Little is known about her except that she changed her mind about wanting to raise a child by herself.

Jeremy was bureaucratically bounced around for 37 days before being placed with Ruth and her husband, his new adoptive parents. But this loving home couldn't relieve the pain already inside this infant's head. Ruth couldn't understand why Jeremy couldn't cuddle and didn't even cry much. She thought it was just an insignificant personality quirk.

Already burned indelibly on this baby's brain was the pain of feeling helpless and hopeless and totally alone at a critical time. When he had clumsily stretched out his little arms and cried for a loving embrace no one was there. His cries received no answer, no nurturing, no smiles. So this baby shut down—to protect himself from further vulnerability.

Jeremy wasn't attached. He didn't have a good model or internalized parent figure that was stabilized in the first few months of life. As a younger child he didn't have the physical capacity to do as much damage to others as he does at 13. He is mad at the world and sticks stubbornly to the belief that he can't trust anyone and that he must always be in control.

When Is It Too Late?

In terms of difficulty, Jeremy can be classified as moderately to highly unattached. The attachment scale varies with the child's symptoms, depending on how he has been impacted by a complex number of known and unknown factors. Among these are genetic predispositions, the degree of bonding break and certain environmental frustrations.

It is generally an accepted maxim that the younger the child the easier reattachment can be. Many therapists believe it is never too late to help an unattached child, but most throw in the towel when confronted with an adult psychopath. Then the issue, unfortunately, becomes more one of control and incarceration than of treatment and rehabilitation.

Foster Cline had serious reservations about taking Jeremy's case. The diagnosis was clear that he was unattached, but there were serious aggravating circumstances. First, his age was above the typical cut off for favorable outcomes. The habits and resistances become so ingrained that anyone over 7 years old with serious problems can be extremely difficult to treat.

A therapist who has worked with Cline says, "Any true vicious psychopath over 16 might as well be warehoused for life because it's just too late. The clay has hardened."

Also working against Jeremy was the fact that his adoptive father was probably a psychopath; he had deserted the family four years earlier leaving Ruth to raise Jeremy and his 8-year-old sister Jean alone.

Cline had agreed to take on Jeremy because he felt sorry for Ruth. He knew that she didn't have much money. And, although his practice was already full, he managed to make time for this special case.

It should be noted that—while Cline's holding therapy has not been without controversy because of its radical new approach — Foster Cline, the man, has been beyond reproach. He is one of the most generous and kind persons the authors have met.

Cline tells a funny tale about childhood mischievousness. When he was a youngster he wanted to surprise his father by painting the family car. He painted the car, the bumpers, the headlights, everything, with jet black paint. And yes, his father, who was Denver, Colorado's district attorney, was quite surprised.

But acting out was the exception for Cline as a child; he now is a leader in his church and "friend" to everyone who knows him. It is probably fitting that this gentle man who seldom gets angry at anyone is now the world's foremost practitioner of Rage Reduction Therapy, helping troubled children to find inner peace and joy.

Cline instinctively knew that Ruth would stand by this difficult child. After the proper consent forms were obtained the procedure was explained to Jeremy, who agreed to undergo treatment. Six experienced body holders were in the room. The three-and-one-half-hour session is explained here. It follows the Rage Reduction model previously described.

Abbreviated Content	Therapeutic Process
Cline: O.K. Jeremy, are you pretty comfortable?	Concern for client's welfare and establishment of fair boss.
Jeremy: Yeah.	
Cline: Well, pal, let's get started. I'm up here on top of you and you're on the bottom and you're being held with your permission by 6 people so who is boss right now?	Phase one: Establish control — "Who's boss issue."
Jeremy: I am (closes eyes).	Egocentric denial of reality and major resistance.
Cline: How interesting you should see things that way. Let's see if you are boss. Try and get up now.	Encouraging patient to check reality.
Jeremy: (Struggles to no avail).	Resistance to controls.
Cline: Is that the best you can do? My grandmother could struggle better than that. Let's see some real effort.	Directing patient to resist and thereby being boss.
Jeremy: Get off me, you bastard (struggling).	Patient testing the controls and trying to establish dominance.

Cline:	An order, you are giving me an order. Who is boss here anyway—you or me? (Light stimulations with finger to rib cage as if lightly strumming—not poking—a guitar, to encourage non-controlling response.)	Correcting patient's role and establishing first major issue to work through.
Jeremy:	(Screaming & struggling) Get off me you jerk!	Patient's anger rising as reality of boss issue becomes more apparent.
Cline:	That's a pretty good yell and for sure we are going to talk about who has been acting like a jerk but that's not the correct answer to my question. Who is boss right now? (more light stimulation to ribs)	Taking control over patient's resistance by directing him to yell more, while correcting his name-calling and directing him back to the issue.
Jeremy:	You are (eyes closed).	Eye-closing resistance.
Cline:	(Stops stimulation) That's the correct words pal, but I want you to look straight at me and say that.	Supporting client while clarifying how therapist wants future responses.
	For the next half-hour Jeremy continues his resistence by coughing, blinking, and looking away from the therapist's eyes. Finally, he acknowledges the first issue.	Eye-to eye connection is critical for untrusting, unattached children. Super resistance and patient control.
Jeremy:	You're the boss (with eye contact and correct speech).	Patient works through initial reservations on issue #1, "who's boss."

Cline:	For sure, pal, I am going to be your boss and be in control so you can learn to be a better what of yourself?	Reaffirming helping role and posing easy therapeutic question.
Jeremy:	A better boss of myself.	Patient's agreement.
Cline:	Now how do you like me being boss?	Confronting patient's controlling.
Jeremy:	(Looking away and mumbling incomplete sentence) Hate it.	Control and resistance.
Cline:	(Rib stimulation and raised voice) I want to hear how much you hate it in a loud and clear voice. Have you got it?	Encouraging patient to let rage out that's deep inside.
Jeremy:	Got it.	Acknowledging doctor as boss.
Cline:	O.K. Good, now go (stops stimulation).	Supportive and directive.
Jeremy:	I hate it when you're boss (normal tone).	
Cline:	I want to really hear it from your guts, unless you're afraid to tell me.	Challenging client to express feelings.
Jeremy:	I hate you being boss (screaming).	Getting into rage.
Cline:	And how are you feeling about me right now? (loud voice and directive control with hand on rib cage but not stimulating).	

Jeremy:	(Screaming) I hate you, I hate you, I hate you.	Primal rage surfacing.
Cline:	(Loud explanation) Good eye contact Jeremy. Now how much do you go around hating?	Supportive of cartharsis or release and going deeper into self-hate.
Jeremy:	(Screaming, then sobbing) I hate all the time, I hate all the time.	Breaking through resistance to deal with negative life script.
Cline:	(Compassionately holding head and wiping away tears) I know you do, pal, and who ends up suffering?	Supportive and still focusing on major life lessons.
Jeremy:	(Sobbing) I do.	Acknowledgment and sadness.
Cline:	For sure, and who do you think can change that?	
Jeremy:	Me (with questioning tone).	Easy therapeutic question designed to educate and support patient.
Cline:	You betcha. But you've got to believe in yourself. Say, "If anyone can change it I can."	
Jeremy:	If anyone can change it I can (said with confidence).	
Cline:	Great. Now do you think you deserve a 10-minute break to stretch your legs?	Break ends on positive resolution.
	Jeremy has a drink and goes to the bathroom and then is back in position.	Phase II, dealing with specific issues.

Cline:	Now that we are back, let's see if you remember who is boss.	
Jeremy:	You are boss.	First issue resolved.
Cline:	That's right. Now tell me about the missing money in your home (Jeremy has been caught repeatedly stealing from his family, as well as shoplifting).	Specific issue, confrontation with common symptom of unattached child.
Jeremy:	I don't know? (eyes looking away)	Denial and resistance.
Cline:	Well, it's time to make a snappy guess. Got it? (hand on rib cage)	If client isn't willing to guess, then we know he's being more resistant since we aren't asking for knowledge or facts yet.
Jeremy:	Got it.	
Cline:	Good, now go.	
Jeremy:	I borrowed some money once (blinking).	Client evasive and untruthful.
	Cline spends the next half-hour breaking down the client's resistances to being honest about facts and feelings concerning his stealing, lying, and controlling behavior. Jeremy's mother verifies accuracy of retold incidents.	Working through resistance on major issues in past.
Cline:	Now, tell about playing with fire.	Therapist centers on major issue and gives client chance to be open.

Jeremy:	I don't know what you mean (left arm twitches and body holders tell Cline).	Non-verbal resistance accompanies lie.
Cline:	Kick your feet until you're ready to answer my question straight and say "ready".	Feet kicking is an alternative technique to rib stimulation. Allows resistant clients another way to express anger in a controlled way.
Jeremy:	(After a couple of minutes of kicking) Ready.	Child has let out some body tension by kicking and is now ready to talk.
Cline:	O.K. Go.	
Jeremy:	I started a fire in the school (an obvious fact since he was caught red-handed).	
Cline:	And why did you do it? (Stimulation of ribs)	Focusing on deeper issue of hate and destruction.
Jeremy:	I wanted to see those teachers burn. (Soft voice and dead cold stare with smirk on face).	Common homicidal desires of unattached children toward anyone who has authority.
Cline:	(Loud commanding voice) Say it loud, Jeremy, and look me in the eyes.	Bringing rage reaction to the surface.
Jeremy:	(Screaming) I wanted to see those teachers burn in hell. (Eyes slanted together and cold).	Beginning identification with devil.
Cline:	(Shouting) And who lives in hell that you know?	Facilitating deeper personal disclosure.
Jeremy:	The devil (soft and sure).	Checking alliances.

Cline: And what do you say to the devil?

Jeremy: I pray to the devil that I can be his favorite child.

> Alliance with negative role model.

Cline: And when do you pray to him?

> Checking frequency.

Jeremy: Whenever I get into trouble.

Cline: What do you say?

> Checking content.

Jeremy: I say, please let me be your child and do your work.

Cline: Why do you do that?

> Checking motive.

Jeremy: 'Cause he gives me power to kill.

Cline: (To holders) Is he twitching?

> He's telling it like he believes it.

Holders: No.

Cline: So, if you can't be good you'll be . . .

> Confirming goal identification.

Jeremy: Bad. A bad-ass killer!

Cline: And is that what happened to your mother's cat? That you said accidentally died.

> Incorporating relevant home issue.

Jeremy: Yes, I choked it until it made a gurgling sound and its eyes rolled backward. It was easy.

> Jeremy has the same look adult psychopaths have just before they kill their victims.

Cline:	And who were you pretending it was that you were really choking?	Going deeper into psyche.
Jeremy:	(Silence).	
Cline:	(Shouting and rib stimulation) Who was it, Jeremy?	Pushing for the core rage reaction.
Jeremy:	My mother.	
Cline:	Say it louder. I wanted to kill my mother.	Admitting deep rage feelings.
Jeremy:	(Screaming) I wanted to kill my mother.	
Cline:	Say why you wanted to kill her.	
Jeremy:	'Cause I hate her for bossing me.	Control and vulnerability issue.
Cline:	Look at her and say it (Cline brings Ruth to Jeremy's head).	
Jeremy:	(Shouting) I hate you, I hate you, I hate you . . .(8 times)	Peak rage coming.
Cline:	Who else do you hate?	
Jeremy:	Sharon.	
Cline:	Is Sharon your birth mom?	
Jeremy:	Yes. I hate her for leaving me.	Cognitive pain and hate awareness.
Cline:	Let it all out now, son.	

Jeremy:	I hate her guts. (Screaming) I hate her so much (total body rigidity and screaming loudly for two and one half minutes, then crying).	Peak rage reaction.
Cline:	And who was there to love you?	Sadness and early rejection feelings.
Jeremy:	(Sobbing and crying, body not tense) Nobody, there was nobody.	
Cline:	And what is it you want more than anything.	
Jeremy:	(Sobbing and direct eye contact) Love, I want you to love me. Please love me.	Breakthrough and core issue of wanting love.
Cline:	(Gently holding Jeremy's head and making positive eye contact)Yes, pal, you have done super well. Ruth, come up here and hold your son's head and give him your answer.	Integrating mom for attachment.
Ruth:	(Crying) Oh yes, yes I will love you and you can count on it. (They embrace, his body is totally relaxed for several minutes).	Equilibrium and release.
Cline:	Now, my friend, we need to discuss how things are going to be different at home and at school. So if you'd like to sit up, I think you're ready.	New structure development.

Jeremy:	Yeah, I think I'm ready now too.	Client affirmation.
Cline:	How do you feel?	
Jeremy:	(Great eye contact and firm voice) Great.	
Cline:	(Arm around Jeremy) Fantastic job, kiddo.	Support and closure.

Following the session Cline went into detail with Ruth about what she should work on with Jeremy until the next session, which was scheduled for that week. After 4 lie-down sessions with Cline and follow-up education with Ruth, Jeremy began to work out many of his problems and became firmly attached to his mother. He soon was making friends at school for the first time in his life. As with all adolescents, there have been some rough spots, but as his mother says, "These have been regular teenage things. Jeremy is doing so well sometimes I just can't believe he is the same child."

Most children do not require such a severe treatment procedure. Character-disturbed children with lesser problems than Jeremy respond well to a modified holding technique. Cline uses this technique with some children, as does one of the pioneers of modified holding, professor John Allan. We explore his treatment in the next chapter.

"If Charles Manson had gotten holding treatment and successfully bonded when he was a little boy things would have turned out much differently . . ."   John Allan

19

Modified Holding Techniques

Not all character-disturbed children have an extreme degree of unattachment and resistance; they don't need full rage reduction holding. It is important not to use an atomic bomb when a simple rap on the knuckles works as well. A young child may simply sit in the lap of the therapist or even in a chair. These modified techniques involve mild confrontive interviewing, balanced with verbal support and face-to-face intervention. The therapist might simply point out when the child doesn't maintain eye contact or ask the child to repeat incorrect statements, and say whether he needs to be louder or less hesitant.

A good therapist is aware of normal childhood developmental stages, obviously, so he doesn't make everything a child says a "control battle." Children deserve some freedom and it would be disastrous to see any negative behavior of a child as justification for a rage session.

To one resistant child who wouldn't talk, Foster Cline said, "That's okay, I have other things to do and when you are ready to talk like a 5-year-old, then let me know. Meanwhile, I'll do some things I enjoy doing." After 20 minutes of silence the child said, "Whatcha doing?" and opened up. All techniques used with unattached children require structure and a guiding hand from the therapist or parent. (personal communication, February 14, 1986)

All children have deep feelings about themselves, even before they can talk. After they learn to talk they still have difficulty expressing their innermost emotions. Treatment with these children can be directed toward the body to help them identify, express and release these feelings. A skillful therapist, for example, can use sensitive touch to reduce the child's resistances. By using holding the therapist acts like a healthy parent figure and communicates to the child, "Your life is not going well and you are upset and I'm going to hold you until some things are worked out."

As we noted earlier, modified holding therapy has reached new heights

227

with the work of Allan who also studied with Zaslow. He places emphasis on releasing feelings through a combination of different holding techniques. Depending on the patient, he will hold for weeping, rage and anger, pleasure or play.

Allan may have as a goal to get the child to respond with smiles and thus promote tension reduction. This often involves fun tickling, swinging, cuddling, rocking, jumping and bouncing together. (Allan, 1986) He may, for example, imitate and echo the child's cries and screams, but in a friendly and playful way. This lets the child know that the therapist is there to have fun and that he isn't upset with the youngster. The child gets the message that he is safe and that spontaneity is okay.

One technique Allan has found particularly useful is holding for weeping; the child is encouraged to talk about how hard life has been on him. The sobbing that results can last up to an hour or more. The therapist then comforts the child. Allan describes what happened in a session with a 7-year-old autistic child who refused to speak normally:

> "Jane was the mother of Timmy. She had never allowed herself to cry in front of her child. Her only wish was to have her son talk in a complete sentence. Progress was slow and finally Jane couldn't hold back her tears any longer. As she cried openly in front of her young son he reached over and touched her cheek and said very clearly, "Tears for Tim.' " (Allan, 1986, p. 156)

Allan also uses children's drawings, as do many therapists. Besides giving the child a creative release, drawings provide a visual record of inner psychological conflicts. Progress can be judged by comparing past and present artwork. Allan sometimes combines dream analysis with drawings.

A 13-year-old boy was referred to Allan after he had killed his 9-year-old sister. He had kicked his sister hard in the stomach during a fight and she had died of a ruptured spleen. Billy knew all about being hit hard; his alcoholic father often beat him. The child's dreams after the death of his sister involved pictures of him riding alongside his sister's dead body. After months of therapy he drew a picture of a mummified monster who came up out of a swamp and lifted up a man as if to strangle him. In a dream Billy saw the monster put the man down and look directly at him.

"He looked me directly in the face, eye to eye, I knew this man was me. I could kill. I could kill my father for what he had done to me but I know I won't. My father has severe problems and needs help."

The dream signified Billy's acceptance of his own aggression and the resolution of a major problem. In follow-up the feelings of resolution continued and after therapy Billy adjusted well into society. He finished school and got a good job. (Allan, 1987, p. 8) (See drawing on page 182e.)

Sometimes drawings can be used as a catalyst for change. A cute 7 year-old-girl named Cathy was referred to Allan for severe depression and elective mutism. (Although she was physically capable of talking, Cathy had decided to remain silent.) It was found that Cathy's mother had suffered a severe case of postpartum depression following her daughter's birth. The doctor asked Cathy to draw a picture of a girl in a cage. After a week of modified holding, Cathy's spontaneity increased and she began drawing the girl out of the cage. It represented a new beginning for her. After additional treatments she began to talk. (Allan, 1987)

In another case, Allan was treating a bilingual child who refused to speak in English even though she was fluent. She would speak only in Japanese. With modified holding he got her to shout, "I do not want to speak in English." She said it in perfect English. (Allan, 1987, p. 7) Allan and Cline both prefer working with younger children (under age 7) and both encourage parental involvement. Therapy can range from a few sessions to 12 months or longer. Overall, the modified holding process is designed to help the child identify, understand and express deeply held feelings. Then the child and parents work on a plan for future happiness.

How Schools Help

School personnel are frequently brought into the process so they can work with the therapist and parents to recognize back-sliding and learn effective techniques to aid in the child's rehabilitation. The teacher, for example, might establish face-to-face contact and say, "Jimmy, you have said that you want to be a good boss of yourself and I will support you when you make good decisions. But disrupting other students in class goes against class rules. Now, would you like to handle this situation or would you prefer that I enforce a consequence?"

Further disruption by the child would result in a variety of consequences previously set up by the parents and therapist. This can take many forms, such as a simple "time-out" or a token system of points for privileges. In one example, the parent said to the child, "Your misbehaving tells me that you want attention and that you feel you aren't getting enough love. Therefore, if you need me to be closer to you then simply misbehave and I'll come sit next to you . . . on the school bus, in your classes, on the playground . . . whenever you need me." (Schaub, personal communications, February 23, 1987)

If the parent comes across to the child as loving and serious, and is prepared to follow through, the child saves embarrassment from his peers by not acting out in school.

Both Cline and Allan spend a great deal of time educating parents and teachers on the correct uses of this therapy. If the parents are properly instructed in how to communicate effectively with and touch their children, the reattachment treatments have a better chance of success.

A Word of Caution

All children have problems at some time in their lives. But not all children are so disturbed that they need holding therapy. Most have a conscience and a sense of right and wrong but from time to time have problems which can fall into the category of neurotic conflicts or adjustment disorders. It is imperative that appropriate diagnosis be made so proper treatment can be given. As one experienced therapist says, "If you get on the wrong train, you are likely to end up at the wrong station." (Schaub, personal communication, February, 1987)

Handled appropriately, these therapies have worked wonders. But they can backfire. Such was the case with Robert Zaslow, who was successfully sued in 1972 by one of his adult clients for a rage reduction session that didn't work. As a result, he lost his license to practice psychology in California. He now can reapply but he is getting older and has elected simply to teach the therapy he developed. Zaslow will probably be seen someday as a great pioneer who pushed back the frontiers for treating severely disturbed children.

For some it is not difficult to see how holding therapy could be controversial. Some uninitiated observers viewing this therapy for the first time might think holding a screaming child against his will is barbaric. Of course it is imperative that the therapist and support personnel be trained professionals and no child should ever be held by an angry adult. Absolutely no one should attempt such therapies without proper training. And all therapists should include parents in the room when the therapy is being conducted. Because of this, holding therapy is in many ways a family therapy. The child *and* parents are being treated as the therapist fosters better communication and interaction between them.

Family therapy is also offering new promise in dealing with Antisocial Personality Disorders, as we see in the next chapter.

"A happy family is but an earlier heaven."
Chinese Proverb

20

More Therapeutic Options

Family Therapy

 No one lives in a vacuum and in family therapy the pattern of family relationships in which a person exists is taken into account.

To be attached implies that you are attached to *something*. The family is the crucible in which we all learn the fundamental lessons in life. It is here we develop our basic strategies for getting love and affection. These must be compatible with those of other family members. If conflict is present the result is often frustration, anger and acting out.

The family therapist's job is to see the whole picture and how each person in the family is attempting to secure happiness. His job is also to see what is blocking this process. The goal of the family therapist is to look closely at family relationships and interrupt or change people's pathological behaviors, replacing them with new patterns that help the family achieve love.

Techniques to accomplish this goal are as varied as the therapist's imagination. The technique may be as simple as having a parent change how he talks to a child or it may involve wholesale role changes in the family.

Many family therapists rely on early pattern interruptions first tried by Milton Erickson. The idea is simple. You interrupt an existing unhealthy pattern of behavior for a more positive one, even if it causes a minor crisis in the family. If the family members rally around the crisis in a more healthy way then you've succeeded.

"Erickson is willing to induce crisis to bring about a change, but he is also more willing than most therapists to influence a small deviation and then build upon it until larger changes occur." (Haley, 1973, p. 35)

One popular technique with unattached children is called the double-bind. In this therapy the child is forced to choose a correct response. For example, when the parents of a 10-year-old child would confront him about

231

bed wetting, as well as urinating in his clothes, the child would hang his head and mumble that it was an accident. Actually, there was no organic problem; the child was angry at his parents. In a double-bind, the child would be told:

> "You know, most smart kids who get mad say so with their mouth, not by peeing in their pants. Now, if you were mad at me right now, what would you do?"

Because it is difficult to have an "accident" in front of the parents, the child is stuck in a double-bind. He can then be rewarded for the correct response.

Another family technique involves the parents restructuring the hierarchy of the family power. This means who tells who what to do. In this therapy the family's concern is refocused on how the child is trying to help the family avoid loss. The theory here, advanced by Cloe Madanes and Jay Haley, is that if the child behaves normally he loses the power that his acting out gives him over his parents. The child's misdirected actions focus the parents' concerns on the child rather than on their own overwhelming personal, social or economic dilemmas. (Madanes, 1984)

In one family situation a little girl had escalated her own acting out, including feigning illness, because she had heard her father say to her mother, "As soon as we settle Janey's problems I want a divorce." The therapist needed to help restore the balance in this family so that the child didn't try to protect her parents in an unhealthy way. (Shaub, personal communication, February 23, 1986)

Other new therapies focus on body awareness.

In the work of former Erickson student Richard Shane breathing and body language are being used to indicate a client's condition. This therapy, known as Integral Therapy, is based on the belief that unattached children who continue to detach from bodily experience are at high risk of becoming adults who chronically separate from their bodies and innermost feelings. Psychopaths are known to be extremely detached from their feelings and can resist normal pain. (1986)

In this therapy the theory is that cold hearts need consistent warmth and love, not anger and punishment. The by-word with this therapy is patience but some therapists feel this technique is severely limited when you are working with violent, uncontrollable psychopaths.

All therapeutic changing of human behavior involves caring for the patients' welfare, but nowhere is that caring more evident than in spiritual therapy.

Spiritual Therapy

Clearly the issue with criminal psychopaths is how to alter man's inhumanity to man. And the prison preacher has been around as long as the prison. Although many such preachers have been successful, the average psychopath is not interested in religion unless there is a strong motivation — such as early release — to seek out this avenue. Others may gravitate toward the church because they see an opportunity to gain power, manipulate others or pass the plate for their private feast.

Some of the worst demigods in America today may be found in the pulpit, leading their sheep into temptation and delivering them into evil. (Schreibman, personal communication, July 8, 1986)

But a few bad apples who are living a lie shouldn't detract from the fact that religious education and conversion have accounted for some of the most significant human changes. Trying to talk a psychopath out of his evil ways is like trying to fill a long-neck bottle by throwing a bucket of water over it. But a true religious experience has been known to go beyond words. The spiritual message of love and redemption is emotionally charged and often experienced in an unforgettable manner. When this spiritual therapy works, the psychopath has become "attached" to God.

Some psychopaths have been known to be converted through religious experiences and this path has looked appealing to some who are incarcerated or at the end of their ropes, whether they be children, adolescents or adults. Spiritual therapy is not new, nor is it limited to the U.S. In Japan a treatment called Naikon Therapy is modeled after ancient Buddhism. (Buddhist priests go into caves and meditate after long periods of time on love and self discipline until they experience Satori— enlightenment.)

In Naikon Therapy a patient is told to sit alone and reflect on his past each day from 5 a.m. to 9 p.m. His only diversions are eating and going to the bathroom. The therapist comes in to assign specific tasks and listen to confessions. The tasks all revolve around three themes: what was received from others, what was returned to them and what troubles were caused to them.

Naikon forces the patient to prosecute himself like an attorney might and own up to his past errors. This resembles the Catholic process of examining one's conscience and making confession.

After days of reflection the patient usually breaks down and cries when he realizes how others have loved him in spite of his selfishness. The patient is then assigned the task of amending past wrongs so future actions can be positive. Often a patient records his thoughts for later playback to therapists or in group sessions.

Because it is ideally suited for those who are incarcerated, Naikon Therapy has been frequently used in the Japanese prison system and in juvenile detention centers. (Reynolds, personal communication, 1981)

Dr. Stanton Samenow, author of *Inside the Criminal Mind*, uses a similar approach when treating psychopaths, including extensive note-taking and tape recordings, to readjust faulty thinking and promote morality.

Moral message therapies have a place in working with psychopaths, but control over the daily actions of the patient is essential. Another program for those with APD is performed, paradoxically, in an environment with no walls or fences . . . just wilderness.

Wilderness Therapy

Eighty feet off the ground, she grabs for a trapeze swinging toward her. But as her fingers reach for the bar she miscalculates the distance and misses. With a terrified look on her face she plummets toward the ground. At the same instant, a safety rope attached to her harness catches, preventing the fall. As the crowd below roars with glee she is gently lowered to the earth.

Applause is her reward for the courage to leave the security of the platform and trust those around her. The therapist expands on this trust as he talks later with her and the other adolescents in this program about self-confidence, support and separation.

Experiential or Wilderness Therapy gives troubled youths a chance to test themselves against the elements and learn about their inner feelings in a totally new environment. Usually two therapists accompany up to 8 children into a wilderness setting. The group of teenagers and counselors are together 24 hours a day, 7 days a week for up to 3 weeks.

The challenges are rigorous but not overwhelming as children are singled out to build skills. At the Santa Fe Mountain Center in New Mexico, for example, activities include white water rafting, rock climbing, canyoneering and cave exploration. Experiences are choreographed so each youth is challenged to learn self-discipline, commitment to action, trust and caring for others and responsibility. When a child forgets to put up a shelter he suffers the natural consequences of sleeping outside. These adolescents learn you can't con Mother Nature.

The group goes over the day's trials each night. Dr. William H. Reid, editor of the book *Unmasking the Psychopath,* says the "wilderness programs offer the most help I have seen for treating severely disturbed youths, including those with APD." (personal communication, December, 1986)

One adolescent talks about his experience on a trip into the mountains near Santa Fe:

> "When this trip starts . . . you despise the weight of the pack, curse every rock, and every dirt mound, condemn every speck of dust, spit at every dirty mud puddle and snarl at every ridge. You will want to hang, tar and feather and burn every . . . around you; you will cringe and smirk at every bug and spider you see, you will hate the sun and love the cold, and you will hate the cold and love the sun, you will resent your very existence and you will suffer every aching pain in your body over and over again. You will push yourself and be pushed both mentally and physically further than you've ever imagined possible, you will endure the seemingly unendurable . . . you will think back over these things, all of them, and you will feel this incredible surge of power over yourself, and all of those things will add up to the most fantastic and cherished adventurous memory you will ever know.
>
> "You will find the people you did not trust, the same people you wanted to destroy, crush and mangle, are just the same as you are; flesh and bone vulnerable and human. Just people . . . it's not happening to you alone; just like when the group watched your back and protected you as you went down that cliff, so shall the groups be in harmony on thought . . . This is the meaning of the wilderness experience." (Kimball, 1986, pp. 27-31)

All of the therapies discussed in this chapter are meant to deal with the character-disturbed child or psychopath within a controlled environment, whether that environment be the family or a clinic or the wilderness. In the last chapter on therapies we will discuss the most controlled therapeutic environment of all — the locked hospital wards.

"It is the very error of the moon;
She comes more near the earth than
she was wont,
And makes men mad."
                                    Shakespeare

21

Hospital Treatment

No one wants to go to a mental health hospital.

This sentiment is shared by more than just Trust Bandits. But Trust Bandits particularly do not think they are sick and find it hard to swallow anything they don't like, including hospital rules.

But this superstructured environment is just what the Trust Bandit needs. Without locked wards the typical psychopath will take a hike as soon as he is confronted about his behavior. Court orders usually are necessary to keep patients in treatment and involuntary containment protects not only the patients but also the public. (Reid, 1985)

A patient such as this usually goes into the institution because he has not followed society's rules. The first treatment goal is to help him gain control over violent, destructive actions so therapy can begin. (Selman, 1986)

Setting firm limits is essential to bring in check extreme acting out behaviors and feelings of omnipotence many patients often exhibit. (Selman, 1986) Why should hospitalization even be considered for psychopaths? Dr. James P. Frosch explains, "There is a consensus that outpatient therapy is of little benefit no matter what the approach. The antisocial personality rarely volunteers for treatment, and even more rarely sticks with it . . . which leaves the therapist feeling as if he is riding a dangerous roller coaster." (1983, p.244)

Behind Closed Doors

Treatment programs in hospitals are using virtually everything but the kitchen sink to work with APD patients. Generally a combination of individual and group psychotherapy, family and activity therapy, behavior modification, cognitive and psychodynamic, and extensive drug therapy are used.

Dr. William Shamblin says a strong advantage of hospitalization is that a full psychiatric, medical, neurological and educational evaluation is available for each patient. (1986, p. 216)

As we pointed out earlier, however, hospital programs—particularly those based on behavior modification—do not seem to have lasting results with Trust Bandits once they are released into the general population.

The goals for many of these programs, particularly with adolescents, are to have the patients take more after-care responsibility for their actions, improve their self-esteem, control their anger and drug use and say no to negative peer pressure. Behavioral systems of rewards and consequences are set up. Family members are often included in the treatment plans. The idea is to provide a forum for family discussions and open expressions of fear, anger, resentment, support and hope for the future.

Because families often overprotect their children or minimize their problems, hospital personnel may focus on bringing this out into the open and help the family to set limits. If the staff can confront the youth's criminal thinking the theory is that the criminal behavior can be changed. One technique has the patient monitor his thoughts throughout the day, writing them down in a journal. This is similar to the previously described Naikon Therapy. Samenow writes in *Inside the Criminal Mind:*

> "First Leroy had to be taught to stop and recollect what he had thought, then to make notes on paper. He was instructed to think of this exercise as though a tape recorder of his thinking were being played back. The reason for the emphasis on thinking is today his thoughts contain the seed of tomorrow's crime."
> (1985, p. 219)

Daily hospital sessions on new, more positive and socially acceptable thinking are extended on an outpatient basis long after the patient is discharged.

Other in-hospital treatment programs have included the use of videotapes for self-examination, team activities to encourage cooperation and even art therapy to explore thoughts and feelings. (Potts et al. 1986) In a hospital setting basic problems can be attacked; the sharp differences between the thinking processes of a Trust Bandit can be contrasted with those of healthy individuals.

All of these concepts operate within what Dr. Maxwell Jones in 1947 called the "therapeutic community." (p.30) Since then, they have been widely used throughout the world in the continuing effort to treat and rehabilitate Trust Bandits. Variations on the hospital themes are used in prisons. In Germany, for example, a special youth prison attempts to rehabilitate youths from the ages of 15 to 21. The Sommerberg House near Koln is special because it utilizes an extensive treatment plan of individual, group, community and occupational therapy. (Silfen, 1983)

The St. Elsewhere Syndrome

If a patient has received treatment which hasn't really helped and the physician is publically asked where the patient was last treated, the doctor might say, "Elsewhere." These "elsewhere" patients can go from hospital to hospital and never really get better. In urban areas, indigent patients—those who cannot pay for medical care and are unwanted by private for-profit facilities—end up at overcrowded public hospitals. These hospitals may be ill-suited to meet the patient's particular medical needs.

A similar fate befalls many psychopaths entering the treatment system. Psychiatric hospitals accepting Trust Bandits often do so because they are legally required to take them in.

Agreeing to treat Trust Bandits and successfully treating them are two entirely different things. Few patients are as difficult. In too many cases, hospitals and staffs try their best, but see no real improvement. Most hospitals couldn't help Trust Bandits even if they wanted to. "The general psychiatric hospital is an inappropriate milieu for definitive treatment of antisocial syndrome," says Reid. (1985, p. 835) Reid suggests that specialized units or hospitals, such as Patuxent Institution in Maryland and a very few others, are sometimes able to establish programs better designed to handle APD patients.

The Patuxent Institution is unique in that it is a therapeutic prison designed to hold up to 500 serious offenders. It was established to act as both a maximum security prison and a mental hospital. But despite well-intentioned plans, the institution became the focus of controversy in 1975 because of several factors. Patients were admitted for an indeterminate time and in the first 18 years only 135 had been considered sufficiently "cured" to be released. There were accusations of guard brutality and overuse of such things as solitary confinement. The enforced treatment policy was thought to be inconsistent with good therapeutic purposes. In 1977 a law ended indeterminate sentencing and provided that those serving at Patuxent now do so of their own free will. (Coleman, et al., 1980) The success of this unique experiment still is not known; only time and a reduced recidivism rate on the part of released psychopathic prisoners will tell. Unfortunately these sorts of programs are expensive and few and far between.

*****

Despite the occasional heart-felt promise to change, the psychopath continues to frustrate clinicians' best efforts. When they've tried everything they can, therapists are faced with two choices: release the patient or refer him "elsewhere." Neither alternative is a cure for this most desolate of human ailments.

These are the patients without a conscience who no one wants and they put everyone else in society at high risk.

Whether they are character-disturbed children or adult psychopaths, their suffering and pain affects all they touch. And, as we have shown, the treatments are still experimental and frequently ineffectual unless these individuals are helped at an early age. Drastic interventions such as Rage Reduction Therapy have resulted in a reasonable cure rate, but only when used at a very young age on character-disturbed children. The outlook for adult psychopaths and any lasting "cure" is bleak indeed.

Prevention is still the best solution for the disastrous AIDS of the mental health field. In the next section we take a look at the social and personal predictors of unattachment. We do not have all the answers to these pressing social problems, but we will make some suggestions which might lead us down a better path.

We have talked about crime and looked directly into the face of the psychopath. We have shown how those with APD get that way and some treatments, including the state-of-the-art therapies. Now we hope to provide parents and future parents with some practical guidelines and suggestions for preventing America's most dangerous and pressing problem.

V

PREVENTING CHILDREN WITHOUT A CONSCIENCE

Toward Solutions

 The problem we have been discussing is so complex because it runs through the entire thread of our society. Americans are scared and they want answers to the violence they don't fully understand.

Working mothers want to know how to balance a career and a family so neither will be slighted. They want to know how to decide whether their child should go to day care, and how to pick a center or a sitter who will not put their child at high risk.

Teachers want to know how to deal with troubled students who disrupt others and nurture violence and evil in the classroom.

Divorcing fathers want help in keeping the attachments they have formed with their children after the separation. And family court judges want and need guidelines for ruling in the best interest of the children when visitation proposals and other divorce issues come before them for decisions.

Employers want to be able to recognize potential employees with APD before money is stolen or careers are ruined.

And single adults want to know how to recognize, and avoid dating, Trust Bandits who will steal their hearts and sometimes put them in physical danger.

The list of questions goes on. Americans want sensible advice about how to protect themselves and prevent guiltless and loveless people from coming into this world.

We will attempt to unravel this confusion one step at a time, giving specific answers to each issue, and suggesting an overall framework for addressing the problems of children without a conscience. Our approach will be educational. We have tried to leave no question unexplored in our presentation of this issue, knowing that describing this phenomenon would be much easier than coming up with answers. The advice of the ancient Talmud Code rings true even today:

The existence of a question doesn't presuppose the equal existence of an answer.

As we examined research and clinical case studies, we began to take the puzzle of antisocial personality syndrome apart. But wisdom comes from putting this puzzle back together.

We will first take a look at what today's parents can do about unattached children. Then we will move into what tomorrow's parents can do.

23

Positive Parenting Practices

Never in the history of mankind has raising children been
more of a challenge than in today's fragmented society. With
more working parents, more divorces and more step-families,
nothing seems constant except change. Families in the '80s are either
multiplying or dividing.

Most parents, despite their situation, try to administer love and discipline
and with unattached children they find neither approach works very well.
Countless control battles mark their relationships with their children and
frustrated parents can end up by giving up.

When a parent gives up on a child, other "parents" sometimes take over,
whether this be school teachers or the police.

When control becomes the main issue, love has taken a back seat. As we
noted in the treatment section, the older a child the more intractable the
problem. Cline notes, "For every dollar we spend on seriously troubled
adults, we get a nickel back. For every dollar we spend on seriously troubled
adolescents, we get 50 cents back. For every nickel we spend on seriously
disturbed infants, we get a dollar back." (personal communication, March,
1986)

Our national spotlight should clearly be on the crib — not on the criminal
— if we are to change the future. Infants who do not receive a warm
welcome into the world will seek their revenge.

In an 1987 *Psychology Today* cover story, senior editor Robert Trotter
writes " . . . children who experience disturbed interaction patterns during
infancy still have similar problems or are having language development and
behavioral problems at 2 years of age." (p. 27) The article addresses a baby's
amazing ability to imitate and learn. It profiles the work of Dr. Tiffany Field,
a neo-natal expert at the Mailman Center for Child Development in Miami,
Florida. "If you don't develop relatively harmonious interaction patterns
early in life, you are going to have difficulty with peer relations and in social

situations. We know that kids who have disturbed peer interactions are the ones most likely also to be delinquent or psychologically disturbed," says Field. (1987, p. 27)

What is truly amazing is that negative patterns have been found to start even before birth! Any difficulty during the pregnancy, either perceived or real, that causes the mother negative stress can impact her fetus. Field says extremely high anxiety in mothers can "contribute to hyperactivity and irritability in a newborn infant." (1987, p. 28) The problem has been found to go beyond psychological dimensions. "Pregnancy anxiety has been linked with cranio-facial anomalies, such as cleft palate and hairlip," says Field. (1987, p. 29) This has been proven in experiments with rats exposed to stress during pregnancy. Prenatal care and precaution, therefore, promotes healthy infants.

As we continually learn about the fetus and the newborn infant some provocative facts are emerging. The old view of a newborn was that he was a helpless, half-blind blob of wiggling protoplasm that couldn't really do anything. But Field says newborns who have spent as little as four hours out of the womb can recognize their mothers' faces. (1987, p. 31) Although a newborn's vision is poor for long distances, most babies are able to focus well at a distance of 12 inches—the distance from the mother's face to her nursing infant. It is apparently nature's plan to promote close face-to-face attachment.

A baby can not only discriminate his mother's face, but recognize her voice as well. The fetus responds to sound in the third trimester; by birth a baby has very sophisticated hearing. A. J. DeCasper and W. P. Fifer in 1980 reported their research findings in *Science* which shows that "a newborn infant younger than three days of age cannot only discriminate his mother's voice but also will work to produce her voice in preference to the voice of another female." (pp. 1174-1176)

A baby's recognition of his mother's voice and face is designed to enhance the bonding and attachment process. As we have noted, it is through the parent-child attachment that the baby's energy becomes regulated, channeled and transformed into healthy growth. This is the start of the socialization process that provides the growing child with an inner sense of trust and well-being. With socialization the forming of a conscience has begun.

As we have shown earlier in this book, the formation of a weak bond or a break in this attachment will lead to non-regulated discharge of a baby's energy, and mistrust and insecurity. Here lies the seed of antisocial personality disorder. This complicated and subtle pattern of interaction must occur between mother and child for a healthy attachment. Mothers are primarily responsible for early socialization, but the infant contributes too. By crying, clinging, eye following, smiling, and sucking, a baby lets his mother know his needs.

Parents should know that infants who seldom cry and seem the "perfect baby" may actually be headed for trouble. Because they need less attention, they can set up a cycle that doesn't promote attachment. A lack of early crying and babbling may result in speech problems later, a common unattached child symptom. A mother or father picking up a crying baby lets him know that he has power in his universe and that he can do something to relieve his stress. This allows the baby to feel he is not helpless and alone.

Other difficulties may surface if a baby has poor reflexes and cannot grasp properly or if an infant has sucking difficulties; this can cause a mother and child frustration. Poor grasping can result in later motor skills difficulties and an infant who cannot suck may be headed for food problems later in life.

Similarly, an infant who smiles will start a chain reaction in others, making the whole world smile with him. Smiles and laughter make for a positive environment and set the tone for a future ability to give and receive joy. Early behavior *by the infant* can have profound effects on how a mother responds. "But it is the smile that rewards the parent, the smile that decisively seals the emerging bond." (Konner, 1987, p. 44)

So we find there are indicators which can signal future problems that may place a baby at high risk. The signs of attachment change, depending on the ages of the children. Each developmental stage—infant, toddler, grade-schooler, teenager—has a particular focus that can be quite complicated.

We have divided the symptoms of low and high risk attachment into two broad sections: infants and beyond. There is some overlap because symptoms that begin in early childhood can continue into late adolescence (such as a 5-year-old unattached girl's seductiveness changing little as she grows into a 15-year-old adolescent).

Just as a trigger does not make a gun, neither should one symptom lead to the conclusion that a child is unattached. A series of high-risk symptoms, coupled with a professional evaluation, is needed before this illness can be confirmed.

There are "easy" babies and "difficult" ones. And not all babies who dislike cuddling are unattached; however, all unattached babies do hate cuddling.

Infants at high risk for unattachment fall into the following categories:

● Genetic history of APD in family members.
● Prebirth trauma — mother taking drugs and under extreme stress.
● Emotionally-disturbed parent.
● Premature birth and low birth weight.

● Birth trauma — serious medical complications during birth.

● Separations at birth with a primary caregiver.

● Other interruptions in the consistency of care — divorce, day care, abuse and neglectful family setting, etc.

The infant under 1 year of age will show signs of unattachment or attachment in the following ways:

Infant Attachment Checklist

Low-Risk Signs	High-Risk Signs
Infant cries to signal unmet need and when gratified will gradually terminate crying.	Weak crying response or rageful crying (without tears) and/or constantly whining.
Infant may sometimes resist cuddling but with moderate touching, and body sculpturing, infant will positively respond to mother's positive nurturing.	Poor clinging and extreme resistance to cuddling and close holding (fights to get free). Arches back when picked up (after first six weeks of life) and seems "stiff as a board".
Baby can fixate on mother's eyes and develop good following response, especially when nursing or smiling.	Weak contact in eye-following response. Infant will highly resist close face-to-face eye contact and consistently avert gaze (even if cuddling is permitted).
Infant may have some nursing difficulty (mother's nursing difficulty, i.e., inverted nipples, etc.) but can adapt and quickly develop healthy response.	Baby has poor sucking response and doesn't motivate to approach mother for receiving nurturance. Can also be due to developmental difficulties, i.e., cleft palate.
Baby gurgles, chortles, and has smiling response, especially when primary caretaker smiles.	Infant resists smiles even when tickled or played with lovingly. No reciprocal smile response.

Infant sparkles with life and a varied combination of emotions from sad to mad to glad. He looks and feels "right."

Infant is extremely passive and lifeless and seems to be in another world with no positive response to humans. Not attached to anything. Later this passivity will give way to rage. Baby looks and feels "like something is wrong."

It is important to remember that strong attachment and bonding involves a positive interplay between the caregiver and the infant and this starts well before birth.

*****

Sherry was ecstatic about her first pregnancy. She was proud that she had waited until after graduation from college to get married to John. Now she had the training she needed, but she was ready to start a family — her career could be postponed. She wanted to have a child "while she was still young." Her mind raced with thoughts about what her baby might look like. How much would it resemble John? Or herself? The thought of dressing up a cute little girl gave her a delightful tingle inside. Should she dare start to buy girl's clothes and decorate the spare room in pink? No, she would wait for the ultrasound and a doctor's report.

As her due date approached she felt the baby kicking. The doctor had loaned them a stethoscope, and she and John would listen to the baby's heartbeat. As she put the stethoscope to her ears and heard the faint echoes of the heartbeat Sherry began to "own" the life deep inside her abdomen. Whatever its sex or size, she knew she loved her baby. The attachment process for Sherry and John and their baby had already begun.

A year and a half earlier Sherry's younger sister, Carol, had also become pregnant. Unlike Sherry and John, Carol had not looked forward to the delivery. She was 17, unmarried, and still struggling through the 11th grade. Her family would not be able to support her. With no skills, no husband, and no help, her future looked bleak. Every kick of the baby threw her into a deeper state of depression. There was no excitement, only dread. Unlike her older sister, Carol seldom discussed the pregnancy and at times wished she could die. She was ambivalent about giving the baby up for adoption, but felt she had no choice. One thing she did know: she didn't want to love that baby. Giving it up would be just too painful if she loved it.

Sherry and John got their wish, a cute little blue-eyed girl. Carol also delivered a healthy baby girl, but refused to touch her. She wanted the whole thing to be over.

Unfortunately, Carol is not alone in her feelings of remorse. Many expectant mothers have such feelings about their babies and this interferes with the attachment process. These feelings can indicate a lack of confidence in mothering skills, a negative self-concept, lack of economic and emotional support or a physical illness. Other feelings interfering with this process might include grief, loss of a job, or the birth of a physically disabled infant.

An alert nursing staff can recognize and intervene when they see a new mother needs educational or psychological help. Here is a partial list of some of the more common parental behaviors (mother and/or father) to look for during the first year of life.

Parental Behaviors

Low-risk Parenting

Mother exhibits positive interest in baby at birth and is eager to interact.

Mother wants to hold, caress and respond to infant's vocalization. Makes positive statements about baby, "She's adorable."

Happy mother is filled with radiance, even, at times, tears of joy.

Mother is attuned with baby's need for a balance of stimulation and quiet time. They develop a healthy rhythm together of play and rest.

Mother frequently establishes face-to-face positioning with eye contact and appropriate smiles.

High-risk Parenting

Mother withdraws and assumes a negative psychological and physical posture regarding baby at birth.

Minimal touching, stroking, or talking to or about baby unless in negative manner. "Be quiet." May hold infant tensely.

Emotionless and flat affect or depressed and angry. Sometimes tears of sadness.

Mother overstimulates baby by too much talking and touching. Mother sometimes plays in inappropriate or hostile ways (cruelly teasing infant).

Mother doesn't establish eye contact except when angry and rarely smiles or does so inappropriately (when infant in pain).

Plays with infant when awake (but doesn't overdo it) and places baby in stimulating area to observe and interact with others. Shows ability to comfort child and appears strongly attached.

Leaves infant, when awake, for long periods in isolation and doesn't show the ability to comfort the baby when needed. Handles baby roughly or in detached manner and may be abusive and neglectful.

Mother provides infant with proper and preventative medical assistance. Concern for diet, diaper changes, and health of baby.

Mother fails to provide basic supplies for well baby care and is angry at most baby behaviors. Mother doesn't seek medical assistance unless a crisis occurs.

Mother is basically happy and satisfied with being a mother and primary caretaker.

Mother is unhappy, frustrated, and angry at being a mother and the primary caretaker.

What About Fathers?

With more women in the work force, there is an obvious void in child rearing which needs to be filled. The role of the father in attachment can be likened to that of the office of vice president of the United States. It looks good on paper but in reality it is an isolated position that has certain expected tasks which seldom receive center-stage attention, unless there is a problem or crisis.

During pregnancy, a father is expected to support the mother so she can bond better with "her" baby. Dr. Jerrold Lee Shapiro, recounts his experience as a second banana in a 1987 *Psychology Today* article. During a childbirth class he spoke up, saying he felt nervous about the actual birth. His questions were ignored. "When I later asked the instructor about this privately, she looked at me in dismay, saying 'What did you expect me to do, get all those pregnant women upset?' "

The message clearly was: "Fathers shall not express nervousness about childbirth publicly." (p. 38) So what can fathers express? Everything necessary to enable them to bond and attach to the new baby. Fathers can attach emotionally to the unborn and nurture and attach to the infant immediately after birth. There is a critical period of father-child attachment during the first three days after birth. This event is called "engrossment" and helps cement a father to his offspring.

It was obvious that Bill had played football sometime in his life. He was a huge man, towering over the nurses in the delivery room. As the birth progressed, his eyes grew as large as quarters. When his son's head emerged Bill seemed to stop breathing entirely. He later explained it was like seeing fire for the first time. When he held his baby his hands almost completely engulfed the infant and all he could say was, "He's so fragile." Then the child looked into his father's eyes and smiled. Tears began to run down Bill's cheeks as he smiled back. The magic of the moment made time stand still. At that second no one else existed except this father and the tiny infant cradled in his arms. He was bonding with his child.

This is what is supposed to happen. Unfortunately, it isn't always that way.

Many things can get in the way of this father-child attachment. These may include maternal reluctance to relinquish child care responsibilities, a father's fear and ignorance, lack of peer support, etc. High-risk fathers follow a pattern like high-risk mothers, including not smiling, no eye contact and other distancing responses to the infant. But fathers can bond with their babies and they should take every opportunity to do so.

Rebonding or Reattaching

The fact that infants can be molded one way or the other with so little effort is a double-edged sword. While many experiences early in life can produce an unattached child, positive intervention can reverse this downward spiral and redirect a child's future. Generally, as we have noted, the younger the child at intervention the better the prognosis. Severe cases of unattachment, such as those resulting from abuse, neglect, or illness, should be diagnosed and treated by qualified professionals only. Less serious cases in the first 18 months can be handled by following the positive suggestions in the low-risk Parental Behavior chart.

It is important to remember that irritable babies are that way because of an unmet need. Certainly every caregiver should exhaust the list of normal possibilities, such as wet diaper, hunger, illness or other discomfort before assuming the issue is an attachment problem. For most babies, normal comforting techniques will work.

Probably the best treatment for an unattached, irritable, whining infant is to pick him up and hold him in a very special way. The caregiver must be able to combine a number of personal behaviors, including loving sensitivity, positiveness and firmness when holding a struggling child. Parents suspecting they have a severely unattached child — despite all their efforts to bring about a solid attachment — should consult a professional.

There are good parents who have done everything "right" but still have difficult babies. Often unattachment is the result of inadequate parenting, but there are cases where this isn't true. Perhaps the baby had some undiagnosed illness, such as an inner ear infection, which distanced him from the loving care he was receiving. In these cases the parents should not feel guilty, but it is important to seek help immediately so they may reattach to this troubled child.

When rebonding is occurring it probably will create a rage response and "stiffening" on the part of the infant. The caregiver helps the baby loosen up by gently flexing stiff arms and legs at appropriate joints. All the time this "repositioning" is taking place the parent is talking calmly to the infant and trying to establish eye contact. Even in small babies this will often produce a rage response (or struggling) which, if contained, will give way to crying and deep relaxation.

There are many other methods of holding an infant but all should be done with loving care, smiles and close face-to-face interaction. Caregivers who are emotionally stressed or overly mad, sad or even overly glad should not be holding troubled infants. Field warns that "over-stimulating mothers" who incessantly talk or interact with an infant can cause the baby to withdraw. (1987, p. 32) Proper handling and tactile stimulation, however, can do wonders for troubled babies. Preliminary research shows that massaging premature infants helps them gain body weight and relate to their caregivers. Field says, "infant massage, like adult massage, gets some type of intimacy going and produces a better baby. And if you have a better baby, you have a happier parent who is going to interact better and be more responsive." (1987, p. 34)

Parents who know about infant bonding and attachment are better able to prevent problems from occurring and to understand how to deal successfully with them should they occur. Problems escalate as the children become older.

There is another factor in parenting that should not be overlooked. All parents are at risk of suffering burnout and a deterioration in the adult relationship. It is important for parents to find a loving and consistent substitute caregiver so they can occasionally renew the romantic bonds between them outside the home environment. It is a question of proper balance.

From Toddlers to Teens

For most parents, it gets easier to identify a problem with their offspring as the child gets older. The "critical" bonding periods and "critical" symptoms surrounding an unattached infant all seem quite subtle. However, as the child grows up, these symptoms become impossible to ignore, depending on how unattached the child is. Remember too, that the attachment process does not stop at a certain age; it is continual and breaks can occur later in the child's life if there is enough provocation. (The classic case of this is Helen Keller, who started out life as an attached child, but later developed severe illnesses and became a rage-filled youngster.)

When evaluating an older child it is important to keep in mind that some children are at higher risk than others, depending on the number and severity of symptoms present. The following high- and low-risk chart explains again important symptoms addressed earlier in the book. Read these symptoms with caution and do not label a child as unattached without professional help.

Toddlers to Teens
Attachment/Unattachment Checklist

Low-Risk Signs	High-Risk Signs
Young child has attached to primary caretaker and is cautious of strangers at first but as time goes by develops trusting view of the world. Child can smile and look at others.	No deep attachment so child not upset when primary parent leaves, unless child wants something. Child can superficially attach to strangers but doesn't trust anyone. Rarely looks others in the eye or smiles.

Child searching for autonomy and sense of self. Some testing of limits and resistance to rules but manageable and allows others to share control.

Child has physical self-control and pride in individual accomplishments. Child's behaviors are generally age-appropriate and regressive behaviors such as bed wetting, etc., are transitional. Child responds well to traditional therapy and can develop healthy self-image.

Generally enjoys supportive warmth and closeness from others. Increasing motor dexterity ability, and any illness is usually temporary.

Child has a good internalized parent to guide him. Can establish realistic goals and understands behavioral rewards and consequences.

Basically likes himself and has normal peer group connections. Can empathize with others' feelings and generally avoids serious fighting and destruction of property. Feels good when he helps others and can follow and align with good models.

Extreme resistance to all controls and is constantly testing limits. Sassy to grownups and argues, whines, and has severe temper tantrums when he doesn't get his way.

Regressive oral and anal problems, such as severe eating difficulties (gorging food), speech problems, bed wetting, soiling pants, hoarding things, etc. Acts immature for age and has hostile dependency relationship with parents, needing constant reassurance. Low self-concept. Child doesn't respond well to traditional therapy.

Body rigidity and resistance to holding, especially in close face encounters. Often motor skill difficulties and complaints of illness. High pain tolerance and accident proneness.

Learning problems and difficulty with logical thinking and normal cause-and-effect consequences. Poor attention span and often hyperactive. Not able to delay gratification.

Cruel to self and others and has a fascination with pain and vicious destructiveness. No long-lasting healthy friendships. Bullies others and fights with siblings and peers. Doesn't share or recognize feelings of others. May play with fire and align with evil forces.

Occasional infraction of rules including infrequent stealing or lying for personal gain but when caught can learn from the experience and correct maladapted behavior. Eye contact hard to establish and maintain when lying.

Habitual stealing and lying, sometimes for no apparent reason. Always projecting blame on others and denying all personal responsibility. Frequently in trouble with authority. Some teens can fake eye contact when lying.

Can play many roles but has a "core" identity which is trustworthy, honest, and reliable. Capable of success in relationships and work.

Manipulative and phony. "Con men" and "seductive women" who are incapable of true intimacy. Poor work histories, unrealistic life goals and no "core" identity established.

Low-risk children who experience some inner turmoil when going against their principles. Conscience securely in place.

High-risk children without a conscience or principles to guide them. No genuine guilt or remorse for wrong doing.

© High Risk, Magid/McKelvey

Parenting Toddlers to Teens

Mark Twain once suggested that children should be raised in barrels and fed through a small knothole until they reached the teen years. Then, sarcastically, Twain suggested that the knothole be plugged up.

Raising children often has parents experiencing some frustration with their children. Parents who have fine children usually have children with fine parents. But unattached children do grow up and become parents of more unattached children. These parents, with unresolved pasts, are unprepared to meet the responsibilities of good parenting. They have never had good role models from which to learn and are often mad, sad and frustrated about taking care of their children. The anger generally promotes abuse and neglect. The sadness can bring on adult neediness and role reversal in which the child becomes the controller.

There are certainly different degrees of attachment for children, as there are for parents. It is important to treat unattached children as early as possible. "Train a child in a way he should go and when he is old, he will not turn from it." (Proverbs 22:6)

Here are some of the high- and low- risk behaviors for parents of toddlers to teens:

Toddlers to Teens
Parent Checklist

Low-Risk Signs	High-Risk Signs
Parent shows interest and excitement in child's development and autonomy and works on building self-concept of child by supporting skill building efforts and emotional closeness.	Parent not intimately involved or interested in child's development, skill building, or self-concept. Unaware or unmotivated to focus on psychosocial needs of child.
Parent expresses a healthy and informed interest in meeting all of the child's environmental needs including personal preferences in clothing, food, room decoration, etc. Parent helps child learn about proper medical and dental care and responds to illness quickly.	Parent doesn't provide for physical needs of child such as diet, adequate clothing, safe housing, medical check-ups and proper care when child is ill. Parent doesn't care about the child's personal preferences.
Parent's priorities are balanced so that frequent time is spent with the children (especially the younger children). Activities are shared and the interaction is usually positive. Child care is warm, consistent, and adequately supervised and children are not left alone for long periods.	Parents neglect child because of their own problems and concerns; drug abuse, prostitution, career priorities, parental overload with other infants, etc. Child is often left unsupervised or with substandard care.
Parent allows child to try tasks independently in order to gain self-awareness and confidence. Parent doesn't over-protect child from experiencing normal cycle of frustration, persistence, and self-accomplishment.	Super anxious and overprotective parents who are constantly hovering over child, never allowing him to risk and fail and learn by himself and gain self-confidence and autonomy. Parent always rescues child who then feels helpless and incompetent.

Parent's usual response to child is loving and nurturing with an ability to comfort the child in a positive way. Anger and sadness are temporary and love is a far greater self-emotion than hate or sadness. Mutuality and healthy laughter and joy are frequently present in the home.

Parent's emotional response to child is usually extreme, either hot (angry) or cold (distant and not caring). Parent rarely comforts child or says, "I love you." May tease child with inappropriate humor or gesture of caring. Sexual and verbal abuse is common.

Discipline is balanced with love, logic, consistency, and fairness. Parent designs chores that help child learn responsibility, pride, and self-respect. Mutual respect is still intact.

Discipline is irregular, unrealistic, and unfair. Chores and limit-setting may not be age-appropriate and are punitive. Control battles are the norm and there is no mutual respect.

Parent supports child's intellectual, spiritual, and social growth by attending school functions, helping with homework, providing religious opportunities, supporting healthy peer and extended family relationships and "being there" when needed. Teaches child positive citizenship and values by good parental modeling.

Parent doesn't actively support child's education or social growth. Rarely attends school functions and prefers to blame academic difficulties on child or school system. Socializing of the child is either too restrictive or without healthy guiding parameters. Teaches child immorality and mistrust by modeling same.

© High Risk, Magid/McKelvey

Solutions for older children and teenagers who are unattached requires far more aggressive intervention, such as that outlined for professionals in the treatment section. Obviously, a single mother with no training would be ill-advised to attempt to confront and physically hold an unattached teenager. Therefore, holding therapy is not something to be attempted by a parent or concerned adult unless it is in conjunction with an experienced professional. A few general rules in the home are a must. Obviously, we feel unattached children need stronger guidance and support than most children.

If your child is younger—and not severely unattached (not displaying many symptoms)—then setting up appropriately structured guidelines with natural consequences and reinforcing every positive move the child makes can often turn things around.

Older children need additional structure and consistent reinforcement but sometimes that isn't enough. Because of the children's hardened habits and physical size, many parents choose to enlist outside help from such resource groups as Tough Love or Parents Without Partners. All parents of unattached children need to have extra patience, stamina and love. Only those who have such children are able to understand truly what a parent goes through. Getting together with others who share a common focus is beneficial, as has been demonstrated by Alcoholics Anonymous. There is strength and comfort in numbers, and an Unattached Children Anonymous organization could be established to help those needing assistance.

A Behavioral Look at Psychopathy

The inconsistencies of parental love (rewards and punishments) in an unattached child's life play a critical role. It's been hypothesized that if a child cannot accurately predict how his actions will get him a reward—or a punishment—while he is doing something, then punishment per se loses its control. Then the only thing that matters is keeping busy until the next positive event occurs (Doren, 1987, pp. 75-131).

In fact, punishment or conflict is seen as part of the normal process of getting one's goal. This helps explain why most unattached children don't have good cause-and-effect thinking about avoiding pain and trouble.

Couple this with the possibility of a genetic chemical predisposition toward seeking more stimulation and you can explain why virtually all unattached children are hyperactive thrill-seekers with short attention spans. The child has "learned" to stimulate himself and endure pain until a reward is reached. He learns to always be in control because he has realized that other people are unpredictable and don't deserve to be trusted and loved.

*****

Suppose you are a good, loving parent, who did everything you could, and you find yourself with an unattached child. The guilt and hand-wringing can hurt any positive effort to remedy the situation. It is not unlike dealing with alcoholism; living with an unattached child requires a daily, step-by-step approach.

As the parent of such a child, you may fall down a thousand times and feel like giving up. It is important to remember that inside, parents are wired for success, not failure. Falling down should be nothing new to you. It is not different from when you were a small child and decided to learn to walk. Though you stumbled and fell flat on your face many times, and you cried, you didn't stay there on the ground. If someone didn't help you up, you got up yourself and tried again, and again, until the goal was reached. It happened one step at a time.

It is the same thing when working with an unattached child. You will fall a lot, and you will cry, but it is important to hang in there. It is your child's life that is at stake. It is also important to learn as much as possible about how unattached children tick. In seeking a professional therapist, make sure he knows about the unattached child syndrome and proper treatment procedures. Be a wise consumer, feeling free to check out the therapist's professional background. Is he licensed? What is his real-world experience? Does he have children and does he have a healthy, loving attitude about babies' rights?

The weakest among us should have the strongest rights. There is an interesting story from the California Gold Rush days, where a mother brought her baby into the theater one night. Just as the orchestra began to play her baby started crying. An elderly man jumped up from the pit and in a loud, booming voice said, "Stop those fiddles and let the baby cry. I haven't heard such a beautiful sound in ten years." The audience was overcome with sentiment and the orchestra stopped while the baby was allowed to continue his solo performance amid unbounded enthusiasm. (Fuller, 1978, pg. 165)

"School days are the best days
of your life . . . provided your
children are old enough to go."
Old vaudeville line

24

Teachers of Future Parents

Matthew is officially in the second grade, but his ranking on an achievement test would put him somewhere below a first-grade level. His father drinks frequently and is verbally and physically abusive to his mother. Last night, his mother became intoxicated and tried to stab her husband with a kitchen knife. The police were called, as they have been many times before, but nothing was resolved.

Matthew is filled with hate and fear and feels more comfortable out on the streets than at home. He says he carries a knife to school "just in case." His teacher worries that he isn't "motivated" and wonders how to help him.

Today it became clear he needs more help than just tutoring. He has just stabbed a first-grade child. (Betsy Geddes, personal communication, February, 1987)

Things are different now in the schools. Never before have we experienced the kinds of problems we now face. In the 1940s, according to a CBS News Report, the top seven public school problems were:

1. Talking out of turn.
2. Chewing gum.
3. Making noise.
4. Running in halls.
5. Cutting in line.
6. Dress code infractions.
7. Littering.

In 1980, the seven top public school problems were:
1. Drug abuse.
2. Alcohol abuse.
3. Pregnancy.
4. Suicide.

5. Rape.
6. Robbery.
7. Assault. (CBS Evening News, February 9, 1987)

Many educators who are on the front lines in the schools know how things have gotten out of hand. Dr. Betsy Geddes, an inner city elementary school principal in Portland, Oregon, has 25 years' experience working with children. "The majority of kids we suspend or expel, almost without exception, have either been sexually or physically abused and have a high incidence of drug abuse in the family. We call them amoral, with no sense of right and wrong, and these kids don't seem to learn from their mistakes. They have no feeling of remorse," says Geddes. (personal communication, February, 1987)

Jim Fay, a Colorado educator with more than 30 years' experience, points a finger clearly at the attachment crisis. "We are finding more and more kids coming into school now who don't like themselves. Their bonding has not been right." He says this attitude sets up an atmosphere for failure, rage and sabotage for teachers and other adults trying to help these children. "These kids are actually destroying their learning opportunities," says Fay. (personal communication, February, 1987)

The bottom line is that we are not preparing seriously troubled children to fit into society, says Geddes. "We are not preparing them to be functioning members of society, to work at jobs, pay taxes, etc. Instead we are turning out children who are going to be just receiving benefits." (personal communication, February, 1987)

The problem is made complex by the double-bind, no-win situations we set up for ourselves. We want teachers to do a professional job with our most precious resource, but we aren't willing to pay for it. School superintendents say their first priority is to have children learn to like themselves and get along better with others, yet they grade themselves, teachers and the students using only basic student performance and three R's test data. For many unattached children, the basics of love and trust were missed a long time ago. They have to start at the very beginning, necessitating parent involvement.

Here is a classic scenario of a no-win situation. The few programs that might help unattached children require parental consent and involvement. But the parents of the most seriously disturbed children refuse to get involved.

Workers in these programs say, "Why should I waste my time working with children whose parents don't give a damn since there is so little chance of success?" One educator, who wished to remain unnamed, says: "We could run PTA sessions at the state pen and get more people there than we do at many of America's most troubled schools." These children are modeling after their parents; they come from very difficult home environments. The overwhelming question is "what is society going to do with all these children no one wants to touch?" Most unattached children don't fit into regular classrooms and they don't fit into special programs. If something isn't done, they will not fit into society.

It is hard to believe how some of these children can disrupt a classroom unless you are there:

> "Jerry was all over the room, hitting and biting kids, yelling, screaming, and causing problems for everyone. When I tried to talk to him, he'd nod his head and with big, innocent eyes he'd say, 'yes,' and then within a few minutes he'd go back to pulling someone's hair or disrupting others. If he was quiet, I also had to worry because he would sometimes just get up and wander out of the classroom and I wouldn't know where he was or what he was doing. I just found out he has been kicked out of seven other classrooms before he was shoved in my door. He is just in the third grade now and the administration tells me they don't have room for him anywhere else. What am I supposed to do?" (C. Smith, personal communication, January 20, 1987)

Unfortunately, the primary grades are just the beginning. As the child gets older, the consequences to society get more severe. Something must be done and done now.

The Solution is Elementary

The great philosopher Seneca said, "The lesson that is never learned can never be taught too often." Children need to learn how to trust and love others before they can contribute positively to society. Teaching children to count isn't nearly as important as teaching children what counts. We cannot call it education unless it also teaches our children honesty, self-respect and respect for others. For children who haven't bonded with their parents, the question is clear — who can they bond with?

"Teachers," says educator Fay. "What's left if no one else is there to help them?" (personal communication, February, 1987)

Geddes agrees, "As educators, we can't all say parents must do their work at home or we won't do our jobs at school. In some cases parents won't or can't. It may be frightening that many of our kids are raised on school food, don't know how to use a knife and fork properly, or don't know what is acceptable social behavior. But if that's what a child needs to learn, then that is where we need to start. It is a great opportunity to help change things and there is no one else to do it." (personal communication, February, 1987)

Of course, teaching teachers how to bond with unattached children is easier said than done. Teachers must first have a positive attitude about themselves and the students if a successful union can be realized. A lot of work needs to be done in this area. Roy Mayer and Tom Butterworth recently wrote in *Psychology Today* that teachers criticize three times as often as they praise. (1984) Teachers need specific ways to increase children's self-concepts. Billions of tax dollars being poured into education will do little good unless the educators change their attitudes toward "troublemakers" and "misfits." If we send away everybody who doesn't fit, there won't be anyone left.

The old saw still rings true: the mediocre teacher tells, the good teacher explains, the superior teacher demonstrates, and the great teacher inspires.

Here are high- and low-risk guidelines for teachers on bonding with children. High-risk teaching methods will negatively impact all children, not just unattached children. These methods are suggested for grade-school teachers working with unattached children still capable of forming positive alliances. No teacher should be asked to work with severely unattached children who are so out of control that they are a danger to themselves or others. These children need to be referred for therapy.

Evaluating Teachers

Low-Risk Signs	High-Risk Signs
Confident, yet willing to learn new skills. Has a trusting, positive outlook about himself and others.	Poor teacher self-concept. Insecure and immature. Not motivated to learn about own weaknesses.
Adequate understanding of childhood developmental stages and how the attachment process works. Experiential training within a multi-cultural setting.	Poor teacher training. No understanding of how to work with unattached or severely troubled children. No real-world understanding of multi-cultural children. Feels frustrated and unprepared.
Positive attitude toward children with persistent "can do" attitude. Always accentuating and looking for what a child does right and without undue praise supporting every positive effort the child exhibits.	Negative attitude and expectations toward students. Teacher and administrators don't expect child to succeed and convey a "born to lose" attitude toward children, who often adopt a negative self-fulfilling prophecy.

A teacher who engenders mutual respect by listening to the students' concerns, not putting them down, using "I" messages when confronting, and looking for win-win solutions. Being firm when necessary and credible (doing what he says) to build trust and respect.

Teacher who allows child to be involved in decision-making processes and to "own" the natural consequences, as well as the self-pride, of his successes. Teacher models good thinking by saying, "I'm going to wear my coat at recess because I don't want to get cold," and then lets Mother Nature be the next teacher without telling the child specifically what to do.

Teacher has flexibility to tailor lessons and delegate student aides to offer individualized help. Resources are adequate and comprehensive enough to meet student needs.

Teacher who threatens children, calls them names, emotionally abuses them, unfairly criticizes them, or makes them feel psychologically small. A teacher who says one thing and does another.

Teacher who usurps the student's responsibility by "owning" the child's problems and rescuing him from any natural learning consequences. Teacher tries to control child by making decisions for him, thus impairing decision-making ability. "Don't make me tell you again to take your coat with you outside. Even first graders know that."

Poor curriculum and facilities. Teacher is faced with forcing round pegs into square holes by not having freedom to teach children what they need to know but rather what is "required." Also, overcrowded classes, understaffing, inadequate physical and social resources (i.e., library, medical, athletics, etc.).

© High Risk, Magid/McKelvey

How early should formal education begin? Certainly the earlier the better for unattached children.

Critics of Headstart programs have long asserted that the benefits of early education don't last, but a study by the Maryland Department of Education suggests otherwise. "There is evidence that the benefits of education of 4-year-olds endure as they progress through primary school," says Dr. Leon Rosenberg, who directed the study. (1979)

Rosenberg, an associate professor at Johns Hopkins University School of Medicine, says it is time to act. "The need is clear for a firm commitment to make the education of 4-year-olds an integral part of our educational system, not just a brief demonstration of what we can do when we want to." (p. 64)

John Allan of the University of British Columbia also believes in starting early. He helped set up an elementary school program in which sixth-and-seventh-grade student volunteers interacted and played with preschoolers while the younger children's mothers attended a counseling group on parenting. The supervised sixth-and seventh-graders did more than just baby-sit. They learned a great deal about how toddlers tick and what parenting is all about. One student remarked: "I understand why my mom gets so mad at me." Observed Allan: "If such training in caring and parenting were part of every elementary school curriculum, great benefits to society as a whole might ensue." (1978, pp. 149-150) A similar type of pre-parenting training has been tried at Adams High School in Portland, Oregon. Students are given instruction on decision-making and child care and work twice a week as "interns" at a day-care center. Videotaped students are evaluated in discussion groups on their parenting techniques. (Wall, 1981)

Educator Fay likes to combine positive programs at school and at home to help a child build a better image of himself. He advises teachers to spend two minutes a day with a child for 10 days in a row just listening and paying attention to what's on the child's mind. At the end of each 2-minute session, the teacher gives the child a strong personal compliment, "described so tightly that the kid can't wiggle out from under it." (personal communications, February 1987)

Parents are encouraged to do the same exercise at home along with something that Fay calls "attribute theory." The parent and teacher are instructed to look only for things the child got *correct* on his school papers. The adults then confront the child about why he got those items right. If he doesn't know, the adults might suggest that he tried hard or is getting better at the subject. "This helps force the child to generate in his mind, or say it in his own words so he burns the lesson into his subconscious forever," says Fay. All these techniques, he adds, make it easier for the child to "fall in love with the teacher and bond." (personal communication, February 1987)

Troubled children need much more than just bonding and attachment. They need to learn new ways of behaving, good citizenship, and telling right from wrong. It is difficult for unattached children to understand the relationship between cause and effect. More courses are needed in developing social skills, such as cooperation and being a good friend, and in solving problems without violence.

An innovative grade-school program in Glendora, California, attempts to do just that. Psychologist Jane Favero helped develop the program. She explains: "We try to teach children to think about behavior to get them to reason, to focus on the ramifications of their actions." (Timnick, 1982, p. 45)

Geddes says that a program in the Portland elementary schools, called Peace and Justice, reviews the laws of the land and teaches that a person has not only rights but also responsibilities. (personal communication, February, 1987) These types of classes are essential for all unattached children, who need the lesson repeated many times.

Elementary schools should also provide classes on sexuality, drugs, avoiding crime and sibling abuse. Children need to be taught about available community resources. Quality after-school programs work in European countries and should be offered to the millions of American latch-key children who come home to empty houses.

Teachers need assistance, too. As we set higher standards for becoming a professional teacher it will be necessary to increase elementary and preschool teacher salaries. As one typical teacher reports, "I can make more money and have a less stressful day by checking groceries at the express lane of my supermarket." (B. Williams, personal communication, January 1987) Preventing teacher burnout must have a high priority. In-service seminars on stress and burnout and hiring teachers to relieve those who need a break are two ways to help.

If high-risk children are to be spotted early and helped, it is vital that all teacher-education programs provide a thorough understanding of the attachment process. Teachers should be familiar with new methods being developed to deal with unruly, unattached children in the classroom. One veteran English teacher who wishes to remain anonymous laments, "I was taught how to teach normal kids, not half-socialized animals. What am I supposed to do with a child that even a psychiatrist doesn't know how to cure? And I have 27 other children to worry about too. It is not fair."

Some action is possible. In a system developed in Canada by Allan, the elementary school counselor uses the power of the entire class to change a student's negative behavior. The child, while temporarily separated from the class, is asked to look at how his classmates treated him and how he feels about it. The counselor then asks the child how he would like to be treated and what he can do to make that happen. The session ends with the student agreeing to behave in specific ways.

The counselor meets separately with the student's classmates, allowing them to air their feelings about his negative behavior and to speculate on why he acts the way he does. They commonly answer, "He wants attention," or "He doesn't have any friends," or "He hasn't learned how to act normally." Then the counselor and the class examine alternatives to just hating the unattached child. Common solutions include ignoring silly behavior, praising good behavior and being friendly to the child but telling him in a normal voice — "what we do and don't do in this class." (Allan, 1983, p. 147-151)

The power of the group is enormous. The classmates make a commitment to help the student while not allowing themselves to act like him when he is being a jerk. Followup sessions are held weekly.

Other ways to help unattached children before they move on to secondary school include setting up behavior-modification programs and providing individual counseling. Once a child gets into secondary school and adolescence, there are additional pressures which make it extremely difficult to "rescue" the child. He has become set in his ways. In the next section we will examine one of the major challenges faced by this nation: teenage sexuality.

25

The Teenage Baby Boom

"Debbie is 16, and in labor with her first baby. The contractions are regular, every 10 minutes or so, and they're starting to get painful . . . She's positive that it's punitive, my denying her this drug her mother told her she could have . . . She begins to scream at me . . .

"After the baby is born, though, Debbie doesn't want to hold her. 'You take her mom,' she says. 'You know what to do.'

" 'She's your baby, you know,' the nurse says, 'you have to learn to take care of her.'

" 'Later, OK, mom?' Debbie says with perfect adolescent intonation."

Perri Klass, 4th year
Harvard Medical School student
(1986, p. 16)

Teenage parents are one of the largest sources of unattached children in America. For teenagers who get pregnant the fun is over. The Alan Guttmacher Institute says 3,000 teenagers are getting pregnant each day in the United States. That is over 1 million pregnancies a year, the highest rate in the Western world. (Sherman, 1986, p. 202)

The outlook is usually grim for teenage mothers and their babies. The mothers' early sexual habits put them at higher risk for pelvic disease, cervical cancer, gonorrhea, chlamydia, herpes and the deadly AIDS virus. And then there are psychological, educational, economic and social handicaps.

269

Because of immaturity, immobility, ignorance and dire financial straits, teenage mothers seldom get good prenatal care. Since most prefer junk food, they know little about proper nutrition. Add to that an unwillingness to give up smoking, drinking or drug use, and you have a high-risk situation.

The bottom line is that all of these negative factors combine to double the risk of having a low birth-weight baby (under 5.5 pounds). Teenage mothers are a primary reason the U.S. has one of the highest infant mortality rates in the Western World. And surviving babies born to teenagers are likely to need years of medical and/or psychological care.

Caring for a handicapped infant requires special parenting skills. Most teenagers are too immature to care for normal infants, much less babies with special needs. Often the pressure is just too much for these young mothers, and their babies end up abused, neglected, or both.

Then the cycle of unattached, amoral children continues. In a 1987 *Newsweek* article Kim Cox, a health educator in San Francisco, says: "They're little kids with grownup problems. They're moved to sex, many of them, not by compassion or love or any of the other urges that make sense to adults, but by a need for intimacy that has gone unfulfilled by their families." (Kantrowitz, 1987, p. 65)

What Can Happen Differently

For a change, Americans need to copy someone who is doing a better job. In Sweden and some other Western countries, there are fewer unwanted pregnancies and the infant death rate is lower. America's teen pregnancy rate is almost double that of Sweden. "Other countries have a far more realistic approach. They say, 'Our kids are having sex. Let's make sure they don't get pregnant.' In our country, we are still trying to pretend our kids aren't having sex," says Sue Yates, formerly with the Guttmacher Institute, (Sherman, 1986, p. 202)

Dr. Kristen Moore, a social psychologist for the research group Child Trends, agrees: "Why can't we stress morals and teach about contraceptives? Certainly, we should be teaching kids to delay having sex until they are emotionally ready, but can't we get them the information they need?" (Sherman, 1986, p. 205)

Most sex education for teens in America has been abysmal. Only 10% of all teens take a course that includes practical information on birth control, and fewer than half receive any kind of family-living education. (1986, p. 205)

Most teens don't care about the biological issues. In a survey by Dr. Sol Gordon of Syracuse University, 50,000 teens showed an interest in questions about sex. But, he says, "Not one teenager asked a question about Fallopian tubes. Young people want to know about homosexuality, penis size, female orgasms, contraceptives, and love." (1986, p. 1-199)

These may be the questions teenagers are asking, but so far in America few adults seem willing to provide the answers. Not only are parents and educators reluctant to discuss sex with teens, but the young people are embarrassed to talk about it with their partners—until after a pregnancy occurs.

The contradiction is that, despite the reluctance to discuss sex and pregnancy prevention, the national electronic media continues to portray sex in a pervasive way. Parents Without Partners has calculated that the average TV viewer sees 20,000 scenes suggesting sexual intercourse each year.

It is encouraging that the few forward-thinking high schools in this country offering realistic prevention programs have significantly reduced their numbers of teenage mothers.

But if we really want to change things, we have to start as early as possible, in the elementary schools. America must follow Sweden's example and establish a sex-education program, for kindergarten through 12th grade, that demystifies sex and teaches the dangers of immorality, disease and unwanted pregnancy. In Sweden, 7-year-olds learn the facts of reproduction and by age 12 can pass a test on prevention and contraceptives. Many American high-school seniors couldn't pass such a test.

Elementary schools should consider having teenage mothers advise pupils about the real-world consequences of getting pregnant and having to take sole responsibility for a baby at such a young age.

Another helpful exercise is to put each youngster in charge of a raw egg for a week. Can the child carry the egg wherever he goes without breaking it? If the egg is left alone, gets cold or is abused, the child loses the game. The lesson, as pointed out by the teacher, is that taking care of a child until he is 18 is far more difficult than caring for an egg for a week. Having a baby is not a game.

Schools also need to teach children how to say no: "No, I don't want to go to bed; "No, I don't take drugs," "No, I don't need to hang out with a gang."

Several methods, including role playing, videotaping and class discussions, can be used to teach children. But the methods must be socially acceptable, motivational and appropriate to the children's ages.

Most programs fail because they don't take into account how children think. If you tell a junior high school student not to smoke because he might get cancer someday, you've pressed the wrong button. It's like telling your child that if he mows the lawn every weekend, you'll give him a gold watch when he's 21. He doesn't care. But if you tell him that smoking cigarettes will give him bad breath and make his teeth look yucky, you've got his attention.

Peers are everything to teens and if you relate to their social world, you've got a chance to influence them. Parents Without Partners realized this when the group distributed anti-pregnancy posters showing a teenage mother holding a baby, and captioned: "It's like being grounded for the next 18 years." Young people understand this: no dating, no freedom, a permanent babysitting job with no pay.

Amazingly, many macho boys aren't afraid of dying of AIDS. But they are terrified of getting the disease and being labeled homosexuals, reported sex educator Medora Brown from St. Paul, Minnesota. "That's the issue — they are more afraid of having people call them gay than they are of dying." (Kantrowitz, 1987, p. 60) As friends die this attitude will change.

Youths are more likely to take responsibility for their actions if they learn how to make decisions based on real-world data. Most can't fathom that today over $100,000 is required to raise the child to age 18. They might better understand if the sum were calculated into the kind of job and home budget they'll need to accomplish it.

How painful is labor, and how would it feel to have a Caesarean section, complete with scar? What about abortion, single-parenting, marriage and divorce? All these issues must be addressed *before* they happen. Teens are required to know the basics of safe driving before they can pass a driver's test, yet we don't insist that they learn how to prevent pregnancy, safely care for a baby or prevent unattachment. It is time to mandate that all high-school students pass a basic course in family living before they are allowed to graduate.

In Wisconsin, a grandparent-liability law makes parents responsible financially for their teenagers' babies until the infants are 18 years old. The law is designed to force parents to teach their children about the consequences of an unwanted birth. The plan has some merit but we fear that it does little to encourage responsibility in the teenagers. It also might prompt more families to opt for abortions because of economic pressures.

It seems to make more sense to educate young potential fathers, who have long escaped their fair share of responsibility for preventing pregnancy ("It's her problem, not mine"). Robert Mnookin, a Stanford University law professor and a member of the National Research Council, recommends that child-support laws be strictly enforced to make clear to young men that one mistake can mean 18 years of child-care bills. (Kantrowitz, 1987, p. 60)

Prevention programs, whatever the form, would seem to be a better use for American tax dollars than paying the tremendous costs of the teenage pregnancy epidemic. The Center for Population Options in Washington, D.C., reports that teenage pregnancy cost state and federal governments $16.7 billion in 1985 alone (Sherman, 1986, p. 202). And that doesn't include the staggering costs of escalating juvenile delinquency resulting from unattached teens giving birth to unattached children.

It's a Crime: Teen Violence

Early in 1987 a gang of youths was suspected of bludgeoning a woman to death with golf clubs in Denver. The incident prompted this response from

Don Mielke, a Colorado district attorney: "A criminal is a criminal is a criminal," whatever the age. (McGraw, 1987 p. 1-A)

Mielke is one of many prosecutors around the nation who are fed up with teenage violence and want the serious cases tried in adult courts. Many of the cases "involve bad actors who should be treated as adults . . . Victims don't care about age," says Mielke. (pp. 1-A, 10-A)

Barry Nidorf, chief probation officer for Los Angeles County, agrees. "We're dealing with a much more serious offender than we're used to; it's appropriate that we deal with them in an adult sense." (Coplon, 1985, p. 166)

The type of young offender at issue here is the typical psychopath who blames the victim and has no remorse. As one 17-year-old mugger says, "If we got to shoot you, we shoot you. It ain't really so we take the money. It's done in anger. You're playing hero, and we get upset. It burns me up. We're serious, and you think this is a joke. You're testing us." (Coplon, 1985, p. 168)

According to a Justice Department survey at least 90% of the 50,000 youths in public detention centers in 1986 were being held for acts that would be considered serious criminal offenses if committed by adults. Almost one of every five were suspects in murders, rapes, robberies or aggravated assaults. ("Survey shows high," 1986, p. 5,6)

Many of the youths who land in detention centers receive no treatment and are quickly released back into the community, where they commit more crimes. Kim Goldberger, a Colorado county judge, explains: "In most states we have a separate juvenile code to deal with juvenile offenders. They are treated as if their crimes aren't as serious as an adult's. It's a fallacy. It's a legal fantasy." (*Hour Magazine*, February 9, 1987)

How could anyone, especially children and teenagers, want to hurt innocent people? Erica Manfred, a former probation officer for Family Court in Brooklyn, N.Y., says: "These kids are human refuse. They are neglected by their parents almost from birth. They live in the streets and don't care if they live or die. They think they're worthless . . . and so they think nobody else is worth anything, either. They're filled with rage, and they take it out on anybody who looks at them sideways." (Coplon, 1985, p. 166)

The answer, of course, is to reduce — and prevent whenever possible — the ways in which children become mistrustful and filled with rage.

In the past, society's approach to crime committed by children has been largely reactive, focusing on control and rehabilitation.

Efforts toward prevention now concentrate on three main areas: modifying conditions in the physical and social environment that lead to crime, such as home care; attempting to identify and help those who might be heading for crime before they get into trouble; and preventing children from repeating crimes. (Wall, 1981)

The Center for the Assessment of Delinquent Behavior and Its Prevention developed a list of the most important factors to be considered in programs designed to help such children. These include social network development, psychological and biological well-being, self-concept enhancement, role development and education. Of these, education and self-concept building are of primary importance in preventing teenage violence, just as they are in the case of teenage pregnancy.

There are a few school programs in the U.S. which have made specific efforts to help prevent delinquency through early intervention. Oregon public school educators are helping elementary school children learn to assume important roles in life, such as learner, individual, producer, citizen, consumer and family member. In Calabasas, California, the school district has instituted a program called "Law in a Free Society." In it, students from kindergarten through 12th grade learn about responsibility, authority, privacy, justice, participation, property, diversity and freedom.

Some anti-delinquency programs concentrate on helping parents with aggressive or out-of-control children. The Family Teaching Center in Helena, Montana, teaches parents child management techniques including discipline and self-concept skills.

In Des Moines, Iowa, the In-Home Support Services program helps the family in need by offering comprehensive therapeutic homemaking and child-care services on the home turf. (Wall, 1981)

There are many other programs attempting to deal with delinquent youths. In most cases developers of these programs may be vaguely aware of the importance of the attachment process. Unfortunately what they are offering is probably too little, too late.

Detecting and treating unattached children early is vital. It is much easier to deal with the rage of an unbonded 2-year-old than with the fury of an unattached 19-year-old.

The sad truth is that many hard-core psychopaths need to be incarcerated to protect the public. Those diagnosed as treatable should be given an opportunity for professional help as described in the treatment section of this book.

Judge Goldberger is upset with the current state of affairs in the judicial system, noting, "I give him (a psychopath) 5 to 40 and he beats me home for dinner." Goldberger laments the situation, and is determined to do something about it. "I want my colleagues to learn more about this subject so that we can make more constructive changes to protect the public. I plan to talk to every judge I meet so that we are in the leadership role again." (personal communication, January, 1987)

We must stop the bonding crisis in America.

Goldberger sees 6,000 cases a year and many of them tug heavily at his heart. "I have a court situation where the 1-year-old is left in the care of the 5-year-old until the 10-year-old gets home from school. What kind of bonding and attachment are those children going to develop?" he asks. "I worry about our future." (personal communication, January, 1987)

*****

We have talked about good parenting practices and good teaching techniques. Of the persistent social problems dogging our society, teenage pregnancy and crime are but two examples. In the next section we will discuss some of the other situations that may be causing unattached children: increasing numbers of parents forced to return to work too soon after childbirth or adoption, the day-care dilemma, the adoption and foster-care system and abusive homes.

26

National Leave Policy

Jean Goebel had a choice: her $35,000-a-year job or her adopted infant daughter.

She chose her daughter.

Goebel testified in 1987 before the Congressional subcommittee considering the adoption of a national 18-week parental leave policy. She recalled her anger at her employer who would not allow her time off to get acquainted with her new infant. She chose the time off with her baby and was subsequently fired from her airline job of 14 years. She said when she began searching for another position, "I found I was being considered for jobs at $12,000 and $15,000. The loss of my job was devastating." ("Fired Adoptive Mom," 1987, p. 4-D)

She testified in favor of legislation which would allow fathers or mothers unpaid leave after the birth or adoption of a child, or to care for a seriously ill child.

The Senate Subcommittee on Children, Families, Drugs and Alcoholism was considering the bill. Senator Chris Dodd, D-Conn., had introduced the senate's version of legislation on parental leaves. Representative Patricia Schroeder, D-Colo., in February, 1987, reintroduced a similar bill into the House of Representatives. It was Schroeder's second attempt to pass this legislation. The 1986 version did not come to a vote. The 1987 Family and Medical Leave Act (HR 925) addressed one of the most pressing problems in this country today—that of allowing young parents enough time to grow comfortable with their new family situation and to establish competent parenting patterns.

Employees should have the right:

- To paid, job-protected leaves with continuation of health benefits for temporary, non-occupational disabilities, including those related to pregnancy and childbirth.

- To elect a job-protected leave of absence for parenting. ("Parental Leave: Options," 1985)

In view of the increasing proportion of the American labor force trying to work productively while raising families, a national policy for all parents must be legislated. Both mothers and fathers should be eligible for appropriate provisions of any program. The Pregnancy Discrimination Act was a beginning. It requires a pregnancy-related disability to be treated as a medical disability. There is no requirement that employers provide temporary disability coverage.

The time generally provided for disability is not sufficient for many parents to launch their families. It is vital that a parenting leave be offered distinct from pregnancy-related disability.

Schroeder's bill exempts companies with fewer than 15 employees and it has three main components:

- It would mandate up to 18 weeks of unpaid leave for employers, male and female, with a newborn, newly adopted child or seriously ill child or parent.

- It would require up to 26 weeks of unpaid leave for workers with short-term disabilities from pregnancy or other temporary conditions.

- It would create a panel to study the feasibility of a national policy on paid parental and disability leave. (MacPherson, 1987)

Although the legislation is a starting point, we do not feel this goes far enough. The nation would be better served if a *paid* leave of at least 6 months were available, with an additional 6 months of optional leave. (Paid leaves of this duration are now common practice in many European nations, including France and Sweden.)

More than two-thirds of the nations in the world, including almost all industrialized nations, have some provisions for parents of infants to take paid, job-protected leaves of absence from the workplace for physical recovery from labor and birth and to care for their newborn infants. (Zigler, 1985) The United States is still in the Dark Ages when it comes to helping develop healthy, intact families.

HR 925 does not provide for monetary help during such leave. This stand needs to be reconsidered. Many in our society — those who need the help the most — would not be able to take advantage of such a leave without monetary assistance.

Edward Zigler agrees this is necessary. He told a news conference in late 1986 that at least one member of a working couple should get a six-month leave of absence with partial pay to prevent lasting damage to families. (Okula, 1986)

At the same press conference, a Yale Bush Center committee proposed granting leaves with 75% pay for three months. The estimated $1.5 billion cost could be paid from an insurance fund into which employers and affected employees would contribute. (Okula, 1986)

The short-term, initial monetary costs of parental leave have fueled the arguments of most opponents, who include some of the nation's most powerful business groups. While acknowledging that such a measure could be a good way to recruit and retain valuable workers, businesses are saying mandating such a benefit would eliminate flexibility.

They say it would cost business $16 billion through lost productivity and replacement workers. "If parental bonding or nurturing . . . is the desired goal, it will not result from government coercion," says Frances Shaine, a Massachusetts businesswoman and chairman of the U.S. Chamber of Commerce Small Business Council. ("Fired Adoptive Mom," 1987, p. 4-D)

In closing remarks to a symposium on parental leave held in 1985, T. Berry Brazelton quoted a Mayan saying from southern Mexico:

> " 'In the newborn baby is the future of the world. The mother should hold that baby close so he knows the world is his. A father should take that baby to the highest hill so he knows how wide and wonderful his world is.'
>
> "In my view that's where we have to go." (p. 5)

*"A man travels the world over in
search of what he needs and returns
home to find it."*
George Moore

27

What About Day Care?

 The debate continues about whether it is harmful for small children to be in day care. The kind of day care and the age of the child seem to be the important factors here.

In one dramatic example of what day care should not be, a 1984 report on Quebec day care centers presented an appalling scenario:

Thirty or 40 children were crowded into quarters designed for a single family. There were large noisy groups with a ratio of 20 charges per caregiver, and poorly supervised children sat glassy-eyed in front of the TV. Two-year-olds marched single file and were obliged to maintain strict silence during meals. There were 3-year-olds kneeling in a corner as punishment and 5-year-olds forced to take naps. The ultimate horror: a 4-month-old infant was found dead. She had suffocated on her pillowcase. (Maynard, 1985, p. 12)

*****

Parents in today's world are caught up in the dramatic events that are changing the ways in which we raise our children. As the trend towards increasing numbers of working mothers continues, parents face a confusing number of alternatives when it comes to day care for their children. In addition to being expensive, day care is often unreliable. Underpaid, overworked sitters and day-care center workers have a huge turnover rate.

Guilt is a pervasive undercurrent as parents fear they are damaging their children's development and weakening the attachment bond when they send their small children to day care.

It is important to review the facts when discussing day care solutions for infants and small children. The Bureau of Labor Statistics estimates that almost half of all mothers with young children work; the total was about 8.2 million in 1986. Some predictions are that 80% of all families will have two working parents by the end of the century. (Meredith, 1986)

What is clear is that this scenario will not reverse itself. Given that, how can parents safely leave their children in the care of others without risking the disruptions that cause bonding breaks? We feel the answer to this question, for infants under 1 year of age, is that *they cannot.*

It is unwise to leave any youngster in full-time substitute care until he is at least 1 year old. After 1 year of age children are in a natural transition that fosters autonomy from the parents. From age 18 months to 2 years is a better time to make the transition from home care to day care.

Studies have shown that older children, in fact, can do well when their mothers work. Parents of children 2 years old or older can take some relief from these studies. There is evidence that older children in quality day care develop just as well socially and intellectually as those with mothers in the home.

Parents of infants can feel no real comfort, however. As we have pointed out, so few studies have been done and their results are so controversial that infant day care is still a high-risk situation.

After the baby is more than 1 year old, parents can begin to ease him into a substitute care situation. Very careful attention must be paid to how long the parents can safely stay away from the child. And the time spent with the baby should be "quality" time. When parents do return to work, they must make sure that the day-care situation into which they are placing their infant is the best available. Parents must not be willing to choose simply "custodial" care; they need good quality, nurturing environments for their children.

What of parents who have no choice but to leave their babies before they are a year old? What of the single-parent family or the working poor? If you *must* return to work and leave your small infant, the overriding concern should be that you find a loving and nurturing individual to care for your baby. This can be a nanny, a relative in your own home or a loving caregiver in another's home if it is of high quality. The ratio of adult caregivers to children should be much smaller with babies than with older children.

Child-care experts believe infants should be cared for with a ratio of no more than three infants to one caregiver; two infants to one caregiver is even better. The substitute caregiver for small babies must be someone to whom the baby can attach, in addition to the baby's parents. Again, the most important attribute of the substitute caregiver is that *she must be a loving, nurturing individual.*

For a baby or very small child the best situation seems to be in-your-home care. This is someone who comes into your home and whose primary responsibility is to love the baby and nurture him.

RECOMMENDED RATIO OF CHILD CARE PROVIDERS TO CHILDREN

1:3	1:4 or 5	1:7-9	1:25
infants	1-2 years	3-5 years	6-13 years

Children under 3 years old should be in groups of 12 or less and 3-5 year olds in groups of 20 or less with appropriate number of providers.

© High Risk, Magid/McKelvey

The second best situation for infants and small children is individual care in someone else's home, such as a relative or family day-care mother who you know is a good caregiver. Next would be a family day-care home, with a kind and loving person caring for no more than three children in her licensed home. (A licensed home, by the way, doesn't guarantee that the person is more capable or loving, but it does show that he or she is committed enough to have gone through the licensing process.) Although it is nice to have someone who is intelligent and well-educated, the important criterion is the ability to love and nurture.

The least desirable situation for smaller children is a day-care center. Most centers have too many children and too few adults to be able to care for and nurture small children properly.

There are two kinds of day-care centers, nonprofit and profit-oriented. These types of centers are good for older toddlers who are beginning to socialize and need to have play experiences with other children their ages.

There is a strong evidence that day-care centers, particularly those with large numbers of children, can be damaging. A 1981 study by the Tavistock Institute, in England, found that such nurseries make children more aggressive and less able to cope with school. The report suggested reorganization of typical staffs if such nurseries are to work. It proposed more staff for nurseries, changes in nursery practice and different training for the staff that would emphasize nurturing instead of teaching children. (New York Times Educational Supplement, 1981)

There are consumer guides for cars, refrigerators and soaps. But the sad fact is there are few such guides for day care settings, or any other human-services institutions. ("Group Care Can," 1980)

Good quality substitute care is one of the most elusive products available in the marketplace. While government and business are making some progress toward aiding working parents, the situation is still fairly bleak. Neither the federal government nor private industry has shown the full commitment needed to solve the persistent problems of child care.

One solution to some of the dilemmas of day care is to develop more on-site child-care programs at places of employment. Unfortunately, the American businessman has not been at the forefront in helping working women cope with the anguish of serving two masters. Few corporations provide some form of day care, despite the growing evidence that such offerings actually save money through increased productivity and high employee morale. About 2,500 companies across the country now offer such benefits. (Peterson, 1986) These companies usually offer some kind of child-care assistance, rather than getting into the business of child care. This might be a reference or referral service, subsidies or vouchers redeemable at a center of the parents' choosing, reimbursement accounts from which pretax dollars are held back to pay for child care, funding of existing community day-care centers and, in a few cases, on-site centers.

These are fairly new human services and, although they are called the perk of the 80s, what is ironic is that we have known how to do this correctly since World War II.

During that war, to meet heavy construction demands, the Kaiser Shipyards in Portland, Oregon, hired 25,000 women and established what has been called the "best day care, ever." (Zinsser, 1984, p. 80)

Kaiser founded an around-the-clock, 365-days-a-year center to help care for the workers' children. The facility was huge (2,250 children in two complexes) and it had:

- A well-paid, thoroughly professional staff;
- The best equipment available (everything from unbreakable juice glasses to easels and scooters);
- An infirmary staffed with full-time nurses;
- A provision for immunizations to save parents from time-consuming visits to the doctor;
- A special-service room for temporary care of children not enrolled in the center;
- Carefully planned, nutritious meals and snacks;

- A pre-cooked food service for workers, who could order the family dinner in the morning from a standard menu and then pick up the meals when they collected their children at day's end;
- A bi-weekly newspaper describing the children's activities;
- Booklets on child care, toy selection, holiday activities and shopping ideas; and
- A lending library of children's books.

The center even had plans for a mother and infant dormitory, a shopping service, provisions for haircuts and photographs.

"We thought that anything that saved the working mother time and energy meant she would have more to give to her child," recalled James Hymes, Jr., who served as on-site manager. (Zinsser, 1984, p. 80) The center was closed at the end of the war and nothing like it has ever been established again.

Why is it that in the 1940s we had much more vision about the needs of families than we do in the 1980s?

Today's businesses would do well to take a long, hard look at who is suffering when they choose not to help the working mothers of this nation. It is the nation which is reaping the bad harvest. The day care situation outlined above was considered the best of its day. But what can parents look for when selecting a day-care center for their older child in today's market?

Day Care: A Parents Guide

Low-Risk

High-Risk

Caregivers in the home:

A warm, intelligent and experienced person who genuinely loves children. You can tell a lot about an individual by the way she looks and talks to your child. She should be openly affectionate.	An individual with a "drill sergeant" mentality who feels children need to mind first and feel second. A person who would verbally scold, criticize or threaten a child or make fun of or ridicule a child.

An individual who comes with excellent references (preferably from a good friend or your family doctor and who is mature).

A young, inexperienced girl who doesn't know about bonding and attachment. She is detached, removed from the child, even when not on a break.

Someone who will share the experiences of the day with the parents before leaving (if she doesn't live in your home).

An individual who dashes out the door complaining about the bad day she had and the trouble your child was.

This person will have the baby "ready to play" with his parents. She will take care of all the routine tasks so a busy mother can sit down and enjoy her baby. She will care about you as well as your baby.

Be wary of someone who seems to have the TV on from the time she enters your home. She may be using it as a babysitter. She leaves the child alone.

A sensible person who knows enough about child-rearing to be able to make gentle suggestions that help busy parents maximize the time they have with their infants.

Watch your child's reaction to the caregiver to tell whether a close and loving relationship is growing.

Caregivers in a center:

There are no more than 1 to 3 infants or small children per adult caregiver. And the total number of children per room should be low, fewer than 10.

Great numbers of children are jammed into rooms too crowded to serve them, and babies are cared for by whoever is available.

One caregiver has the responsibility for your infant in particular. This is *most* important if your child is under 18 months old. At least one person should have formal training in early childhood development among the supervisory staff.

Most of the caregivers seem young (barely out of their teens) and no one with real authority seems to be in charge.

Make sure caregivers get along and work well together. They have been at the center for a reasonable length of time.

There are not enough caregivers to handle the children and many are new to the center. (Beware of a turnover rate of 15% or more.)

Nurturing individuals sense when children need a pat or a hug. They do not leave distressed children to cry but pick them up and hold them. Soft toys and blankets are available so children can hold them. Teachers know when a child needs help or encouragement and are there to provide it.

Children are directed about with no one really paying attention to the children's individual differences. Youngsters cry to themselves, some in corners of the room. The children get lost in the middle of the general chaos.

Competency is fostered by teachers who help children work on self-help skills. They praise children when they accomplish such tasks as cleaning up after playtime or helping clear a table.

Orders are given and the teachers "do for" their charges instead of helping the children form a sense of self-worth. No praise is heard.

Babies and children are talked to, even during diaper changing. Children are asked questions requiring more than a one-word reply. Books and reading are encouraged and are often part of the day's activities. And children are shown props (such as fingers and toes) when learning new words. Hugs, smiles and claps accompany new words and language skills.

The caregivers don't seem to know the children's individual names, but call out to the children with "boy," "girl" or "hey, you." No attempt is made to communicate with the children on a one-to-one basis.

Caregivers are fun-loving and enjoy participating in games and playing with the children. They join in and show by their enthusiasm that the world is a good place and that curiosity is a healthy emotion. They treat children courteously.

There seems to be little enjoyment from the instructors' point of view. They primarily stand around and watch the children, without participating themselves.

They understand a baby's need to have sensory stimulation, such as sucking, stroking, tasting and messing. They accept this sensual side of small children and convey the message that the children's bodies are good.

Children are rigidly controlled and they are discouraged from using their "security blankets" or favorite toys. A baby exploring his body is chastised.

If children are naughty, the caregiver wards off pending trouble by staying alert. This is a happy place and the caregivers are firm and loving. Children are made to feel secure.

Children are spanked or treated roughly. Some may be placed in a seat against the wall or ignored.

When the opportunity to teach comes up, teachers seize it, but teaching is not the god here. Teachers take time to show children cause-and-effect thinking and are always ready to explain and enhance at any time.

The situation seems tense and children are not very happy. You get the impression that it is out of control or indifferent.

The Facilities: Centers and in-home:

The surroundings are safe and clean with plenty of room for the babies or toddlers to play and move around.

Be wary of a home setting that is too fastidiously clean and meticulously arranged. Such a setting may not give children the freedom they need.

Certain areas are set aside (like a darkened bedroom in a home setting) for nap and quiet times.

Centers that have just one large room or too small an area for the number of children will not foster both quiet play and more aggressive pursuits.

A fenced yard with plenty of space for play, running, jumping, climbing, swinging, and tricycle riding. Such activity will encourage coordination and will help children develop hearty appetites.

Make sure you don't see hazards, such as sharp objects or rusty toys or equipment. Things don't have to be brand-new, just well kept.

This environment should be safe and well-maintained. Emergency phone numbers and parents' numbers are clearly posted. The menu includes healthy food that meets the daily food-group needs of growing children. (Special diets are taken into consideration.)

Look for hidden dangers: these might include unprotected outlets or stairs, sharp table edges, cleaning supplies at floor-level and not locked up, or hot surfaces at child level. Make sure floors are non-slippery and have no splinters (carpet is best). The house smells like ammonia, or dirty diapers. An unclean environment spreads infection easily among young children.

The best toys are those children can do something with, such as jack-in-the-boxes and wind-up music toys. There are plenty of props that encourage children to use their imaginations and play "make-believe."

Broken toys are frustrating and can be dangerous if there are sharp edges. Ripped books or puzzles with pieces missing only discourage children.

The program:

Of course, a more formal program will be followed at a center than in a home setting. But you can ask what is done during a typical day. Usually both kinds of care will include problem-solving activities as well as creative ones (such as matching shapes or painting). Toy-play helps children with hand-eye coordination and understanding cause and effect.

Children do not do well when they must conform to a strict schedule that requires them all to do the same task at the same time in the same way.

The center's program has flexibility for special events, such as birthday parties. Those tending the children have the freedom to deviate from the day's plan should the children seem disinterested or particularly restless that day.

Ask if children are allowed to watch TV, and if so, for how long and what programs. Poorly run centers often have caregivers who show children too much, not allowing for individual discovery.

The best centers plan outside activities, such as visits to the zoo and parks. When a child is found to need special services, community resources are tapped or suggested.

Perhaps one of the most telling signs of a good caregiver or center is how parents are encouraged to participate. Parents should be asked to share their knowledge and concerns about their child and they should always feel welcome to drop by.

If outside trips are planned make sure the center's vehicles comply with child-restraint laws. A large number of children accompanying a few caregivers on an outing spells trouble.

Be suspicious if the center wants you to call ahead before dropping in for a visit. Parental involvement should always be encouraged. When it is not the center or caregiver may have something to hide. It could be poor child-minding, or it could be something much worse.

© High Risk, Magid/McKelvey

We have talked about the attributes a good caregiver must have and what an employer can do to help with employee child-care problems. There is another option not used often enough to help ease working mothers back into the workplace. It is called flex-time. Presently, this option is often the result of individual negotiation and depends a great deal on how valuable the employee is to the company. Working part-time or from home or at reduced or flexible hours (4 days a week, for example) may take its toll on the working mother's career advancement, however.

Some mothers are making this a viable alternative. Many law firms, for example, are allowing new mothers to work on revised schedules.

Susan, a computer operator, was able to negotiate an arrangement to work out of her home at full salary and with benefits. She used a computer hook-up with the office and said the only thing she missed was the social interaction and not being there when major decisions were made.

Fewer than 2% of the white-collar population now works out of the home. "While the total number of 'telecommuters' doing office work today is relatively small — around 15,000 people — the potential for growth is enormous," says Mary Murphree, a New York-based regional administrator for the Women's Bureau of the U.S. Department of Labor. "Estimates of the number of teleworkers doing office work in 1990 range from 5 million to as many as 18 million." (Rubin, 1987, p. 35)

Women all over the country — in small numbers — are beginning to negotiate for flexible time so they can care for their small children themselves and preserve their seniority and positions.

Another woman, vice-president for a major tour company, was able to take a maternity leave and hold meetings in her home during the interim. She then arranged to work shorter hours for a reduced salary until she could return full-time.

She says the company receives an added benefit: "I can do as much in three or four days as I did in five. I am not as distracted with petty details. I am more focused. People know I'm only here a certain amount of time, so they take on more responsibility themselves." (Rubin, 1987, p. 35)

Women trying to negotiate for flexible hours may have to try several approaches. They can point out that part-timers save the company money, says Jane Bryant Quinn in the March, 1986, issue of *Woman's Day* magazine. (p. 20) An employee might work full-time, then devise a plan for dividing responsibilities and reducing hours. Or she can suggest how the company can save money by letting her share a full-time job with a partner with similar skills and experience. The most common job-sharers are teachers, social workers and other professionals.

Most part-time workers, however, do not receive benefits; workers needing these are probably better off with large corporations. Quinn notes that part-timers have two disadvantages: no job security and slower advancement. (1986, p. 20)

These sorts of special accommodations are not made for everyone, however. An editor at a large daily newspaper tried to negotiate so that she could work from her home computer when her new son was born. But management refused, saying that allowing her to work from home would "open a can of worms." Because she could not afford to lose her well-paying job, she went back to work full-time.

Many companies, however, are finding that being generous with working mothers and/or fathers pays off in the end. "There's no question that our child-care program has helped us compete very effectively for talented people," says Leonard Silverman, vice president of human resources at Hoffmann-La Roche. The company began sponsoring child-care services for employees in 1977. It is one of the few companies (there are about 150 who do so) in the U.S. operating its own center — a block from its New Jersey headquarters.

Silverman said benefits to his company (and others who have provided child-care benefits) include: increased retention of trained employees; reduced tardiness, absenteeism and turnover; and greater productivity. Silverman sums up the company's experience: "We consider support for child care to be an investment — one that has already paid us handsome dividends." (Micheli, 1986, p. 132)

There are four very good business reasons for corporations to become actively involved in creating first-class child care for their employees: tax advantages, public relations benefits, employee satisfaction and cost-effectiveness.

The child-care crisis for the middle class and the poor must be addressed. The ad hoc, fragmented, inadequate network currently in place has services that range from minimal to dangerous. "The once-private matter of child care," says Elizabeth Ehrlich in a recent issue of *Business Week,* "has become a public policy issue that demands action." (1986, p. 52)

To assure quality care to serve growing numbers of disadvantaged children, for instance, "government has to get more resources in the system," says Rep. George Miller, D.-Calif., chairman of the House Select Committee on Children, Youth and Families. (Ehrlich, 1986, p. 52) Affordable, excellent child care is an idea whose time has come.

Unquestionably, the future is looking better for working parents. Child-care perks are not just for women, but for fathers and families and the companies that provide them. The ultimate winner will be this country. While relieving working parents' anxieties, good care for their children allows these workers to concentrate more on their work and results in healthier children, too.

New options are opening up in the work force for parents as they try to juggle the responsibilities of making a living with those of their families. As more women move into the work force and into positions of management, these options will open even wider. Employees can help a company get involved by doing research on the needs and benefits and presenting their requests to management.

Businesses and government can help solve the day care dilemma. In San Francisco, for example, a new city law makes child care an official priority. Last October, Mayor Dianne Feinstein signed into law a measure requiring developers of new office buildings to include child-care facilities in the plans. If such facilities are not included, the developers must make contributions to a city-administered child-care fund. It is the first law of its kind in a major U.S. city. Just as developers in most big cities now must provide for an adequate number of parking spaces, San Francisco is requiring they find space for parents who need good solutions to their child-care problems.

Congress also needs to help by making flexible-benefit programs more tax-beneficial for employers.

Child care is a national issue and it needs national attention now if we are to reduce the risk of unattached children and ease the minds of working parents everywhere.

"Do they miss me at home — do they miss me?
'Twould be an assurance most dear,
To know that this moment some loved one
Were saying, 'I wish he were here'. "
                                    Caroline Atherton Briggs Mason

28

Adoption and Foster Care

 There was the pre-teen boy who was sexually molesting his adoptive family's 3-year-old daughter. She still awakens, screaming in the night.

There was a 5-year-old girl who refused to eat in her new home. Eventually she heaved vomit across the room when she was forced to eat.

There was the young man who tried to set fire to the trailer where he lived with his adopted family.

And there was the boy who goaded his father into slapping him in the face. The adoptive father realized he couldn't go on.

All of the youngsters above have been involved in disrupted adoptions. (Hornby, 1986)

There is also the child who spent his first few months with his adoptive family abusing the family animals. Diagnosed as "character-disordered," he doesn't have the capacity to tell right from wrong. His adoptive mother said: "We have made a commitment to him. Even if he winds up in jail some day, we know we will have given him his best shot." (Hornby, 1986, p. 7)

These are all children in serious trouble. They are products of the foster-care and child-adoption system in the U.S. Some are in trouble because of past abuse and neglect, others because of delays in the adoption process. They have all suffered attachment breaks. Bureaucratic delays are causing these kinds of breaks — children are becoming unattached through the very processes designed to help them. Adoption and foster care can, indeed, be hazardous to their health.

Some of the most problematic children are those who have lost their ability to trust, to show affection and form lasting relationships. In addition, children in their early adolescence may confuse the normal desire for independence with their rejection of parents in a new adoptive home. For some, adoption is not even a believable concept because they hold memories of other significant grown-ups and have idealized families in their past. (Hornby, 1986)

These children do not have to be so tragically unattached. Research underscores the need for agencies to make the most timely, permanent plans for children. It should be a crime that some infants are left in limbo, languishing in foster homes or hospitals. They must be permanently placed with their adoptive parents as soon as possible. Recent reports have shown that even days-old infants have already begun the attachment process.

Of children available for adoption, the most likely to have disruptions are those in their pre-teens. But all children are entitled to have a permanent home. The key to making these adoptions work is preparation of parents and the adoption agencies' own practices and services. (Hornby, 1986)

Foster or adoptive parents should know that the road ahead is littered with potholes, and they should be aware of the danger signs. They should realize that younger children need help if the effects of attachment breaks are to be mitigated.

Parents seeking foreign infants to adopt must also realize that these children — particularly those who come from orphanages — may already be seriously damaged. Many of these children require years of expensive therapy and even then may never be whole.

Those involved in social-service decisions regarding the placement of children and their removal from their original families must know the dangers these children and families face. Education and preventative intervention are vitally necessary in suspected abusive families.

When a child must be removed from his home, he should be prepared for the move if at all possible. Most children's initial reaction to abrupt separation from their parents, whether through removal or abandonment, is intense anxiety. A talented social worker will tell children at a time like this, "Most kids are really scared when they move into a new home." This frequently opens the door for a child to talk about his feelings.

Next we discuss the steps that foster families, agencies and adoptive families can follow to make the transitions for these children easier:

Children in Transition

Low-Risk

High-Risk

Foster families:

Help a child who has left his family to express his feelings. Take on the job of helping him deal with these feelings. Children who don't work through sad or angry feelings will do poorly in the long run.

Minimize the child's feelings. Say, "Don't be sad" or "You aren't at fault." A child's pain will not disappear by being ignored.

If future moves are planned, to another foster home or to an adoptive one, prepare the child. The best way may be with a "life book." This includes pictures of important events in the child's life and descriptions of how he felt. Such things might be toys he liked or what he was afraid of or particular childhood illnesses. This provides a sense of continuity.

In the past some foster parents were instructed not to get emotionally close to the foster child. This has now been proven wrong. It is now believed that if a child can bond with a foster parent he most likely can bond with a permanent family.

Get physically close to the child, if possible, even if he will not allow you to get emotionally close. If a child withdraws, sit with him or hold him (do not hold a violent child) but do not insist on his talking, and do not feel you must talk.

Expect the child to conform at first to "family rules" such as eating a normal breakfast or making his bed.

Although it may be painful, encourage visits from the child's natural parents if this is possible. This will alleviate the child's fears and help him deal with his feelings of anger or pain.

Children in foster-care often are terrified that their natural parents are dead. This is true even if the parents were abusive.

It is crucial that foster parents respond by trying to establish an atmosphere of trust with the child.

The foster-care system itself fosters breaks and parents can worsen them by not helping a child make an attachment.

Adoptive parents:

Insist on a complete history of the child you are adopting. Make sure you can handle the situation. Enter the agreement, particularly with older children, with both eyes wide open.

A home that has an environment that is inflexible, is humorless or has no sense of adventure will be in trouble from the start.

A positive "we have a lot to give" attitude is a plus. Tailor your aspirations to what the child can deliver.

Parents with a "save-the-world approach" are headed for trouble. They may be naive. Love will not conquer all with these children.

Make sure the child you are adopting will be compatible with your family. If conflict arises do not allow yourself to be brought down to the child's level.

Force the child to conform in ways not possible. Some children are messy by nature, for example.

If you know there will be adverse circumstances from the beginning (say you are adopting an abused child), you should have a plan of action. By taking a child on as a challenge, you and the child may be better served.

Problems that escalate worsen when the parents are caught off guard.

Accept some credit for improvements children make, but do not buy into their failures. Look beyond the child's superficial words and behaviors to see his most basic needs and feelings.

Adoptive families who see the new child's behavior as a reflection of their own ability to parent can run into serious trouble.

The agencies:

First and foremost, get the child into permanent placement as soon as possible. Children placed at younger ages and with fewer traumatic moves always do better. Do not shortchange the child's preparation for adoption, however. Make sure you are giving this child the best possible chance of survival.

Delays in the decision-making process can be catastrophic for these children.

Actions by placing agencies can help mitigate problems: earlier therapy and individual counseling, and more thorough assessment of the child's needs, problems, history and capabilities.

Poorly matching a child to a family can result in the tragedy of a disrupted adoption. The blame can be placed squarely on the agency's insufficient work to help the child and the family.

Adoptive parents should be thoroughly prepared with counseling and helped with administrative and legal matters. And it helps to put them in contact with other adoptive families.

When the placing agency does not have custody this can hinder having a complete background on the child.

Once a child is placed, the agency's job is not over. Consistent, open communication and assistance is imperative to help the child and family over rough spots.

Inadequate contact between social worker and the adoptive family will spell trouble. They must be in constant contact and adequate support must be available.

© High Risk, Magid/McKelvey

Adoptive or foster care parents can help unattached children if they follow some techniques for encouraging attachment. It is possible, although difficult, to help "make up" for the lack of healthy attachments a child has suffered. Vera Fahlberg, in *Attachment and Separation*, outlines ways that adoptive and foster parents can modify the initial bonding cycle for infants so they may help older children.

Recall that the First Year of Life Cycle involves four separate interactions between infant and parent: Need, Rage Reaction, Gratification or Relief, and Trust. Using a similar pattern this cycle can be adapted for older children. Fahlberg calls this the Arousal-Relaxation Cycle. In this cycle, the child first has physical or psychological needs. These lead to a state of high arousal. If the need is satisfied then relaxation of tension is achieved. Out of this can come security, trust, and eventual attachment.

The pattern followed here is much like that used in the Rage Reduction Therapy. "The important thing is that these needs create intense feelings or states of high arousal in the child," says Fahlberg. (1979, p. 53)

These intense feelings can be negative, such as fear, anger or rage, or they can be positive, such as joy or excitement. Fahlberg says in working with older unattached children the parents' role is not so much to satisfy the need themselves as to be with the child and encourage his expression of feelings until the body tension that accompanies his intense feelings subsides. It is at this time that the child is most open to bonding.

"For example, when a child gets extremely frustrated and has a temper tantrum, at the end of that tantrum he relaxes and is very open to bonding. When a child is ill and faces a trip to the doctor, he is likely to be highly aroused. A parent who stays with the child through any painful proceedings and allows the child to express his feelings encourages bonding." (1979, p. 54)

Another way to encourage attachment is by the parent starting positive interactions. These might include going on special outings, teaching the child to cook or bake, saying "I love you," and teaching the child to participate in family activities.

Initiating "claiming behaviors" is another technique. This encourages a child to claim a family as his own. For example, the family might send out adoption announcements or hold a religious or other ceremony that welcomes the child into the family or add a middle name of family significance. All such activities encourage a child to feel he belongs to the new family.

Those working in the social-services system *must* continually promote attachment between these children and their adoptive or foster parents.

Only a select few parents will be able to adopt newborn infants each year, but thousands of older children are currently in foster care around the country awaiting adoptive homes. These children come with a past but this should not scare away potential adoptive parents. Such adoptions *can* work if parents are properly prepared for the challenge they will meet. Even if adopted children are not unattached they usually have special worries. They wonder about their place in the family and about their biological parents. The ways in which children react to this situation, of course, depends on whether they are infants or older children, are from another country or racial group and whether other children are already present in the adoptive family. Children from other cultures or ethnic backgrounds, most child psychologists believe, should be encouraged to remember and participate in aspects of the original culture which can fit into their new home.

Most agencies recommend, as do the authors, that the adoptive mother stay home most of the child's first year with the family. This may mean taking a leave of absence from her career, but these are children who have already lost at least one parent figure (and sometimes many more) and need the security of a full-time mother. Fathers can fill this full-time caregiving role too.

Parents having trouble with an adoption should turn to their agency for help. But there are national organizations which also help with problems and function as support groups. Two of the most prominent are International Concerns Committee for Children, in Boulder, Colorado, and the North American Council on Adoptable Children, in Alexandria, Virginia. The National Committee for Adoption maintains a 24-hour hotline for all sorts of adoption concerns.

"A wrathful man stirreth up strife:
but he that is slow to anger appeaseth
strife."
The Bible: Proverbs

29

Interrupting the Cycle of Abuse

Abusive parents make promises to themselves that they cannot keep.

Donna was unable to keep her promise. This is her third visit to the emergency room this month with her 2-year-old son. As he sits quietly beside her his eye is swelling shut and a large, ugly purple bruise appears. Donna tells the nurse that he fell, hitting the edge of the coffee table. She remembers her mother saying the same about her.

Mary was also unable to keep her promise. She calls the doctor, frantically explaining that her son has pulled a hot pan of soup from the stove, all over his stomach, "They won't suspect I did it," she thinks. When she was a child her mother scalded her by pouring hot water down her legs.

"Violence breeds violence. If a parent beats his child, there is a risk that the child will also use violence in the future to achieve his aims. Corporal punishment shapes the child to an authoritative pattern and seems unfitting in a society which aims to develop the child into a peace-loving independent individual." Such was the belief of the Swedish Government in 1979 when the Riksdag outlawed physical punishment of children in Sweden. A child in Sweden also cannot be subjected to humiliating treatment. (Salzar, 1979. p. 3)

This is a far cry from treatment of children in the U.S. where annually more than 1 million youngsters fall victim to abuse at the hands of their parents, friends or neighbors. As stated earlier, child abuse is a pervasive problem in this country. It is the nonaccidental physical injury, physical neglect, sexual abuse or emotional abuse of children. (Cohn, 1986)

Families with abusive backgrounds must be singled out for help and education.

"The most powerful cause of violence today, as in the past, is neglect and physical abuse of children. This usually turns children into aggressive and

301

often criminal adults . . . Mistreatment of children can occur at all economic and educational levels," said Dr. Benjamin Spock in a 1979 article. (p. 64) It is still true.

In addition to neglect and parental rage, there is a great deal of "casual" mistreatment of children in the U.S. — parents hitting children in supermarkets, angrily yanking them along the sidewalk, frequently and irritably shouting at them.

"Children subject to a lot of abuse become adults who in turn beat their spouses or children, thus passing on the unfortunate pattern," says Spock. (1979, p. 64)

Industrialization, the concentration of more and more people in large, impersonal cities, the breakup of the family, the tendency of people to move often—all tend to weaken positive ties between people and release their antisocial impulses. By and large, however, it is the history of an abusive and neglectful childhood that parents who abuse have in common. The hurts they receive as children influence their entire lives, and ours as well. These childhood histories are commonly reported by many adult criminals and juvenile delinquents. And their children are at very high risk for unattachment.

Several things can be done. When there are greater-than-average tensions between husband and wife that affect the children, families can seek counseling at social agencies, mental-health clinics, private therapists' offices or marriage-counseling bureaus. The same applies to parents who find themselves getting inappropriately angry with their children.

In seeking jobs, parents can pay less attention to questions of money and prestige and more to friendliness of atmosphere and possible enjoyment of the work. Corporations interested in preserving the family should reevaluate their transfer process, which often has junior executives moving every couple of years. This process tears up the roots of every family member and robs them of the comforts that come from being a permanent part of the community.

We must also address the causes of poverty in this country that doom many children not only to near-starvation conditions but promote an atmosphere conducive to violence.

"The greatest of evils and the worst of crimes is poverty." (George Bernard Shaw)

There is a sad irony in that many of those who are child abusers really do love their children. They often find themselves in life situations beyond their control and they do not know how to cope. Because of their abusive backgrounds, many abusers have unrealistic or inappropriate expectations of their children. They set standards that are impossibly high, that the children cannot possibly achieve. When the children don't meet their parents' expectations they are beaten.

One mother replayed her nightmarish childhood through her child. When visitors came to her home, they saw a very clean and neat 5-year-old whose hair was always nicely combed.

This polite and attractive child always smiled and had hugs for everyone. But she was unusually attentive to her mother's needs. She would, for example, bring her glasses of tea or fluff up her pillows or offer to comb her hair. And the mother made the child wait on visitors hand-and-foot. Despite the child's obvious efforts to please, the mother often berated her, telling others how "sloppy," or "ugly," or "mean" she was.

Why was she so hard on her daughter and why did her daughter seem not to mind, but fulfilled all her mother's needs? Because this child, to protect herself, had become parent to the parent. Parents like this mother need parenting themselves. They expect their children to provide the things they aren't getting. This mother unleashed her rage when her 5-year-old daughter couldn't meet all of her needs. So the child, like her mother before her, assumed responsibilities that were normally her mother's. The cycle of abuse continued.

What can be done to stop escalating physical and mental abuse? Prevention is the key, and it requires the help of the community. We need to strengthen our families so that we strengthen our society for later generations.

Ways to strengthen families have been discussed in the section on parenting and teenage pregnancy. New parents need to be taught such things as prenatal bonding. We need to prepare people to become parents so we can foster the development of a loving relationship and strong attachment between parent and child.

Those who have had abusive backgrounds need to be provided information about child development and taught skills in child care. For parents whose problems seem to be piling up, who feel stress and don't know what to do about it, the National Committee for Prevention of Child Abuse (NCPCA) has materials available, including tips on parenting.

Some of the danger signs for parents include:

- Do you feel troubled or nervous?
- Do you feel lonely or isolated with no one to turn to for help?
- Do you feel inadequate as a parent? Unable to cope?
- Are you often depressed?
- Do little problems seem overwhelming?
- Are you frightened about what you might do to your children?

- Do you sometimes physically hurt your children when you're angry with yourself?
- Do you feel that you were mistreated as a child and are now repeating your past?
- Do you feel confused concerning your sexual feelings toward your child? (Cohn, 1986)

Seek help if you answered "yes" to several of these questions. Most communities have child-abuse hotlines or family service agencies offering assistance. Some communities even have crisis centers where stressed parents can leave their children for a short time until they have a chance to calm down.

Other resources for parents who abuse, or fear they will abuse their children, include: programs that help abused children and young adults deal with crises, seek help and succeed as adults, especially as parents; self-help groups such as Parents Anonymous, foster grandparents or parent aides; family-support services for counseling and other emergency help.

If you find stress building up to the point that you might lash out at your child — perhaps you've recently lost your job, or you have a headache, or the washing machine has gone on the blink — the best advice is to stop and cool off. The NCPCA has put together alternatives to help you cope with the moment of frustration without hitting or hurting your children:

1. Stop in your tracks. Step back. Sit down.
2. Take five deep breaths. Inhale. Exhale. Slowly, slowly.
3. Count to 10. Better yet, 20. Or say the alphabet out loud.
4. Phone a friend, a relative or go visit someone.
5. Still mad? Hug a pillow. Or munch on an apple.
6. Thumb through a magazine, book or newspaper.
7. Do some sit-ups.
8. Pick up a pencil and write down your thoughts.
9. Take a hot bath. Or a cold shower.
10. Lie down on the floor, or just put your feet up.
11. Put on your favorite record, or radio program.

(Cohn & Gordon, 1986)

Every parent should be familiar with the causes and symptoms of child abuse and with the remedies. Abuse is not restricted to any single area of our country or any socioeconomic class. It happens everywhere, even in upper-class American homes.

Those who can't contain their frustration and abuse their children as a result often have failed in another aspect of their lives; they may feel worthless. Perhaps there is trouble on the job, or in the marriage. As we have noted, these people often were abused children themselves. Friends and relatives of parents they suspect are abusing their children should contact authorities so that the family can receive help. This can be done anonymously. But it must be noted that many, including members of Victims of Child Abuse Laws, feel some families are being falsely accused of abuse. This can lead to the children being removed from the home and placed into a foster home. Child abuse is not something to report without evidence; children do tend to bump and bruise themselves.

An abusive parent who finds that the self-help steps outlined above do not work should not hesitate to find professional help. Many counseling methods are helpful, including individual and family therapy. For help you can call the National Child Abuse Hot Line.

In September, 1984, the U.S. Attorney General's Task Force on Family Violence issued its Final Report. Two quotes from this report are significant to this discussion:

> "Violent crime is a major problem in this country. The possibility that any of us might be injured or have our homes invaded by a stranger is frightening to contemplate. But hundreds of thousands of Americans face an even more devastating reality. They are harmed, not by strangers, but by those they trust and love. They are victimized, not on the street or in the work place, but in their own homes. The shadow of family violence has fallen across their lives and they are forever changed.
>
> "We must admit that family violence is found at every level of our social structure. We must let victims know that they need not hesitate to seek help. We must listen with an understanding heart and we must act in ways which prevent, protect and support." (Colorado Domestic Violence Coalition, press release, February 26, 1987)

We must stop the cycle of abuse that is putting thousands of our children at high risk for unattachment.

How can an individual assure that he or she does not enter into a relationship with an abusive Trust Bandit? Dating singles need to know the danger signals so they can avoid the violence that can result when you fall in love with an individual with APD. The next chapter explores relationships.

"The prince of darkness
is a gentleman."
Shakespeare

30

Relationships

The No. 1 goal of most singles in America is to find Mr. and Mrs. Right. Their No. 1 fear is ending up with Mr. or Ms. Wrong. As 36-year-old eligible single Renata says, "Life would be 100% perfect if only I could meet the right person to share it with." (Olson, 1986, p. 69)

Renata got her wish and soon was madly in love with her new acquaintance, Randall. For a short time, life was blissful; they went everywhere and did everything together. Renata thought about Randall constantly and felt alive again. But within 30 days, she had been swindled out of her life savings as Randall conned her into a phony business deal. As she looks back, Renata is angry. "This may be the ultimate rape. In some ways it's worse than that because I was a willing party in it." (1986, p. 72)

Writer Kiki Olson explains the process: "The woman suckered by an artful con suffers far more than the one whose wallet is lifted from the bar when she's asked to disco. . . . Not only is there usually a more significant amount of money at stake in a con, but a woman is robbed of her trust, her confidence (which is how the con man got his name) and very often her love. What she loses, besides her cash, is often her self-respect and her optimism, which frequently is replaced with self-recrimination, loathing and bitterness." (1986, p. 72)

Being conned is not the only type of trouble that can cross the paths of dating singles. Mr. and Ms. Wrong cheat on their mates, carry diseases that they don't disclose (herpes, AIDS, etc.), lie whenever it suits them and sometimes even resort to violence.

Often marriages occur before the truth about the Trust Bandit surfaces. But surface it does, because evil minds and deeds are like fire — they can only be hidden a short time before we begin to smell smoke.

Usually a violent adult has experienced some violence in his home when he was a child. Wife-beaters, for example, are emotionally insecure and find it very hard to handle their rage. Dr. Elaine Hilberman, a psychiatrist at North Carolina School of Medicine, describes wife-beaters as "childlike, dependent and yearning for nuturance" when they aren't being overtly aggressive. (Edmiston, 1979, p. 102)

Sometimes, it is impossible to please Mr. Wrong, as one 24-year-old recalls:

> "Nothing I did was right. Dinner was too hot, too cold, too late, too early. The baby's crying annoyed him. He didn't want me to go out, he didn't want me to have friends . . .In the midst of an argument, he threw the baby on the floor. That was the first time I got it, when I stepped between him and the baby." (Edmiston, 1979, p. 99)

Once violence starts, it generally doesn't stop. As psychiatrist Natalie Shainess says: "Once a wife has been hit, it is likely to recur; some standard has been lowered, some barrier broken down." (Edmiston, 1979, p. 99)

The fact that dating violence seems to be starting earlier has educators and parents concerned. Dr. Mary Riege-Laner of Arizona State University reports that 60% of the male and female students on that campus acknowledged experiencing violence while dating. (Crichton, 1982, p. 337)

Even high-school students, who are just starting to date, are falling victim to violence. A study by Drs. June Henton and Rodney Cate of Oregon State University found that 12% of teens reported abuse in dating relationships, with the first such experience occurring at an average age of 15. (Crichton, 1982, p. 337)

Henton and Cate found similar accounts of abuse being committed by both sexes at the university level. And surprisingly, more than half of the students said they chose to stay with the abusive partner. (Baker, 1983, p. 313)

Why did they stay, and how did they get into abusive dating situations in the first place?

Riege-Laner says, "Those students who experienced childhood violence were more likely to have courtship violence as well." (Baker, 1983, p. 313)

Writer Nancy Baker profiles a typical case:

> "Miranda Hopkins did suffer repeated childhood beatings at the hands of both her parents, especially her father. But Miranda also remembers his frequent neglect—and somehow that was even worse. 'I now see that I did a lot of bad things to get my father's attention,' she admits. 'If I was good, daddy ignored me. So I stayed out late, stole from stores and didn't go to school; that got me his attention.' And a beating. Miranda learned that the kind of attention she 'deserved' was violent. When she later became involved with abusive lovers, she believed she had caused—deserved—those beatings too. The fact that men hit her convinced Miranda that they cared about her." (Baker, 1983, p. 313)

Dr. Gloria Hirsh, clinical director of Friends of the Family, a Los Angeles family-counseling and educational center, agrees that problems start early. "We define love by what happens in our family." (1983, p. 313)

Many children living with unattached parents are neglected and abused, and they end up with extremely poor images of themselves. This is one reason why, depending on their own degree of unattachment, they become either victims or perpetrators of violence in the dating market. They are afraid of being alone and will take the first partner who comes along, especially if the new relationship resembles the familiar one they had with their troubled parents.

People stay in abusive dating relationships for other reasons as well. They may be afraid to leave, or they may have a desire to "reform" their mate, believing that things will be better someday. Many times, their explanation is simply, "I love him."

But what if you don't want to fall in love with the wrong person in the first place? You can follow Benjamin Franklin's sage advice: "Keep your eyes wide open before marriage and half-closed afterwards." In other words, if you encounter love at first sight, it's best to take a second look and develop insight. What you think you see may not be what is actually there.

Author Jeffery Ullman offers these examples of impressions of famous people before and after marriage:

> Richard Burton, about his second wife, Elizabeth Taylor:
> Before: "Elizabeth's body is a miracle of construction and the work of an engineer of genius."
> After: "She is too fat and her legs are too short."
> Diana Dors about her first husband, Dennis Hamilton:
> Before: "If I am subdued, he woos me gently. If I am gay, his lovemaking is boisterous and wild. When he takes me in his arms, I forget everything and give myself to him joyfully and unstintingly."
> After: "Let's face it. He was oversexed." (Ullman, 1986, p. 115-118)

It's true that love is an unusual game. There are either two winners or none at all. But the problem is that we often confuse love with infatuation. Infatuation quickens all the physical senses, but not common sense. Our heartbeat and respiration speed up, our eating and sleeping habits change, and our brains secrete an amphetamine-like substance that keeps us perched high on cloud nine. We are obsessed with constant thoughts about that special someone.

But how can we know whether we are making a good decision, especially when our bodies are topsy-turvy, half-drugged and in a condition that Plato once referred to as "temporary insanity?" The truth is that we can't always tell. We project our fantasies onto our lovers and make them temporarily come true in our minds.

The fantasy starts with unrealistic assumptions and expectations about what kind of lover we need to make us happy. We gravitate toward the "beautiful people," or at least the ones with dazzling personalities. Like moths drawn toward the light, we like to associate with people who exhibit a flair for living and appear confident and powerful. We assume that they can make us feel more confident and alive, too.

And besides, they rarely look and act like a Trust Bandit.

Olson writes: "While the con man himself has no 'giveaway' look, it's safe to say he's good-looking, charming, glib, self-assured, manipulative, and no doubt quite loveable. What woman, after all, is going to hand over her money to a stammering, stumbling oaf of a guy who's no fun to be with?" (1986, p. 72)

Men, of course, can be equally stung by sexy, beguiling, unattached women who seductively wrap them around their little fingers.

It is wise to approach infatuation the way you would a roller-coaster ride. Once you get on and it starts moving, you can't jump off without getting hurt. Of course, roller-coaster rides can be fun, especially if your partner is a well-bonded person with a conscience who can care about you. But never make a lifetime commitment while you are on a roller coaster. Just hang on and have fun until the ride stops. Then, if you are not sick to your stomach or scared to death, work to establish a mature, loving relationship.

What's love, anyway? It is more easily demonstrated over time than defined, especially when trying to detect a clever psychopath. An article in *Psychology Today* reports that "most people are poor lie detectors. Even those who can recognize a lie may be unable to tell what a liar really feels." The most reliable "leak" that reveals whether someone is lying is a discrepancy between two different channels of communication. Is the person smiling while talking in an agitated or angry voice? (Coleman, 1982, p. 16)

Fortunately, there are other signs that can help singles chart a positive course through the dating maze. It is important to note that there are different types and levels of psychopaths. Some Trust Bandits in executive boardrooms and halls of Congress won't exhibit the same symptoms as those in pool halls and prostitutes' bedrooms.

Nevertheless, they all share a common trait. They once were children without a conscience, and now they are adults without a conscience. Here are some helpful hints:

Relationship Checklist
(For Both Sexes)

Low-Risk Signs

You are attracted to him but you still maintain your own sense of self. You share the spotlight with mutual give and take. You are more concerned with enjoying the present moment than banking on the future rewards and happiness. You are aware of his human side and you decide to wait before making commitments. For now he is "Mr. Maybe."

Your partner is open and honest about his childhood and appears to have attached to a consistent loving caretaker(s) despite early childhood traumas or separations. He has resolved most of his childhood problems and can act mature and responsible. He is willing to seek counseling if needed.

He can both give and receive orders and is able to get along with fair bosses or teachers. Any problems with the law have been transitory and not habitual. He can make a friendship that lasts through thick and thin and is willing to introduce you to his friends. His previous relation-

High-Risk Signs

He is able to cast an almost irresistible hypnotic spell which draws you toward him. You are fascinated with his charm and you love to listen to him. He quickly wants to include you in his grandiose plans and future successes. You are excited that you have finally met "Mr. Right," since you can't see any obvious personal flaws.

You can't seem to find many specific details about his troublesome childhood. He was possibly abused or neglected. He has unresolved bonding breaks including: a lengthy illness of himself or a primary caretaker; conflicted family; a divorce, or delayed adoption. He has unresolved childhood problems and is frequently childish and immature.

He seems to have serious difficulty with authority figures such as bosses or law-enforcement officials. He may have had habitual run-ins with the law as a juvenile and as an adult which he may boast about. When you go out with him it's either by yourselves or with his "new acquain-

ships were not all fly-by-night or of short duration.

He displays a quiet sense of self-assurance and usually doesn't lay "power trips" on others. He can express some humility when appropriate and likes to listen to your concerns.

His life patterns seem stable and well-organized and you can usually reach him when needed. He confronts issues openly and honestly with you and is willing to own up to his share of blame when things go wrong. He can feel your pain and experience genuine remorse when he goofs.

You feel comfortable with him sexually because it's not a constant high-pressure sales tactic. Your partner is able to balance strength with gentleness and is concerned with meeting your needs as well as his own. He can commit to one partner and doesn't use sex as a manipulative tool.

tances" since he doesn't seem to have friends who go way back. His past loves have not been long lasting relationships.

He appears powerful and super self-confident, almost to an exaggerated point. He definitely likes to control others through words (conning), money, or physical strength. He is egotistical and very self-centered. He is either moody and quiet or very talkative.

He comes and goes and you don't really know where or with whom. You have mixed feelings about trusting him, and at times he seems sneaky. You think that he lies but he's hard to pin down and he won't accept blame or express remorse when it is clearly his fault. He can sympathize but not empathize.

You notice that he approaches sex in an aggressive, forward way. He usually has a voracious sexual appetite, especially at first, and you sense that he has been extremely promiscuous. He acts interested in you but he is primarily interested in seeking his own pleasure rather than sharing sensitively with his partner. He may become rough and interested in sado-masochistic practices. (Note: females are extremely seductive, flirtatious, and manipulative with their sexuality.)

He can be spontaneous and exciting but he's also stable. You note that his previous work history has added some continuity, purpose, and meaning to his life. His personal goals seem realistic and achievable and he is self-confident enough to take well-thought-out calculated risks.

One of the things that impresses you is his ability to share and exhibit more genuine kindness to others than they actually may deserve. He can display caring without having to get something back because it makes him feel good.

Finances are balanced with other concerns. He is fair and reasonable about money matters and willing to be generous at times without making a big deal about it. He tries to pull his own weight with chores and doesn't want to borrow money he can't legitimately pay back. He shares his material items and respects your individuality.

Although your new partner may not be a teetotaler, he doesn't abuse himself with drugs. He doesn't need drugs to escape or to be able to relate intimately with you. His temper is controllable and not abusive. He can argue without resorting to threats or violence.

He always seems impulsive and unsettled and rarely carries through on projects, saying he is now moving on to "bigger fish." He is always looking for more stimulation and excitement and takes unbelievable chances. His job history and education are usually scattered and unfinished, although he says that's his choice.

You realize that he is manipulative, controlling and conning toward others and rarely displays kindness unless it's for direct personal gain. He may be kind to a cute waitress or sales client but is abusive and cold to a waiter or a clerk. He is shallow and superficial.

He appears closer to money than to anything else. He is either tightly controlling and stingy with material items, letting you know how much everything costs, or he is parasitic in wanting to live off your labor. Be especially careful if he wants to borrow or invest large sums of your money. He believes that he owns you and is extremely possessive and jealous.

Be careful if he regularly consumes any drug, including alcohol, even if he tells you it's recreational and he can take it or leave it. Addictions are easy to cover at first so beware of mood changes. Be especially aware if he has a short fuse and displays any indications of violent behavior.

He may or may not belong to a church but he has a deep appreciation and reverence for the spiritual side of life. He is sustained by his faith in love and goodness. His sense of humor may be offbeat, but it isn't cruel.

You love him because he demonstrates in words and deeds that he can be trusting and loving. You like yourself enough to associate only with someone who can enhance the quality of your life and gradually, but realistically, grow into "Mr. Right."

He may profess a religion but his actions indicate that he secretly delights in aligning with evil and the dark side of life. You sense that he has a cruel nature inside because he smiles at people's misfortune and pain.

Finally, he is so believable and charming that despite many obvious high-risk symptoms you think that the problems between you are as much your fault as his and you just have to "love him" more to make a difference, even though deep inside you know he is Mr. Wrong.

© High Risk, Magid/McKelvey

We have additional tips for daters who want to lower the risk of hooking up with Mr. or Ms. Wrong. If you are going out with someone for the first time, proceed slowly and perhaps meet in a public place for breakfast or lunch. It's not only safer, but it puts less pressure on both parties about how to end the date. It also offers a more business-like atmosphere for asking questions and learning about each other.

We also recommend that singles carefully examine their own values and goals about the preconceived qualities that define their Mr. or Ms. Right. Unfortunately, many single men are looking for a playmate of the year, while single women yearn for a hero.

Writer Signe Hammer describes the typical Mr. Right:

> "The hero will be a tower of strength and sexual potency. He will rescue us from indecision, self-doubt and a precarious self-supporting future. He will earn a lot of money. He will hail cabs in the rain and take us out to dinner. With him, we can live in a bigger apartment or house. " (1979, p. 117)

Hammer goes on to say that the real hero is the nurturing one who diapers the baby and brings his mate chicken broth when she has the flu. But he's not considered a No. 10 in Hollywood's eyes.

Unfortunately, most of us have fairly stereotypical and rigid guidelines about male and female beauty. As a result, we miss some of the best relationship opportunities.

Many semi-attractive or shy people have developed personality qualities that make them look like winners to anyone who has the good sense to take a deeper look. These can include a strong capacity for true intimacy, and an ability to share feelings, interests and mutual concerns. For example, shy people tend to listen more and are rarely obnoxious, over-aggressive or pretentious.

Don't put boundaries on yourself. Occasionally try seeking out seemingly bashful bores. Inside, many of them are talented and beautiful people. Mr. or Ms. Right may be easier to find than you thought.

Before making any lifetime commitments, it is wise to consider getting a professional premarital evaluation to see whether you and your prospective partner are compatible. You also might compare views on economic and career goals and how to attain them, child-rearing practices, educational and cultural backgrounds, religious preferences and, certainly, money and sex.

Also, understand that passionate love and compatibility are two different things. You can "love" some people with whom you can't live happily.

*****

Some of the guidelines when looking for companionship also translate to the business world. It is important that potential employees are carefully evaluated for their compatibility with a particular company. American business has been a frequent and easy target for Trust Bandits.

> *"The market is the place set apart where men may deceive each other."*
> *Anacharsis*

The Psychopath's Favorite Playground: Business Relationships

Not too long ago in Japan a man's word in business or government was his bond to society. If he was caught lying or if he "lost face" he might lose his life, and often by his own hand (hara-kiri). Even in this country, not too long ago, a man's word and firm handshake seemed to mean something. Certainly, there have always been shysters and crooks, but past concern was focused on ferreting out incompetents rather than psychopaths. As Owen Young put it, "It is not the crook in modern business that we fear, but the honest man who doesn't know what he is doing." (1980, p. 38).

Unfortunately, all that has changed. We now need to fear the super-sophisticated modern crook who does know what he is doing . . . and does it so well that no one else knows. Yes, psychopaths love the business world.

"Uninvolved with others, he coolly saw into their fears and desires, and maneuvered them as he wished. Such a man might not, after all, be doomed to a life of scrapes and escapades ending ignominiously in the jailhouse. Instead of murdering others, he might become a corporate raider and murder companies, firing people instead of killing them, and chopping up their functions rather than their bodies." (Harrington, 1972, p. 18)

Up until the early 1987 Wall Street woes involving insider trading, white-collar crime was largely not something we focused upon. Certainly, the "penalties" administered in the business world are far less severe than those for "blue-collar crimes." As Houston Police Chief Lee Brown reports in the book *Crimewarps*, "Police do not devote their efforts to get the white-collar criminal. The crimes we devote our efforts to are the ones the public is more concerned about — street crimes. I don't foresee that changing." (1987, p. 105)

Of course, the consequences to the average citizen from business crimes are staggering. As criminologist Georgette Bennett says, "They account for nearly 30% of case filings in U.S. District Courts — more than any other category of crime. The combined burglary, mugging and other property losses induced by the country's street punks come to about $4 billion a year. However, the seemingly upstanding citizens in our corporate board rooms and the humble clerks in our retail stores bilk us out of between $40 and $200 billion a year." (1987, p. 104)

Concern here is that the costume for the new masked sanity of a psychopath is just as likely to be a three-piece suit as a ski mask and a gun. As Harrington says, "We also have the psychopath in respectable circles, no longer assumed to be a loser." (1972, p. 20) He quotes William Krasner as saying, "They — psychopath and part-psychopath — do well in the more unscrupulous types of sales work, because they take such delight in 'putting it over on them', getting away with it — and have so little conscience about defrauding their customers." (p. 20) Our society is fast becoming more materialistic, and success at any cost is the credo of many businessmen. The typical psychopath thrives in this kind of environment and is seen as a business "hero." Authors Norman Mailer and Michael Glenn recognized the increasing presence of this type of individual in society and have warned that this Trust Bandit may be better adapted to meet the goals we have now set for ourselves in defining "success." (Sanchez, 1986, p. 89)

Certainly, both entrepreneurs and psychopaths love excitement, and they use manipulation of others as their primary method of succeeding in business. "Manipulation is the primary method of eliciting admiration, 'love' and even envy. It is also a favorite technique for expressing aggression without the threat of retaliation because the aggression is masked," says Dr.

Ethel Spector Person (1986, p. 262). But the important differences, once again, revolve around conscience, rage and aggression.

The entrepreneur can be fiercely competitive but still maintain good cause-and-effect thinking and not become sadistic or evil. The businessman/ psychopath has no such boundaries and is cunning, immoral and ruthless. Both can be highly successful and the trick is determining which is which and who can be trusted. Here are some suggestions on how to avoid getting involved with a high-risk business partner.

Avoiding Psychopaths in Business (Male and Female)

1. What is his family background? Was it a rocky road in the first few critical years of life? If so, was he able to attach to a significant other?
2. Did he have severe discipline problems at home or school and did he get into trouble with the law?
3. Is his resume accurate? Check out previous job history and several references. Double check all credentials, including identification (psychopaths commonly forge or substitute documents). Are the stated time frames in his resume accurate? Does he have a reasonably stable work history with evidence of some continuity?
4. Does he have a history of any long-term friends and/or intimate relationships? Does he seem preoccupied with "scoring" or being seductive?
5. What is his method of relaxation? Is he constantly on the move, with his eyes or physical mannerisms?
6. Does he have a past or current history of drug use? How does he define "just a little for recreational purposes"?
7. Is he consistent in words and actions? Does he frequently lie or grossly exaggerate?
8. Does he consistently have a new "pie in the sky" or "big deal" brewing which lures people from tasks at hand? Can you detect that he is a con artist, casting "spells" over those he interacts with, especially strangers?
9. What's his relationship to money? Does he borrow from others and not pay it back? Does he ever loan money to others or give to a charity? Does he use money for "thrills" and seem incapable of judicious spending or saving for the future?
10. Can he truly empathize with those who are weaker and have less power than him? When he gets angry, can he control it or does it get out of hand?

11. Is "trouble in the office" commensurate with his presence? Does he sabotage others at every opportunity while strongly professing no culpability? Does he blame others for his mistakes?
12. Does he respond to moral issues regarding customers or colleagues with a sense of integrity, even if he may not receive personal gain? Do you sense he can genuinely trust anyone else? Can you trust him?

It's once again important to remember that one or two negative symptoms does not necessarily make someone a Trust Bandit. Refer to the ranges of people without a conscience described in the human conscience chart in Section I.

It was Calvin Coolidge who once remarked that "business will be either better or worse." Unfortunately, the future doesn't look promising in terms of America's stock in ethics and fair play. Sociologist Jose Sanchez warns about . . . "a society in which personal needs are given primacy over group needs, in which 'love' has lost its meaning; expediency is emphasized over morality; appearance is given greater importance than 'innerworth'; morality is no longer clearly defined. Such a world can serve as a fertile ground for the use of the psychopathic personalities."

The business world must remember that there are non-violent white collar psychopaths. "The non-criminal psychopath's talent for impression, management, calculation, and charm, which he shares with all of us, makes it difficult to distinguish him from the vat of society." (Sanchez, p. 93)

Although it is possible to paramatize and control business executives who have psychopathic tendencies, it is a tricky operation and involves "challenging" them with special projects which are exciting but tightly controlled. Another strategy involves implementing special business workshops offering role-training and situation-ethics seminars to reprogram wayward tendencies. Using tailor-made audio and video tape packages in conjunction with group psychotherapy can also be effective, but prognosis is guarded in severe cases.

Suffice it to say, in the business world it's best to hire and work with honest people. Honesty is one business policy that will never have to be changed to keep up with the times. We must keep psychopathic thinking in check. Polygraphs and handwriting analysis should be used only in conjunction with an expert therapist who is familiar with diagnosing psychopathic personalities.

If we are to *prevent* Trust Bandits we must do so with the help of leaders in the fields of business, mental health, law, education and religion. In the next chapter we discuss educating the experts.

"Men who know the same things
are not long the best company
for each other."

Emerson

31

Educating the Experts

Sweeping reforms are necessary across the social structure of the United States to prevent more unattached children from coming our way. Rather than knee-jerk reactions, we need well thought-out plans which incorporate sound leadership.

Unattached children are a reality that many Americans are already struggling with. A handful of experts do know about the phenomenon of unattached children but many more have never heard of the concept.

The sad truth is that few of our leaders in the fields of mental health, law, education, religion, business and politics understand that psychopathology can result from even "minor" amounts of deprivation, abuse or neglect. It is imperative that our leaders become better informed.

Unraveling a Mental Health Mystery

The challenge facing mental-health workers in dealing with future Trust Bandits is enormous and the public will desperately be looking to experts for help. Better training and facilities are needed to meet this challenge.

Any mental health worker who says he completely understands a patient with Antisocial Personality Disorder should be referred immediately to another mental-health worker for therapy on his delusions of grandeur.

Most mental-health workers are hampered by a lack of knowledge about how to prevent, diagnose and treat psychopaths. It is possible that a street-wise policeman on the beat is better able to detect a clever psychopath than the average mental-health expert. Remember, the Hillside Strangler fooled court-appointed psychiatrists and psychologists into believing he was a multiple personality, rather than a psychopath.

No extensive training programs exist to help those working directly with psychopathic populations. Often only hard-earned experience is the teacher. Those working with APD patients are frequently fooled, especially

319

at first. Lessons spelling out how to deal with this type of patient need to be incorporated into curriculums, preparing students to deal with Trust Bandits.

In professional jargon, curriculums need to deal with the psychobiological, psychosocial, and phenomenological aspects of children without a conscience.

The mental-health worker needs a clear understanding of childhood developmental stages and how to make his clinical diagnosis of a high-risk child.

Symptoms other than those included in the DSM-III (and discussed earlier in this book) need to be taught so that proper diagnosis can result. Countertransference is the greatest danger in the treatment of unattached children or adult APD patients. (Countertransference is how the clients' issues can negatively affect the therapist.)

When countertransference does occur, the therapist can approach this emotional response with an attitude of friendly curiosity, perhaps saying to himself: "How interesting, I wonder what it is inside me that caused such a strong emotional reaction to this patient."

If a mental-health worker can be aware of the traps, he can be in a better position to avoid them. Here is a partial list of guidelines for therapists treating Trust Bandits.

Treatment Checklists
for Therapists

Low-Risk Treatment	**High-Risk Treatment**
Therapist is attached and has a good cause-effect thinking process. He can model trustworthiness, honesty, and loving commitments. He has a strong conscience to guide him.	Therapist has unattachment issues of his own that haven't been worked through and doesn't provide good modeling to others. Faulty thinking processes and lack of conscience development evident.

The therapist has learned about the unattached-child syndrome and is prepared to deal with patients who don't have a conscience. Besides textbook training, he received "hands-on" internships or workshops.

The therapist doesn't fool himself about his abilities and realizes that he is dealing with constantly challenging patients. He knows that it's what he learns after he thinks he knows it all that counts. He encourages peer supervision and frequently consults with colleagues.

A realistic approach is taken by the therapist. When a danger exists, adequate but not unnecessary precautions are taken to insure safety. He may utilize other therapists or do group activities. He instills hope for a new future in the patient.

The therapist attends to his own inner feelings as a barometer of what countertransference might be occurring, and does mid-course corrections as necessary. Therapist can counteract by saying to himself, "How can I use this mutual involvement for a productive outcome."

The lure of being gullibly drawn into the Trust Bandit's "exciting life" is checked by clear thinking about not supporting immoral behavior and being aware of the patient's seductive process.

The training of the therapist is impaired or lacking. He has inadequate training or experience with unattached children or psychopathic adults. No real-world understanding of the unattached child syndrome.

The therapist has an overinflated sense of his own ability. He is naive about the power of a psychopathic patient and therefore is open to victimization by the client who subtly controls the therapy process and outcome. This is a form of denying his own vulnerability.

The therapist has an overinflated sense of the Trust Bandit's ability. He is fearful, overly suspicious, and over-compensates by victimizing the client (overmediation, punishment, etc.). He has a defensive posture and is afraid of violence or manipulation and sees the patient as totally evil without possible rehabiliation.

The therapist is bored, which is possibly a defensive response to try to escape a difficult reality which he doesn't want to deal with. He may act disinterested and detached.

The therapist is overly excited and involved with the patient and possibly being drawn into the Trust Bandit's web of vicarious excitement, thus indirectly condoning immoral or illegal behaviors.

Rules are critical when working with clients who don't have a conscience. Through clear structuring, the active therapist helps the patient control his thoughts and actions, delay immediate gratifications, and establish responsibility and trust with others. Immediate rewards and natural consequences are also set up.

The therapist avoids undue frustration by realizing his patient's progress is usually slow and tedious. He doesn't allow the Trust Bandit's emotional swings of support or rejection to be a criterion for his own success as a therapist.

Great facilities enhance the positive prognosis for trust bandits. A good facility can not only insure the safety of everyone involved, but can also provide necessary psychological and medical evaluations and interventions. The supportive staff is trained to deal with Trust Bandits' manipulative behaviors and works together to challenge, monitor, educate, and correct faulty thinking processes. Rewards and natural consequences are clearly structured and a positive attitude toward patients and staff is evident.

The therapist has not established fair and clear rules or helped the client develop specific goals to achieve during treatment. There are no clear parameters or structure set and the therapist is passive. Rewards and consequences for inappropriate behavior are not monitored or controlled.

Guilt and depression are evident in the therapist who doesn't make rapid progress with the Trust Bandit and sees himself as a failure. The therapist feels hopeless and helpless when the client rejects him. This frustration may be turned back at the patient in the form of anger.

The facilities are inadequate or inappropriate. The staff members aren't prepared to securely contain dangerous or highly manipulative patients for a lengthy stay. The mental-health staff doesn't work with concerted and consistently effective therapeutic goals. Inconsistent controls in monitoring of patient behaviors are evident, which also reduces patient progress and increases staff burnout. The atmosphere is gloomy and negative.

The therapist prepares the patient to meet the challenges of the real world and monitors ongoing support systems such as family, friends, job progress, social activities, etc. so that relapses don't occur or are handled immediately. Followup sessions and contacts are essential to insure long-term patient progress.

Followup and extended support systems are lacking and the patient returns to old haunts and habits. The patient is not prepared to counteract negative influences on his own and a support network of family, friends, and meaningful career objectives has not been incorporated in the therapeutic process. Followup is based on crisis-oriented need only.

© High Risk, Magid/McKelvey

If a therapist faces difficulties in treating a psychopath, an equally difficult challenge awaits the medical expert who can play a key role in prevention and education regarding unattached children.

The Medical Experts

The primary-care physician can do a great deal to reduce the bonding crisis in America — if he is properly trained and armed with the latest research.

Second to parents, physicians are in the best position to first notice unattached children. They can intervene at an early age when they spot high-risk situations. Physicians can play a key role in educating soon-to-be parents about the importance of the bonding-and-attachment cycle. Prevention is much better than trying to find a cure. As John Scott says in the book, *Psychopaths*:

> ". . . What is the cure for the person who has developed the strong habit of violent behavior over a period of years? This kind of person is often described as a psychopathic personality . . . .
> At present there is no conspicuously successful method of dealing with the psychopath . . . . We can only conclude that prevention of violence is far more effective than its cure."
> (Harrington, 1972, p. 244)

Most physicians aren't prepared to meet that need. Says Dr. Martin Kiernan, director of Family Practice Education at St. Joseph Hospital in Denver, "It's unfortunate that physicians, especially those in the primary-care areas, are so uneducated as to the importance of the attachment-and-bonding process. These physicians, with their great opportunity to educate young mothers about attachment, are significantly untapped links to promoting effective and secure bonding between mother and child." (personal communication, February, 1987)

An average physician will see about a quarter of a million patients in his working lifetime, but many opportunities to educate parents are lost. "You can't teach what you don't know," says Kiernan. "I believe that it is vitally important that medical students and residency programs include training in the effective development of attachment and bonding in their curriculum." (personal communication, February, 1987)

Dr. Craig Watson, another veteran Colorado physician, agrees: "I see so many cases where the parents could unintentionally go the wrong way and end up not forming a strong bond with their infants. They need up-to-date information on how to maintain solid attachment to their babies, and doctors just don't focus enough on that issue. We need more guidelines." (personal communication, January, 1987)

Many hospitals have had policies which interfere with critical early bonding (such as separating healthy babies and parents immediately after birth). More hospitals are now responding to this critical need by relaxing these policies. Practices, such as wrapping babies so securely that their mothers end up having limited skin contact and interaction with their babies, do not encourage bonding.

Attachment experts such as M. H. Klaus and J. H. Kennel recommend that the new baby be united with the mother for the first half hour or more after birth to cement the bond. (1976) Postnatal tests of the infant can be done while a baby is lying on his mother's stomach warmly covered. A baby is alert immediately after birth and this is a good time to make sure positive bonding has started. Some hospitals are now delaying putting antibiotic ointments or silver nitrate in the baby's eyes for a few hours after birth so that eye-to-eye contact can continue uninterrupted. Fathers should also be encouraged to hold and caress their newborns right after birth.

Restrictive hospital practices that separate new mothers from their families need to be changed. These few guidelines will help enhance the bonding and attachment between the new baby and his parents. Here is a checklist of some of the factors physicians should consider as they help educate new parents to the bonding-and-attachment cycle:

Before Birth Checklist for Physicians (Prenatal)

	Low-Risk Yes	High-Risk No	Comments
1. Is sufficient rapport established so that the patient can feel comfortable asking difficult questions or sharing fears (not distant and impersonal)?			
2. Does the parent seem attached herself? Does she seem capable of bonding with the new baby? Did she have a positive early childhood? Does she have a stable work history, and positive personal relationships? Can she maintain eye contact? Does her life history and present mental status suggest that she has a conscience and genuine sensitivity to others?			
3. Does the parent take active interest in the present and future welfare of the fetus, i.e., taking prenatal classes, reading books, asking relevant questions.			
4. Does the parent understand the relationship of self-health to the unborn infant's health, i.e., improper nutrition and risk of low-birth-weight baby, or the dangers of drinking, smoking, drug use, or other high-risk behaviors?			
5. The parent does *not* have to deal with serious physical problems, i.e., poor eye sight, hearing problems, etc., and especially consistent pain which might interfere with the attachment-bonding process.			

	Low-Risk Yes	High-Risk No	Comments
6. Parent does *not* have to deal with an ongoing mental or psychological problem which might inhibit bonding or produce an attachment "break", i.e., overwhelming stress or severe depression such as grieving over the recent loss of a job, failed love relationship, death of a previous child, extreme guilt, anger, or negative attitude about being a parent.			
7. Parent has no interfering family problems such as unattached or jealous siblings (or husband), conflicted or impending divorce, over-controlling or under-supportive in-laws or parents.			
8. The parent is aware of support resources available in the community such as La Leche League (breast feeding), government agencies, self-help tapes and books, counseling services, etc.			
9. The parent has realistic expectations about parenting tasks and understands the bonding-attachment cycle and that infants need consistent loving care and nurturing.			
10. High-risk mothers, such as young teens, addicted and terminally ill or emotionally disturbed parents, and others considered extremely high risk, are referred to special supportive services.			

After Birth Checklists for Physicians (Postnatal)

	Low-Risk Yes	High-Risk No	Comments
1. Parent is attentive and interested in personally connecting with the baby in positive ways; i.e., touching and talking to the baby who seems interested and alert, smiling and having the baby reciprocate, nursing without problems, cuddling and having the baby be receptive, establishing eye contact and noting the baby can focus and follow the parent's face.			
2. The parent notices the baby's individuality and behaviors — "Look, baby Billy is smiling", and observes the infant's physical condition, "Is it OK that his head is so soft on top?".			
3. The parent wants to integrate the baby into the family, i.e., "He looks just like his daddy," or "Say hello to your big brother, he's going to help me take care of you."			
4. The parent's self-esteem remains high (not decompensating). The parent is mature and can handle adult responsibilities (rather than wanting to be taken care of). The parent is functioning reasonably well with life stressors (not hostile, depressed, withdrawn, or manipulative). The parent is bonding well with the infant.			

	Low-Risk Yes	High-Risk No	Comments
5. The parent is in sync with the baby's needs and can adapt her behavior to meet the changing requirements of the infant, i.e., "You look tired of playing so now I'll give you a rest." The parent is attentive to the baby's crying and searches for causes and an appropriate solution. The parent handles the baby lovingly and sensitively (not roughly or verbally abusive). She doesn't ignore the baby for long periods or overstimulate the infant.			
6. The parent continues to demonstrate well-baby care, i.e., proper nutrition, medical checkups, and positive regard for the infant's well-being. The parent knows how to maintain strong attachment and bonding to the infant, while still remaining connected to other family members and the outside world. The parent is satisfied with her caregiving role.			

(In the above checklist all "no" answers need further investigation.)

© High Risk, Magid/McKelvey

Obviously, the physician helps guide parents with new issues as a baby grows — such as speech and toilet training, proper discipline, selecting an alternative caregiver, sibling rivalry, accident prevention, etc.

De-mystifying the Medical Mire

How to Find a Good Doctor

Finding a good doctor is no less difficult than finding a good automobile mechanic. Just how bad the situation really has become is hard to say, but there is reason for concern. One statistic gleaned from a congressional investigation reported that there were more than 10,000 practicing physicians who were imposters (Bennett, 1987, p. 136).

Many of these quacks receive phony degrees from diploma mills. Others may have been licensed but received inadequate training from substandard foreign medical schools and relocated in your town. Most physicians, however, are reputable and do a satisfactory job. But what if you want more than an O.K. job? What if you want a notch above average?

How can you go about finding a great physician, or a great mental-health professional, besides taking potluck in the Yellow Pages? There are no guarantees, but here are some suggestions to help lower the risk of being dissatisfied.

Consumer Suggestions for Locating Physicians and Mental-Health Professionals

1. Ask respected friends, relatives and coworkers whom they might recommend and why they like that person.
2. Inquire about recommendations from organizations concerned about attachment and bonding issues such as the La Leche League, Lamaze childbirthing classes, hospital birthing centers and organizations offering prenatal or parental education classes.
3. Use the vector approach. Contact hospitals, nurses, physicians or mental-health workers and ask for three recommendations of someone to treat your specific problem. Call those professionals and ask them for three additional names. Stop when you obtain the same name(s) repeatedly recommended.
4. Ask questions: Is the professional qualified and competent? Does he have appropriate training and licensure? Physicians should have completed a residency program from a well-respected hospital and be board-certified in their specialty. The Directory of Medical Specialists is a valuable source of information about doctors, and most libraries carry it in their reference section. It tells where a doctor went to school, his current hospital affiliations and much more. Mental-health specialists also should be licensed by their respective state boards which can be contacted for specific information about prospective therapists (qualifications and training, grievances, special recognition, etc.).
5. Interview the professional. This can be by phone or through a personal visit. Some busy professionals do charge for this time but it may be worth the initial expense before committing to extensive treatment. Ask their views on attachment and bonding and notice if they listen attentively to your concerns. Be cautious of defensive or authoritarian

professionals who patronize patients. Does he explain treatment in ways you can understand? Has he ever treated a similar problem before? Is he involved with his community and especially children's issues (i.e., Scouting, church, schools, etc.)? Has he won any special recognition or written any books or taught any classes in his field of specialization? Do you like him and feel comfortable sharing difficult feelings with him?

6. Do you feel comfortable with his support staff (nurses, assistants, etc.)? Do they appear happy at their jobs and present a positive attitude to the public?

7. Does the professional have good connections with other resources in the community, i.e., medical and psychological treatment centers as well as liaisons with other professionals outside his own field of specialization? Can he be reached in time of crisis?

8. Are his fees reasonable? Are they covered by your insurance plan? Can you afford his services? Is he willing to learn about attachment?

This is just a partial list and choosing a good professional can be complicated. For example, many health consumers are now subscribing to HMOs, which are prepaid group-practice organizations that provide a wide range of health-care services for a fixed monthly fee or premium. The flexibility of choice may be narrow and become a problem if you locate a qualified specialist on attachment issues who doesn't belong to your HMO plan. Other difficulties include problems involved with grievances and litigation. Just because a physician has been sued doesn't necessarily mean he is not a competent doctor, especially in a society in which such suits are becoming commonplace. On the other hand, there are also legitimate grievances brought against some doctors which should be investigated.

If, as a consumer, you realize that you aren't happy with a professional, make sure he knows about your complaint to see if positive changes can't be made. If you don't get a positive response, then you always have the right to seek other help.

Research

As we have noted, psychopathy is a mental illness caused primarily by the environment but possibly involving a genetic predisposition. Without certain environmental triggers, the disorder will not be fully manifested. However, the right combination of genetic characteristics and circumstances — such as the bonding breaks we've discussed — may be just the catalyst that causes a particular individual to become a Trust Bandit.

A strong predisposition for APD probably requires only a small environmental push to send a child over the edge. If, however, the baby has little predisposition toward APD, it takes more abuse and neglect to knock him off balance. This helps explain why some children turn down the wrong road while their brothers and sisters may not.

It is clear that new research on attachment will affect us all. Tiffany Field has demonstrated that the classic early assumptions on how and when a baby attaches are now obsolete. Her research has dropped a bombshell on the long-held view that newborns can't discriminate between their mothers and strangers. That view held that babies couldn't attach until the seventh month or later. "Evidence from our laboratory suggests that recognition of the mother's face occurs as early as the first day of life," Field says. (1985, p. 435) Her theory is that significant attachments occur not just in infancy but at all stages of life, including those with friends, colleagues, lovers and parents. Likewise, Field believes "breaks" can occur anywhere along the life span.

"Large numbers of attachment disruptions and disturbances, as manifested in child abuse, spouse abuse, divorce, psychopathology, loneliness, depression, suicide, homicide, disease and death mandate a deeper and broader understanding of the psychobiology of attachment." (Field, 1985, p. 450)

As we have noted earlier, the attachment issue is vital to all that comes after. Psychodrama expert Carl Hollander says those who did not bond well as infants are destined to replay the hurt. ". . . Later, if critical people in their lives leave, then they not only grieve the termination and look for a replacement, but they resurrect the pain that was first experienced as a child." (personal communication, March, 1987)

The mental-health profession is undergoing extreme change as research broadens. Brain chemistry researchers, for example, in early 1987 isolated a gene which they feel is responsible for manic-depressive illness.

No similar biological breakthrough has been found to explain children without a conscience, but some interesting paths are being charted.

Some intriguing questions require answers: Why is it that psychopaths produce offspring with a greater likelihood for the disease and how does their brain chemistry differ from others? Harrington (1972) concluded that early experiments that injected adrenalin (which excites most people) into psychopaths' bloodstreams caused them to temporarily stop searching for criminal excitement and feel more at peace.

And work by Gerald Brown and Frederick Goodwin suggests the possibility of chemical differences in violent criminals' brains; they report variations in levels of the mood-altering compound CSF-5HIAA in criminals' brains (which relates to levels of excitement). But Brown and Goodwin don't rule out environmental factors. (1986, p. 148) If we are to further our understanding of the basis of aggressive behavior in humans, we must be careful not to exclude contributions from any discipline. Certainly the answer is still unknown.

Poverty as an environmental factor has always played a role in the development of criminals. But criminologist Georgette Bennett says in her book, *Crimeworks,* that poverty is not the sole cause of the psychopath. "His crimes are spawn of an expanding pool of unwanted, malnurtured children who are unsuited to civil life." (1987, p. 41)

Certainly, everyone has limits, and children living in bad situations are at higher risk of growing up without a conscience. Inconsistent parenting and "hyperlike" children combine to produce situations ripe for psychopathy. The high activity levels are largely explained using biological answers (low cortical arousal and limbic system dysfunction). Inconsistent rewards and punishments tend to produce children who are conditioned to block out depression and helplessness by mercilessly driving themselves toward short-term gains regardless of consequence or morality. (Doren, 1987, p. 1-267)

The Judicial System

In the old days, hanging judges were often the rule. They were just as likely to suspend the bad man as suspend the sentence. In some countries, such as China, they still do. In China, justice is swift. A trial usually lasts less than an hour. A report on the Chinese prison system in the *Columbus Dispatch* notes: "Anyone in China who attacks a policeman has to know that he is going to die. That person is not considered worth saving." (Brooks, 1985, p. 72B6)

But in America, judges spend a lot of time determining who is worth rehabilitating. How much do they really know about psychopaths? Can they spot one in their courtrooms? Once again, the experts need more training.

Says Judge Kim Goldberger, "Never do we find out in law schools how to deal with these people and how to sentence them. They look good, they talk good, and act good in court. They can fool a judge or an attorney into thinking that they have 'changed' when really their word means nothing to them.

"Judges are sentencing people blind now." (personal communication, January, 1987)

Plea-bargaining, probation and early parole are also part of the system; a system that is not working.

The probation officer's dilemma is equally difficult. His official job is to rehabilitate the defendant while protecting the public. But how is he to really know whether his probationer is going to make it or not?

Massachusetts probation officer, Andrew Klein, reported in *Judges Journal* that one third of probationers who commit new crimes in that state, while on probation, do so within the first month. Almost 90% do so within six months. (1986)

We must also deal with the moral question of whether treatment for psychopathy can make these people better criminals. Social worker Carol Anderson says ". . . If he plays a losing game, we show him how he can make himself into a more successful psychopath. We say, 'If you're going to manipulate, learn to do it better.' We teach him to be a better psychopath. Then he can become an insurance company president." (Harrington, 1972, p. 220)

It is important to educate judges and law-enforcement personnel about the symptoms and modus operandi of clever psychopaths. An old joke around the courthouse is that a jury reported back to the judge, "We don't want to get involved." Many frustrated judges feel the same way.

Judges need to become involved; they have enormous power to change things. But how can they tell the really bad apples from those who can be rehabilitated?

A 1982 study by the Rand Corporation gives some clues. Researchers came up with a half-dozen tell-tale signs — many of which are identical to those Hervey Cleckley used to identify typical psychopaths 20 years before. (Moore, 1983) The key is someone who manipulates without a conscience.

Certainly, true criminal psychopaths need to be identified and incarcerated. Dr. Phillip S. Hicks, chief psychiatrist at San Quentin Prison in California, wishes a separate research facility could be set up for these individuals. "I would set up a research institute like the National Institute of Mental Health, addressing the APD issue. We need to study them." (personal communication, November, 1986)

Of the 3,500 prisoners San Quentin holds, Hicks believes that most have character disorders. "Our sociopaths all have developmental disorders based on a lack of appropriate parent-child affective interpersonal relations. We need to learn more about this phenomenon," he says. It's also important to segregate psychopaths so others won't be negatively manipulated and contaminated.

On the positive side, some judges are learning how to identify unattached children at high risk for delinquency, truancy and other offenses. The sooner these children are diagnosed, the sooner corrective measures can be started.

Chief Juvenile Court Judge Thomas McGee of Louisiana notes, "If we accept the premise that abusive children can beget criminal behavior, then juvenile judges must become involved with the social-services system that provides for abused children to develop preventative measures." (1985, p. 22)

The judicial system needs help. Certainly we can give stiffer penalties to psychopaths and use electronic bracelets and closed-circuit television for monitoring probationers. But what is really necessary is educating the "experts," who can help by nipping small problems in the bud. They must understand how children turn rageful and grow up without a conscience. "Judicial education is essential with unattached children for the orderly administration of justice and the protection of society," states Judge Harry Scholitz Jr. of Scottsdale, Arizona. (personal communication, March, 1987)

Children of Divorce

The divorce enigma, especially, requires understanding about what is truly "in the best interest of the children."

Judges in Wisconsin and five other states have statutory power to require counseling for parents who can't agree on how to deal with their children during divorce proceedings.

The move toward mutual parental responsibility is noted by California Superior Court Judge Byron Lindsley, who says, "If protection of the children's best interest is our function, then we should be doing all we can to create a post-divorce environment in which the children share their lives with both parents. We should try to achieve as free an exchange between parent and child as possible." (1985, p. 22)

Many judges are not aware that they are actually hurting the attachment process when they rule on complicated visitation schedules in divorce cases. Infants and young children, as we have noted before, have different time references than do adults. They, therefore, need differing amounts of contact with their primary caregivers so that bonding will stay intact.

Judges ruling that children can be sent to another parent, perhaps in another state, for a long period of time are jeopardizing the attachment with the primary caregiver.

Below we offer guidelines for parents and/or the legal community in the difficult decision-making process of establishing post-divorce schedules and living arrangements between parents and children.

Ware notes that when "both parents have made arrangements to maintain good parent-child relationships, children are not likely to suffer developmental interference or enduring psychological distress as a consequence of the divorce." (1979, p. 80)

The two main factors affecting any arrangement regarding continued contact between children and both parents are the child's age and nature of the original relationship. The specific guidelines presented here are derived from the most recent information available regarding optimal child development and are recommended to be used in conjunction with these factors:

1. The nature of the contact;
2. The physical and emotional state of the child:
3. The environment into which the child is being taken; and
4. The amount of attachment between each parent and child.

These guidelines can help maintain parent-child attachments and can help youngsters in their emotional and social development:

Parent/Child Time-Sharing Guidelines

Recommended Frequency of Contact between Either Parent and the Child/ren

Age of the Child	Continuum of Frequency of Contact		
	Preferable	Acceptable	Threshold of Harm*
Under one year	2 days	7 days	More than 7 days
One through two years	3 days	10 days	More than 10 days
Three through five years	1 week	3 weeks	More than 3 weeks
Six through nine years	2 weeks	4 weeks	More than 4 weeks
Ten through thirteen years	4 weeks	6 weeks	More than 6 weeks
Fourteen years plus	6 weeks	9 weeks	More than 9 weeks

*Contacts which are less frequent than suggested by the "Threshold of Harm" are likely to result in developmental problems as outlined in the text. (Magid & Oborn, 1986)

© High Risk, Magid/McKelvey

These guidelines assume shared parental responsibility whereby each parent has equal access to and limited separation from the children.

Religious Experts

In Proverbs it says, "Wickedness loves company — and leads others into sin" (16:29). Many religious leaders believe evil cannot be disguised, but unfortunately the roots of some evil people go very deep and are well hidden.

It's important for religious experts to fully understand the true psychopath so they aren't conned and do not subject their followers to a victimizing scam.

Probably the best way to understand the true Trust Bandit is to look at the Ten Commandments as seen through his eyes:

The Ten Commandments

1. Thou shalt have no other gods before me.
   Trust Bandit — "I'll worship money, sex, power and the devil himself if I please. I give allegiance to no one, ever."

2. Thou shalt not take the name of the Lord, thy God, in vain.
   Trust Bandit — "I like being vain and I'll say anything I want to if it impresses, seduces, controls or destroys others."

3. Thou shalt sanctify the holy day.
   Trust Bandit — "The only holy day is when I get my way, and the darkness is my best friend."

4. Thou shalt honor thy father and mother.
   Trust Bandit — "I secretly hate and despise my parents and all those authority figures who want me to be loving and do things their way."

5. Thou shalt not kill.
   Trust Bandit — "I enjoy killing living things and watching the hopelessness and helplessness on my victims' faces. I like killing other people's happiness and dreams."

6. Thou shalt not commit adultery.
   Trust Bandit — "Every woman (or man) is fair game for sexual conquest."

7. Thou shalt not steal.
   Trust Bandit — "If I see it and I want it, then it's mine."

8. Thou shalt not bear false witness against thy neighbor.
   Trust Bandit — "I can lie with more confidence than you can tell the truth. Conning, slandering, and verbally manipulating others is what I do best."

9. Thou shalt not covet thy neighbor's house.
   Trust Bandit — "I see no good reason why not, since I deserve it more than him."

10. Thou shalt not covet thy neighbor's wife.
    Trust Bandit — "If it hurts him and makes me feel good for the moment, nothing else matters."

Sometimes the words of the psychopath are sophisticated and sometimes they are not, depending on the person's education and background. A clever psychopath can hide behind a blue collar, a white collar, or even a church collar.

Some religious experts believe they can simply destroy the psychopath with kindness. Usually things don't happen that way; the adult psychopath doesn't identify with true love — only hostility and his twisted logic. Trying to help someone with APD by blindly counseling them with love is naive and nonproductive. As Harrington says, "Out of kindness I am telling you; 'you have no identity, not even the identity of a bastard, because I won't let you be a bastard. I will be divine and truly forgive you.' But it's not true. I'm human and by forgiving you too readily, I destroy your achievement, even your bastardly achievement, and in doing so destroy your integrity, and practically guarantee that you will go out and do something worse in order to prove yourself." (1972, p. 227)

Psychologist Stanton Samenow believes that APD patients need to be confronted and forced to admit their mistakes before they can learn right from wrong. "By using the tactic of self-disgust, we make him look into the mirror of the evil within" (1984, p. 10).

The point is that psychopaths can be extremely complex. Religious counselors and leaders need more help in understanding and working with Trust Bandits, even when the counselors' hearts are filled with love.

I believe that children are
our future,
Teach them well and let
them lead the way
Show them all the beauty
they possess inside
Give them a sense of
pride,
To make it easier
Let the children's laughter
Remind us how we
used to be

Epilogue

No one program can possibly solve the many social problems now associated with the unattachment syndrome. We believe it is possible, however, to find a new direction in this country regarding our children's future. No one wants to see increasing populations of individuals with antisocial personalities.

But the solutions must come from many elements of our society: federal, state and local legislatures and government agencies, the schools, the churches, parents, the media, youth organizations, health and social agencies.

We all want to know what is going to happen in the future. The challenge is great.

William and Joan McCord put it succinctly, "Psychopaths . . . threaten the safety, the serenity and the security of American life." (Harrington, 1972, p. 17)

Georgette Bennett issues an ominous warning in *Crimewarps:* "unwanted, antisocial, abused children will become our most fearsome criminals." She sees shifts in criminality from violence in the streets to more professional crime, such as high-tech stealing and victimization. (1987, p. 11) Whatever the crime trend of the future, it still revolves around the issue of how one fails to develop a basic sense of right and wrong.

We fully expect highly educated psychopaths to continue to flow into the ranks of big business, government and anywhere else where they can blend in and victimize. One concerned physician has even suggested that no one be allowed to take a powerful governmental post until tested for APD. (Bierer, 1977, p. 303)

"Increased psychopathy among the more prosperous classes of American society will most likely create a social world in which expediency, impersonality, narcissistic manipulation and corruption will continue to replace morality and sensitivity. On the other hand, the under classes of our society will be a source of fear for us all," says sociologist Jose Sanchez. (1986, p. 93)

But violence does not have to be part of the American lifestyle. We hope that in these pages we have provided some of the information needed to understand the nature of the problem, what is being done to solve it, and the enormous unmet needs that still exist. It will take a national effort to reach these goals. But our children are worth the effort.

Without positive change now, this country's future will be at high risk . . . from children without a conscience.

Bibliography

Abagnale, F. W., Jr. (1980). *Catch me if you can*. New York: Pocket Books.

Adler, A. (1977). Individual psychology and crime. *Police Journal, 17*, reprinted in *Quarterly Journal of Corrections*, 7-13.

Staff. (1987, September 4). AIDS babies suffer neglect; foster, adoptive parents hard to find, hospitals say. *Rocky Mountain News*. Denver, Colo. p. 4.

Ainsworth, M. D. S. (1973). The development of infant-mother attachment. In B. C. Caldwell & H. R. Riciuti (Eds.), *Review of child development and research* (Vol. 3, pp. 1-94). Chicago: University of Chicago Press.

Ainsworth, M. D. S. (1978). *Patterns of attachment*. Hillsdale, NJ: Lawrence Erlbaum Associates.

Alan Guttmacher Institute. (1981). *Teenage pregnancy: The problem that hasn't gone away*. New York: Author.

Allan, J. (1977). Use of holding with autistic children. *Special Education in Canada, 51*, 11-15.

Allan, J. (1978, July). *Training in caring: A practical program for sixth and seventh graders with pre-schoolers*. Paper presented at the International Round Table for the Advancement of Counseling, Oslo, Norway.

Allan, J. (1983). Scapegoating: Help for the whole class. *Elementary School Guidance and Counseling, 18*, 147-151.

Allan, J. (1986). The body in child psychotherapy. In N. Schwartz-Salant & M. Stein (Eds.), *The body in analysis* (pp. 145-166). Wilmette, IL: Chiron Publications.

Allan, J. (1987). Holding therapy outline. Unpublished paper—faculty of education. University of British Columbia.

American Psychiatric Association. (1980). *Diagnostic and statistical manual of mental disorders* (3rd ed.). Washington, D.C.: Author.

Association of Junior Leagues, Inc. (1982). In C. Berman (Ed.).*Women, work and the family*. [Conference report]. New York: Author.

Association of Junior Leagues, Inc. (1985, March). *Parental leave: Options for working parents* [Conference Report]. New York: Author.

Baker, N. (1983, August). Why women stay with men who beat them. *Glamour*, pp. 312-313, 365, 367.

Barley, W. D. (1986). Behavioral and cognitive treatment of criminal and delinquent behavior. In W. H. Reid, D. Dorr, J. I. Walker, & J. W. Bonner III (Eds.), *Unmasking the psychopath* (pp. 159-190). New York: W. W. Norton.

Barnes, M. (Producer & Director). (1984). Inside the criminal mind. *Frontline* [TV Documentary]. Seattle: Network of Public Broadcasters.

Basler, B. (1986, December 7). Careers and motherhood: Stage two of the women's movement. *New York Times Syndication Sales*.

Belsky, J. (in press). The "effects" of infant day care reconsidered. *Early Childhood Research Quarterly.*

Belsky, J. (1986, Sept.) Infant day care: a cause for concern? *Zero to Three.* (Vol. VI, No. 5) Washington, D.C.: Bulletin of the National Center for Clinical Infant Programs.

Bennett, G. (1987). *Crimewarps: The future of crime in America.* New York: Doubleday.

Bierer, J. (1977). Can psychopathic behavior be changed? *International Journal of Social Psychiatry, 23,* 291-303.

Bloom, F., Lazerson, E., & Hofstadter, L. (1985). *Brain, mind, and behavior.* New York: W. H. Freeman & Company.

Bolton, F. G., Jr. (1983). *When bonding fails: Clinical assessment of high-risk families.* Beverly Hills, CA: Beverly Hills Sage Publications.

Bowlby, J. (1973). *Separation: Anxiety and anger.* New York: Basic Books.

Bowlby, J. (1979). *The making and breaking of affectional bonds.* London: Tavistock Publications.

Bracey, G. W. (1985, November). Does day care increase aggression? *Phi Delta Kappan,* pp. 227-228.

Brazelton, T. B. (1986, October). A speech to parents at the Auraria Higher Education Center, Denver, CO.

Brazelton, T. B. (1985) *Working and Caring.* Reading, Mass.: Addison—Wesley Publishing Co., Inc.

Bridgeman, A. (1987, February). The bully syndrome. *Child,* pp. 24-25, 106.

Brooks, S. (1985, July 19). Chinese prison: Wholesome yet repressive. *Columbus [Ohio] Dispatch,* p. 72.

Brown, G. L., & Goodwin, F. K. (1986). Human Aggression: A biological perspective. In W. H. Reid, D. Dorr, J. I. Walker, & J. W. Bonner III (Eds.), *Unmasking the psychopath* (pp. 132-155) New York: W. W. Norton.

Burling, S. (1986, November 16). Teens' offspring cost state millions in social services. *Rocky Mountain News,* Denver, Colo. p. 6.

Cadle, K. (Segment Producer). (1987, February 9). Children without a conscience. *Hour Magazine* [TV Show]. Hollywood, CA: ABC.

Capote, T. (1966). *In cold blood.* New York: Random House.

Staff. (1987, January 30). Childcare strongly affects productivity. *Rocky Mountain News,* Denver, Colo. p. 79.

Cleckley, H. (1964). *The mask of sanity.* St. Louis: Mosby Books.

Cleckley, H. (1982). *The mask of sanity.* St. Louis: Mosby Books.

Cline, F. (1979). *Understanding and treating the severely disturbed child.* Evergreen, CO: Evergreen Consultants in Human Behavior.

Cloninger, C. R. (1978, August). The antisocial personality. *Hospital Practice,* 97-103, 106.

Cohn, A. H. (1986). *It shouldn't hurt to be a child*. Chicago: The National Committee for the Prevention of Child Abuse.

Cohn, A., & Gordon, T. (1986). *Tips on parenting*. Chicago: The National Committee for the Prevention of Child Abuse.

Cole-Alexander, L. (1982). Issues. In C. Berman (Ed.), *Women, work, and the family*. New York: Association of Junior Leagues.

Coleman, J. C. (1984). *Abnormal psychology and modern life*. Glenview, IL: Scott, Foresman.

Colorado Domestic Violence Coalition. (1987, February 27). *Data on domestic abuse* [press release]. Denver, CO: Author.

Conger, J. J. & Miler, W. C. (1966). *Personality, social class, and delinquency*. New York: Wiley.

Coplon, J. (1985, August). Young, bad and dangerous. *Ladies Home Journal*, pp. 124-125, 165-166, 168.

Cosmopolitan. (1986, April 25). International adoptions. *Associated Press Features*.

Craft, M., Stephenson, G., & Granger, C. (1964). The relationship between severity of personality disorder and certain adverse childhood influences. *British Journal of Psychiatry, 110*, 292-296.

Crichton, S. (1982, August). The riddle of dating violence. *Seventeen*, pp. 336-337, 362-363.

Staff. (1985, March 11) Day care infants face trauma, expert says. *The Denver Post*. Denver, Colo. p. D-3.

Staff. (1987, August 30). Day care worries tied to troubles in the workplace. *Rocky Mountain News*. Denver, Colo. p. 40.

DeCasper, A. J., & Fifer, W. P. (1980, June 6). Of human bonding: Newborns prefer their mothers' voices. *Science*, pp. 1174-1176.

Despert, L. L. (1953). *Children of divorce*. Garden City, NY: Doubleday.

Doren, D. (1987) *Understanding and treating the psychopath*. New York: Wiley p. 75-131.

Dorr, Darwin & Woodhall, Peggy K. (1986). Ego dysfunction in psychopathic psychiatric in patients. In W. H. Reid, D. Dorr, J. I. Walker & J. W. Bonner III (Eds). *Unmasking the psychopath*. New York: W. W. Norton. p. 128.

Edmiston, S. (1979, May). If you loved me you wouldn't hurt me. *Redbook*, pp. 99-105.

Ehrlich, E. (1986, October 6). Childcare: The private sector can't do it alone. *Business Week*, pp. 52-53.

Emmons, N. (1986). *Manson in his own words*. New York: Grove Press.

Erikson, E. H. (1968). *Identity, youth, and crisis*. New York: W. W. Norton.

Erikson, E. H. (1965). *Childhood and society*. London: Hogarth.

Fahlberg, V. (1979). *Attachment and separation: Putting the pieces together*. Michigan Department of Social Services, DSS Publication 429.

Fein, G. G. & Moorin, E. R. (1980). Group care can have good effects. *Day Care and Early Education.* New York: Human Services Press.

Associated Press. (1987, February). Fired adoptive mom backs leave bill. *The Denver Post,* p. 4-D.

Fishbein, H. (1984). *The psychology of infancy and childhood: Evolutionary and cross-cultural perspectives.* Hillsdale, NJ: Lawrence Erlbaum Associates.

Flynn, T. (1986, November). When teenagers rock baby, we rock boat. *Rocky Mountain News/Sunday Magazine,* p. 4-M.

Fraiberg, S. (1977). *Every child's birthright: In defense of mothering.* New York: Basic Books.

Franklin, B. (1909). The autobiography of Benjamin Franklin. In C. W. Eliot (Ed.), *The Harvard Classics* (Vol. 1). New York: P. F. Collier & Sons.

Freedman, A. M., Kaplan, H. I., and Sadock, B. J. (1975). *Comprehensive textbook of psychiatry* (Vol. 2). Baltimore: Williams & Wilkins.

Freud, S. (1949). *An outline of psychoanalysis.* New York: W. W. Norton.

Frosch, J. P. (1983). The treatment of antisocial and borderline personality disorders. *Hospital and Community Psychiatry, 34,* 243-248.

Fuller, E.(Ed.). (1978). *2,500 anecdotes for all occasions.* New York: Avenel/Crown Publishers, p. 165.

Fuller, E. (Ed.). (1980). *Witty remarks and epigrams.* New York: Avenel/Crown Publishers. p. 38.

Garbarino, J., & Groninger, W. (1983). *Child abuse, delinquency, and crime.* Chicago: National Committee for Prevention of Child Abuse.

Gaylin, J. (1986, August). Do children need a stay-at-home mother? *News from Redbook.* New York: Solters/Roskin/Friedman.

Gerhardt, G. (1986, August 31). Psychiatrist has criminals on his mind. *Rocky Mountain News,* p. 8.

Goldie, D. (1986, December 29). Congregation's help repaid with betrayal. *Rocky Mountain News,* p. 43.

Goleman, D. (1982, August). Can you tell when someone is lying to you? *Psychology Today,* pp. 14-18, 20, 22-23.

Gordon, S. (1986). *Reprints from the teenage survival book and when living hurts.* Irvine, CA: News America Syndicate.

Guidubaldi, J., & Perry, J. D. (1984). Divorce, socioeconomic status, and children's cognitive-social competence at school entry. *American Orthopsychiatric Association, Inc.,* p. 459.

Haley, J. (1973). *Uncommon therapy.* New York: W. W. Norton.

Hammer, S. (1979, July). Why nice guys finish last with women. *Mademoiselle,* pp. 117-119, 168.

Hare, R. D. (1986). Twenty years of experience with the Cleckley psychopath. In W. H. Reid, D. Dorr, J. I. Walker, & J. W. Bonner III (Eds.), *Unmasking the psychopath* (pp. 3-27). New York: W. W. Norton.

Harrington, A. (1972). *Psychopaths.* New York: Simon & Schuster.

Heinicke, C., & Westheimer, I. (1965). *Brief separations.* New York: International Universities Press.

Hellwig, B. (1986, November). How working women have changed America. *Working Woman Magazine,* pp. 129-144.

Henderson, M. A. (1985). *Flim-flam man.* Boulder, CO: Paladin Press.

Hester, G., & Nygren, B. (1981). *Child of rage.* Nashville: Thomas Nelson.

Hewlett, S. A. (1986a). *A lesser life: The myth of women's liberation in America.* New York: William Morrow.

Hewlett, S. A. (1986b, November). Why we need a national policy to help working mothers. *Glamour,* p. 194.

Hodges, W. F. (1986). *Intervention for children of divorce.* New York: John Wiley.

Hornby, H.C. (1986, July-August). Why adoptions disrupt . . . and what agencies can do to prevent it. *Children Today.* pp. 7-11.

Hubbel, C. (Ed.), (1987, January). *Creative Thought Magazine,* p. 66.

Hulse, J., & Bailey, K. (1986, October 16). War on child abuse escalates into hysteria. *Rocky Mountain News,* Denver, Colo. pp. 6-7, 60-61.

Hunter, B. (1986, February 21). Breaking the tie that binds. *Christianity Today,* pp. 31-33.

Jones, E. F., Forrest, J. D., Goldman, N., Henshaw, S., Lincoln, R., Rosoff, J. I., Westoff, C. F., & Wulf, D. (1986). *Teenage pregnancy in industrialized countries.* London: Yale University Press.

Kagan, J., Kearsley, R. B., & Zelazo, P. R. (1978). *Infancy: Its place in human development.* Cambridge, MA: Harvard Press.

Kantrowitz, B. (1987, February 16). Kids and contraceptives. *Newsweek,* pp. 54-65.

Kantrowitz, B. (1986, March 31). Changes in the workplace. *Newsweek,* p. 57.

Kaplan, L. (1978). *Oneness and separateness: From infant to individual.* New York: Simon & Schuster.

Kegan, R. G. (1986). The child behind the mask: Sociopathy as developmental delay. In W. H. Reid, D. Dorr, J. I. Walker, & J. W. Bonner III (Eds.), *Unmasking the psychopath* (pp. 45-77). New York: W. W. Norton.

Kennell, J., Voos, D., & Klaus, M. (1976). Parent-infant bonding. In R. Helfer & C. H. Kempe (Eds.), *Child abuse and neglect.* Cambridge, MA: Ballinger Publishing.

Kimball, R. (1986, March/April). Experiential therapy for youths: The adventure model. *Children Today, 15,* 26-31.

Klass, P. (1986, May). The fantasy and the reality of teenage motherhood. *Discover,* pp. 14-16.

Klaus, M. H., & Kennell, J. H. (1976). *Maternal-infant bonding.* St. Louis: C. V. Mosby.

Klein, A. R. (1986). Punishing probationers who skip prescribed treatment. *Judges Journal, 25* (4), 10-40.

Konner, M. (1987, March). The enigmatic smile. *Psychology Today*, pp. 42-44, 46.

Kovel, J. (1976). *A complete guide to therapy*. New York: Pantheon Books.

Krasnow, I. (1986). The tough job of blending families. *UPI Lifestyle.*

Lamb, M. (1982). Parent-infant interaction, attachment, and socioemotional development in infancy. In R. Emde & R. Harmon (Eds.) *The development of attachment and affiliative systems*. New York: Plenum Press.

Lamb, M. E. (1981). *The role of the father in child development* (2nd ed.). New York: John Wiley.

Lamm, D. (1986, October 19). The cycle of abuse. *The Denver Post/ Contemporary*, Denver, Colo. p. 2.

Lang, M. E. (1985, October). Research: Child-care policies. *Yale Alumni Magazine*, pp. 42-45.

Levine, S. B. (1987, March). Caring about child care. *Ms.*, p. 31.

Levitin, T. (1983). An overview of the effects of divorce on children: Problems, questions, and perspectives. *The Psychiatric Hosptial, 14*, 149.

Lindsley, B. (1985). Ruling without bias. *Judges Journal, 24 (1)*, 19-22.

Ludlow, R. (1987, August 16). Slayer would find killing easy working county hospital halls. *Rocky Mountain News.* Denver, Colo. p. 38.

Maccoby, E. E., & Jacklin, C. N. (1974). *The psychology of sex differences*. Stanford: Stanford University Press.

Macheli, R. (1986, June). The perk of the eighties. *Working Woman*, p. 132.

Macpherson, K. (1987, February). Parental leave proposal gets new breath of life. *Rocky Mountain News*, Denver, Colo. p. 18.

Madanes, C. (1984). *Behind the one-way mirror*. San Francisco: Jossey-Boss.

Magid, K., & Oborn, P. (1986). Children of divorce: A need for guidelines. *Family Law Quarterly, 20*, 331-340.

Makins, V. (1981, July 24). Day nurseries damage children. *New York Times Educational Supplement*, pp. 1, 3.

Mann, J. (1984, August 3). Child care. *Washington Post*, p. 40.

Mayer, G. R., & Butterworth, T. (1984, May). Save our schools — Love a vandal. *Psychology Today*, pp. 17-18.

Maynard, F. (1985). *The child care crisis: The real costs of child care for you — and your child*. New York: Viking Penguin Books.

McBroom, P. A. (1986). *The third sex*. New York: William Morrow.

McGee, T. (1985). Preventing juvenile crime. *Judges Journal, 24 (4)*, 20-23.

McGraw, P. (1987, February 12). DA to get tough on violent teens. *The Denver Post*, pp. 1-A, 10-A.

Meister, D. (1986, July 22). Childcare. *Christian Science Monitor News Service.*

Meredith, D. (1986, February). The nine-to-five dilemma. *Psychology Today,* pp. 36-39, 42-44.

Meyerhoff, M. K. (1984, January). In response [Letter to the editor]. *Young Children,* p. 2.

Michaels, J. (1986, January). "The teacher hurt me, mommy." *Redbook,* pp. 106-108, 142.

Michaud, S. G., & Aynesworth, H. (1983). *The only living witness.* New York: Linden Press.

Moore, G. (1983, November). The beast in the jungle. *Psychology Today,* pp. 38-45.

Mussen, P. H., & Conger, J. J. (1956). *Child development and personality.* New York: Harper & Brothers.

National Association of Homes for Children. (1986, Spring). *Caring, 11,* 4-7. Millbrook, NY: Author.

National Commission on Working Women. (1985). *Women at work.* Washington, DC: Author.

National Commission on Working Women. (1986). *Child care fact sheet.* Washington, DC: Author.

Staff. (1987, February 14). National statistics on teen crime. *Sentinel Newspapers,* p. 2.

Newhaus, C. (1982, April 12). Scorned and swindled by her bigamist husband, Sharon Vigliotto got mad, then got even. *People,* pp. 5-6.

Oberkirch, A. (1985). Psychotherapy of a murderer: Excerpts. *American Journal of Psychotherapy, 39,* 499-514.

Ode, K. (1985, November 19). More attention being paid to dynamics of dual career couples. *Scripps Howard News Service.*

Okala, S. (1986, November). Committee calls for universal six-month maternity leave in the U.S. *AP wire story.*

Olson, K. (1986, October). The con man's new victim. *New Woman,* pp. 69-72.

Orr, S., & Haskett, G. (1985). *Parental leave: Options for working parents.* New York: Association of Junior Leagues.

Staff. (1986, November). The parental leave bill — help get it passed! *Glamour,* p. 194.

Peck, M. S. (1983). *People of the lie.* New York: Simon & Schuster.

Person, E. S. (1986). Manipulativeness in entrepreneurs and psychopaths. In W. H. Reid, D. Dorr, J. I. Walker, & J. W. Bonner III (Eds.), *Unmasking the psychopath* (pp. 256-273). New York: W. W. Norton.

Peterson, N. (1986, November 6). U.S.A. gives more working moms little support. *USA Today,* p. 30.

Potts, L., Barley, W. D., Jones, K. A., & Woodhall, P. K. (1986). Comprehensive inpatient treatment of a severely antisocial adolescent. In W. H. Reid, D. Dorr, J. I. Walker, & J. W. Bonner III (Eds.), *Unmasking the psychopath* (pp. 231-255). New York: W. W. Norton.

Powledge, F. (1985). *The new adoption maze.* St. Louis: C. V. Mosby.

Pride, M. (1986). *The child abuse industry.* Westchester, IL: Crossway Books.

Prins, H. A. (1977). Who is the psychopath? A rejoinder and a comment. *Medical Science Law, 17,* 241-245.

Quinn, J. B. (1986, March). Many facts: Good news for working women. *Woman's Day,* p. 20.

Reid, W. (1985). The antisocial personality: A review. *Hospital and Community Psychiatry, 36,* 831-837.

Reid, W. H., Dorr, D., Walker, J. I., & Bonner, J. W. III. (1986). *Unmasking the psychopath.* New York: W. W. Norton.

Reite, M., & Field, T. (1985). *The psychobiology of attachment and separation.* Orlando, FL: Academic Press.

Robins, L. N. (1978). Aetiological implications in studies of childhood histories relating to antisocial personality. In R. D. Hare & D. Schalling (Eds.), *Psychopathic behaviour: Approaches to research.* Chichester, England: Wiley.

Roby, P. A. (1973). *Child care — who cares?* New York: Basic Books.

Rogers, C., & Stevens, B. (1967). *Person to person: The problem of being human.* Walnut Creek, CA: Real People Press.

Rogers, C. C. (1984). *Fertility of American Women: June 1983.* (U.S. Bureau of the Census, Current Population Reports, Series P-20, No. 395). Washington, DC: U.S. Government Printing Office.

Roman, M., & Haddad, W. (1978). *The disposable parent: The case for joint custody.* New York: Penguin Books.

Rosenberg, L. A. (1979, September/October). Four year olds in school? *Today's Education,* pp. 62-64.

Rosenthal, M. S. (1970). A three-year report. In *Phoenix House,* p. 5. New York: Phoenix House Foundation.

Rubin, K. (1987, March). Whose job is child care? *Ms.,* p. 35.

Rule, A. (1980). *The stranger beside me.* New York: Signet.

Rutter, M. (1981). *Maternal deprivation reassessed.* New York: Penguin Books.

Salzer, E. M. (1979, July). To combat violence in the child's world; Swedish efforts to strengthen the child's rights. *Current Sweden,* p. 3. Stockholm: The Swedish Institute.

Samenow, S. E. (1984). *Inside the criminal mind.* New York: Times Books.

Sanchez, J. (1986). Social crisis and psychopathy: toward a sociology of the psychopath. In W. H. Reid, D. Dorr, and J. I. Walker, & J. W. Bonner III (Eds.), *Unmasking the psychopath* (pp. 78-97, 93). New York: W. W. Norton.

Sanko, J. (1986, July 16). Children having children. *Rocky Mountain News*, Denver, Colo. p. 21.

Schroeder, M. L., Schroeder, K. B., & Hare, R. D. (1983). Generalizability of a checklist for assessment of psychopathy. *Journal of Consulting and Clinical Psychology, 51*, 511-516.

Schroeder, P. (1986, October). Opening remarks at a speech to parents at the Auraria Higher Education Center, Denver, CO.

Schroeder, P. (1986). Parental leave: a working family's issue [Press Release], p. 1. Denver, CO: Author.

Schulins, N. (1986, June 16). Kids who kill. *AP Newsfeatures*. New York.

Schwartz, P. (1983). Length of day-care attendance and attachment behavior in eighteen-month-old infants. *Child Development, 54*, 1073-1078.

Seliger, S. (1986, April). What is best for the children? *Working Mother*, pp. 77-78.

Selman, R. (1986). A therapeutic milieu for treating the antisocial substance abusing adolescent. In W. H. Reid, D. Dorr, J. E. Walker, & J. W. Bonner III (Eds.), *Unmasking the psychopath* (pp. 221-230). New York: W. W. Norton.

Shalala, D. (1982). Introduction. In C. Berman (Ed.), *Women, work, and the family*. New York: Association of Junior Leagues.

Shamblin, W. (1986). Inpatient treatment of antisocial youth. In W. H. Reid, D. Dorr, J. I. Walker, & J. W. Bonner III (Eds), *Unmasking the psychopath* (pp. 208-220). New York: W. W. Norton.

Shane, R. (1986). *The foundations of integral therapy*. Unpublished manuscript, Integral Therapy Institute, Boulder, CO.

Shapiro, J. L. (1987, January). The expectant father. *Psychology Today*, pp. 36-39, 42.

Sherman, E. (1986, October). Teenage sex. *Ladies Home Journal*, pp. 199-206.

Silfen, P. (1983). Clinical criminology: youth prison as an institute for rehabilitation. *Medicine and Law, 2*, 27-37.

Spitz, R. A. (1965). *The First year of life*. New York: International Universities Press.

Spock, B. (1979, November). Your child: raising children to make a less violent world. *Redbook*, p. 64.

Stautberg, S. (1986, June 30). How new personnel policies help families. *New York Times Syndication Sales*.

Talan, J. (1986, October 19). The children of divorce. *The San Jose Mercury News*, p. 4L.

The Swedish Institute. (1982, Octoboer). *Fact sheets on Sweden: Child care programs in Sweden*. Stockholm: Author.

Thomas, G. (1987, January 3). Experts sound alarm about rise in crimes committed by kids. *Rocky Mountain News*, p. 8.

Timnick, L. (1982, August). Now you can learn to be likeable, confident, socially successful for only the cost of your present education. *Psychology Today*, pp. 43-45, 47-49.

Trotter, R. J. (1987, January). The play's the thing. *Psychology Today*, pp. 27-34.

Ullman, J. (1986). *The singles almanac*. New York: World Almanac Publications.

USC News Service. (1986, January). *Maternal preparation programs help first time mothers*. Los Angeles: University of Southern California.

Vaughn, B. E., Gove, F. L., & Egeland, B. (1980). The relationship between out-of-home care and the quality of infant-mother attachment in an economically disadvantaged population. *Child Development, 51* 1203-1214.

Wall, J. (1981). *Reports of the national juvenile justice assessment centers*. Washington, DC: U.S. Department of Justice.

Wallis, C. (1985, December 9). Children having children. *Time*, pp. 79-90.

Walshe-Brennan, K. S. (1977, December 15). The psychopathic personality. *Nursing Mirror*, pp. 29-31.

Ware, D. (1979). *Sharing parenthood after divorce*. New York: Viking.

White, B. L. (1985, October). Should you stay home with your baby? *American Baby*, pp. 27-28, 30.

Widom, C. S. (1977). A methodology for studying noninstitutionalized psychopaths. *Journal of Consulting Clinical Psychology, 45*, 675-683.

Wilson, J. Q., & Herrnstein, R. J. (1985). *Crime and human nature*. New York: Simon & Schuster.

Wolfgang, M. E., Figlio, R. M. & Sellin, T. (1972). *Delinquency in a birth cohort*. Chicago: University of Chicago Press.

Women's Day Magazine and Yankelovich, Skelly, & White. (1986, June 10). *A woman's choices*. New York: Author.

Woolley, P. (1979). *The custody handbook*. New York: Summit Books.

Yale Bush Center Infant Care Leave Project. (1985). *Facts on parents in the workforce and infant care*. New Haven, CT: Author.

Yarrow, L. J. (1965). Research in dimensions of early maternal care. *Merrill-Palmer Quarterly, 9*, 101-114.

Zaslow, R., & Menta, M. (1975). *The psychology of the Z-process*. San Jose, CA: San Jose State University.

Zigler, E. F. (1985, November). Recommendations of the Yale Bush Center advisory committee on infant care leave.

Zigler, E. F. (1985, October 17). Recommendations of the Yale Bush Center advisory committee on infant care leave. *Hearing on parental leave HR 2020 before House Subcommittees on civil service, labor management relations, labor standards, and employee benefits.*

Zigler, E. F., & Brazelton, T. B. (1985). Medical/psychiatric and child development perspective. In S. Orr & G. Haskett, *Parental leave: Options for working parents*, (pp. 4-5). New York: Association of Junior Leagues.

Zinsser, C. (1984, October). The best day care there ever was. *Working Mother*, p. 80.

Index

A

Abagnale, Frank, Jr., 10
Acquired Immune Deficiency
   Syndrome (AIDS), 21, 156, 206,
   272
Adler, Alfred, 9
Adoption, 147-159
   Danny (case study),
   51-57, 152, 153
   Danny's drawing, 182a
   John (case study), 147, 148, 151
   Nancy (case study), 149, 150
   Patrick (case study), 152
Adoption and Foster Care,
   147-159, 293-299
Adoption Services in the States,
   154
AFL-CIO, 141
Aid to Families with Dependent
   Children, 161
Ainsworth, Mary, 3, 60, 61
Alcoholics Anonymous, 259
Allan, Dr. John, 93, 94, 205, 227,
   228, 229, 230, 266, 268
   therapy drawings, 182a
Alan Guttmacher Institute, 162,
   163, 164, 165, 167, 169, 269, 270
Alexander, Dr. Lenora Cole-,
   111
American Academy of Pediatrics,
   143
American Can Company, 136
American Humane Association,
   174, 175
American Proverb, 18, 107
American Psychological Associa-
   tion, 118
Anacharsis, 315
"Anal cycle," 101, 102, 103
Anal Stage, 101, 102, 103
Antisocial Personality Disorder
   (APD), 3-8
Arizona State University, 308

Arousal-Relaxation Cycle, 298
Association of Junior Leagues,
   Inc., 111, 113, 140
Attachment, 51-69
   affect of separation, 61-63
   definition, 58-60
   how it helps child, 59
   how it is formed, 60, 61
   long-term detachment,
   67-69
   love isn't enough, 52-58
   when attachment fails, 63-66
The Attachment Continuum, 67
Attachment Process, 208-209
Attachment and Separation, 60,
   154, 298
Aynesworth and Michaud, 60,
   63, 64, 65, 91

B

Baby Boom, teenage, 269-275
The Bad Seed, 95
Bailey, Jeffery, Jr., 1-2, 29-31
Baker, N., 308
Barland, Gordon, 176
"basic trust," 73, 193
Barley, W. D., 198
Basler, B., 134
Bathurst, Kay, 133
Behavior Modification, 196,
   197, 198
Bennett, Georgette, 316, 329,
   332, 339
Berkowitz, David, 2
Belsky, Jay, 124, 125
Berman, C., 117
Bersharov, Douglas, 155, 156
Bianchi, Kenneth, 2, 15-18
Bible, 18
Bierer, J., 339
Blake, William, 173

Bloom, F., 5
Bolich, Sally, S., 41
Bolton, F. G., 177, 178
Bonding, 6, 7
  extremely attached, 6
  extremely unbonded, 7
  slightly impaired bond, 6
  partial bonding, 7
  weak bond, 7
  well to average bond, 6
Bonding Breaks, 107-190
  Laura (case study), 107, 108
Bonding Crisis, 110-119
The Bonding Cycle, 71-77
Boston's Children's Hospital, 113
Bowlby, John, 59, 61-62, 67-69,
  107, 128, 130, 157, 158, 193
Bovee, C. N., 243
Brazelton, T. Berry, 69, 113, 114,
  116-118, 121, 127, 130, 143, 279
A Breeding Ground for Psycho-
  paths, 1-47
Bridgman, A., 179, 180
Brock, William, 145
Brooks, S., 332
Brown, Gerald and Goodwin,
  Frederick, 331
Brown, Medora, 194, 272
Buber, Martin, 73
Buddism, 233
Burling, S., 169-171
Bundy, Theodore, 2, 20, 62-65,
  91
  handwriting analysis, 40-41
  homicidal psychopaths, 37-43
Burton, 183
Burton, Richard, 309
Business Relationships with Psy-
  chopaths, 315-318
Business Week, 123, 292
Butterworth, Tom, 264
Byrd, Judge James, 31

C

California State University, 132,
  133
Capote, Truman, 64
Carnegie Corporation, 118
Catch Me if You Can, 10
Cate, Dr. Rodney, 308
CBS News Report, 261-262
Center for Assessment of Delin-
  quent Behavior and Its Preven-
  tion, 274
Center for Parent Education, 127
Center for Population Options,
  272
Character-disturbed child, 13,
  34-35, 293
  percentages of, 34-35
  profile of, 13
C. Henry Kempe National Center
  for Prevention and Treatment of
  Child Abuse and Neglect, 175
*Child Abuse, Delinquency and
  Crime*, 178
Child Care—Who Cares? 126
Child Development, 130
Child of Rage, 155
Childhood Symptoms, 79-99
  angry parents, 80, 92, 93
  control problems, 80, 88-90
  crazy lying, 80, 98-99
  cruelty to others, 80, 83-84
  eye contact, 80, 91-92
  inability for affection, 80-82
  lack of long-term friends, 80,
  96-98
  learning disabilities, 80, 96-98
  phoniness, 80, 84-85
  preoccupation with blood, fire,
  80, 93-94
  self-destructive behavior,
  80, 82-83

speech pathology, 80, 86-88
stealing, hoarding, gorging, 80, 85-86
superficial attractiveness/ friendliness, 80, 95-96
Children in Transition, 295-297
adoptive parents, 296-297
agencies, 297
foster families, 295-296
Citizen's Committee for Children, 165
City on the Hill Church, 45
"Claiming Behaviors," 298
Clarke-Stewart, Alison, 133
Clark, Florence, 165
Cleckley, Hervey, 4, 5, 8, 9, 12, 14, 19, 193
Clement, Jim, 45
Client-Centered Rogerian Therapy, 196
Cline, Foster, 3, 11-14, 25, 35, 62, 65, 71, 73-75, 80, 81, 85, 86, 89, 92, 95, 96, 101, 148, 149, 151, 182b, 182c, 205, 207-208, 210-212, 214-226, 227, 230, 245
Cloninger, C. Robert, 8
Cohn, A., 301, 304
Coleman, J.C., 11, 239, 310
Coplon, J., 273
Colorado Domestic Violence Coalition, 305
Columbia University, 115, 143
Columbus Dispatch, 332
Conger, John J., 20
Corona, Juan, 2
Cosmopolitan, 152, 153
Council on Maternal and Infant Health, 166
Counter transference, 202
Cox, Kim, 270
Craft, Stephenson and Granger, 68
Crichton, S., 308

Crime and Human Nature, 19
Crime Warps, 316
Crimeworks, 332
Critical Time — Attachment, 51-103
The Custody Handbook, 187
Cycle of Abuse, 173-181, 301-305
Donna/Andy (case study), 173, 174
Sandy Meyer (case study), 180
Cycle of Abuse, Interrupting The, 301-305

D

Day Care, 121-137
Westpoint Child Development Center, 120
Day Care, 281-292
facilities, 288-289
guide to home caregivers, 285-286
guide to center caregivers, 286-288
programs, 289-290
ratio chart, caretaker/child, 283
DeCasper, A. J., 246
Defusing a National Time Bomb, 207-214
Ruth and Jeremy (case study), 207-208, 215-226
Demara, Ferdinand Waldo, Jr., 10-11
Diagnostic Dilemma, 202, 203
Diagnostic and Statistic Manual (DSM-III), 7
Directory of Medical Specialists, 329
Dismukes, Lucille, 166

Divorce Disrupted Children,
    183-185
    Jason Rocha (case study),
    183-185
Dodd, Senator Chris, 277
Donahue, Thomas, 141
Doren, D., 259, 332
Dorr, Darwin, 195
Dors, Diana, 309
Douglas, Lloyd, 101
Drawings by unattached children,
    182a, 182d
DuSable High School, 169

E

Edmiston, S., 307-308
Educating the Experts, 319-337
Ehrlich, Elizabeth, 123, 292
Ellwood, David, 170
Emerson, Ralph Waldo, 71, 319
"engrossment," 251
Emmons, Nuel, 22-24
Erickson, Dr. Milton, 205, 231,
    232
Erikson, Erik, 73, 102, 193
Eron, Leonard D., 179
*Every Child's Birthright: In De-
    fense of Mothering*, 63
Evaluating Teachers, 264-265
"Ewing, J. R.", (Dallas), 5
Experiential Therapy, 234

F

Fahlberg, Vera, M. D. 59-62
    72, 88, 97, 154, 158, 298
Family and Medical Leave Act, 144,
    277
Family Practice Education, 323
Family Teaching Center, 274
Family Therapy, 231, 232
Favero, Jane, 267
Fay, Jim, 262, 263, 266

The Fear Game, 203
Feeding Program for Women,
    Infants and Children, 163
Feinstein, Mayor Dianne, 292
Field, Dr. Tiffany, 161, 162, 245,
    246, 253, 331
Fifer, W. P., 246
"Fired Adoptive Mom," 277, 279
First Year of Life Cycle, 74-75,
    298
    gratification, relief, 74, 75
    need, 74, 75
    "non-responsive" infant, 76, 77
    rage reaction, 74, 75
    trust, 74, 75
Fishbein, H., 59-60
Flynn, Joe, 9, 154
Flynn, Trisha, 153-154
Flim-Flam Man, 18
Ford Foundation, 136
Fortune Magazine, 136
Foster Care, 147-159
    John (case study), 157-158
    what a family provides, 158
Fraiberg, Selma, 5, 57, 63, 64, 66-67
Franklin, Benjamin, 1, 44, 45
Frontline, 15-17
Freedman, A. M., 5-8
Freud, Sigmund, 9, 101, 196
Frosch, Dr. James P., 237
Fuller, E., 259, 315

G

Gadhafi, Moammar, 75
Garbarino J. and Groninger W.,
    178, 180, 181
Gaylin, J., 112, 113
Geddes, Dr. Betsy, 261, 262, 263,
    267
Gerhardt, G., 26
Gestalt Therapy, 196
Gilmore, Gary, 2, 57
Glamour Magazine, 142, 144

Glick, Paul, 185
Goebel, Jean, 277
Goldberger, Judge Kim, 273, 274, 332
Goldie, D., 45
Goodwin, Frederick, 331
Gordon, Dr. Sol, 270
Gottfried, Allen, 133
Gottfried, Adele E., 132
"Grace," 73
Griffin, E., 72
"Group Care Can", 284
Guidubaldi, John, 132, 185, 186, 187, 188
The Guilt-Gotcha Game, 203, 204
Guttmacher Institute, 165, 169

H

Haley, Jay, 231, 232
Hamilton, Dennis, 309
Hammer, Signe, 314
Hansen, Jo-Ida C., 118
Hare, R. D., 14, 194
Harrington, A., 316, 323, 331, 333, 337, 339
Harvard Medical School, 113, 170
Harvey, Donald, 18, 19
Haskins, Dr. Ron, 133
Headstart, 265
Heinicke, Christopher and Westheimer, Ilse, 62
Hellwig, B., 114
Henderson, M.A., 9, 10,
Helter-Skelter Murders, 2
Henton, Dr. June, 308
Herman, Alexis, 121
Hester G., and Nygren, B., 154, 155
Hewlett, Sylvia Ann, 114, 143, 144, 145
Hicks, Dr. Phillip S., 333
Hilberman, Dr. Elaine, 307
Hillside Strangler, 2, 15

Hirsch, Dr. Gloria, 309
HMO's, 330
Hodges, William, F., 187
Hoffman-La Roche, 291
Hoffman, Lois Wladis, 132
Hollander, Carl, 331
Homicidal Psychopath, 37-43
Hornby, H. C., 293-294
Hospital Treatment, 237-240
Hour Magazine, 273
Hubbel, C., 199
Huff, ix
Hulse and Bailey, 174, 175, 176
Hunter B., 124
Hurst, Marsha, M. D., 117

I

IBM, 136
In-Home Support Services, 274
Infancy: Its Place in Human Development, 114
Infant Attachment, Low risk/High risk, 248-249
    Sherry/Carol (case study), 249-250
In Cold Blood, 64
Inge, Dean, 51
Inside the Criminal Mind, 9, 19
Integral Therapy, 232
International Concerns Committee for Children, 249
"internalization of good parent," 73
Intervention for Children of Divorce, 187
"I-thou" relationship, 73

J

Jacklin, Carol Nagy, 35
Jefferson, Thomas, 37
Jeremy: An Abbreviated Case, 215-226

Johns Hopkins University, 266
The Join Me Game, 204, 205
Jones, Dr. Maxwell, 238
Jones, Elise F., 163, 167
Judges Journal, 332
Judicial System, the, 332-334
Judy, Steven, 175, 176

K

Kagan, J., 114
Kaiser Shipyards, 284
  day care center, 284
Kamerman, Sheila B., 143-144
Kantrowitz, B., 136, 145, 270
Kaplan, L., 185
Kazdin, Alan, Ph.d., 33, 34
Kegan, K. G., 102, 103, 114
Kemper, Edmund, 2, 28
Keniston, Kenneth, 118
Kennell, John, 58, 324
Kent State University, 132, 186
Kiernan, Dr. Martin, 323-324
Kids who kill, 27-35
Kimball, R., 235
Kissimmee Police Department, 1
Klass, P., 269
Klaus, M. H., 324
Klein, Andrew R., 332
Klein, Ethel, 115
Konner, N., 247
Kovel, Dr. Joel, 196, 198
Krasnow, I., 185, 186
Krugman, Dr. Richard, 175

L

Laeser, Abe, 32
La Leche League, 329
Lamaze, 329
Lamb, M., 188
Lamm, Dottie, 180
Lang, M.E., 140
Larsen, 42

"Law in a Free Society," 274
Law, Susan H., 123
Lazarus, Dr. Martin, 33
"Legally competent," 195
  criminals who "fall through the cracks," 195
  sane or insane, 195
Legendre, Judge Ronald, 29, 31
A Lesser Life: The Myth of Woman's Liberation in America, 114
Levine, Ellen R., 115, 116
Levine, Steve, 32, 116
Levitin, T., 185
Lifetime knowledge, 71
Lindsley, Judge Byron, 334
Linnoila, 194
Lucas, Henry Lee, 2

M

Maccoby, Eleanor Emmons, 35
Macdonald, Dr. John M., 26
Macpherson, K., 278
Madanes, Cloe, 232
The Mad-Glad Ploy, 204
Mailman Center for Child Development, 245
Magid, Dr. Ken, 201
Magid and Oborn, 186, 187, 188, 336
"Magical Cycle," 73
Manfred, Erica, 34, 273
"Mania Without Delirium," 8
Mann, J., 135-136
Manson, Charles, 2, 22-24, 69
Manson in His Own Words, 22
"Manson myth," 23
Mask of Sanity, 4
March, William, 95
Mason, Caroline Atherton, 293
Maternal Deprivation Reassessed, 3
Mayan saying, 279
Mayer, Roy, 264

Maynard, 281
McBroom, Patricia, 113
McGee, Judge Thomas T., 333
Meister, D., 137, 141
Mengele, Joseph, 7
Meredith, 124, 133, 134, 282
Meyerhoff, Michael K., 127
Meyer, Sandy, 180
Michaels, J., 129
Micheli, 291
Mielke, Don, 273
Miller, Jerome, 113, 174, 175, 176
Miller, Wilbur C., 20
Minnesota Mother-Child Project, 178
Mnookin, Robert, 272
Modified Holding Techniques, 227-230
Mood-altering chemical, 194, 331
Moore, Dr. Kristen, 270
Moore, George, 121, 281, 333
Mothers in the Work Force, 122
Mount Sinai School of Medicine, 117
Mullen, Barbara, 186
Mussen, P. H., & Conger, J. J., 97
"Mutual trust and empathy," 196

N

Naikon Therapy, 233, 234, 238
National Association for Child Care Management, 125
National Association for Women Business Owners, 143
National Association of Homes for Children, 148, 149, 150, 151, 152
National Center on Child Abuse and Neglect, 155
National Center on Institutions and Alternatives, 113, 174

National Child Abuse Hotline, 305
The National Commission on Working Women, 121, 122, 123, 134, 140-141
National Committee for Adoption, 299
National Committee for Prevention of Child Abuse, 303, 304
National Crime Wave, 42
National Institutes of Health, 185
National Leave Policy, 277-279
National Organization for Women, 143
National Research Council, 272
National Time Bomb, 207-214
Necessary Losses, 153
Newhaus, C., 44
Newsweek, 270
Nidorf, Barry, 273
The Night Stalker, 2
Nixon, Richard M., 122
North American Council on Adoptable Children, 299
Northwest Child Development Council Inc., 123

O

Oberkirch, A., 203
Ode, K., 118
Okula, S., 279
Olson, Kiki, 307, 310
The Only Living Witness, 64
Oregon State University, 308
Orr and Haskett, 144
Oborn, Dr. Parker, 188

P

Parental Behaviors, 250-251
Parental and Medical Leave Act, 128, 141

Parental Leave, 139-145, 278
  Ann (case study), 139
  Sue (case study), 139-140
  Thomas, Louisa, 144-145
Parent/child Time-Sharing, 335
Parents Without Partners, 259, 271
Patuxent Institution, 239
Peck, M. Scott, M.D., 21
People of the Lie, 21
People Magazine, 44
Pennsylvania State University, 124
Person, Ethel Spector, 25, 196, 316, 317
Peterson, N., 114, 145
Perturka, Beth, 31
Physicians' Prenatal Checklist, 327-328
Physicians' Postnatal Checklist, 327-328
Piaget, Jean, 189
Pinel, P., 8
Planned Parenthood Federation, 163
Polaroid Corporation, 136
Positive Parenting, 245-259
Powledge, F., 154-155
Pregnancy Disability Act, 141
Pregnancy Discrimination Act, 278
Pregnancy Profile, 170
Prevention of Unattached Children, 243-337
Pride, M., 154, 155, 176
Prins, Herchel A., 8
Proctor and Gamble, 136
Provence, Sally, 144
Proverbs, 256, 301, 336
Psychoanalysis, 196
Psychology Today, 245, 251, 264, 310
Psychopath, characteristics of, 14

Psychopaths, 323
Psychopathy, disease of, 6-11

Q

Quinn, Jane Bryant, 291

R

Rage Reduction Therapy, 182b, 182c, 190, 205, 209, 240, 298
  treatment structure, 209-214
  the process diagrammed, 212
Rand Corporation, 333
Ramirez, Richard, 2
Rasputin, 194
Reality Therapy, 196
Redbook Magazine, 112, 113, 124
The Referral, 201-206
Reid, Dr. William H., 235, 237, 239
Relationships, 307-318
Relationships Checklist, 311, 314
Religious Experts, 336
Research, 330-332
Reynolds, 234
Rice, Dr. Ruth, 72
Rice Infant Sensory Stimulation, 72
Riege-Laner, Dr. Mary, 308
Robins, L. N., 34
Roby, Pamela A., 126, 127
Rocha, Jason, 183-185
Rockwell, Norman, 114
Rogers, Carl, 196
Roots of Violence, 31-34
Rosenberg, Dr. Leon A., 265, 266
"Ruth," 207
Rosenthal, M. S., 5
Rubin, K., 290-291
Rule, A., 38, 42
Rutter, Michael, 3

S

Sadists, 7
Salzer, E. M., 301
Samenow, Stanton E., 9, 19, 20, 234, 238, 337
Sanchez, Jose, 318, 339
Sandy Meyer Clinic for Human Advancement, 180
San Jose State University, 194, 208
Santa Fe Mountain Center, 234
San Quentin, 333
Seliger, S., 132
Selman, R., 237
Seneca, 263
Schaub, 230, 232
Schreibman, Walter, 13, 15, 19, 45, 46, 76, 233, 234, 245
Schroeder, Patricia, 128, 141, 142, 143, 277, 278
Schroeder, M. L. and Schroeder, K. B., and Hare, R. D., 14
Schwartz, P., 186
Schweitzer, Albert, 6
Science, 246
Serial Killers, 7
Serotonin, Mood-Altering Chemical, 194
Shakespeare, 307
Shalala, Donna, 111
Shamlin, Dr. William, 238
Shane, R., 232
Shapiro, Dr. Jerrold Lee, 251
Shaw, George Bernard, 302
Sherman, E., 269, 270, 272
Shulins, N., 32-33
Silfen, P., 239
Silverman, Leonard, 291
Slaby, Ronald, 33
Smith, 263
Son of Sam, 2
The Song of Phoenix, 180

Spenkelnik, John, 176
Spiritual Therapy, 233, 234
Spitz, Rene, A., 57, 67
Spock, Dr. Benjamin, 301-302
Stallbaum, Pastor Dan, 45
Stanford University, 272
Stautberg, S., 135, 136, 142
St. Elsewhere Syndrome, 239, 240
Stepfamilies Association of America, 186
Stevenson, D., 185
Superficial Mask, 11-13
Sutton, Willy, 103
"Survey Shows High", 273
Syracuse University, 270

T

Talan, J., 185, 187
Task Force on Family Violence, 305
Tate, Dr. Deanna, 135
Taylor, Elizabeth, 309
Talmud, 243
Teachers, 261-268
Teachers, evaluating, 264-265
"Teen Pregnancy Epidemic," 161-171
  Kim (case study), 165, 166
Teenage Pregnancy in Industrialized Countries, 163
"Teenage Pregnancy: The Problem That Hasn't Gone Away," 162
Teenage Sex Survey, 168
"Tender years doctrine," 188
The Ten Commandments, 336-337
Teresa, Mother, 6
Texas Womens University, 135
"Therapeutic Community," 238
Therapist traps, 202
Therapists Treatment Checklist, 320-323

Theognis, 161
The Third Sex, 113, 116
Thomas G., 28, 31
Thomas, Louisa, 144, 145
Three Faces of Eve, 4
Timnick, L., 267
Toddler to Teen, 254-259
    Attachment/Unattachment
    Checklist, 254-256
    Parent Checklist, 257-258
"Token reinforcement," 196, 197
Tough Love, 259
Traditional Therapies, trouble with,
    193-199
Transactional Analysis, 196
Transference, 202
Treatment, 193-240
Trotter, R. J., 245
The "Trust Bandits," 1-27
The Tylenol Killer, 2

U

Ullman, 309
Unattached Children Anonymous,
    259
Unattached Child, symptoms, 13
University of British Columbia, 266
University of California, 133
University of Illinois at Chicago, 131
University of Michigan, 132
University of Minnesota, 118
University of North Carolina, 133
University of Southern California,
    165
Unmasking the Psychopath, 235
U.S.C. News Service, 165, 169
U.S. Department of Labor Women's
    Bureau, 111

V

Vaughn, Brian, E., 133, 134

Victims, 37-47
Victims of Child Abuse Laws
    (VOCAL), 176, 305
Vigliotto, Giovanni, 44
Violence, Teen, 272-275
Viorst, Judith, 153
The Vulnerable, 21-26

W

Wall, J., 266, 273, 274
Wallis, C., 163, 167
Ware, D., 334
Watkins, Connell, 11, 58, 66, 75, 76,
    82, 85, 87, 95, 148, 149, 150
Watson, Dr. Craig, 324
Watson, William, 79
Wattleton, Fay, 163
West Point Child Development
    Center, 129
Widom, C. S., 43, 44
Wiggins, 204
Wilderness Therapy, 206, 234,
    235
Williams, B., 267
Wilson, J. Q., and Herrnstein, R. J.,
    177, 179, 185
White, Burton L., Ph.d., 69, 123,
    127, 128, 134
Wolfgang, M. E., 34
Woodhall, Peggy, 195
Woolley, Persia, 187
Women's Bureau, U.S. Labor Depart-
    ment, 290
Women's Day Magazine, 115, 291
Women, Work and the Family, 111

Y

The Yale Bush Center in Child
    Development and Social Policy,
    112, 114, 116, 144, 279
Yale University, 69, 121

Yankelovich, Skelly and White, 115,
    169
Young Children, 127
Young, Owen, 315

Z

Zaslow, Dr. Robert, 194, 208-209,
    211, 230
Zigler, Edward F., 69, 113,
    121, 124, 127, 133, 143, 278, 279
Zinsser, C., 284
"Z Therapy," 194, 209